THE LYTTELTON
HART-DAVIS
LETTERS
Volumes 3 and 4

THE LYTTELTON
HART-DAVIS
LETTERS

Correspondence of George Lyttelton
and Rupert Hart-Davis
Volumes Three and Four 1958–59

Edited and introduced by
RUPERT HART-DAVIS

Correspondences are like small-clothes
before the invention of suspenders;
it is impossible to keep them up.
SYDNEY SMITH

JOHN MURRAY

Lyttelton Letters
pp 1–178 © 1981 Humphrey Lyttelton
pp 179–357 © 1982 Humphrey Lyttelton
Hart-Davis letters and notes
pp 1–178 © 1981 Sir Rupert Hart-Davis
pp 179–357 © 1982 Sir Rupert Hart-Davis

First published in paperback 1986
by John Murray (Publishers) Ltd
50 Albemarle Street, London W1X 4BD
Printed in Great Britain by
The Bath Press, Avon

British Library CIP Data
Lyttelton, George
The Lyttelton Hart-Davis letters: correspondence
of George Lyttelton and Rupert Hart-Davis.
1. English letters
I. Title   II. Hart-Davis, Rupert
826'.914'08   PR1347
ISBN 0-7195-4290-1

INTRODUCTION

The delightful people who have read and enjoyed the earlier volumes of this correspondence, and written to tell me so, will need no further introductory words from me, but newcomers may like to know how it all began.

In 1926 I had been taught by George at Eton, where he was an outstanding teacher and housemaster. He taught mostly classics but in my last year he had started an English course, and it was then that I fell under the spell of his infectious enthusiasm for literature. After I left Eton our ways parted. George taught for a further twenty years before retiring to Suffolk. We met again in 1949 and thereafter saw and wrote to each other occasionally, but the origin of this correspondence was a dinner-party in 1955 during which George complained that no one wrote to him in Suffolk and I accepted his challenge.

To avoid repetitive footnotes I should say that Comfort was my wife; Bridget, Duff, and Adam my children. Ruth Simon had been my beloved prop and stay since 1946.

As before, in the first letters I have retained the opening and signature, which are afterwards omitted, since they are almost always the same: any variation is printed. Similarly I have given our full home addresses in the first two letters and then abbreviated them. From Monday to Friday I lived in a flat above my publishing office at 36 Soho Square. At the beginning of this volume George was almost seventy-five and I was fifty.

RUPERT HART-DAVIS

Marske-in-Swaledale
1981–86

*This double volume is dedicated
by its editor to*
JOCK AND DIANA MURRAY
and to the memory of
ROGER AND SIBELL FULFORD

4 January 1958

My dear George

Many happy returns of the day. I have, alas, no gift to send you—only affectionate good wishes—but I will at least try to post this tomorrow, so that it reaches you on your birthday.

Many thanks for yours from Eton and Cambridge. Has the famous hat reached you safely? Mr Pooter is indeed a new rôle for you, but Adam[1] was certainly unaware of it, since after your departure he expressed his delight in and approval of your coming—a rare tribute from a fourteen-year-old who normally takes everything—including his parents' friends—for granted.

Captain Starlight's horse certainly figured in the film,[2] but anonymously. I too was a fanatical *Black Beauty* fan in early youth, and can still remember—or rather re-experience—my thrills of pity and terror when the stables caught fire.

Last week began with four nights-out running. On Monday I dined quietly with friends in Regent's Park but didn't get home till midnight. On Tuesday I was taken (for the second time, after almost a year) to the two-man review *At The Drop of a Hat*, which I enjoyed all over again. They mostly use the same material, but include one or two topical songs: I rather liked this one of four lines:

> Russia is red, dilly, dilly,
> England is green.
> They've got the Moon, dilly, dilly,
> We've got the Queen.

Afterwards I had to put in an appearance at a New Year's Eve party in Chelsea, but managed to escape before the chimes rang out. Next day I travelled to Brighton in the afternoon, stayed with some friends, and after supper addressed the Hove Quill Club on Oscar

[1] My younger son.
[2] Of *Robbery Under Arms* by Rolf Boldrewood.

Wilde's Letters. Some thirty stalwarts turned up, including (rather disconcertingly) a little girl of nine! Also a fine-looking old boy called E.H. Visiak, an amateur scholar of means who lived with his mother till she died in her late nineties: he edited the Nonesuch Press *Milton* —whether ill or well I know not. Also present was an elderly, amiable and shaggy Oxford don called J.B. Leishman, who has translated most of Rilke's poems into English. I had prepared nothing, but simply let loose on them a hurricane of words, facts and quotations which kept going for three quarters of an hour. They seemed satisfied, even pleased, and we adjourned for some (by me) much needed drinks. Then came a brief visit to some other friends of mine who live nearby, and I got to sleep by one a.m. Next morning I caught an 8.30 train and reached the office just in time to give our assembled travellers a two-hour exhortation on the Spring Books. Lunch with an old friend up from the country, and in the evening *five* hours on the proofs of Diana Cooper's book. To-day we (the family) all drove, mostly through fog, to Moreton-in-Marsh to lunch with Comfort's stepmother. Phew —what a week! And what a lot of licences seem to need renewing— thank heaven we have no dogs, menservants or crests on our carriages!

Sunday morning

I slept for *eleven* hours! and am still so drenched with sleep that there is no sense in me. Adam has volunteered to bicycle to the post office with this, so I must hasten, lest his ardour cool. Needless to say, neither the car's 'log-book' nor the insurance certificate can be found. Duff may know where they are, but he is construing Demosthenes in the drawing-room and I am loth to disturb such unaccustomed assiduity.

The total absence of domestic help is going to produce an intolerable situation when Comfort starts teaching again in a fortnight's time, and I simply don't know what to do about it. There must be people who would be pleased to live here for nothing in return for doing a little housework—for instance a young woman writing a book, and God knows there are plenty of *them*! Perhaps an advertisement in the *New Statesman*? Forgive this drooling: I'm still half-asleep.

Yours ever
Rupert

8 January 1958

My dear Rupert

Your Adam is a good lad—just the sort of look about him that a housemaster likes to see coming into his house—and however stupid housemasters are, they do get rather good at looks, though of course a good many thirteen-year-olds' faces are so to speak neutral. What do you think could have been noticed in George Moore's face at that age? Mere blancmange!

I look forward to meeting T.S. Eliot. Shall I ask Sir Malcolm Sargent if he knows he is known in the music world as 'Flash Harry'? Perhaps not—they are a jealous and backbiting lot, and anyway they can't deny that his tailcoat is the best-fitting in all London. Henry Wood's was a mere bag of ferrets in comparison. I shall see you beforehand and go through my usual hoop of ringing all bells and banging all knockers except the right ones at about 6 p.m. With my new pocket-diary I shall get all 1958 dates right.

Even you must have found that week tiring, but you would, I know, greet any advice to go slower with the same contempt as Johnson, full of dropsy and melancholia and asthma, felt for the Frenchman who said *'Ah, Monsieur, vous étudiez trop'*.

I like that absurd little quatrain. Why is the addition of 'dilly, dilly' so effective? It reminds me of an epitaph told us by my father sixty-five years ago. Have you ever heard it? It is frightfully silly:

'When I am dead, diddle, diddle, (or if you prefer it 'dilly, dilly')
As it may hap,
Bury my head, diddle, diddle,
Under a tap.'
'Under a tap, diddle, diddle!
Pray tell me why.'
'That I may drink, diddle, diddle,
When I am dry.'

It is better than anything in Ezra Pound.

I should like to have heard you on O. Wilde, unprepared, all bubbling out of you, fresh and inexhaustible. It was always said that the time to sit listening to Porson[1] was when he was quite sozzled and went on hour by hour 'hicupping Greek like a helot'. Only in one particular is the parallel inexact. I bet it was immensely worth hearing. I greatly enjoyed Harold Nicolson's book.[2] Why do some call him conceited? It is the book of a particularly likeable and *un*conceited man, don't you agree? I have just begun Jonah's book[3], reading very slowly, as an epicure deals with his cutlets, 'soubees' and cheese 'remmykin'. His writing is full of delicate flavours, as always, and anyone who appears in his pages is most clearly and pleasantly drawn. But I remember some curmudgeonly reviewer saying of his previous book 'Do we want to hear about Balliol characters of half-a-century ago?' A typically *saugrenu* question of course, but won't they be saying it again of the world of Jonah's prime? Among all your publishing confrères you stand out as the one who first of all publishes a book because it is good and not because it will pay. And I am glad to see that in nearly all reviews of your books the external attractiveness is mentioned; they really are beautifully got up.

We are both sympathetic to the verge of distress about your domestic predicament. Perfectly and flawlessly damnable! Advertise wildly and widely. As you say, there *must* be someone somewhere who would gladly come. It is these puttering squalid harassments that get one down. We really long to hear that the situation is saved. And in all this pudder you fill your day, and write to me, and send on my loathsome hat (a million thanks to you both) and are charming to everyone and run the Library and the Lit. Soc. The truth must be frankly faced (*not* 'up to') that you are an exceptionally good man!

Yours ever

G.W.L.

15 *January 1958*   *Grundisburgh*

Damn that germ![4] We all missed you very much. There was a fine

---

[1] Richard Porson (1759–1808), Regius Professor of Greek at Cambridge.
[2] *Journey to Java* (1957).
[3] *Georgian Afternoon* by L.E. Jones (1958).
[4] I was in bed with influenza.

gathering, the new ones (to me) being T.S. Eliot, Sir Malcolm and Pryce-Jones. I had luck, being—without any design—between T.S.E. and Sir M. and opposite P.-J. My two neighbours were most friendly and excellent company. I had a good chuckle with T.S.E. A very good man, I thought, with no affectations etc at all. Flash Harry too I liked; he looks extraordinarily young and fresh, which perhaps is not surprising as he said he *enjoyed* (like another I know?) being at work twenty-five hours in the day.

And I was delighted to meet P.-J. again—first time since he was up to me! I was glad to find he is adamant about anonymity in the *T.L.S.*—just as adamant as he was in the most benign manner about the plethora of foreign writers given all that space in his columns.

The *only* snag in these delightful evenings is that one wants to have a crack with practically everybody there. I got hardly a word with Roger, or Peter F. or Bernard F. or Somervell. *Embarras de richesses* with a vengeance. Roger has discovered an occasion in the annals when Spencer Lyttelton and Lord Curzon were the only attendants. Very embarrassing for old Uncle S., who hated a tête-à-tête. He was a superbly handsome and vigorous man, but, well, when E.F. Benson asked him if he had ever kissed a girl, his answer was 'Once—on the brow'. A Victorian old bachelor but somehow not at all spinsterish.

I get this off at once, more than suspecting that, whatever your temperature, you may have written. Please get well at once or sooner.

19 *January 1958*   *Bromsden Farm*

At last I have succeeded in disappointing you—and a good thing too if it brings down to earth your much too flattering estimate of my kindness and capabilities. I did intend to scribble a few lines last week-end, but as I lay sweating with fever, eyes, nose and whole head occluded by a streaming cataract, I found myself unable even to read or to concentrate for more than a minute or two. It was like a wakeful delirium, neither restful nor enjoyable. I was much concerned about the efficient cancellation of all my plans, and only pray that you were warned in time to prevent a fruitless visit to Soho Square. So glad you enjoyed the Lit. Soc. Tom Eliot is a pet, isn't he? So natural, humorous and unpretentious. Flash Harry (though clearly a bounder) is good company occasionally, and very friendly. Did I tell you how once at the beginning of a big dinner-party at Hamish Hamilton's I was approached by a very pretty girl whom I scarcely knew? 'Will you promise me something?' she asked earnestly, out of the blue. 'Anything,' I gallantly replied, strengthened by a powerful Martini. 'Promise me,' she said, 'that whatever happens I shan't have to go home alone in a taxi with Malcolm Sargent.' I duly promised, but later regretted my quixotry, since we had to wait till the small hours before Flash Harry gave up the chase, and then of course I had to escort the lady to South Kensington.

Poor old Jonah, every minor detail concerning his new book (have you read it yet?) has gone wrong. Ages ago we arranged that he should come in shortly before publication (next Friday) and sign some copies for special friends, which I would then send out. He chose to come when I was away: my secretary nursed him with blotting-paper and labels: she assured him the books would not go out for a week, and then went to lunch. When she got back she found that the packer, seeing the books ready and thinking to be helpful, had packed and despatched them all. It didn't matter a jot, but it upset poor Jonah unduly. On Friday I got a charming note from Roger, marked on the envelope 'TO AWAIT RETURN OF STRENGTH', which I rather liked.

Still no sail on the domestic ocean, but various local steps are being taken. Duff is back at Oxford, and Adam returns to Eton on Tuesday, after a day and night in London with Dad: he goes up with me in the morning. I shall give him dinner at the Garrick and take him to a theatre, get his hair cut, and try to buy him some flannel trousers and a tweed jacket. He is as tall as many grown men, but has no hips or shoulders to speak of.

I have, as you can imagine, little news to recount, save incoherent sickroom musings. Next Wednesday I am to dine with Tommy Lascelles and wife in their grace-and-favour apartments in Kensington Palace, and on Thursday with old Heygate's daughter Liza, an old friend of my sister's and mine. I must redouble my London Library efforts, to make up for lost time, and you've no idea what four days' absence does to my office desk.

I have got Oscar out of prison now, basking in the summer sunshine of Dieppe in the brief lull before the poverty, squalor and degradation of his last three years. The story still has power to move me, and I think will always affect those who are susceptible of being purged by the pity and terror of a man's destiny. When I've finished the annotation (there will be more than a thousand footnotes) I shall rough out a general introduction and brief prefaces for the nine parts into which I have divided the book. Then I shall have to read the whole damned thing through again, adding new footnotes, supplying endless cross-references and generally tidying up. Meanwhile new letters still trickle in, and I hope they'll continue to do so until my first proofs have gone back to the printer. When will that be?

23 January 1958   *Grundisburgh*

Shakespearean hunch: I am sure in my own mind that the adjective 'whoreson' came into *his* mind from some experience in Suffolk of a day like 22 January 1958; there is no other completely fitting epithet. I was in Ipswich and at precisely 12.21 midday fell headlong on the pavement—without, I may say, the smallest damage or even discomfort; I might have been a slalom champion in embryo. The only discomfort was caused by two citizens, who thought they were helping me, 'offering unneeded arms, performing dull farces of escort' (do you know those superbly absurd hexameters of Clough's *Bothie*?). To-day the sun is here, but, like Bet Flint vis-à-vis Mrs Williams's disapproval, the frost 'makes itself very easy about that.'[1]

I do hope you are being *immensely* careful not to overdo it after that flu. It is a vindictive germ, and Suffolk is full of men who are nursing cardiac murmurs and upsets of various kinds through resuming hard work too soon. But I suspect you are one of those good men who pay not the smallest attention to such advice—or indeed any.

[1] 'I have known [said Dr Johnson] all the wits from Mrs Montagu to Bet Flint!' 'Bet Flint!' cried Mrs Thrale; 'pray who is she?' 'Oh, a fine character, madam! She was habitually a slut and a drunkard, and occasionally a thief and a harlot . . . Mrs Williams,' he added, 'did not love Bet Flint, but Bet Flint made herself very easy about that.' (Fanny Burney's Diary, August 1778).

How right you are about T.S.E. and Flash H. The former said several excellent things, but, as Dr Johnson praised in Beauclerk, without a trace of self-consciousness. And the genially bounding Flash H. I have always heard that his morals were less admirable than e.g. the sit of his tail-coat, which is admirable. Your tale of that girl is very sinister. H.G. Wells was like that—and so was Mr Pepys, whose propensity I have seen mysteriously and unconvincingly ascribed to his stone in the bladder—not that that is more ridiculous than some of the Freudian excuses for criminals. Soon they will be whitewashing Neill Cream,[1] as Graves has Palmer.[2] (Have you read *They Hanged my Saintly Billy*? I haven't.) Or rather he seems to hint that P. was innocent. But Dr Kenealy recorded that P. gave him an impression of absolute evil. Sir Guy Stephenson who married my cousin told me that he and Bodkin (lately dead) both had the same feeling about George Joseph Smith (Brides-in-Bath), almost a sort of lowering of one's temperature, as Utterson (was it?) had in the presence of Mr Hyde. Interesting, if not *ex post facto*.

I have just read Hesketh Pearson's *Gilbert*—a dreadfully tiresome man—huffy and irascible, and at the same time thinking much of his fame, and despising the achievement which created it. Very like Conan Doyle, who thought highly of *A Duet* and scorned Sherlock Holmes. Have you ever read Gilbert's plays? Frightfully feeble and soft and stilted. But the man who could pour out such lines as 'An affection à la Plato for a bashful young potato, or a not-too-French French bean' shall surely remain immortal.

I have also read Sir Russell Brain's *Tea with Walter de la Mare*. Slight but enjoyable, though there is rather too much about the difference between the brain and the mind etc. Did you know him? Manifestly a delightful chap. There is one tremendous gaffe: Brain says that de la Mare thought 'A Mr Wilkinson, a clergyman' was an actual line of Wordsworth's, and then adds that it was invented, as a

[1] A bald-headed squinting doctor who was executed in 1892 for murdering a number of women with strychnine.

[2] In 1856 William Palmer, a young surgeon of Rugeley in Staffordshire, was executed for the murder by poison of John Parsons Cook. It is almost certain that he had previously murdered many other people, including his wife, several of his illegitimate children, and his brother.

typically bad W. line, by Flecker!—when in several books on Tennyson and FitzGerald it is recorded that both claimed the authorship. He (R.B.) misquotes 'Golden lads and lasses must' which is of course what Shakespeare ought to have written but—most inaccountably—he wrote 'and girls all must'. Very odd, surely.

And a neighbour has lent Pamela Clare Sheridan's Diary—title forgotten—which with her outlandish experiences strikes me as not quite as good as it ought to be. But surely her heads in plaster or bronze of Lenin, Gandhi, and Winston are fearfully good? All the same one constantly feels a mild wonder that no one has killed her.

Must stop. *Foul* music by Gordon Jacob just over, in which the pianist stamped on, kicked, butted, thumped and finally threw out of window the long-suffering piano. Now *The Unfinished* removes the nasty taste; though George Hurst, the conductor, is taking it as fast as he bowled. I love the way Schubert (like Beethoven) falls in love with his air and simply cannot say goodbye to it. Bless them both— and you too.

26 January 1958   *Bromsden Farm*

As though to herald the cold spell, last week-end some sort of burglar broke into my office (apparently by using builders' ladders from next door) and stole my only warm overcoat. I was too busy to do anything about it till Friday, when the cold drove me to buy a fine new coat, for which I trust the insurance company will pay. If they do I shall be better off than before, since the old coat had weathered twelve winters and was rather tight. Nothing else seems to have been taken, and I can imagine the intruder gnashing his teeth over so many useless books and papers.

I do hope that fall really did you no harm. Large men fall heavily. Please keep away from treacherous ground.

Jonah's book has started off quite well, with a full-page leading review in *Punch*, a fine one in the *Telegraph*, tolerable ones in the Sunday papers and a good recommendation from the Critics on the wireless this morning. The dear old fellow is now deaf even on the telephone, where most deafness seems to disappear.

Russell Brain is a member of the Johnson Club, and a very agreeable fellow (the two statements are not necessarily contradictory). I enjoyed his book very much, because I could recognise old de la Mare's authentic voice in the conversations, and I admired the unpretentiousness of it all.

Last Monday I took Adam up to London, got his hair cut, gave him lunch, and sent him for the afternoon with one of my staff to the Imperial War Museum—Adam's choice and much enjoyed. Then steak and claret at the Garrick and on to *At the Drop of a Hat*. It was my third visit, but I enjoyed it as much as ever, especially since A. adored it. He slept in the flat, and in the morning I bought him a tweed jacket and some flannel trousers, and put him in a taxi to Paddington.

On Wednesday I dined with the Lascelles. They have made a lovely flat out of the old stables of Kensington Palace, quiet and warm and comfortable. Lady L. (daughter of Lord Chelmsford) is charming, and so is their daughter Lavinia, who was there with her husband. Also present were Tony Thesiger and his wife (née Virginia Graham, daughter of Harry G. and a life-long friend of mine), and Mrs Mulholland (née Harcourt) who is just about to take off for the Antipodes with the Queen Mother. All very agreeable and easy.

Next night I dined with Liza Heygate in Chelsea, in company with Hester Chapman (novelist and another old friend), Mr Justice Upjohn and wife (rather disconcertingly called Bubbles), and a middle-aged Jewish pansy from Manchester. Also agreeable, but I must try and keep some evenings for the work which now threatens to overwhelm me. Diana's proofs are uppermost, and it looks as though I shan't get them to press without a visit to Chantilly. I may go on Friday, and return on Sunday, so perhaps you'd better write to Soho Square this week.

In one of his letters to Diana, written from the front in 1918, Duff praises Meredith's 'The Story of Chloe' as one of the best short stories in the language. I read it last night—with some difficulty, since it's almost impossible to see the story for the words, but there is one excellent chapter (where Chloe plans her suicide), and in some way the effect of the whole story is greater in retrospect than at the time. If you've got it, do try it and let me know what you think.

Did you read Alan Moorehead's stuff in to-day's *Sunday Times*?

Jolly good, I thought, though I'm sure that Arthur Ransome, with whom I dine tomorrow, will pick holes in it. He was in Russia from 1913 to 1918, and nobody else is right, bless him—and you.

30 January 1958   *Grundisburgh*

First to make you green with envy (but not, I am confident, with hatred and malice) let me tell you I am writing this in the summer-house. The eye of the sun, I grant you, is hardly more than squinting at me over the wellingtonia, but I can detect a little heat in it, though, like other cynical visitors, I suspect that you might say that most of it is supplied by my imagination. Unlike Bolingbroke I find no difficulty in wallowing naked in December snow by thinking on fantastic summer's heat.[1] But I am not in this respect so offensive as Toddy Vaughan[2] who was popularly supposed not even to possess a great-coat. I say, how sickening about yours and that damned burglar. Mind you press the insurance folk hard; it may be just the sort of claim they like meeting for the advertisement. But they are a little apt to ask tiresome questions as to how old the lost coat was. You must stress the sentimental value of the dear old coat, what superior cloth old coats were made of etc. The builder whose ladder helped the chap ought to have a slightly uneasy conscience, but probably builders don't keep such things.

What has happened to John Heygate? He wrote a worthless much-puffed book about Eton nearly twenty years ago (*Decent Fellows*) and nothing ever again. His father was a colleague for some years—not an unamiable man, and immensely efficient in a philistine way. Mrs H. was a grim sardonic woman who knew all about football and rowing and had a sharp edge to her tongue. I treasure a remark of hers that the only thing Eton boys learnt thoroughly was the one thing Eton masters knew least about, i.e. good manners. Not bad.

Did you know M.D. Hill who died last week—as he told me a fortnight ago he was about to do, quite placidly. What had clearly happened to him is, I suppose, common at eighty-five, i.e. a complete loss of interest in all that is going on—a sort of *uncoupling* of one's mind from world affairs, human interests, old habits etc. He was a

---

[1] *Richard II*, Act I, Scene 3.   [2] Former Eton master.

blunt, matter-of-fact scientist but, *not* being a Wykehamist, had plenty of humour and could laugh even at himself. I liked him and we corresponded pretty regularly. My chief Eton correspondent is Wilfrid Blunt, who published recently a perfectly delightful book *Persian Spring—disgracefully* reviewed, by the way, in the *T.L.S.* Sneering at him as Mr Chips, wrapped up in Eton, prejudiced, intolerant and mocking about oriental ways etc—the truth being *exactly* the opposite of all these sniffy epithets. Do read it; it doesn't take long. It contains one witticism of real brilliance, referring to those old codgers who throng to Henley in July, what he calls the 'Leanderthal' type. And if that isn't of Oscarian vintage—well I ask *you*?

'The Tale of Chloe.' I read it at Cambridge, I think, and had it at Eton, where some boy borrowed and failed to return it. I remember nothing of it—except, wasn't there somebody in it called The Duchess of Dewlap? And in the same volume there was an excellent tale called 'General Ople and Lady Camper' which I remember thinking very funny. Was I right? Will Meredith ever come back? The world his people lived in is so completely dead. But then so is Henry James's and he apparently is reviving, though I don't suppose John Osborne reads him; how could he? There is as far as I recollect *no* allusion to a water-closet in either Meredith or James. Mugwumps! Mandarins! Stuffies! What can such old mokes know about *LIFE*?

I hope you are *quite* restored to health? You don't say a word about it. My fall left no ill effects, though 'between the stirrup and the ground,' so to speak, I remembered Amsler's[1] saying that a very large percentage of big men over seventy died from the effects of a fall. But not yet!

I must stop—having a slight but persistent feeling that my letters are getting too long, just as I have an equally persistent but far from slight conviction that I talk too much. Like Gilbert, who was disconcerted by the unexpectedly loud laughter when he jokingly said some people thought him quarrelsome. I see grins all round the table when I say I talk too much, hoping to be contradicted.

P.S. When Heygate's won the football cup, the players were presented by Mrs H. with Bibles bound in the house-colours (blue and yellow).

[1] Eton doctor.

Writing in your summer-house in January! Please go indoors at once, and try no more alfresco composition until the swallow dares. We have aconites and many snowdrops in flower: can spring be far behind? Yes, it bloody well can, as we shall doubtless see.

The insurance company has paid the whole cost of my new overcoat, and I remember how old publishers used to pray for 'a fire at the binder's', which would turn their unsaleable stock into much-needed cash. Did you read the article on Publishing in yesterday's *Times*? I think I told you they asked me to write it, and I'm doubly glad I didn't, since I couldn't possibly have mentioned my own name. I thought it quite good and pretty accurate, though, as they say, 'slanted' from the point of view of the big battalions. I must discover who wrote it.

I'm delighted to tell you that *Georgian Afternoon* is booming. We sold 550 copies last week (its first), and the booksellers had first to get rid of their pre-publication orders. Jonah is in high fettle, delighted with all his reviews and letters, and markedly less deaf! One of the places I saw him was at Ursula Ridley's. When I arrived, there were five women (very charming ones) and no men. I drank a whisky-and-water briskly, and when Ursie said 'Help yourself to another', I poured out a stiff whisky and filled up the tumbler with what I thought was iced water but turned out to be strongish Martini! Ursie wanted to throw it away, but I insisted on drinking it, and I can now tell you that a tumbler of Martini containing a large whisky is a great tongue-loosener. I held the five women in thrall, and when Jonah and Evy arrived they must have wondered at my eloquence. Later this same drink, backed up by a glass or two of this and that, sustained me through dinner at White's with my father and the Duke of Argyll. The Duke is dullish and rather pompous, but in my ultra-uninhibited mood I remembered that he spent years trying to fish up a Spanish treasure-ship from the sands of Tobermory Bay, and so encouraged him to describe the whole enterprise.

John Heygate has retired to Ireland, where he very happily does nothing with his third wife and some assorted children. He is amiable but irredeemably silly.

I was sad to read of Piggy Hill's death, and of Lubbock's. I was up to both of them, though, as I have often told you, the only beaks who inspired me were you and Wickham. The others were nicer or nastier, cleverer or stupider, but *not* inspiring.

I think that the 'uncoupling' of the mind at eighty-five, such as you describe in Piggy Hill, might well be a blessed state, though eighty-five needn't be the age for it.

Next Friday at 10 am I leave Victoria in first-class comfort, looking forward to a superb lunch on the French train. Diana will meet me in Paris and drive me out to Chantilly. Saturday will be devoted to the proofs of her book, and on Sunday morning I return by the same route. Write to Soho Square and I'll scribble an answer in the train. Shall I send it to Grundisburgh? When do you come to London? I shall expect you at 6 on the Tuesday—what fun!

I can't remember whether you've read Faber's *Jowett*—forgive my stupidity. I've just got down to it and am enjoying it enormously. The opening chapters are beautifully written, and I don't mind G.F's occasional thrusting in of himself (a habit in biographers which usually maddens and disgusts me).

Adam is up to Bobby Bourne and says he is 'v. nice'. Duff looked in for lunch from Oxford: he is still finding Greats tiresome after his military and other excursions, and I dare say a year of Oxford is all he will take.

I have just listened to Bertrand Russell propounding a new theory of the universe on the radio, but I had to leave the room in the middle and lost the thread—which I daresay I should have done in any case. Science is a closed book to me, and there are so many others I badly want to open.

5 February 1958   *Grundisburgh (summer-house!)*

It is spring-like this morning and, as with you, the garden is dotted with snowdrops 'hailing far summer with uplifted spear'[1] (which I warn you I quote *every* February every bit as unrepentantly). Your comment on Shelley's optimistic query I actually found pencilled

[1] Quotation untrac‹

14

in the margin of an Ipswich library book some time ago, proving once again that what Suffolk thinks today London does to-morrow.

Very good about your overcoat. Mind you get a really good one, and avoid having flu twice in the winter. Yes, I read that article on publishing with interest, as your name suddenly caught my eye. Did you know old George Longman, an immensely worthy, straitlaced, rather ungenial man? Fifty years ago he said that he always gave the same advice to any young man who thought of going in for publishing, viz 'Don't'. However he wasn't head of the firm, and his second son Bobby (a great friend of mine at Eton and Cambridge and very rarely seen since) did go into the firm and has just retired, not I gather bankrupt, so G's advice looks a little timorous. He was a very good bat in the early 70's. I can remember about ten individual strokes that I saw made since 1897. One of Trumper's in 1905 stands out because it was unique, i.e. in none of the books, and never made before or since. Oddly enough one was a square *cut* by Rhodes, who later forbade the Harrow boys ever to cut (or 'coot') as it was unsafe. ('But, Wilfred, a cut's the greatest fun.' 'Cricket's not meant to be foon'—which ought to be in the *Oxford Book of Quotations*, being on the same level as Goering's 'Guns are better than butter'.)

But I weary you. I imagine the success of Jonah's book will help him with the Lit. Soc. Good! I was immensely tickled by your saying it had diminished his deafness; publishers must see human nature with frightening penetration. Also I enjoyed your rake's progress from Martini to Martini—making glad the heart of both R.H-D. and His Grace of Argyll. Was he at Eton? If so, no doubt called Hamilton. *All* dukes at one time or another seem to be called Hamilton. (It is drenching at the moment, and the rain on my tarred felt roof makes a fine tattoo.)

Jowett: yes, indeed, but surely I told you how much I had enjoyed it and added some probably irrelevant comments about the resemblance between J. and Hitler, i.e. some genital inadequacy or oddity. But I expect it was towards the end of a letter, and very faint and few are those who get as far as that—as Macaulay said of those who were in at the death of the Blatant Beast (which, in cold fact, hasn't happened by the end of *The Faery Queen*. It must have been the only book which Macaulay didn't finish).

15

(The sun is emerging. They that endure to the end shall be saved.) I look forward as always to next Tuesday. The only members I have never seen there are E.V. Knox, Balcarres, Laurence Irving and John Betjeman—excluding some like Harold Caccia in another continent and of course the P.M. *He* has just left N.Z., and my nephew, the Governor-General, found him very aloof and inattentive, but charitably supposes he may have been tired. But he does add how disappointing great public men are to meet—as Max Beerbohm once said, I believe. I haven't met many P.M's or ex-P.M.s. Eden was an icicle, Attlee amiable but wholly non-committal, Winston as Laski described him—'like a great actor playing a part'. Baldwin seemed more human at the top of Lord's pavilion during a Test Match, but he fell asleep long before any test could be applied. And years ago A.J.B. shed over all the company streams of that impersonal geniality which leaves one with the firm conviction that fundamentally he doesn't care a straw about anyone. Birkenhead was tight the first time I met him, and showed off interestingly but rather repellently on the second occasion. Half the present cabinet have or ought to have touched their hats to me,[1] but that won't save the country, though in a few years' time it may well be that the country wishes they were back.

9 February 1958   *36 Soho Square*

I meant to write to you on the ship to-day, but I had eaten so heavily and so well on the French train that when the time came I spent the brief sea-voyage half-asleep in an armchair. And now I am sleepy and silly after a long day's journey.

On Friday morning I just had time to look through the post before catching the ten o'clock train and there was your faithful letter, bless you. I read it in the icy train. The snow started in mid-Channel, and my train was three quarters of an hour late in Paris. At Chantilly all the telephone lines were down—and still are. The only other guest was Loelia (née Ponsonby), last-but-one Duchess of Westminster. I spent most of yesterday going through the proofs with Diana. The house is centrally heated, and one can't get used to that in one day.

[1] As boys at Eton.

16

Last night Frank Giles, the *Times* Paris correspondent, came to dinner with his wife (a daughter of Lord De la Warr)—nice young gay people. The whole expedition was quite an amusing change, though considerably less restful than my usual week-end.

I shall expect you here about six on Tuesday, to admire the clock *in situ*. Malcolm Sargent is coming again to the Lit. Soc.: you must have charmed him! The election went as I forecast last week, so you will soon be able to test Jonah's hearing. His book is still going well, I'm glad to say.

Forgive this miserable snippet of a letter. Next Sunday I will resume my normal rhythm.

67 Chelsea Square
London S.W.3

13 February 1958

This cannot be more than a scrap designed mainly as a gesture of defiance to the absurd notion that seeing you on Tuesday could be considered a valid reason for not writing to you on Thursday.

The dinner, as always, was immensely repaying. I sat between the same two as I did a year ago on my first appearance when I was most graciously put at my ease by Tommy Lascelles and surely the nicest of all lawyers, Sir D. Somervell.

I told Peter F. of the pleasant article in the February *National Review* by John Verney (signed 'Trix' and with a good deal of reference to 'Strix'[1]) and your penetrating eye will to a great extent gather from it what sort of chap he is (curious how clearly one sees that in many cases but emphatically not in all). Tommy L. was much amused with the additional chit about Charles Morgan in *The Times*, commending him as a conversationalist. We recalled a dinner at which we all were which C.M. nearly killed till (according to T.L.) I, if you please, talked him into silence. The evidence that I am the most garrulous of ancients grows steadily. I must do something about it. Don't be surprised if, when we next meet, all you get from me is a beautiful smile tinged with sadness, and no words at all. Not all that easy, I suspect, and I remember Hensley Henson's summing up of his

[1] Peter Fleming's pseudonym in the *Spectator*.

Dean, Welldon: 'a man who can neither speak with effect, nor be silent with dignity.' What a grandly perceptive eye *he* had—and the crispest possible style. I must stop, but I leave with you, after all this drip, one thing of his which you will appreciate. It hits an old house-tutor full in the wind. His comment on 'that strange institution the public school': 'I cannot think that the conscientious and devoted governess method, sublime in its self-dedication and Pharisaic in its scrupulosity, can be altogether wholesome for the development of character.' Well, there you are; the old brute (whom I love) doesn't attack the system, as do others, at one of its *weak* points, but at what is usually thought its strong point.

Still I did always try to follow that shrewd advice of C.M. Wells to A.B. Ramsay: 'Ram, I'll tell you a thing; don't see *too much* of your chaps.' It is *very* wise. And when one saw boys *drained* of individuality by too conscientious tutoring one realised it to the full.

Perhaps 'scrap' isn't altogether *le mot juste* for this letter. It is *your* fault. I start, and then I see your face and hear your voice, and remember half-a-dozen things you said, and the thoughts (too big a word?) begin to throng. How horribly duller my old age would be if this correspondence had never started!

P.S. Charles Morgan died in his sleep. His wife has just told Diana. They had been discussing the poet Traherne.

16 February 1958   *Bromsden Farm*

Your splendid 'scrap' from Chelsea was awaiting me here on Friday evening. Clearly the motto on the paper, *Ventis Secundis*, must stand for Second Wind. Jonah's joy at *his* election was unbounded and most touching. Directly he got Tommy's letter on Friday morning, he rang up to say it was the nicest thing that had ever happened to him, and he was so very grateful to you and me for putting him up. That same morning Jonah's book was magnificently reviewed all over the centre page of the *T.L.S.*—by Alan P.-J. himself, I feel sure—so the old boy's Valentine was a pretty good one.

Some day you must introduce me to John Verney: Peter told me to-day that he had read that article in the *National Review* and thought it excellent. Have you by any chance got a copy of it to lend me? I much enjoyed Hensley Henson on public schools: did you know him? Is there a good biography? With letters?

I have had a charming letter from Hilda Morgan, Charles's widow. She is naturally distressed by the inadequacy and mediocrity of most of the obituaries. I am telling her not to worry about C's literary reputation, which will inevitably find its own level in the end, and I'm sending her that Emerson passage which I sent you a few weeks ago. I shall go to the memorial service at St Margaret's on Thursday: it starts at noon, and at one I have to take the chair for a bookseller at a lunch-time meeting at the National Book League in Albemarle Street. A fast taxi will be needed, in which I shall reverse my double-sided jersey from black to scarlet, and whip on another tie, so as not to depress the assembled booklovers. There was a splendid row at last week's meeting of the Royal Literary Fund, during which the secretary and the treasurer accused each other of idleness and incompetence. If only all committee meetings were as lively!

This springlike weather is most beguiling. We have snowdrops, scyllas and yellow crocuses in flower, and yesterday I saw a pair of pied wagtails who showed every sign of setting up house. Today we lunched out of doors, and I imagined you in your beloved summer-house.

Since then, apart from an hour's gardening of the rougher kind, I have been reading one manuscript after another, until I never want to see one again—and so many books all round waiting to be read! Also I spent an hour on poor neglected Oscar, whom I have now got to Naples in the autumn of 1897—the beginning of his decline. Although I now know his whole life backwards and forwards (which is often the way I have to work at it) I still feel moved as I retrace every step of his terrible journey. How tickled he would be to know that someone was spending years of patient work on the minutiae of his life's correspondence!

Diana Cooper's first volume is now, thank goodness, passed for press, and soon I shall have to start work on the second volume, which is already in rough typescript, waiting for me to cut it into chapters, correct the spelling, supply punctuation and generally

19

knock it into shape. She is even now starting to write the *third* volume!

Duff writes from Oxford to say that he and a friend are meditating a drive across the Sahara in a Land Rover. I have written back sternly, saying that I have seldom heard of a more pointless idea. What next? My daughter Bridget writes from New York to say that Alistair Cooke thinks he can get her a baby-minding job in Arizona. She, bless her, always manages to pay for herself, and I have encouraged her to go, though it would be nice to have her home for a bit to help with the housework. A London flat, which a daily woman can more-or-less clean in an hour, has its advantages. Can you manhandle a Hoover? Nor can I.

19 February 1958   *Grundisburgh*

The snow is responsible for this beastly Biro, because I ought to be in the summer-house. In the drawing-room I am a sufferer from that strange feminine dislike for a masculine table a-drip with masculine gadgets which must not be touched, so I am condemned to an arm-chair and Biro. I used to employ an ordinary pen and an inkpot (full of midnight-black indelible ink) poised on the arm of the chair. I cannot say it was a popular set-up, and for quite a time could not understand why. But I did in the end. My plea that, on that occasion, the fact that the chair-covers were away at the cleaners showed that the Almighty was on my side was not well received. Hence an occasional spell of this graphological abortion.

I also had a delightful letter from Jonah. Last Friday certainly was a good day for him—though he modestly says P.-J.'s *T.L.S.* review must be discounted as he is a personal friend, and indeed a relative of his wife's. But I saw nothing in the review which could be faulted on this ground, though of course it was conspicuously benevolent—and yet quite different from those too numerous reviewers who nail every other book with words like 'masterpiece', 'genius', 'irresistible' and 'exquisite'. How much, by the way, some of them are irritated by Harold Nicolson. Some by things in his Java book (which I greatly enjoyed) but chiefly, apparently, by his *Observer* reviews. A silly (I know) young (I suspect) man, who calls himself Humphry Clinker, in a paper called *Books and Art*, has an article called 'Nicolson's Disease', which apparently consists in having an urbane and cultured manner. It seemed to me quite toothless, all bark and no bite; and how tired I am of such adolescent wisecracks as saying that H.N.'s writing gives H.C. 'the kind of sensation which might result from the sound of a silver-plated bassoon down which someone had carelessly stuffed one of the late Lord Curzon's socks'. If that isn't damned bad and silly writing, then I must go back to Remove again. I feel, on reading that sort of stuff, exactly as I did when reading *Lucky Jim*, which, alas, Jonah tells me he thought very funny. There is no doubt I am 'unprofitably travelling towards the grave' (is anything much better than a *good* Wordsworth line?).

I tried to get a *National Review* in Ipswich yesterday, but failed— though one bookseller has heard of the thing. I read it—not all through —in the Borough Library. Hasn't your club a copy? But I suspect you have no time to go there. Next to John Verney is an excellent critique by another old pupil John Bayley—now of New College (called by David Cecil his best English pupil some twelve years ago). He seems to me to hit off one or two aspects of Kipling and Conrad very happily.

There is a two-volume biography of Henson (by Braley) and two vols of *Letters* and *More Letters.* You can skip quite a lot in both, for I suspect your appetite for œcumenical affairs of forty years ago is no stronger than mine, but there is plenty besides. Of course you know his episcopal charge on 'Buchmanism'? A superb and shattering description with exactly *one* derogatory adjective and no more. Out of print now, but if you haven't read it do let me lend my copy to you. It won't take an hour to read, but, my hat, you will enjoy it.

Who did the *Times* obituary of Charles Morgan? Because wasn't that rather distinguished? I suppose he was not a man it was easy to feel *warm* affection for. I liked him on the two or three occasions when I met him—also all his *Reflections in a Mirror* and two plays which were really about something. I hope you managed your quick change in the taxi, and had no such contretemps as the absent-minded peer who arrived at the graveside wearing an I.Z.[1] tie.

What a spirited family you have! Of course there is no point in

[1] I Zingari, a cricket club, whose colours are red, yellow and black.

crossing the Sahara in a Land Rover, but how reassuring that there should still be young men who think there is. And a daughter baby-minding in Arizona must cheer the heart of any father except a James Forsyte ('She'll be knocking herself up one of these days, gadding about like that').

Your committee-meetings sound better fun than mine, in which even questions like 'Should there be a lavatory adjoining the school armoury?' raise no real heat in discussion. But at Ipswich the mutual hatred of the HM and the Bursar shows signs of developing on interesting lines. But what petty tiffs we have now compared with e.g. that of old Butler, Headmaster of Shrewsbury, with his Lower Master. For *thirty-six* years they did not speak to each other, and transacted all the school business by letter. And some still regard the Victorians as 'cissy'!

Jonah's happiness continues, for I have ordered a second impression of *Georgian Afternoon*. By the time it arrives in the middle of March the first edition (6000) should be exhausted. (I am exhausted now, but that is habitual, and beside the point.)

I had better leave Hensley Henson for my old age: if only he had flourished *sixty* years ago I could justifiably hunt through him for side-lights on people Wilde knew.

Ploughing through Emerson for that missing quotation I keep coming on copy-worthy bits. Whether you know it or not, here's one:

A foolish consistency is the hobgoblin of little minds, adored by little statesmen and philosophers and divines. With consistency a great soul has simply nothing to do. He may as well concern himself with his shadow on the wall. Out upon your guarded lips! Sew them up with packthread, do. Else, if you would be a man, speak what you think to-day in words as hard as cannon-balls and to-morrow speak what to-morrow thinks in hard words again, though it contradict every thing you said to-day. Ah, then, exclaim the aged ladies, you shall be sure to be misunderstood. Misunderstood!

It is a right fool's word. Is it so bad then to be misunderstood? Pythagoras was misunderstood, and Socrates, and Jesus, and Luther, and Copernicus, and Galileo, and Newton, and every pure and wise spirit that ever took flesh. To be great is to be misunderstood.

One doesn't hear any uncompromising voices like that nowadays, more's the pity. The telling phrase (rhetorical though it may be) looks like dying with Winston. How indomitably that old warrior battles on! Pneumonia and pleurisy at eighty-three can't, even to-day, be negligible complaints. Perhaps pickling in old brandy is the best prophylactic.

Charles Morgan's memorial service was well attended, and the choir (some dozen men) sang beautifully—the closing Nunc Dimittis was especially moving. But the service was torn in two, and its emotion dissipated, by what the programme announced as THE ORATION. Instead of a man with powerful lungs mounting the pulpit and roundly proclaiming Charles's virtues for all to hear, a chair was placed in the aisle between the choir, and to it was helped Dame Edith Sitwell, her bizarre beauty obscured by a fur coat and a huge black mushroom of a hat. Only her fingers, on which clustered emeralds the size of billiard balls, suggested her customary eccentricities. Having with difficulty extracted her spectacles and adjusted them, she began to read softly from a typescript, in which she several times lost her place. To me, scarcely a third of the way down the church, only an occasional word was audible: to the majority behind me, virtually nothing. Douglas Woodruff, who was sitting in front, told me next day that I hadn't missed much. The whole thing was a grotesque error of judgment.

The service finished at 12.40, and by great luck I immediately got a taxi, in which I dexterously managed my quick change. The National Book League had mercifully saved me some sandwiches and a glass of whisky, and I just had time to knock them back before facing the audience of forty or so, mostly feminine and elderly. I introduced the bookseller, who was supposed to talk for thirty minutes, after which a discussion of the same length should follow. To my horror, after speaking jerkily for *six minutes*, the bookseller dried up and sat down. There was nothing for it but for me to resume, and to keep up some sort of noise until the audience joined in or the bookseller recovered. Somehow I did this, and at the end of the hour I had to apply the closure to what by then was a tolerably lively discussion. Phew!

On Friday Comfort came to London for the evening. We had a good dinner and went to *The Potting Shed*,[1] which we both enjoyed. It's a preposterous play, but up to the end of the second act it's dramatically gripping. The third act is a feeble anticlimax.

As you may have seen, *Time and Tide* looks like closing down next month. This will be a great blow, since I have reviewed detective stories for them uninterruptedly for fourteen years, and have become used to both the books and the money.

26 February 1958   *Summer-house*

John Verney has had a charming letter from 'Strix' about his article and J.V. is arranging a dinner in March where we shall all meet. You must meet him some time. Poor Bernard Darwin, like that Norse hero (was it?), is slowly turning into a tree, and will never attend the Lit. Soc. again. I was always surprised that he was really such a commonplace talker. I remember once at a small party he contributed very little, though not apparently bored, and then some weeks later a *Country Life* article, largely based on this party, was full of humorous, shrewd comment which would have greatly added to our fun, had it issued in speech. Is he like Goldsmith, who once allged that, though he never had sixpence in his pocket, he could draw for £1000? Or Kipling?

How right you are about Emerson. Why has he gone *pro. tem.* so completely down the drain—just as Browning has, who, the Leavises now say, had, if you please, 'an inferior mind and spirit,' which is, surely, just silly? I like E's saying that 'the weak point about good resolutions is the fact that, even while we indulge the luxury of framing them, we know in the background of our minds that the task of carrying them into effect will have to be entrusted to the same old incorrigible law-breaker who has so often betrayed us in the past.'

[1] By Graham Greene.

That has more perception, human nature, and humour than many of G.B.S.'s much better known wisecracks.

Your account of Charles Morgan's memorial service is delicious. Why do very clever people behave so stupidly so often? Couldn't a brother or someone have told E. Sitwell that she is inaudible? As old Henson always averred, illegible writing and inaudible talking are both forms of bad manners—and very tiresome ones. Roger spotted you there, and maintains, *more suo*, that half of you was acutely observing who was or was not there, while the other half was fervently and melodiously proclaiming the desire to fly to the bosom of Jesus. Do you remember Horace Walpole's brilliant description of 'the burlesque Duke of Newcastle' at George II's funeral—holding his spy-glass to his eye with one hand and mopping his tears with the other?

Really your quick-change escapades! And then having to fill in the time (which, in passing, I bet you did jolly well). Don't organisers tell speakers roughly how long they are expected to hold the floor? Don't speakers ask beforehand? There are too many asses about.

Time and Tide yes, tragic—and very bad luck on you. Can *any* decent weekly survive—*John o' London's Weekly, Truth, T. and T.* What squalid times we live in. Nature too is quite mad. The sun is shining, a thickish snow is falling with a strong S.W. slant, though the wind is N.E. Sheer Lewis Carroll.

I am glad about old Churchill. These resilient old men are very heartening. On March 21 I dine with C.M. Wells—his birthday party. He is eighty-seven. But Plum Warner—eighty-four I think—is fearfully fragile and almost transparent. Odd that in his prime he particularly enjoyed the fastest bowling; he can't have weighed much more than the ball propelled by Kortright.

I am posting this on Wednesday, as the postal service here is 'looking both ways for Sunday' as George Bonnor used to say the English bowlers would if he could only remember that balls hit along the ground cannot be caught. He never did learn it. Ruskin said he was physically the finest man he had ever seen. He drank like a fish.

I'm glad to say there seems some hope of a reprieve for *Time and Tide*. I am in close touch with the charming young lady who dishes out the review copies. She tells me that Lady Rhondda has told the staff (who are naturally apprehensive and despairing) that the paper will certainly continue beyond the fatal March 22, and maybe indefinitely. We all breathe again. Did you see all the letters in the current issue? The subscribers may be few, but they are certainly loyal.

Last week was a bad one around here. On Tuesday morning Comfort spent four hours vainly trying to drive herself and five children to her school near High Wycombe, some fifteen miles. After skidding, sticking, being dug out, trying another road, she abandoned the struggle, took the children to their various homes, and eventually got back here frozen, wet, dirty and much agitated. (I don't know if I ever told you, but she suffers from blood-pressure so high as to be scarcely credible, which leads to periodical collapses, despite the quieting (and depressing) drugs which she is given by the doctor.) Clearly she was in a bad way when she got home, and the first letter she opened was one from Fred saying that Adam had been flogged by the Headmaster for helping another boy with his Maths Extra Work after twice being warned not to. Comfort has always had a horror of corporal punishment, and of the children being beaten, so this news, coming as it did, was the last straw. Poor darling, she collapsed completely, with nausea, giddiness and general weakness. She rang up Soho Square, but I had gone out to lunch, with a meeting afterwards, so heard nothing till the evening. She was quite alone here, and mercifully she had the sense and strength to drive over to a friend a mile or so away, where she stayed for forty-eight hours. This was just as well, since this house was cut off for the whole of that time—and her school too. I did what I could to reassure her on the telephone, and wrote to Adam telling him to do the same. He rang her up on Thursday, very cheerful, but even that didn't restore her. She got to school on Thursday and Friday, but directly I got down I took her to the doctor, who gave her some magical pills called Purple Hearts. I imagine they are made of Benzedrine or some such stimulant: God knows what they'll do to her blood-pressure, but they have removed all the other symptoms.

To-day we drove over and took Adam out to lunch at Bray. He was well and cheerful, and clearly not bowed down by either guilt or shame. He told us all about his crime. He is in C. Select for Maths (not bad considering he's only fourteen and a half), and in his Tutor's is a lad called X.Y., who is (clearly quite wrongly) in D. Select. He was apparently quite incapable of solving the problems he had to do out of school, and was so worried by his inability that Adam helped him. The warnings were not given to them specifically, but to the Maths divs in general. I pointed out to Adam the folly of this action, since he clearly couldn't carry X.Y. for the rest of his schooldays, and the sooner he's moved down to a div. within his capacity, the better. Adam was entirely frank and philosophical about the whole episode, which has clearly done him no harm. Comfort is, I think, finally re-assured, but I have asked Fred to send any further bad news (pray heaven there is none) to Soho Square. In fact he knows perfectly well I'm there all the week, and didn't think. Sorry to inflict all this on you, but it has naturally filled most of my week. And now I am supposed to write a 'Profile' of Diana Cooper for next week's *Sunday Times* in 350 words—an almost impossible task, which I haven't yet begun. Have I sent you the Wells-James book? Clearly not, but I will. I am reading *Sartor Resartus*, which is as clotted as Colin Wilson but much more rewarding.

6 *March 1958*   *Grundisburgh*

What a perfectly detestable time your poor lady and you must have had! I positively ached with sympathy as I read it, and so did Pamela. When we came to the execution of Adam, she, with that contempt for men's laws and that clear commonsense which all good women share, said 'Why did they want to flog him for that? Don't they approve of kind acts?' And somehow the case one puts up for the necessity of rules, and hard cases making bad law etc, invariably sounds rather thin and mean. I hope Birley had the sense to make it a token flogging

27

so to speak—and anyway I hope Comfort now sees that she has fundamentally been given additional reason for being proud of her son. Just before I took on Brinton's, a boy, moved to the heart's core by a sermon, went out onto Slads and presented a tramp with his new shirt and of course got six of the best from the captain of the house. Brinton, that worthy old sadist, told me the tale with glee. However God defeated Mammon in the end as the boy became a parson. The last time I saw him, I think the tramp had given him back his shirt, having found a better one on a scarecrow.

Last night I began the James-Wells book. What a little *cad* H.G.W. became when his temper was lost, and how easily he lost it—in the most literal sense, because everything he then said or wrote was untempered, e.g. to label poor old Percy Lubbock as a 'pretentious, academic greaser' who showed 'extravagant dirtiness' in boycotting Rebecca West's article on H.J. is surely right off the map. P.L. was never the *T.L.S.* editor, and what evidence is there that he had anything to do with what articles were or were not inserted? (By the way, might it not be a good thing to extract and print P.L.'s *T.L.S.* reviews? There must have been a good many, and the quality of them was very high. Arnold Bennett once said in one of his *Evening Standard* causeries that there was a man writing in the *T.L.S.* about Henry James in such a way that he had decided never to write another word about H.J. himself. Percy said A.B.'s remark *could* be construed as a condemnation, but, as Field Marshal Robertson said to the Cabinet, 'Well, I think different.')

I am always fascinated by the flexibility and rich resource of H.J.'s vocabulary and phrasing, even if he is saying only 'I hope to call on you some day', but I am surprised at his incomparably acute sensibility not spotting that he puts 'so' before too many adjectives and adverbs. Hypercritical? Perhaps.

I met F.L. Lucas once and liked him very much. I didn't notice his deafness (it was fifteen months ago). Have I a voice like Trollope's which brought the putty rattling out of the windows? *Of course* he ought to have been in the Johnson Club years ago—and David Cecil too. I liked his review of H.J. and H.G.W. in the *Sunday Times*. (By the way what an outstandingly attractive appearance, binding, print etc all your books have. I suspect you have always made a special point of all that. And how speedily your books are dealt with by reviewers. Quite rightly!)

I am delighted to hear you are re-reading *Sartor* which I shall at once do myself. It has superb things in it—the picture of London at night, the Alps ('a hundred and a hundred savage peaks') and the reduction to uttermost simplicity of such things as war ('What quarrel had these two men? Busy as the devil is, not the smallest', but they proceed to blow each other's brains out), and justice—Judge in red, man in the dock in blue. Red says to blue, 'You be hanged' and blue accepts it meekly and *is*. I don't quote—merely recollect from undergraduate days. It is odd to realise that so many professed lovers of literature fail to see, with all its blemishes, the enormous power (*yes*, and *fun!*) of Carlyle's writing. The 'pig philosophy' in *Latter-Day Pamphlets* makes one laugh out loud. And I wish your chap who anthologised him had put in more of his excellent letters (only G.W.L. and Max B. have realised how good *they* are! He said so while eating a *filly de sole* at Butterwick's table in 1943).

9 *March 1958*   *Glyn Felin, Neath, Glamorgan*

Comfort faithfully forwarded your letter, and it reached Soho Square before I left yesterday. The train was so cold that in my first-class carriage (ticket paid for by W.H. Smith, the sponsors of the so-called Brains Trust) I wore my greatcoat and muffler for the whole four and a half hours and shivered withal. I am staying with the octogenarian and stone-deaf (but nevertheless delightful) widow of a tin-plate magnate, who lives in this huge and arctic house with her unmarried daughter. In the old days they had five indoor and five outdoor servants: to-day they spend most of their time clearing up after themselves and the one grudging woman who works for them. It is snowing hard, and I have visions of the rest of the Brains Trust being held up, and my having to hold the audience single-handed for upwards of an hour. Not that I anticipate many turning up at half-a-crown a head. Hitherto I have always performed for helpless schoolchildren, dragooned into the hall. The full horror shall be reported to you on Tuesday.

So glad you're enjoying the Wells-James book. I've had an amusing letter from Percy Lubbock about the reference to him: you shall see it on Tuesday. I feel pretty sure P.L. would say his *T.L.S.* reviews were too unpolished for book-publication, though you and I would probably disagree.

Clearly your trumpet-notes crashed through F.L. Lucas's deafness, which has deterred feebler talkers for twenty years.

I am appalled to read in the current number that *Time and Tide* needs £450 *a week* to keep it going! How on earth can they secure that?

I am thoroughly enjoying *Sartor*, but my word, you have to dig out the nuggets! All those capital letters, German words, and the number of lines beginning with inverted commas must deter the faint-hearted. At Balliol in my day all Freshmen had to read a weekly essay to the Master or some other don. My first week the alternative subjects were Proportional Representation and *Sartor Resartus*. The first I didn't (and still don't) fully understand, and the second looked to me unreadable, so with the utmost pusillanimity I went sick.

I fear that note on Diana Cooper was poor; I struggled with it for days: the most difficult bit of writing I've ever attempted. Forgive this scrap. Tuesday 6.

10 *March 1958*   *Grundisburgh*

Sickening! We are so infested with climatic vagaries that I cannot leave Pamela to cope with them alone—pipes threatening to freeze, snow to seep through, and the moment a thaw comes the certainty of a flooded cellar and possibility of the automatic pump sticking. Like all pumps it is as temperamental as a prima donna. Only yesterday we exhorted ice and snow to praise the Lord, but alas the Lord's all-seeing eye spotted that I thought this exhortation ridiculous, so sent us an extra packet.

I am particularly sorry to miss this meeting, as I should have liked to add my welcome to old Jonah, but there it is.

I telephoned to No 36 this morning and a bright feminine voice said it would be all right *qua* the Garrick and warning them, and your secretarial soul will not be excoriated by having a dinner for seventeen and only sixteen guests to eat it.

And I had *so* much to talk to you about. Damn!

13 March 1958   *Grundisburgh (summer-house)*

Your Wales trip doesn't sound to have been pleasant, but I always regard you as one of those highly—and justly—praised by the psalmist, who, 'going through the vale of misery, use it for a well'. How deliciously characteristic that you should have been staying with the stone-deaf widow of a tinplate magnate. As to Lucas's deafness, and my not noticing it, I am afraid your diagnosis may be too kindly. I suspect he spotted that my conversation was not such as he need pay much attention to, and it would do to meet it with those inarticulate murmurs which H.G. Wells described as resembling responses in church. Have you read F.L.L.'s book?[1] I haven't yet. There was the sort of review I particularly dislike by John Raymond in the *New Statesman*, but I have a suspicion that L. *does* rely on too many quotations, apt as they always are. What do you think? His width of reading seems to be enormous—in several languages (but I wish he would translate his quotations from Italian and Spanish). And I look forward to making the same protest to P.-J. at the next Lit. Soc. Did you read that grim article on medieval Spanish playwrights some weeks ago?

I was interested to read in *Punch* that Anthony Powell always found H.G.W. unreadable. Odd—but I suppose to *his* generation W's speculations and prophecies and impatient omniscience were all becoming rather tarnished. *My* generation simply battened on him—not so much, in my case at least, his prophecies etc as his humour and frequent penetration. Who was the man at some wedding breakfast who 'had just taken a mouthful that amounted to conversational suicide'? And I bet old H.J. savoured such things too. But, Gosh, how dead H.G.W.'s books are now, while H.J.'s are not—though I gather in the man Amis's last novel, a character surveying another's shelves, and reading the titles, bursts out '*Portrait of a Lady*! Oh my God!' But even the youth of 1958 will soon be finding out that what Amis—with

[1] *The Search For Good Sense* (1958).

31

many others—says doesn't matter at all. I look forward to hearing what Percy L. said on finding himself labelled 'a greaser'. I believe H.G. *could* be delightful in company, and much must be forgiven to the man who invented the Christian name Altiora for Mrs Bailey, i.e. Beatrice Webb, in *The New Machiavelli*. I cannot help hoping that for a moment it pierced even her armour of self-satisfaction.

How right you are about *Sartor*; it *is* hard going, but as *he* said of Coleridge's monologues, wonderful sunny islets do sometimes emerge from the general haze. I was always attracted by the thrawn old dyspeptic, his poor tummy fermenting with what he (mistakenly) called 'an innocent spoonful of *porridge*' last thing at night. But, gosh, what marvellous pictures he had in his head. Do you remember the account of Robespierre's execution, ending 'Samson, thou canst not be too quick', with the dreadful reason why?

We liked your 'profile' of Diana Cooper, though Pamela—*more feminarum*—observed that her charm in old days was more perceptible to men than to women. Not that she was hinting at anything at all derogatory, but merely that D.C. got the masculine votes more easily than the feminine—which, when I look at it, is rather a bad platitude, bad because it seems to hint at something sinister in the background. But it doesn't—and P. is *never* 'feline', any more than was Hugh Walpole's biographer! (X's book still has not come my way. I am pretty sure I shall dislike *him*, as I always do a writer who is hailed by the 'chorus of indolent reviewers' as 'having no nonsense about him'. One knows at once he is going to throw mud of some sort at better men than himself. And one is *not* prejudiced in favour of a man who describes *Middlemarch* as 'insincere humbug' because the author lived in what one's grandmother called sin with the 'little ape' Lewes. On the whole *M* is my favourite novel. Was it V. Woolf who said it was almost the only grown-up novel of nineteenth-century England?)

I spent a day or two ago among the March monthlies much im- or de-pressed by an article on 'Scriptistics', but immensely cheered by the name of its author, which, believe it or not, is Dr Virgil Wigwam. Probably you know all about 'Scriptistics'? Those who master it (or them?) know *all* the rules about composing poetry. Another article follows it, by a Russian young woman who says—of course—that they have known all about it in Russia for years, and that Dr Wigwam

has slipped into several grave errors. Is there *any* limit to the anfractuosities of the human mind?

15th March 1958   *Bromsden Farm*

My Welsh trip was on the whole agreeable, though the Brains
Trust itself wasn't much cop. Some three hundred demented citizens
had paid half-a-crown each, and they filled rather less than half the
hall. The 'panel' consisted of Lionel Hale (in the chair), L.A.G.
Strong, Lettice Cooper (a nice Yorkshire novelist), myself, and an
ebullient Welsh schoolmaster (and, I gather, television star) called
Gwyn Thomas. On him we had to depend for answers of some sort to
such questions as: 'Do you consider that the flowering of Welsh
literature can be partly explained by the fact that Wales escaped early
from the domination of the Roman Catholic Church?' I found it easier
to cope with 'Are books too expensive?', while 'What do you consider
the greatest novel ever written?' produced a mixed bag of answers.
There were preliminary drinks in the Mayor's Parlour, but I managed
to avoid the subsequent dinner. Lionel Hale told me next morning
that all the Welshmen spoke until the Goddess Reason tottered on her
throne, and he had no doubt that any two English doctors would have
certified them all *in situ*.

Other Lit. Soccers besides you fell by the wayside on Tuesday, but
we sat down eleven. Tommy had Tony Powell and Jimmy Smith beside him, so I took charge of Jonah, who had Leslie Hartley on his
other side. Donald Somervell was on my left. Jonah seemed slightly
bemused and a trifle deaf, but he ate and drank heartily, and enjoyed
talking about quasi-theological literature with Donald. The latter delighted me by telling me that when someone asked Renan whether
he was turning Protestant, he replied: 'I have lost my faith, but not
my reason'. I expect you knew that already.

I have just read William Plomer's new book *At Home*. Having
known and loved W.P. for twenty-six years, I find it hard to judge his
books dispassionately, but I enjoyed this one immensely: it was just
like listening to him talking at his wisest and wittiest: do try the
book. Some of his jokes are first-rate, like his translating 'near-miss'
to a Frenchman as *demi-vierge*.

33

I don't think Tony Powell is wholly representative of his generation in his attitude to Wells. I am only a year or two younger than Tony, and in my youth I lapped up H.G.'s novels. *Mr Britling* was the first wholly adult modern novel I ever read, and I was as impressed with it as with my own advancement. What should I think of it to-day? One day I must try.

I realise that the profile of Diana wasn't nearly good enough, but it filled the space and delighted Lord Kemsley (owner of the *Sunday Times*), who called his staff together and told them it was the best one they'd had for years! Since they had written most of the others, they received his words somewhat sourly. Diana too was pleased, though horrified by the photograph. In a postcard from Rome she wrote: 'Glass[1] should be broken, and whoever wrote the praise exhalted.' (Her spelling is always her own.)

I am writing this on Saturday, because tomorrow morning I have to drive to London Airport to meet my American friend Leon Edel, the great Henry James expert (have I sent you the first volume of his biography of H.J.? He is now at work on the second). I'm bringing him here for the night, and taking him up on Monday to the flat, where he will stay, off and on, till April 5. Perhaps he'd enjoy the Johnson Club? You'd certainly like him.

I shall think of you carousing with C.M.W. on Friday. I am eagerly watching *The Times* for your next grandchild—'and still they come'. Have you any daffodils in flower? We have a few in bud, threatened by frost and ice. Poor Comfort had toothache all last week, on top of all her troubles, but to-day all is well. Duff comes home from Oxford on Thursday; their terms are all too brief; I only hope he will do some work in the garden.

20 March 1958   *Royal Empire Society*

I am at the furthest pole from the summer-house—the large and stuffy lounge of my club, among coal-black bishops talking volubly no doubt about God in various languages, all of which resemble the

[1] Douglas Glass, the photographer.

cries of alarmed cock-pheasants. Two are wearing tight skull-caps which, as no doubt you know, contrive to give the most saintly a criminal aspect. Is there some sect which regards a bald head as indecent exposure? Your Welshmen sound pretty garrulous too. Is there a great efflorescence of Welsh literature? It hasn't reached East Anglia yet. But if the idiom is that of that *delicious* book *How Green was my Valley* I hope it soon will. I don't think I have ever heard your opinion of that masterpiece. I wish R. Llewellyn would write a sequel to it, though I rather respect him for not doing so.

Jonah obviously enjoyed his first Lit. Soc. evening immensely, though a little distressed at the early departure of the older members, recalling the Doctor's dictum that any man who goes to bed before twelve is 'a scoundrel' (I have, not for the first time, the grim suspicion that I have told you all this before, and I can't look up your penultimate letter to see). I must get W. Plomer's book; it sounds good value. Is there *any* man of contemporary letters whom you *don't* know? *Demi-vierge* is brilliant. I am glad you are not an anti-H.G.W. H.J.'s admiration of his enormous richness and vitality was clearly deep and genuine, but I suppose with that up-bringing he could never get rid of all the chips on his shoulder. I should have liked to tell him what a grand bowler my father said his father was nearly a hundred years ago. Or did he regard bowling as G. Meredith regarded tailoring?

I say, London!! A dreadful place to live in. I sit in the Underground, deeply depressed by the scores of clayey faces all round me, 'all silent and all damned'[1] surely—absorbed in evening-papers but showing no sign of enjoyment, interest or any reaction whatever. And my seat is always opposite one of those emetic advertisements of Amplex. Last night at the rush hour I nowhere near got a seat and was almost flattened by the press. No one got out between Tottenham Court Road and Archway, where *all* got out. Does every clerk and typist etc live in Highgate? I had never heard of Archway till it became my brother's station.

Edel's Vol I is about the only book you have not sent me of all your rich output. Why not bring him to the Johnson Club? A good man—especially an American—*ought* to see J's house. I think it might be one of the better evenings with Roberts and Christopher Hollis—who

[1] Wordsworth, 'Peter Bell'.

now for some reason as obscure to him as to me has to sign his *Punch* articles Percy Somerset. Editors are strange folk.

We had a good week-end. Diana has produced a son and is over the moon with joy, and so is her good man. And on Monday Humphrey defeated the Barnet R.D.C. over his 'cowshed'. The surveyor was fool enough to say his proposed house was 'anti-social', which slow full-pitch was duly despatched to the boundary by H's law-man saying that a house deliberately designed to enable him to trumpet away without annoying the neighbours was about as non-anti-social as anything could be. And the hanging-judge cordially agreed.

I agree with you about the ridiculous brevity of university terms. The sums paid for twenty weeks' residence p.a. are extortionate. And I do wish the doings and sayings of Oxford striplings were not always front-page news. The young men can hardly help thinking themselves very important.

I have had two school G.B. meetings this week—not very interesting. The last thing ever discussed is education, and my views on finance and architectural plans are practically non-existent; nor have I ever really fathomed the difference between direct-grant schools and grant-aided, or whether it is or is not better to have a three-stream entry or a two-stream. The educational world is in labour with a scheme to prevent the Labour Government from mucking-up the public-schools, but I expect it will be stillborn. The Archbishop of Canterbury is a very good chairman of the G.B.A. and a charming man, but I suppose fundamentally a light-weight. Do you think he ought to have said to my brother recently (who told him a son of Geoffrey Fisher's had been in my brother's battery) 'And who the devil are you'? Very genially and all that, but can you hear Anselm or Sancroft or Temple saying it? 'Sir, this merriment of parsons is mighty offensive'.

The black bishops are sunk in slumber and are not looking or sounding their best; the waistcoat of one is sprinkled with cigarette-ash. Down below-stairs the Lord Alanbrooke is discoursing to a large audience on birds. I am afraid you may think this short measure, but my ideas flow more freely in the summer-house where there is no bishop, or babble, or snore, or Amplex—nothing but a score of daffodils, a robin or two (and of course an occasional flake of snow).

All last week I was busily occupied with Leon Edel. He is the most intelligent, charming and undemanding of men, but he hasn't been in England for twelve years and was clearly agog for literary and other society, so I did my best.

On Tuesday I dined him at the Garrick and took him on to a party at Rosamond Lehmann's, where he scored a right and left with the American Ambassador, Mr Whitney, and T.S.E., very mellow in his wedded bliss. Also present were Stephen Spender, Dadie Rylands, Hester Chapman, together with sundry wives and extras.

On Wednesday I went as a guest to the dinner of the International P.E.N. at the Criterion Restaurant. I sat between the elderly wives of the Esthonian Minister and the French Chargé d'Affaires. They were both very nice, but conversation was laboured until the Esthonian began in the greatest detail to tell me about her thrombosis. They had just got her into the ambulance when the speeches began. A French writer called André Chamson made a good speech (in French) which included a moving tribute to Charles Morgan and some good jokes. He said that wherever he goes he is asked the same two questions: '*Qu'est ce que vous pensez de Françoise Sagan?*' and '*Qu'est ce que vous pensez des Jeunes Gens Furieux?*' Then Leon Edel made a brief and fitting speech, Richard Church a long flat one, and then a ghastly bearded Scottish Nationalist professor spoke for what seemed hours. The Scotch *are* tiresome people, aren't they? Particularly when they're trying to be funny. 'I'm sorry to disappoint the ladies by not coming in my kilt—not that I've pawned it'—and so on interminably.

Next day I took Leon to a lunchtime lecture at the National Book League, on T.J. Wise by a reputedly redoubtable librarian from Texas called Fannie Ratchford. She proved mild and nervous, and said nothing new. All the bibliographical and bookselling boys were there, so that the discussion afterwards was better than the lecture.

On Friday I gave a Jamesian luncheon-party for Leon in the small private room at the Garrick. There were eight of us, and I think it was a great success. Now Leon is spending the week-end at Ewelme with the Nowell-Smiths, and is to rejoin me on the train tomorrow morning. (It is late and I am writing this so fast that I fear the sentences don't construe: pray forgive.)

I have never read *How Green was My Valley*, but almost thou persuadest me.

Lord Kemsley, still delighted with my snapshot of Diana C., rang up to ask me to do to-day's on Celia Johnson. I begged off, and suggested Bernard Fergusson, who wrote most of it, though the insertion of theatrical details of which he was ignorant rather spoiled its shape.

27 March 1958   *Grundisburgh*

No, it won't do![1] It is all very well for our stout eupeptic secretary to say that a fork supper (at £1.0.0 per head!) does not cause him a moment's embarrassment, but it ought to. And that hugger-mugger collecting of chairs at literally the last moment—was dear Dr Powell supposed to sit on the floor? It wasn't otherwise a *very* good evening. The paper was all right (was it *conspicuously* above B+?); and I wanted to have *you* within conversational range, though both Roberts and Hollis were excellent value (Roberts's little speech I thought the best thing of the evening). Were the many parts of that American's speech that I couldn't hear a) better, or b) worse than the parts I did hear?—which I wished the Doctor himself could have heard, and we should have had something to put beside his advice to the young man to have his head fumigated, 'for that is the peccant part'. And I should have done better with you and Roberts afterwards. Hollis was all right, Sir Russell was amiable but rather watchful and silent, and that nice, richly-stomached guest of Hollis's, whose name I have forgotten, was fighting a losing battle against sleep most of the time. Hollis is a good Johnsonian, by which I mean his annoyance about the catering sprang from a sense of insult, not to his stomach, but to the Doctor and the Club. Nobody will bring a guest to such meagre entertainment, but I fancy I saw that crusading glint in your eye, which the committee of the London Library knows and trembles before—in fact you have already got to work and roped in two new

[1] The recent dinner of the Johnson Club.

38

members who are sound in wind and limb and under seventy. Good Dr Chapman would have pursed his lips over them, I feel.

John Verney gave us an excellent dinner, and it really was a good evening, not ending till 12—except for Peter Fleming who came in 'faultless evening dress' (with medal-ribbons) as he had to go to some posh reception. He and J. Verney seemed to get on very well. I sat next to Lord Altrincham, who seemed an extremely pleasant fellow—much younger than I expected; John Murray the publisher, whom no doubt you know, and John Bayley of New College, an old pupil of mine, who writes poetry and criticism well above the head of his erstwhile tutor, and is married to Iris Murdoch, who, according to him, has far superior brains to his own. You would like him—in fact you would have enjoyed the evening and I wish you had been there.

I look forward very much to hearing what you think of *How Green*. I *cannot* believe you won't enjoy the English—or how you can fail to fall in love with Bron. When is your birthday and where?—your Yorkshire fastness, I suppose. I have no meetings for a month (except the Lit Soc—unless these blasted strikers dish that) and then we are soon in June when the dreariest of all ceremonies—school prize-givings —are thick on the ground. Tell me what to say to the boys of Bromsgrove, which will divert them from a career of crime and the weekly perusal of *Reveille*, which I heard an elderly man once sum up as 'all bosh and bosoms' which, however, doesn't distinguish it from many other journals.

I expect you have noted the death of my beloved half-aunt Mrs Alington. She was much crippled, and generally speaking full of broken machinery, but she had got home, after a week or two's nursing-home, went to bed and placidly failed to wake up. She was as good a human being as one could hope to meet.

Isn't there something in *Sartor* about how we 'haste stormfully across the astonished earth'? Never for a moment did Carlyle forget the mystery and the brevity and the incongruity of human life. A trait which I always liked in him. In fact all writers ought to have it—not necessarily *ever* to appear.

The Henry James biography Vol I arrived just before I left. In a minute I am going in to tea, then I shall open that delicious parcel—

39

and gloat. (Is there any greater pleasure?) I shall start reading it the moment I have finished *Middlemarch*, of which there are still 250 pages (out of 1200—one of the very few books that really are long enough). According to old Saintsbury very few are; he must be the only man who ever lived who wanted more of *The Faery Queen*. Have you read any of it? I once managed about ten pages and have ever since rested content with that.

I agree with all your strictures on the Johnson Club. I've no doubt that I *could* get it right, but I simply haven't the time. Why shouldn't the Club own its own liquor? Even that pitiable and extravagantly dear collation the other night could have been taken at the accustomed long table. Certainly no-one would twice inflict such pigging on a guest, and I can see some looming resignations as well. When Williams (the President) gets back, I'll have a go at him.

I'm planning to take three weeks' holiday immediately after the Fourth of June, in my Yorkshire fastness (don't tell Roger). There, apart from reading *Middlemarch* and *How green etc*, I hope to polish off the introduction to the Wilde letters, so that I can send the whole caboodle to the printer in July. But no doubt my reach exceeds my grasp—or is it the other way round?

I was so sorry to read of the death of Mrs Alington. I never knew her, but she was in every sense a great figure in my youth, and I never heard any but good words of her. You have unerringly put your finger on Carlyle's greatest quality—that constant feeling of man in relation to the mysterious immensities of the Universe—and one can forgive him a lot of his crotchetiness on that account.

Stephen Potter once wrote of George Saintsbury: 'It is recorded that for eighteen years he *started the day* by reading a French novel (in preparation for his history of them)—an act so unnatural to man as almost in itself to amount to genius.' He also quotes G.S. as writing in his *History of Criticism*: 'Grillparzer's natural limitations appear to have been further tightened by his playwrightship and by the influence of Joseph Schreyvogel, a sort of Austrian Nisard, of whom I do not know so much.' Both these splendid passages are to be found in S.P.'s entertaining book *The Muse in Chains*, a history of the teaching of Eng. Lit., published by Cape in 1937, when I was there. In it you will find, among many diverting details, the fact that F.D. Maurice was responsible for introducing Chaucer's *Prologue* into the syllabus.

On Thursday evening I took Leon Edel to see *Lysistrata* (which they pronounce LISS-ISS-*TRARTER*). It is tolerably amusing with some good bawdy jokes, but would be improved by the removal of much song and dance, which were clearly introduced to pad out the play to something like an evening's worth. I am enjoying Edel's visit very much, and shall miss him when he leaves next Saturday, though I must confess it will be convenient to have a little time for my own work. He is the easiest and most congenial of guests.

The Society of Authors, hitherto poverty-stricken, has come into something like a fortune by getting a small percentage of the royalties of *My Fair Lady*, and is now setting out on a programme of goodwill dinners, designed to bring authors and publishers together informally to discuss matters of mutual interest. The first of these occurred last Wednesday: it began with a dozen oysters each, and continued with bortsch (into which cream and brandy were liberally flung), excellent chicken, sweet and savoury. Two good wines, brandy and cigars. I was between a nice literary agent and Arthur Bryant, who was most agreeable. The idea that monopolised most of the talk was that publishers should pay a voluntary royalty of 1% on all out-of-copyright books, the money to be put into a fund to help literature, poor or old authors, scholarship etc. Like all such ideas, it is admirable *in theory*. Anyhow Arthur Bryant and I have been detailed to ask Tommy Lascelles—off the record—whether he thinks the Pilgrim Trust could possibly act as trustees to such a fund. Meanwhile I gather that our old campaign for new legislation on Obscenity in Literature (the Herbert Committee) may soon be brought to a victorious conclusion by the Government's bringing in a Bill very like the one we caused to be introduced.

For people to vote Liberal in disgust at the other two parties may be natural, but seems to me pretty pointless. I see no solution, and shall go on voting Tory until something better turns up. *Et toi?*

41

Your holiday is still a long way off—how you love overwork! I wonder what you will make of *Middlemarch*. Somebody at that Barmecide feast said he used to love it, but, on trying it again recently, could not make any headway in it. And now comes H.G. Wells's byeblow telling us that George Eliot was an impostor; he is reviewing her letters, in which he sees 'the slow perfection of a technique of self-deception that in the end equipped its possessor to become a perfect supplier of soft solder to *l'homme moyen sensuel*, the swamped and ignoble Tartufe (sic) of industrial society'. To which, as was once said, the only answer is 'resonant, monosyllabic, and plural'. For her great admirers were people like Mr Gladstone, Tennyson, Leslie Stephen, Birrell etc. It is true that old George Moore called her intellectuality 'studied brag', but that might have been expected. But what made Ruskin write 'that disgusting *Mill on the Floss*'? He may have been just about to go off his head—or have just gone. Of course one may well be derisive of all that solemnity, as of some sibyl receiving a string of worshippers, but I doubt if among them were to be found many *hommes moyen sensuels*. A. West like so many clever young men (but *is* he so young?) is much better—often good in fact—about what or whom he admires than on those *unsympathisch* to him, when, *me judice*, he often drivels. All he writes is from the personal angle—about the authors, not about their books. He gives you a pretty good chit apropos of Hugh Walpole, whose weaknesses of course he sees, but not much more. Your life 'told with tact and a feline discretion,' he says, is 'much more interesting than anything H.W. managed to write'—which I agree with, but I have never been a great novel-fan. He shows no signs at all that he thinks Maugham's 'Alroy Kear', depicted just at the moment when it would do H.W. most harm, the action of a cad. Surely the really final thing to be said about H.W. by people like God, R.H-D., G.W.L. etc is that he was a much nicer man than most of his detractors, and did a great many very kind actions. I do wish more critics had the art of indicating defects in others without contempt, or complacency ('I haven't such failings'). But perhaps that wouldn't please their public.

The other book I got from the library yesterday was Lord Elton's

biographical sketch of Bishop King of Lincoln—certainly the most
saintlike man I ever saw: it was unmistakable. Nothing solemn about
him, or hearty either. I once stayed with my aunt's husband, Bishop
Talbot, at Kennington, and the rest were Bishop Gore, Bishop Paget,
Bishop Lang, Scott Holland, Tommy Strong of Christ Church and
Bishop King. I was twenty-two; it was great fun. They all had the
greatest admiration and affection for old King, but, led by Gore, drew
a delicious and convincing picture of him (in his presence) as a
worldly, grasping materialist, of low tastes and habits, sipping beer
of an evening and falling asleep in his chair, after giving out that he
always had an hour's meditation before retiring. Old King played up
splendidly, and admitted that there often seemed to him no better
place to end his days in than 'a small public-house on the Harrow
Road'. You would have loved it, but Anthony West would probably
have been quite certain they were all hypocrites, and King an *homme
moyen sensuel*. A young cleric, elected to serve on some committee,
arrived late and frightened at its first meeting. Old King in the chair,
an atmosphere of the heaviest solemnity, only one seat left, next to
him. The youth stood appalled, but K. beckoned him to the chair
next his, and as he sat down bent and whispered to him behind his
hand 'We aint so good as we look'. But probably these mild tales of
clerical life bore you? It is very probable that you have never really
come across a saint. Blunden has something of the look of one, I
thought more than once. Is that right off the target? Oh, but yes, you
have, i.e. Mrs Alington; she certainly wasn't far off. That thing of
Robert Birley's in *The Times* was first-rate. The only thing lacking to
a complete picture was her magnificent *wrath* at anything mean or
vulgar. I remember a film in the School Hall in which the whole and
sole point was that nearly everyone in it was drunk. She came out at
the end, her face crimson and lowering, and standing on the steps in
her bell-of-doom voice cried 'Damn,' and added a few blistering words
about the results of long and expensive education. She had latterly
every kind of ache and pain, and lameness and blindness, and never
paid the smallest attention to any of them. She was the last of that
generation, her eldest half-brother being my father, born in 1842.

I like that saying about old Saintsbury, a man no one surely could
help liking and respecting; that tremendous gusto for everything in

life and literature from sandwiches to Swinburne. I remember hearing Housman say (after some pretty sharp words about S's style) that it was meritorious—a *very* high word of praise on A.E.H.'s lips—that anyone who wrote so much was so rarely off the mark in his literary judgments. Do you agree with his dictum that whenever you are offered fried sole, whatever may be the alternatives, fried sole should be your choice? I do rather, but C.M. Wells, though not antagonistic to this view, said that in his opinion cold ham was the only thing that deserved such a high place in the list. But he admitted that there must be nothing wrong with the feeding, the killing, the curing, the cooking, and the carving. I do like food, don't you, though, unlike Agatha Christie, we shall never say so in print? What is that love-poem which ends

> Seared is of course my heart, but unsubdued
> Is and shall be my appetite for food?

It was one of Mrs A's few weaknesses that food to her was mere fuel. I remember her vivid ejaculations, three quarters horror one quarter reluctant laughter, at an advertisement of some restaurant, one man glossy and taut with food and wine saying to another: 'Well, I think that's the best dinner I've ever eaten.'

That is lovely—'Joseph Shreyvogel, of whom I do not know so much'. G.S. must have been about the last of the polymaths. Do any of the Youngs and Bryants and Toynbees qualify? Who are these illiterate producers who always get names wrong? Lysistrata for instance, and I remember in the *Caesar and Cleopatra* film Britannus was always Brittanus, just as *every* lower boy for some reason used to pronounce Achilles as a dactyl. We have a good man on the County Council here who never will let pass controversy (as in 'of') or hospi*t*able. The only really sensible change in my lifetime has been 'laboratory', which, when I was young, was practically indistinguishable from lavatory, and now isn't. Except for the trivial circumstance that now no children are starving or ragged, practically all other changes have been for the worse!

I believe I have been more intolerably lengthy than ever. This paper? I know you like a juicy sentence. Here is what Meredith said in a letter of old Carlyle: 'Swim on his pages, take his poetry and fine grisly laughter, his manliness, together with some splendid

44

teaching . . . I don't agree with Carlyle a bit, but I do enjoy him.'
And 'He speaks from the deep springs of life . . . but when he would
apply his eminent spiritual wisdom to the course of legislation, he is
no more sagacious nor useful nor temperate than a flash of lightning
in a grocer's shop.' Perfectly true—and the grocer's standpoint
steadily ousts the seer's, and Mrs Sidney Webb rests in the Abbey
and Carlyle at Ecclefechan.

Easter Sunday, 6 April 1958   *Bromsden Farm*

In the snowstorm I began to fear that I should never get Leon Edel
to the airport, but all was well. Somehow Comfort managed to pick
him a bunch of daffodils, which, he reports this morning in a cable
from New York, stood the crossing well. I shall never grow accustomed to the annihilation of time and space. Leon's three weeks' stay
has been a great pleasure, but I had to spend most of my spare time in
his service, to the detriment of the long-suffering Oscar.

Adam redeemed his misdeed by once again doing well in Trials: he
just missed a Distinction (scoring 997 instead of 1000) but carried off
the Trials Prize for Lower C—which I call good at 14.8. He spent his
prize-money on a one-volume Shakespeare, *The Faber Book of Comic
Verse* and T.S.E.'s *Old Possum*—quite a good choice, and he said there
wasn't much else in the shop worth having. Apparently Fred
Coleridge is going to move into the new house as soon as it's ready:
the boys are being told that its inaccessibility and lack of a squash
court will be set off by central heating and (some say) hot and cold
water in every room!

I do indeed love food, and certainly put fried sole very high on the
permanent list.

Those bits of Meredith on Carlyle are superb: where do they
occur? I have won through to the end of *Sartor*, and am now em-
barked on *Heroes*. You always know the bits I send you, but here's one
on *Fashionable Novels*:

Of such Sacred Books I, not without expense, procured myself
some samples; and in hope of true insight . . . set to interpret and
study them. But wholly to no purpose: that tough faculty of

reading, for which the world will not refuse me credit, was here for the first time foiled and set at naught . . . At the end of some short space, I was uniformly seized with not so much what I can call a drumming in my ears, as a kind of infinite, unsufferable, Jew's-harping and scrannel-piping there; to which the frightfullest species of Magnetic Sleep soon supervened. And if I strove to shake this away, and absolutely would not yield, there came a hitherto unfelt sensation, as of *Delirium Tremens*, and a melting into total deliquium: till at last, by order of the Doctor, dreading ruin to my whole intellectual and bodily faculties, and a general breaking-up of the constitution, I reluctantly but determinedly forbore.

That's what the old hero wrote where we should say 'The book was unreadable'. I once drove through Ecclefechan, but had no time to drop a tear on T.C.'s grave. My God, what a depressing place!

Easter Monday morning
Another cold, grey, snow-laden-looking day. I shall not stir very far abroad. Adam is off to a point-to-point with a thermos of hot soup and a mass of sandwiches. Comfort is driving him to the house of the friends who are taking him, and the only chance of getting this posted is for her to take it. Hail is now sharply rapping the window.

Last week Eric Linklater turned up, unannounced as usual, and bore me off to lunch at the Savile Club. The food there isn't bad, but it seldom serves to absorb the quarts of liquor which are dispensed at the bar beforehand. As I left, Eric was ordering me a double Kümmel, and if he drank that as well as his own, he must surely have spent the afternoon lying down.

Did I tell you about my dentist? I have been to the same man for thirty-five years, and when he died last year I felt quite lost. Now, through the enterprise of my sister (who always went to the same chap), I am transferred to a charming Canadian, who makes tapestries and seems gentle and efficient. I paid my first visit to him last week, and came away much relieved. I have a horror of false teeth, which I have so far avoided. Martin Secker, the publisher, has still got all his own teeth at about your age.

The new Ian Fleming, *Dr No*, is pretty poor: after a brilliant opening chapter, the whole story becomes so improbable that, although his narrative gift makes one read on, unbelief is not for a moment suspended. I am supposed to devote 500 words to it in the moribund *Time and Tide* ('it's dead but it won't lie down') and don't want to hurt anybody's feelings.

9 April 1958   *Grundisburgh*

Never has spring been so long a-coming—or does one say that four years out of five? Bad year for daffodils they say; anyway only about a quarter of ours are out, and there is hardly a sign of that reddish mist about the trees which precedes the green. And R.L.S. was not saying a word too much when he called the N.E. wind 'snell, blae, nirly, and scowthering'—not that I really know what any of the four words means. I must ask Ivor Brown at the Lit. Soc. on Tuesday. Can you bear that I should drink with you beforehand, as usual? (No answer desired or deserved!)

I should have liked to see something of Leon Edel. Does he know Percy Lubbock? Clive Carey and I tried once at Lerici to find out from him why (if he knew) some not unintelligent people find H.J. positively nauseating, e.g. Swinnerton's friend who said that he was like (1) a formal suet-pudding, and (2) a rat (which is *not* very like a f.s.-p.!) and Laski who described him as 'a second-class mind dealing with fundamentally third-class ideas'. But you may well say (a) Laski was a sh-t (b) like H.G.W. a journalist rather than an artist (c) and liked denigrating. All quite true. But we really got nothing out of Percy—and one evening when we both said one of the H.J. stories— read aloud by me—seemed to be a lot of fumbling and fuss about practically nothing, we saw a not very distant danger-signal and changed the subject. Laski said H.J.'s letters made him vomit, with their excessive affectionateness and gush. Well, there it is our old friend allergy—such for instance as made W. Raleigh hateful to Swinnerton, though most people found him immensely likeable.

Adam sounds to have done well; in any case trials-prize and flogging in the same half I should think is a record. My son-in-law says he is a good boy, and he doesn't praise easily. He (B. Bourne) made himself, he says, very unpopular a fortnight ago at Putney, when he told the Oxford coaches (who were saying that Oxford had improved miraculously into a class crew) that he thought it was a thoroughly poor crew. I watched the race on TV with him. After *one* minute he said 'The race is over'—and it was! It is all very odd. When I was a boy, Cambridge never dreamt of winning the race.

How nice it is to find someone appreciating the flavour of old Carlyle as you do. I always have, but generally find myself in a minority of one. So few recognise *power* when they come across it. They boggle at his 'message' or his politics or religion (just as they do about Kipling's 'imperialism', as if that put *The Jungle Books* and *Captains Courageous* out of court). The Meredith sentence comes from a letter—let me go and find it—yes 1865 (no month or day given) to Captain Maxse.

Ecclefechan is a grim little spot, though I believe much less so than Craigenputtock, which I never saw. I asked a native of E. about Carlyle, and he had never heard of him. And I read some time that soon after his death a native, asked the same question, knew *all* about the others, but as to Tom 'Oh aye there was Tam, but he went up to Lunnon and I never heard as he came to any good'. It was he or another who summed up the whole family as 'pithy, bitter-speakin' bodies', like T's father (not mother) who at family prayers read the story of Joseph and Potiphar's wife, closed the bible and said 'Aye, and thou wast a bitch, woman' in a loud angry voice as if she was sitting there. That passage of T.C.'s about novels is just what I mean by his being full of flavour; all the many feelings the novels had given him are there, distinct and vivid. It reminds me—how shocked the old man would have been!—of what some woman told George Moore she felt in sexual intercourse. Now where on earth did I come across that? You will know. My uncle Alfred was taken to see T.C. in 1878 or 9 by Ruskin, and told us the old man was very dreamy and melancholy and, as R. said afterwards, already half out of this world. My uncle said R. was charming with him, so gentle and motherly. ('Now, now, this is too bad', as someone recorded was often his way of restoring some kind of equanimity. If T.C. despaired of civilisation in 1878, what would he have done in 1958?)

I gather you did not go to the point-to-point, and suspect that you may share my view that it is about the poorest of human pleasures—almost on the level of the sheep-dog trials in Westmorland (though I grant you the pleasure of seeing a dog on one side of a broad valley obeying the inarticulate cries of a shepherd on the other side, about two-thirds of a mile distant).

Your vignette of Eric Linklater calls him up vividly. Is he going to be at the Lit. Soc.? I agree in resenting false teeth, though I have long been in the state of Miss Bobby Bennett's mother 'who imparted to me the surprising confidence that she had only two teeth in her head, but thank God, they met'. It is tragically sad that Œ.E. Somerville lost all her love of the Irish at the end of her life. The rebels had burnt her brother's house, though the S. family had always been popular with the neighbours and done a great deal for them. She was a friend of Mrs Vaughan's and I very nearly met her at Willowbrook. I should have liked to tell her that my father, my sister and I *all* had *The Irish R.M.* at our bedside.

I shall not read Ian Fleming's latest. He has really gone off the rails in the matter of murders and beatings, and tortures, and impossibility, and lust; Bond I thought was becoming a bore in the last book, and must have made it now. Did you read the analysis of *Dr No* in last week's *New Statesman* by Paul Johnson? I was prepared to mock at P.J. but couldn't help thinking that, if his résumé was accurate, the boot was on the other leg.

13 *April 1958*   *Bromsden Farm*

Whoreson is too gentle a word for this penetrating and incessant wind. I daresay your summer-house trapped the sun to-day, but here the blast mocked the sunshine, though the boys manfully got the motor-mower into action. By hugging the library fire I have managed to drag Oscar another fifty footnotes towards completion. My present knowledge of the Parisian underworld of letters in the late Nineties would fill an issue of the *News of the World*, though all dates and facts are hard to pin down. I have also read (or at any rate plodded glumly through) Stephen Potter's new and allegedly funny manuscript. *Gamesmanship* made me laugh a lot, and its two successors were just

49

good enough (all three still sell prodigiously), but the world has moved (deathwards, you may say) in the last ten years, and Potter hasn't budged an inch. In truth the joke is played out, but he won't face the fact. This manuscript consists of a bunch of marginal articles, written during the past six years and slung together with the minimum of care. What am I to say to him? Some dreary compromise, I suppose—what a bore!

On point-to-points (or points-to-point), my dear George, we think as one. I'm thankful to say I've avoided all such for twenty-five years, but my children's appetite for them seems insatiable. On the other hand I have *never* been to a sheepdog trial, and would much like to, just once, preferably on my beloved Yorkshire moors. The ordinary farmers there can make their dogs do anything by long-range whistles, and I'd love to see them in competition with others. After that I daresay it might pall.

I never met Miss Somerville either, but I corresponded with her, and won her approval by playing up to her belief that Miss Ross was still collaborating with her *d'outre tombe*. I fancy Miss S. was a great spiritualist in her latter days.

Last week, walking to the London Library, I passed the little dead-end called Apple Tree Yard, between Jermyn Street and St James's Square. William Nicholson had a fine studio there for many years, and I was often a visitor. His great delight was to give one lunch in a tiny dark harness-room (the whole place had been a stable)—either herrings or lobsters, both of which were obtained from an adjacent fishmonger's with the splendidly eighteenth-century name of Dash & Bellamy. The shop is still there, but its name has marched downhill with the Common Man.

Don't you love names of pith and character? Our Henley butcher (though long run by others) retains its original name, Gabriel Machin, and the pleasure of writing it helps to alleviate the boredom and irritation of the monthly cheques.

Apropos of names, I here shamelessly copy out a suggestion I made in 1948, in a review of Henry James's *Notebooks*. I had always been struck by the extraordinary names he gave his characters—did ever a novel have such an off-putting start as 'She waited, Kate Croy'?—and ventured this:

And then there is the absorbing question of the names. At intervals throughout the notebooks James jotted down lists of proper names, taken it seems mostly from the front page of *The Times*, on which he afterwards drew for his characters. One list, for instance, begins: 'Chattle—Voyt—Podd—Tant—Murrum—Glibbery,' and continues in that style for five lines. What emerges is that when James came to select from these lists he tended more and more to choose a particular kind of name—gritty, aseptic, impersonal—Stant, Verver, Theale, Croy, Strether, Densher, Stransom. Was he determined to avoid the overtones which hung about his contemporaries; in Hardy the romantic-pastoral (Yeobright, Oak, Winterborne, Everdene); in Meredith the flamboyant-aristocratic (Patterne, Feverel, Wentworth, Beauchamp)? Was he deliberately seeking names which might be as near algebraic symbols as possible and yet remain names? Certainly few heroines have been saddled with such rebarbative syllables as Fleda Vetch.

Leon Edel told me afterwards that there was nothing in this theory: James just thought them good and suitable names!

17 April 1958   *Grundisburgh*

As always, a red-letter evening, particularly the hour beforehand (after I have recovered my breath!) which always passes much too quickly. It was the first time I have had Ivor Brown as a neighbour, and found him excellent value—a dry wine perhaps, but full of flavour —and even, as old Carlyle might have put it, of 'unutterabilities'. Did I gather that he has to be careful about his health? He repudiated beer to top the evening with, offered by Bernard F., and said he was going to drink milk at home.

Roger rang me up the next morning and was in good chuckling form after sitting next to old Cuthbert, who was in characteristic mood. He looked morosely towards our end of the table, and said that now he didn't know half the members (i.e. Tim, I.B., you, Bernard F. who have been in the Society for years, and me whom he has known since about 1912). He then mentioned Jonah: 'Of course you realise he'll come every month', which is very shrewd, but surely is not to be regarded as a black mark? However he beamed at me like December sunshine, which I attribute entirely to your having told him what I had said of him (*did* I say it?).

Yes of course you must go to one sheep-dog trial, but if you are with s-d *fans* remember to have a pressing engagement in, at longest, an hour. Then you will enjoy it. It is the third hour which gets one down. Best of all of course is to come accidentally across a fell-side shepherd on, say Helvellyn, giving orders to his dog on Skiddaw. I forget if you are a lover of dogs. Have I ever seen one at Bromsden Farm? I am not really, though I like our sheepdog collie which has a curiously attractive blend of cleverness and absurdity and friendliness—except of course to the postman—and when Pamela is there, pays no attention to anyone else.

Following on—or in the modern jargon further to—our talk about names, the *Daily Telegraph* has a good paragraph this morning which I shouldn't like you to miss, so send it. The Alingtons some years ago found a man at their gate knocked out by a motor-car. Lavinia their doctor-daughter had him brought in and put on a sofa, and then came and told her parents 'Believe it or not, but his name is Gotobed'. Yet I have a feeling that it is not as rare as one might think—like Lord Emsworth's pig-man 'Wellbeloved'. John Christie's game-keeper had the Christian name of Eli, which was quite right in a household where oddity was normal. I am pleased that a leading scientist who once stridently declared 'the spark-gap to-day is mightier than the pen' should be called Hogben. That vast tome of his called *Science for the Million* contains obiter dicta such as 'Time will come when Johnson will be remembered, *if at all, for his ineptitudes*'! I am sure he is a man to whom one can safely apply the adjective 'rebarbative', a word I have never used before and doubt if I ever shall again, any more than I have and shall the word 'ambivalent' which is compulsory in almost any *New Statesman* review.

Old Henry James's ear or touch failed oddly sometimes, as David Garnett pointed out in the introduction to *Fourteen Stories* (perhaps the first book you gave me) when he changed 'He looked like a young soldier on a battlefield' to 'He was all the young soldier on the gained field,' and Rebecca West bluntly says his corrections were often ruinous. Had he a vein of Daddy Wordsworth in him? My son-in-law Bourne has just read your *Hugh Walpole* with great pleasure and many chuckles. He ended by liking H.W., greatly disliking Maugham, and very impatient with H.J.'s tortuous letters. I cannot find in your book any evidence that supports Swinnerton's saying that H.W. 'no longer cared for H.J.' Didn't he merely outgrow the period of tutelage? But I may be quite wrong.

I have been reading a Simenon novel in bed—not a detective story, and, as so often with the modern novel, am put off by the ridiculously acute and comprehensive understanding which most of the characters are said to have of all the complicated feelings behind every word, look, and movement of everyone they are talking to. But all you pundits, I gather, put Simenon very high. If you are a S. fan, tell me what to read of his.

20 *April 1958*   *Bromsden Farm*

That *was* a good evening, wasn't it? It's always a good sign when the club servants think it's time the party ended. I didn't gather what was the matter with I. Brown: he ate quite heartily, but stuck to white wine and refused the savoury. While you were talking animatedly to Jonah and Bernard, I felt it my duty to have a crack with Cuthbert. He was affable, and as usual thawed after a judicious application of melted butter, but I can't say I find him an enlivening companion. He told me that no candidates ever got elected to the Lit. Soc. unless proposed by the President or Secretary, and that for him (Sir C.) to propose anybody was a certain way to ensure his non-election. I pooh-poohed it all, but in fact the second part of his statement is true. Why can it be?

I am definitely *not* a dog-lover, which is why you have never seen one here, but I don't object to other people's, especially in small doses and preferably out of doors. How shocked Pamela will be!

I'm delighted to know of your son-in-law's reading and approving of my book: one expects people (perhaps) to read a book when it's new, but a message like yours six years after publication is most heartening. It's quite false to say that Hugh ceased to care for Henry

53

James. In the last few years he may not have been quite so assiduous in his attentions, but the War was partly to blame. After H.J.'s death early in 1916 Hugh blamed himself for not having taken more trouble to see H.J. during his last leave from Russia, though in fact the old boy was probably too ill to see anyone.

Yes, I am a Simenon-fan all right, but naturally he has his ups and downs. How could he fail to, writing at least six books a year? Unfortunately I can't now remember which are the best ones, so can't advise you.

Yesterday we all drove to the Cotswolds to lunch with Comfort's stepmother, and on the way I snatched half-an-hour in Blackwell's, where I picked up one or two trifles. Nowadays I find motoring increasingly tiresome—so many cars on the road oblige one constantly to brake, stop and change gear. The first gleams of sun bring out L-drivers like flies out of winter-quarters.

What else can I tell you? On Thursday I lunched with Cecil Beaton at his house in Pelham Place: superlative food served by butler and parlourmaid, and a delightful party of eight, including Margot Fonteyn—a bright, intelligent, gay little monkey. Nowadays I so seldom attend such a luncheon-party in a private house that an occasion like this, besides being highly enjoyable in itself, brings back nostalgic memories of *la douceur de vivre* and the golden age.

On Wednesday I lunched in Soho with Tommy Lascelles and Arthur Bryant, to discuss a new scheme for raising a fund to help authors in difficulties. Also I attended a meeting of learned Counsel in the Temple to discuss Diana Cooper's tax problems, with which I will not bore you. Tax-experts are a new—and not altogether welcome—class of men, though they certainly have their uses.

My daughter is due to arrive on Tuesday on the *Queen Elizabeth*, and everything is swept and garnished for her approach. I must try to see that her young man has adequate access to her when she gets here.

I heard today that my only uncle—my father's elder brother—died yesterday. He had been dotty for years, apparently quite happy in some sort of home unless any of his family visited him, when he went off the deep end. He spent all (or most of) his life in the Colonial Service—Gold Coast, Fiji, and Cyprus. When the mob rose in Cyprus they came first to his house to destroy it. He came out and addressed them, saying: 'I am your friend. I have spent years working for you. If you must burn something, please go and do it somewhere else.' Inspired by his oratory, the mob went straight off and burnt Government House to the ground, whereby Ronald Storrs lost all his books, pictures, carpets and other treasures. I once said to R.S.: 'I'm afraid my uncle was responsible for your losing everything.' Generously he replied: 'We must believe he thought he was acting for the best'. Now it doesn't much matter to either of them.

23 April 1958   *Grundisburgh*

The reign of chaos is not yet at an end in this corner of the world—or in any other, judging by the newspapers. *Is* this the workaday world, or is it some species of fairyland? You will wonder at the question till I tell you a series of facts. Last *Thursday* Pamela was rung up by the B.B.C. and told Humphrey was to be the victim in the 'This is your Life' programme on *Monday*. Would she or I come and take part? No. Could his old nurse or governess? Both dead. His old tutor? Abroad, address not known. His friends? Well, yes, we told them the names we could think of. His sisters? One possibly from Eton, but alas the one who knew him best, Mary, was in Malaya, so of course couldn't come. Oh couldn't she! We'll fly her over, and back. And so they did for her seven or eight minutes with H. We saw the half-hour; it was quite amusing. The best thing in it was H's face when he heard Mary's voice outside. M. says the flight must cost them about £350, and others were flown in from all over England. Does it make sense to you? Didn't Macaulay take a year to get to India? The number of people who watch TV is staggering. I went in to Ipswich yesterday, and *everyone* I met, except two, had seen the show, and reproached me for not being in it. It is obvious that it will soon be regarded as a *duty* to appear if asked. Also that in ten years or less a house without a TV will be as out of date as one without a water-closet.

I am glad at what you say about Hugh W. and H. James. It is quite natural that they met and communicated less often latterly. I am two thirds through the Edel volume. Am I stupid or what in thinking we should have liked H.J. more as an old than as a young man? How odd is the effect of his brother's presence—the merely physical effect —almost as inexplicable as the old King's don found the fact that whenever he played the piano his fire smoked—the cause, not discovered for some time, being that the undergraduate in the rooms above on these melodious occasions climbed out of a window and put a slate over the chimney-pot.

Apropos of what you said of H.J.'s bad names, it is amusing to read (on p 213) that he was highly sensitive about names, and actually said to call someone Kate instead of Katherine might be *fatal* to the story! But why did he think Kate Croy better than Katherine Croy?

Let me know the name of a good Simenon when you remember. After H.J. I embark on Gordon Ray's Thackeray volumes, once again trying to find out why I dislike T. as a man. Is it (in the words of that very far from stupid man Hugh Kingsmill) because of his 'claret and Ecclesiastes melancholy, and nervous insistence on his gentleman-liness'? Something of the kind, I think. I used to love *Esmond*, but I remember P. Lubbock once saying that after a time you 'began to see how it was done' and that spoilt it. He who must not be named[1] has, I believe, the lowest opinion of it.

Motoring. How right you are. It is clear that in fine holiday weather the situation really does approach the impossible. And what of ten years hence? Man will very soon choke himself with his own inventions, quite apart from the explosive ones. Meanwhile the pleasant old crafts like the blacksmith's and the thatcher's steadily diminish. A tree, a yard in diameter, is felled in a few minutes by the motor-chainsaw; it used to take two to four men half the day. The Hagley blacksmith, like Handel's village b., had muscles as strong as iron bands; the head woodman could use an axe with the grace and precision with which Sergeant Troy used his sword.[2] Both would be out of work now, or minding a machine, and whereas old Wolryche (the smith) played draughts of an evening in the Nineties, he would in the 1950s be watching 'Life with the Lyons'.

[1] F.R. Leavis.
[2] In Hardy's *Far from the Madding Crowd*.

I'm late starting my letter tonight, because I've just spent a whole hour listening to a broadcast of an interview with Harry Truman. I've always had an immense admiration for him, which this talk only enhanced. I wonder whether you heard it? He seems to me a wonderful argument for the American political system at its best. A little haberdasher from Missouri who had to decide to drop the first atom bomb, to intervene in Korea, to run the Berlin air-lift, to fire General MacArthur—a man of immense courage, honesty and common sense. I only wish he was still there!

Bob Boothby, whom I dined with the other night, told me he'd just seen Monty, newly returned from the U.S.A., who said that Eisenhower is firing on one cylinder and can't string two consecutive sentences together: it really is appalling. Boothby also said that Winston was so decrepit when he went to the House last week that they can't believe he'll last very long. This dinner was at White's, where my usually somewhat glum dinner with my old father was turned into a feast of fun by Bob's presence. He is the best company in the world, though among my father's friends I should say your cousin Oliver ran him close.

Needless to say, the Headmaster has refused Adam permission to come to my father's eightieth birthday lunch. If only Fred had been half as enlightened as G.W.L. he would have given permission himself: it's infuriating.

Your account of Humphrey's television performance is fantastic: if they can really afford to spend such sums fetching supporting members of a half-hour broadcast, what must the stars receive!

When you say Handel's village blacksmith, you must mean *Longfellow's*. Handel's was more harmonious than muscular.

I was very fond of Ronald Storrs. His public manner may have been a trifle pompous, but he had a fine sense of humour and an enormous love of life and letters. Apropos of my book, I asked him whether the sovereign says 'Rise, Sir Ronald' or 'Arise, Sir Ronald.' He answered: 'Although I received my knighthood by cable rather than by accolade, I understand that "Arise" is reserved for the Resurrection.'[1]

[1] In fact the monarch says nothing.

I am still reading Carlyle on Heroes, and some of Max's essays, and some Emerson, and a mass of miscellaneous stuff to do with the 1890s. I got photostats of twelve new Wilde letters from America last week.

30 April 1958   *Grundisburgh*

I agree with you (as so nearly, and I hope not boringly, always) about Truman, who met great seas of derision, pity, patronage, advice, and detailed denigration with unvarying calm, and, without any roaring or lashing of tail, was clearly as brave as a lion, and perfectly clear too about what he meant to do. But I am merely dotting your eyes! (i's). As for poor Ike—one longs for another heart-attack. And one's misgivings about the government of the world are not diminished by this morning's picture of Khruscheff and Nasser smiling at each other across a table. Burke smiling at Hare, Browne at Kennedy,[1] Himmler at Goering.

I sent a copy of *A La Carte*[2] to Ivor Brown, who was fully worthy, and is a man whose praise is worth having (I have of course handed on what he wrote in reply, to Jonah). I.B. said in his letter, after saying, as Jonah did, how much he enjoyed a good long session, 'I had known some dull occasions when people drifted off at 9.30. Rupert and Lascelles have made a great and admirable change' (so there!). Pay *great* attention here. I shall be at my daughter Diana's from 13 to 15 May and she wants you to come and dine on the 14th. They both want to know you, and she thinks that my being there would break any ice you might (though I assured her wouldn't) feel about it. Do take this *very* seriously. They would of course love to have your lady too, but I remember you said week-days in London were no use for her.

Yes Longfellow, of course; Handel's blacksmith never broke into song. I forgot, for a moment, the unwinking editorial eye.

I wish I had met R. Storrs again after Cambridge: he was so obviously worth knowing (he made a crisp appearance in Harold

[1] They were hanged for killing a policeman in Essex in 1927.
[2] By L. E. Jones (Jonah).

Nicolson's *Some People*), and I always noticed that good men (e.g. Alec Cadogan—and indeed James Agate who may not have been good but certainly had an eye for what was) always liked him. He had no business to die so young. All the sayings attributed to him are invariably full of flavour—sensible or witty or both. I had never heard that one about 'arise'. Fancy being able to quote yards of Meredith—of all difficult stuff to memorise; of course, though, both he and your mother went through all 'Love in the Valley' stanza v. stanza like parson and congregation, which Middleton Murry said was cheap, but unfortunately backed his judgment by quoting 'Lovely are the curves of the white owl sleeping', to which someone modestly pointed out that Mr Murry had the right to think so if he chose but there was no reason to suppose Meredith did, since he wrote 'sweeping', a very different kettle of fish (as my father invariably said). That hatred of beauty in verse and indeed in words all through the late Twenties and Thirties is very odd. I remember a letter of George Orwell's in which he maintained that 'loveliness' was a 'mushy' word. I suppose his ear found more satisfaction in the *Brekekekex, co-ax, co-ax* of Aristophanes's frogs.

Next Monday I go to Bromsgrove School to talk to the boys about reading. On Wednesday I shall be at Eton (c/o R.M.A. Bourne Esq, The Briary, E.C.) where I hope to find a letter—in which I want you to say if *you* are a Thackeray fan. Somehow I don't expect you are. I continue to dislike him, but rather less. I mean the man. His early stuff remains intolerably unfunny and foully mushy in places. All that resolute jocularity is very trying, don't you find? Yet the old chap had guts and never threw up the sponge. But too often he makes me hot all over, and I hate heat. (Gosh, what a day—exactly the right temperature, a world of daffodils and bird-song all round me, all the green of exactly the right tint, etc etc—mix according to taste with suitable quotation from almost any major or minor poet. I need hardly say I am in the houseen on which you poured such derision.)

I have just been reading T.S.E.'s latest essays.[1] Very good especially on Milton, Johnson and Kipling—and I expect you will say on Yeats, whose later work always finds me a little out of my depth. T.S.E.'s

[1] *On Poetry and Poets* (1957).

tone is admirable—never scornful or prejudiced, or shallow, or pretentious. A good man.

I must go to supper. There will be haddock cooked in—I think—cream, as Pamela knows how to do it, and a French cheese by no means to be cursorily dismissed. To end, I shall eat a ginger-nut (with my coffee) which must come from Huntley & Palmer and no one else. Then I shall read some more Thackeray with some little bouts of senile sleep—and a Wodehouse short story in bed.

P.S. And bed will not be before midnight.

Saturday, 3 May 1958Bromsden Farm

My father's eightieth birthday lunch passed off pretty well, though Adam was much missed. I think the old boy enjoyed it as much as his depressing temperament will allow him to enjoy anything. I hired a large car with a chauffeur for the day—to get him to my sister's in Hampstead and back—but he never even noticed it!

Diana Cooper flew over from France for the first night of *My Fair Lady* and I saw her briefly.

I hope you got my note confirming the date of the Lit. Soc. as May 13. Alas, I am already hopelessly committed for the evening of the 14th—it's most disappointing. Please thank them very much for asking me: I hope they'll do so again.

I don't know whether I'm a Thackeray fan or not: certainly I'm not strongly agin him. I loved *Vanity Fair* in youth, and *Pendennis* later, and *Esmond* sometime, but I never liked that arch way of taking the reader aside, and treating the characters for the moment as puppets. Some of his journalism is good: I remember 'The Second Funeral of Napoleon', but I never cared for *The Rose and the Ring*, which my father always thrust down our throats. How I should love an opportunity of re-reading W.M.T.'s complete *oeuvre*: how long, oh Lord, how long?

Last Wednesday I took part in a sort of amateur Brains Trust *chez* the British Council. With me were a bookseller and a printer. The audience consisted of nineteen foreign publishers, male and female, black, brown and white, from the Lebanon, Holland, Iceland, the

Sudan and heaven knows where. They all seemed to know English well, and we answered quite good questions for over an hour. Next day the A.P. Herbert Committee on Obscenity had a meeting—and so it goes on.

Oh yes, I must tell you that I have agreed to appear in *The* Brains Trust on B.B.C. Television on the afternoon of Whit Sunday, May 25. I fear I shan't be very good at it, but they pay thirty guineas for an afternoon's work, and it seemed silly to refuse it. Bob Boothby told me the other day that the whole thing is simply a question of practice, and that when you've done it more than two hundred times (as he has) you simply don't notice the cameras at all.

Sunday evening

No interruptions so far, except for seven bullocks which got into the garden. Luckily the ground is so hard that they didn't do much damage. We got rid of them by breaking down a section of fence, cutting two strands of barbed wire, and shooing them through the gap.

Another heavenly day. I mowed all the grass, and then relaxed sleepily in the garden with a manuscript and the Sunday papers. Luckily I don't rely on buses, so the strike ought not to affect me too much. Doubtless taxis will be difficult to find, and goodness knows when some of the staff will get to work. My excellent secretary is leaving at Whitsun: she got married recently: and a new one is starting on Monday. It's a frightful nuisance having to explain everything all over again. And she may be a dud.

Somehow, before I leave for Yorkshire on 6 June, I must contrive to spend an afternoon in the British Museum, and another in their newspaper department near Hendon. I'm also going to compile a full list of all the people, facts and quotations which I still lack for my Wilde footnotes, and circulate it to all and sundry. You must certainly have a copy, just in case something rings a bell. This may not be possible till after my Yorkshire recess. You must forgive my constant harping on Oscar: the whole thing is forever on my mind, and when the book has finally gone to press, I shall feel like a woman delivered of a child, as I did with *Walpole*—a mixture of pride and relief.

Did I tell you that I was unofficially asked whether I'd consider writing the life of Charles Morgan? I said I really didn't think I was qualified, and it would surely be very thin stuff after Hugh—particularly with a widow and two children to be considered. I dare say I shall hear no more of it. The chap who asked me was Lovat Dickson, a director of Macmillan's and a close friend of Charles's. I told him he'd much better write the book himself.

The Briary
Eton College

8 May 1958

It is the *man* Thackeray I cannot get to like—hardly any of his letters seem to me at all interesting, and their humour is such fourth-form Victorian (why does he always call his horse his '*oss*—and does 'duty' spelt 'jewty' split *your* sides?). But *V.F.*, *P.*, and *E.* I grant you are *good* but for the button-holing. I expect Dickens was a good deal of a twirp, Forster clearly was dreadful.

On the way to and from Bromsgrove I read and greatly enjoyed Plomer's *At Home. Full* of good stuff, and I remember your saying so. My impression that he is a very likeable man was strongly corroborated here by Wilfrid Blunt who knows him (why isn't he in the Lit. Soc.?). I have marked about twenty things in Plomer's book for immortal embalmment (spelling?) in my book (why call it a commonplace book when practically nothing in it is commonplace?). Oliver Van Oss wrote an article about Ruskin in the April *National Review* which had a sentence I think highly of and should like to know if you agree: 'He had the romantic's gift for seeing the inanimate world as if it had that moment left the hand of the Creator'. Jolly good, surely?

'Sir, a cow is a very good animal in a field, but we turn her out of a garden.' We have had bullock trouble too on occasions, and they can do a lot of damage, mainly through blended stupidity and fright (like people). A lot once invaded Luxmoore's garden here, were in it only for ten minutes, but in that time neatly bit out the centre of *every* lettuce. According to the boys, Luxmoore ate nothing but beef for weeks afterwards, till someone told him *no* beef came from milch-cows. How little one knows about such things. A neighbour at Grundisburgh proposed to make a fortune out of selling ten old willows to Gradidge, Gunn and Moore etc., but was disgusted to be told that only a certain kind of willow was any good for bats, and it was not *his* kind.

I am never bored for a moment to hear about your Oscar Wilde researches. Unless the land is on fire when it comes out surely it will have a big sale. I have been told any book about W. is a sure draw, but you know how true that is—or false. I feel pretty sure you were right to refuse to do Charles Morgan. How on earth will all that *dry*ness be made palatable? I don't know his novels at all—except one about a judge which I remember liking, but somehow those Sparkenbrokes etc passed me by. Wasn't his reputation abroad *much* higher than in England, and why?

What fun memorial services of beloved relatives are, when there is no tragedy about the passing—and how dear old Hester Alington would have relished the very general pleasure at the meeting of old friends after singing her requiem in Lower Chapel. Some of my contemporaries do look every bit as decayed and scruffy as no doubt I look to them. One is frequently reminded of that remark of some old peasant-woman in Synge that 'Old age is a poor untidy thing' and of course Winston's reference to 'the surly advance of decrepitude'.

11 May 1958   *Bromsden Farm*

I am writing this at the unaccustomed time of Sunday morning, having only just realised that I should post it to-day if it is to reach you before you leave for London. This afternoon I am to pay a brief visit to a TV-conscious neighbour and watch to-day's Brains Trust: it seems sensible to get some inkling of what I'm in for. I shall post this, short or long, on my way.

Yesterday morning I drove to Oxford, which was looking its loveliest with all its trees green or blossoming. I spent an hour in the Bodleian, looking up Wilde oddments, and then visited Basil Blackwell, who agreed to present the London Library with a free copy of every book and periodical he publishes. (I have now visited some thirty-five publishers, and all but one have agreed to do this!)

I am prepared to go all the way with you about Thackeray the *man*, though I shall do so with more conviction after reading Gordon Ray's two vols. Diana's book only came out on Friday, with the satisfactory advance sale of 11,800 copies. Look for my advertisement on the 'Court page' of tomorrow's *Times*. So glad you enjoyed the Plomer book. He is an odd but very likeable chap.

After lunch

I have now done some gardening, read the Sunday papers (very good on Diana) and eaten a huge lunch. My daughter is protestingly mowing the meadow. The hot sun is neutralised almost everywhere by the strong cold wind: clearly what I need is a revolving summer-house!

You're right about Charles Morgan's greater popularity and esteem in France: the same is true of Rosamond Lehmann, and I think perhaps they both have something, in their style and their subject-matter, which translates particularly well into French—though otherwise they have little in common.

I am now re-reading all Wilde's own books and plays, looking for references etc, and most of them are still entertaining. His quip, 'Nowadays all great men have disciples, and it is usually Judas who writes the biography,' was fully borne out by the efforts of Frank Harris and Alfred Douglas. I think you're right in assuming that *any* book about O.W. is off to a flying start: and surely a new book of his own, fuller and more varied than any of his published ones, should cause some stir. Doubtless it will be translated into several languages, though that won't benefit me.

Four weeks to-day I shall be blissfully on my Yorkshire mountain-top. I look forward to this respite from year to year, and about now begin counting the weeks like a schoolboy. Everything up there is almost a month later than it is here, so one has all the fun of seeing a second flowering and burgeoning.

On Tuesday I am going to the dentist at 5, and should be home by 6, but the bus-strike makes the finding of taxis problematical, so it might be better if you came at 6.15. You'll simply *have* to come by taxi: the underground during the strike would cause Dante to add another circle to his Inferno. We should get a taxi to the club quite easily at 7. I hope the busmen starve, after slaughtering their shop stewards.

This must be the merest scrap, as I have only just arrived home, there is a meeting this afternoon, and to-morrow is positively costive with mainly tedious chores. Tuesday evening, as always, was most enjoyable; I found to my astonishment that James Smith was once up to me at Eton—which I had totally forgotten and indeed went on forgetting, though I have a dim recollection of a handful of boys serenading me at the end of a half with a glee, madrigal, or catch, which apparently he organised. I *ought* to have remembered it and him. Anthony Powell too was excellent value. You did not, I hope, regard my Philip Sidneyish intention of sitting next to Sir Cuthbert as bogus, but he came in only just in time for the gulls' eggs, and nothing could be done about it. To all appearance he got on extremely well with Jonah. On Wednesday I lunched most agreeably with Ivor Brown and (also as before) found him excellent company. His judgement on men and books seems to me very sound. In return for *A La Carte* he gave me an anthology *England*, edited by himself, shortly coming out, a glance or two at which reveals any number of items well off the beaten track—which is what one would expect.

You would have enjoyed the dinner at my daughter's last night—two absolute charmers, Mrs du Boulay and Mrs Mannheim, both Americans—and are not really nice American women as good and easy company as you could want? One of the husbands after dinner told one of those stories which—well, here you are—A man in a railway-carriage after studying the *Financial Times*, threw it on the floor, exclaiming 'The Stock-Exchange be b—d'! and then saw to his horror that he was not, as he thought, alone, but that there was an elderly lady in the far corner He apologised profusely, but all she said was, 'I am afraid your wish cannot be granted, as I read this morning that the bottom had fallen out of the market.' Too contrived, I think, but *perhaps* very funny, I simply don't know—Mr Gladstone would not have liked it. Swinburne would, but Watts-Dunton would have checked it as 'going rather too far, Algernon'. Shall I tell it at the G.B.A. meeting in July when the Archbishop is in the chair?

I read *The Stricken Deer*[1] at the Hoods'. Of all unnecessary sources of insanity, is there any more absurd than the fear of everlasting Hell-fire? Odd that our ancestors never for a moment realised what utter condemnation the theory establishes of the character of the Creator. Also that eternal torture is impossible. One would get used to it, or go so entirely mad as to be unconscious of it.

But I have no reason to suppose you are at all interested in eternal punishment. Probably you might even refer to the figure of God in a religious picture as Roger Fry did when lecturing to students, viz as 'this important mass'—one of the nice things in Plomer's book.

I never asked about your session at the dentist. Most unimaginative and unsympathetic of me. Fifty years ago I experienced *all* the sensations possible at the dentist's—from the clear, clean flame-like agony of a nerve extracted without *any* anaesthetic to the degraded humiliations of a stump *gouged* out with a sharp spike. Country dentists in the Nineties were medieval in method and callousness. Local anaesthetics—when known, which they often weren't—were regarded as effeminate. The true manliness in the chair was that of Robert Browning in 'Prospice'. 'Let me taste the whole of it, fare like my peers, the heroes of old.' Was that your attitude last Tuesday? I like to think so.

17 *May 1958*   *Bromsden Farm*

Even with our pre-prandial hour, all these Tuesdays seem to flash by before I have said half my say, or you half yours. But may be if we tried to tire the sun with talking, we should tire ourselves first—though I doubt it. Your 'merest scrap' arrived punctually this morning, to my great and accustomed delight. Fancy Jimmy Smith having serenaded you! It reminds me of Anatole France's story *Le Jongleur de Notre Dame*: each man can give only what he has. I duly perceived the good fortune which absolved you from your Cuthbertian

[1] Lord David Cecil's biography of the poet William Cowper.

66

vow. As you saw, I was weighed down by the inevitable Lockhart, though I managed to talk to dear old Brand most of the time.

What can I tell you? This morning Duff announced by letter that he has changed his mind, and decided he would like to stay at Oxford for two more years. I can only wish him well, and wonder where the hell the money is coming from. He says his decision was largely influenced by his philosophy don, but I suspect it in fact came from his girl-friend, through her parents, who clearly feared that his going down might be the prelude to an early engagement. I don't think they have anything against the boy except his poverty, and I suppose that secretly all parents would like their daughters to marry rich dukes. Did you?

Driven in from the garden by persistent drizzle, I listened to cricket commentaries, from Lord's where Milton was batting, and Chesterfield where Savage was bowling to Johnson (happy conjunction) with Spenser in the slips.

Sunday night

This afternoon, preparing for my ordeal next Sunday, I went to another friend's house and watched my second Brains Trust. It was less dreary than last week's and I am ever so little relieved. My co-Trustees are to be James Fisher, the bird expert; his wife Margery Fisher, of whom I know nothing; and a poetess called Ruth Pitter. *Ora pro nobis!* All depends on what questions we get.

Next week looks like being a hellish rush: into an already crammed engagement-book are bursting Elisabeth Beerbohm and (separately, *bien entendu*) Alistair Cooke. They will both expect time and attention —oh for June 6 and my lodge in the wilderness! Unlike you I am not at heart a social or gregarious person. The fact that I am tolerably good at coping with people is misleading. I much prefer near-solitude, at any rate for long periods. Maybe too much of it would drive me back to the world of men, but I've never had enough leisure to test the theory, and see little chance of it for years to come. So, on with the dance, let joy be unconfined.

One night last week I gave a dinner at the Garrick for Kathleen Coburn, the Coleridge expert, and two other friends. Afterwards we took a taxi to K.C.'s flat for more talk. I told the driver '26 Brunswick

Square,' and he said in a cultured voice: 'Let me see, which one is that? I always get confused between those Hanoverian squares.' And sure enough, he took us to Mecklenburg Square. I thought his remark a curious *trait de moeurs*: one expects New York taxi-drivers (who have no partition between them and their fares) to launch immediately into a discussion on democracy and free will, but in London no such matter. What next?

In Yorkshire, despite the 'Telly', I shall find simpler folk:

"bright and fierce and fickle is the South,
And dark and true and tender is the North."[1]

Them's my sentiments exactly, but I daresay it's just the Cockney's longing for rusticity as the annual holiday approaches.

21 May 1958   *Grundisburgh*

It is *almost* blasphemy even to hint that we could tire ourselves with talking. But perhaps I should speak only for myself, and you may be finding it heavy work. I always like to think I am pretty quick at noticing the glassy eye and those little convulsive maxillary spasms which reveal that yawns are being stifled. (John Bailey used to complain bitterly that some physiological perversity made him yawn when in fact he was immensely interested; he thought *inter alia* that it suggested that Providence had a schoolboy sense of humour.) Anyway next Lit. Soc. let it be firmly laid down that I sit next to you. Never mind who is on the other (as Clem Hill said when Victor Trumper died: 'he was the best bat I ever saw, I don't know who was the second'). Lockhart *looks* a bore before he has opened his mouth.

The Strachey book[2] has interesting things, but is on the whole heavyish going, with much repetition. His eulogies are not indiscriminate, but the volume of them tends to make one think they are. L.S. (who somehow was rather repellent, physically) is like those people (I know several) whom one always rather dislikes when they are not there. One does, so to speak, outgrow much of *Eminent*

[1] Tennyson, *The Princess*.
[2] *Lytton Strachey: his Mind and Art* by C.R. Sanders (1957).

Victorians, but last night I took up *Elizabeth and Essex* and by gum! anyone who sneers at his style is surely a fool. Just have *one* look at the description of the Queen in chapter 2 (or 3) and tell me it isn't masterly and I shall get me to a nunnery, and read nothing but Thomas à Kempis. The real flaw in S. is not that he had no religion, but he had no understanding at all of anyone who had; he didn't know what it, or they, meant. How hard it is to tell the truth, and how few do it. I treasure Housman's sentence (omitted from his famous lecture at the last moment): 'Not only is it difficult to know the truth about anything, but to tell the truth when one knows it, to find words that will not obscure or pervert it, is in my experience an exhausting effort.' Sanders says that Mrs Humphry Ward wrote 'an angry letter' to *The Times* about S's essay on Dr Arnold. No doubt she may have been angry (it was a very naughty performance) but her letter was extremely calm and dignified; I remember it well.

I don't think we had any matrimonial feeling about dukes, and I think realised pretty soon that our daughters' plans did not include any special deference to parental hopes and wishes. We trusted their basic good sense, and all turned out well—which does not mean that sometimes we didn't wonder, and still wonder, whether we were not amazingly and undeservedly lucky. Who knows, except God, and He won't say?

That is a very pleasing conjunction of names, though I am afraid it was Herbert Spencer in the slips and not Edmund Spenser. If he is a bowler, he must have discarded the ear-plugs which he used to insert whenever the conversation fell below a certain level. Perhaps he leaves it to the wicket-keeper to hear a snick.

Do you remember the one occasion on which we flatly disagreed? I said that humility was an essential basis of greatness, and you wouldn't have it. In last weeks *T.L.S.* my view has the valuable support of Miss Bogan—of whom I have never heard—and apparently of Yeats. Look at p 268, column 3, line 16 etc, after which, like that prig Brutus, I pause for a reply. And it won't be any good throwing Napoleon at my head, for apparently, according to M. Savant, he must have been the complete man of four letters (the word I hate!). By the same token a good many others are dished too.

You call me 'social and gregarious'. I grant you I never draw breath when in company, but I repudiate 'gregarious'. I flatly refuse almost all cocktail parties and recently the Lady Albemarle who lives not far off told someone she understood I was *a recluse*. Long may she think so. And 'gregarious' from you whose affability to all and sundry is a byword in two continents! Not that I disbelieve you about yourself. Surely no really good and intelligent man is gregarious, or is that too strong? Two or three I have known are certainly bores, and you must know scores. What a costive week threatens. You *can't* have time to write your weekly letter, but what's the good of my talking? I have often urged you not to let it ever be a burden, as of *course* in a really heavy week it must be, but you pay exactly as much attention as Pamela does when I say she mustn't do too much.

Your taxi-driver! The re-grouping of the classes? I heard last week that a markedly 'wet' old boy of mine, whom I had never heard from or of since he left thirty years ago, is now the station-master at Swindon, i.e. the most important junction in S. England! What on earth does one know of anyone?

P.S. If you would like to give real pleasure, send a brief word to old P. Lubbock whose birthday is June 4. He would love it.

Whit Monday, 26 May 1958   *Bromsden Farm*

I am a day late in writing, but yesterday was too crowded, and I may yet succeed in posting this to-day. I am trusting—and hoping indeed—that you didn't see my TV nonsense yesterday. I drove up in the morning to Soho Square, where I changed into one of my less dilapidated suits and had a stiff whiskey. Then walked down to Scott's, where the B.B.C. provided an excellent lunch, rounded off with a man-sized Churchillian cigar. Apart from the producer and his secretary, the company was Ruth Pitter the poet, James Fisher (O.E., KS.) the bird expert, his wife Margery (always known as Angus) and the question-master Norman Fisher, an ex-education officer. They were all charming, and under the influence of food and drink the talk was brisk. Then we were driven to a studio in Hammersmith, where we were clustered together in front of some very bogus-looking scenery, and given some trial questions (all much more amusing than the real ones later). Then we were made up, more or less; the ladies in what is called a 'light street', and the men with a few extra chins painted out, bags under eyes camouflaged and eyebrows extended. Then back to the studio, with three cameras and two microphones in action. Blinding lights and much heat therefrom. Then a terrifying pause, filled with backward counting—'Two minutes . . . one minute . . . thirty seconds . . . ten seconds . . . Now!' My mouth became, and remained, as dry as a sand-dune (James Fisher, who has done it hundreds of times, told me afterwards that his is always the same). On the whole the questions weren't too bad— part literary, part ornithological, part general—and the chief difficulty is in having to give an *immediate* answer. 'Yeats wrote "Too great a sacrifice can make a stone of the heart". What is the Brains Trust's opinion of this?' 'What books would you recommend as a picture of the 1920s?' 'Why are no great hymns written nowadays?' And so on. After brief reflection one could cook up some sort of an answer, but out of the blue, under all those hot lights, it's hard—until, I suppose, one has done it a number of times. Comfort said I looked very nervous to begin with—as indeed I felt. Goodness knows what the other *three million* viewers made of it all! Mercifully the number is so large as to be almost unimaginable. Anyhow I retired the richer by forty-five guineas, and shall certainly do it again if I am asked—which I very much doubt.[1]

Afterwards I drove to the Dorchester for a drink with Alistair Cooke and his wife, who are in London for a few days (I am giving a little dinner for them at the Garrick tomorrow). Alistair particularly wanted to meet Ken Tynan whose writing he admires, so I asked him and his wife to come to the Dorchester too. K.T. is tall and thin, with long hair and an intermittent stammer. His wife is small, pretty, American, and recently published a successful first novel called *The Dud Avocado*. They all got on very well, so at 7 I left them, collected the car from Soho Square and drove back here, quite exhausted.

How quick of you to spot my Spenserisation of the Leicestershire player. I'm sure you must have read *Home Life with Herbert Spencer*—

---

[1] I never was.

a delicious book. I remember particularly enjoying his railway journeys in a specially slung hammock.

I hate to disagree with you, but I'm certain I never denied humility as a necessary ingredient of greatness—quite the contrary, and a search through the 40,000 turgid words of all my letters to you will only confirm this fact. Or do you claim that I made this idiotic remark in conversation? Incidentally, how would you define the difference between pride and vanity? And is humility the opposite or absence of both? You see what effect the Brains Trust is having on me!

I readily withdraw the epithet 'gregarious', realising that, like myself, you are a natural recluse, who talks tremendously when he has to, or feels in the mood. Not that I take your shunning of cocktail parties as evidence: all shun them who are free, white and forty-one.

Tim Nugent is staying with Peter—and playing in the cricket match. He came over for a moment on Saturday. He can't come to the next Lit. Soc., as it clashes with his regimental dinner. I always avoid mine, but then I was merely a temporary and inglorious soldier.

In a fortnight I shall be on my Yorkshire mountain-top. I can't tell you how I welcome the prospect—but first comes the perennial problem of whether I can possibly tidy up everything before I go. And there are several committee meetings intervening—London Library and others—*and* the Fourth of June.

Of course I'll write to Percy L. How good of you to suggest it.

28 May 1958   *Grundisburgh*

Well, God be thanked, Bank Holiday is over. I spent it travelling to Oxford, where on both days the place was positively costive with humanity and traffic and din, and whatever dreams come to the spires must nowadays be mere nightmares. Moreover the proportion of really ugly women in the throng was markedly high (Have you, like me, a strong and definitely personal dislike of ugly women? I can't begin to be tolerant or charitable about them).

We were not within reach of TV on Sunday. I should have liked to hear you, though I can't imagine how *any*one could deal, not only convincingly but at all, with such questions as you mention. Ten minutes' preliminary thought would find me still speechless. It really does sound a pretty grim ordeal, for all the forty-five guineas, and that bumping-race marking of the time. G.K. Chesterton, Shaw, Alington, William Temple are the only men I can think of who could answer immediately and convincingly, but one only heard *them* after they had had much practice. It is interesting to know that Rebecca West (much the cleverest woman in England) is a flop on any Brains Trust—just as the omniscient Lecky after five minutes' agonised thought in that paper-game (all the famous people you can think of whose names begin with H.) is said to have produced Hengist and Horsa and no more. We know, or did know, the two Fishers, a very amiable pair. Your only question I could have answered at all is the one about hymns (why no great ones today?) the answer being that the demand is less, and the existing supplies are ample. Though 'O Valiant Hearts' is as good as any—and many streets better than e.g. 'There is a fountain filled with blood, Drawn from Emmanuel's veins' which M.D. Hill used to say made him feel physically sick (besides being manifestly untrue).

I was staying with friends at Oxford and we had one excellent evening when John Sparrow dined. What good value he is—and, as no doubt you know, he loves the Lit. Soc. Why hasn't he written more? Perhaps the All Souls Wardenship fills his time—but there is nothing of which a Cambridge man knows less than of All Souls.

Who wrote that charming review of Lady Diana's book in the *T.L.S.*? The book has been in the dining-room (a big name for it) here, and I have practically re-read it when P. was away, or late. And I agree more and more with those who praise it highly. I remember your saying once that good reviews have disappointingly little effect on a book's sale, but I have a pleasant feeling—I hope correct—that a good many people *are* reading this, and that the R.H-D coffers are consequently bursting.

Humility. I tried to find the passage last night (this is May 29) but I found that it is impossible to skim your letters—they have to be *read*, so one doesn't get very far in a mere evening. It occurs to me that it may have been, not *greatness*, but *genius* to which you denied humility as an essential element. I will keep you in touch.

Pride and Vanity. Just the sort of distinction I sometimes gave my

Extra Studies chaps to worry, and—are you surprised?—A. Huxley, Haldane, Orwell, Connolly, Hart-Davis and Fleming often produced something pretty good. I won't attempt definition (*you* TV Brains Trust chaps can throw one off in a moment) but put it to you that e.g. Milton, like all Puritans according to Macaulay, had invincible pride before men and utter humility before God, that there is no evidence that he was proud about his poetry, but plenty that he was vain about his blindness *not* spoiling his looks; that J. Caesar wasn't a bit proud of straddling the world like a colossus but *was* vain of his looks, and liked the senate's permission to wear the laurel-wreath on his bald head more than all his other honours; that Dizzy was invulnerable to censure or abuse, but it demanded the greatest tact to dissuade him from inflicting his abominable French on the Berlin Conference. But you know lots more.

How right you are about my 'talking tremendously'. After two days at Oxford I practically have clergyman's sore throat. And I *can't* stop. It is terrifying, just as a drunkard or drug-taker *knows* he is killing himself but cannot do a thing about it. My state is even worse, as it is not myself I am killing but my friends. I see nothing for it but a Trappist monastery. And I suspect my letters begin to resemble the young man's description of what he was reading—the young man of Aulla

> who read all the works of Max Muller
> When they asked, 'Are they dull?'
> He replied: 'Very dull'.
> They get duller and duller and duller.

1 June 1958   *Bromsden Farm*

The Glorious First of June has proved wet and dull. The laburnums droop like yellow tears, and the cuckoo calls through a waterfall. Surely my Yorkshire mountain-top will be kinder. Meanwhile we have the Glorious Fourth to splash through, and I suspect only one umbrella among nine (five of us—the first full reunion for almost a year—and four Linklaters). I have a new (off-the-peg) suit for the occasion, very chaste in dark clerical grey, as becomes my age and figure. By the way, all the known 'viewers' agree that the television cameras treated me to a benevolent elongation, so that instead of Holbein's Henry VIII, which they expected, they were served up an old Cavalry Colonel painted by El Greco.

I thought you might enjoy this quotation from Adam's last letter: *plus ça change*: 'During the week I've taken two wickets and made 43 not out, 8 and 50. My window-box is v. flourishing, but in all this gale I've had to stake all my antirrhinums, and it's used most of my pencils.' His cricket must have come on, for, however poor the bowling, one doesn't make 50 without some assiduity and concentration. I swell with vicarious pride.

I so agree about ugly women, though occasionally compassion breaks momentarily through my distaste. Thank God that, with all our disabilities and annoyances, we're not a brace of hideous girls!

I am devoted to Sparrow, but his idleness is not due to the duties of his Wardenship, which are almost non-existent. He suffers (don't we all?) from a delightful congenital idleness, which this post (the plum of all academic jobs in the country) has gently fostered. Almost ever since I have known him (we met as undergraduates in 1926) he has been meditating and preparing a book on Mark Pattison. Did you know that he was a boy-prodigy? He edited Donne's *Devotions* for Cambridge, also Cowley and Bishop King for the Nonesuch Press, soon after he left Winchester.

The *T.L.S.* review of Diana was written by Alan Pryce-Jones.

The reason you can't skim my old letters is that they are, in every sense, unreadable; but the reason you can't find me against humility is not that you have lost some sheets, but rather that I never said it. The discussion must have been with another, or between two quite different men. I hate to think how my early letters must have bored you with complaints of business worries and ill-health. Mercifully the ill-health was entirely caused by the business worries, and ever since Heinemann bought the shares from my friends and relations, both have disappeared. I don't in the least care whether Heinemann's lose their money or not, and ironically, but naturally, my indifference has left me freer for my proper work, and the business has prospered accordingly.

Last Tuesday Comfort and I gave a dinner party at the Garrick for the Alistair Cookes. Peggy Ashcroft came, and it was strange having both my wives at the same table. Peter was there, Rosamond Lehmann and Joe Jackson, the head of Scotland Yard. He was at Piggy Hill's and was a heavyweight boxer. Now for the larks and curlews!

Framingham Chase
Norwich

4 June 1958

Have you ever stayed at a 'Chase'? Do you know what a 'Chase' is? (I don't.) One seems somehow in a Scott-Lever[1]-Trollope atmosphere, and there is even something of Mrs Knox's establishment about it— you remember, a miserable soup in a marvellous old silver tureen followed by a perfect salmon on a cracked kitchen dish. Well here (*chez* Mrs Geoffrey Colman, Pamela's sister) there are trees of primeval age and majesty, a breathtaking blaze of rhododendrons and other flowering shrubs, and flowers so richly and variously coloured that the 'high midsummer pomps'[2] of June can only be seen as an instance of meiosis or even litotes. Very well, but when it comes to writing-paper and envelopes, a good deal of thoughtful research is necessary, and as for pens—well, '*where* is that pen I am sure I saw last week on that table—or perhaps it was the table next door?' (Failure in that quest explains the reappearance of this repulsive Biro.) But it is all very delightful and hospitable, and after all those who originally dwelt in Chases had no truck with pens and paper. Communication with all and sundry was via varlets and scurvy knaves astride of palfreys or stots perhaps of pomely grey, pricking over moor and fen. From where I am writing, I can see cedars of Lebanon that are said to have been planted in the reign of Queen Bess. They make me feel a mere ephemerid, a grasshopper (I speak of the soul rather than of the body). It was Bismarck who always said he preferred trees to men, and in the heart of a Chase like this one sees why—with a great deal of sympathy.

This is the Norwich Festival and this evening we hear Menuhin

---

[1] Charles Lever, Irish novelist (1806–1872).
[2] Matthew Arnold, 'Thyrsis'.

play the Beethoven Concerto, and if you know anything much better than that, kindly tell me what it is. And the B.C. if you please was a 'flop' till Joachim played it! And back to G. to-morrow.

There was what Balfour called 'a frigid and calculated lie' in your letter—no, the epithets don't really apply, but dash it all you said that your early letters to me were unreadable and boring. I have just been re-reading a good many, and they are as full of flavour as a nut or an apple. And arising out of them are several points of moment (1) There are several references to your next visit to Finndale House. Why a' God's name has it never taken place, and is rarely or never now referred to? I suspect you have filled your day impossibly and criminally full and that your nose is a permanent fixture on the grindstone. But please perpend the matter—unless of course you were bored—by no means impossible.

(2) You mentioned two books you would send if I liked them, viz *Abode of Snow* (all about mountaineering) and *The Essential Neville Cardus*. Surely I didn't keep silence, or does it merely show that I was less unblushingly cadging in 1956 than in 1958?

I like to think of you in your northern fastness—its name and whereabouts never breathed by me to any living soul (you remember how Mr Melas shuddered under a similar injunction which, if he disobeyed, 'May the Lord have mercy on *your* soul', and how he disobeyed and escaped by the skin of his teeth, but *not* through anything the Lord did about it).

You are right. Fifty cannot be made with the bat without some skill; wickets can be taken without any—e.g. one taken once at Hagley by the gravedigger, because the batsman couldn't stop a sneeze (hay fever) as the ball was delivered. I like Adam's blend of cricket and horticulture.

John Sparrow. What you say is most interesting. That exhaustion of the precocious happens more often than it should to Wykehamists because frankly they do work their best scholars too hard. They win everything at Oxford and peter out by thirty. But not only at Winchester. Even Raymond Asquith was making *no* mark at the Bar, and told someone not long before the war that he 'found life singularly lacking in motive'. Well, Wellington (the fool of the family), Churchill (who had to cram to get into the army), Birkett (pass degree at Cambridge, I believe) never found it that. And what about your uncle Duff who made so magnificently good?

I took up last week the letters of T.E. Lawrence—which clearly should have been edited by you. You would have eliminated much of that endless jaw about the *Seven Pillars* and his ultimately repellent utterances about its entire worthlessness, which never strike me, at least, as quite sincere. I don't wonder that many of far less venomous spirit than Aldington have been allergic to him, but I expect you have noticed that, like G.B.S., everyone loved him who knew him in person and not only on paper. He had a very wayward literary judgment; has anyone else found *The Odyssey* artificial and third-rate?

That must have been an interesting Alistair Cooke party. Man is of course naturally polygamous, and it is certainly an advance in civilisation that, as often happens today, a divorce leaves the two perfectly friendly afterwards. Byron couldn't do that, but then of course he wasn't quite civilised. He was also extremely stupid not to see that Miss Milbanke was the last wife in the world for him.

I remember old Joe Jackson—a first-rate boxer who lost the heavyweight cup on points because, so rumour said, he didn't like to hit his opponent hard for fear of killing him. Ulysses in *The Odyssey* when fighting the beggar Iras had a similar merciful impulse and instead of killing him with one blow, merely hit him behind the ear so that the surface previously convex became concave. Joe J. refrained even from that. I never knew him, but I doubt if anyone suspected he had detective gifts or tastes.

I say, Rupert, your address in the new O.E.A. books is given as 1 St Michael's Alley!! If this is as it ought to be, my God I have it unto Thee, as T.E. Brown wrote about a much less dreadful happening—death of a child or something.

Does all this bore you? I fear, I greatly fear. You were rather flat about the Max Muller limerick. Probably you knew it.

9 June 1958

The worst of living deliciously in lotos-land is that it *is* always afternoon—in the words of the harassed theatrical landlady, 'Half-past four, and not a po emptied.' I meant to write yesterday, and now I shall have to give this to the nice farmer when he comes up this evening to milk, and if he remembers to post it, you may get it on Wednesday. Blame the delay on to my blessed state of relaxation. I haven't shaved or seen a newspaper since last Thursday, but locusts are plentiful and it looks like a good year for wild honey. Each time I come here I am overwhelmed all over again, first by the beauty of the surroundings, and then by the majestic *silence*. Except for an occasional moor-bird's cry or bleat of distant sheep, there is simply *no sound* from dawn to dusk, and I sit entranced with wonder at this simple fact. You remember the lines about silence coming like a poultice to heal the wounds of sound: well, that is just my state, poulticed, grateful, but not in any way very active. Three glimpses yesterday of a redstart behind the cottage (never seen one up here before) were enough to occupy me for the day. Forgive me if I have said all this before (as from that morbid re-reading you will know): it is a recurrent delight and particularly strong this year.

Your letter was waiting for me in the farmer's house at the bottom of the hill when I arrived on Friday. You shall have *Abode of Snow* when I get back to London, and *The Essential Cardus* too if I can find a copy. Alas, in my ignorance the allusion to Mr Melas is lost on me: please enlighten.

As for 1 St Michael's Alley, I had been hoping to keep that address from you, with its dark hints of contangos, bears and bucket shops, but truth will out, and now you know, or suspect, the worst. In fact the building does also house my father's ultra-respectable stock-broking business, so I must write to the O.E.A. and point out their tactlessness and incompetence.

The last few days before I escaped up here were rackety beyond belief. On Tuesday a London Library committee, followed by a Georgeless Lit. Soc. I just managed to insulate myself against Lockhart by persuading Martin Charteris to sit on one side of me, and

Donald Somervell on the other. The latter told me several anecdotes he'd told me before, including one I'd told him, but made up for it by quoting verbatim (he has a splendid memory) Gibbon's superb footnote on the Giraffe. Jonah said he was against all footnotes, since they simply serve to distract the reader. Having now composed nearly a thousand for Oscar, I felt compelled to disagree. Afterwards Roger came back to Soho Square for a drink, and we then briefly joined my son Duff and his girl in a nearby restaurant. Roger had never met him and wanted to talk about the present state of Worcester College.

Duff stayed the night with me, and next morning we picked up the Linklaters at their hotel (in a friend's car) and drove them to Eton. They were both more than a little apprehensive, Marjorie being theoretically against public schools in general and Eton in particular, Eric feeling the natural *gêne* of a non-Etonian, and neither of them ever having been to the Fourth of June before. By a miracle everything went perfectly: hot sun shone: we immediately joined forces on Agar's with Comfort and Bridget (in our car), found the boys (our Adam and Magnus L.), enjoyed delicious cold chicken and strawberries, brought by Comfort, meeting several Scottish friends of the Linklaters, avoiding all the worst bores etc. The nuisance of Absence[1] etc I avoided by making Duff take the boys in one car, while we escaped (via Maidenhead where we picked up a Linklater daughter) to Monkey Island and an excellent dinner. Parked the cars in Fred Coleridge's drive, enjoyed the fireworks, and I got the Linklaters back to their hotel soon after midnight, exhausted but grateful.

Next day (my last) I desperately tidied up everything, despite interminable intrusions of authors in person, by telephone, in shoals of letters. Lunch with Elisabeth Beerbohm, a long hour with Stephen Potter and the proofs of his new book of nonsense. Then a new committee (at the Arts Council), of which I was reluctantly insinuated into the chair. You shall hear about it next week, for now I hear the farmer's tractor in the distance.

Oscar has come with me in his accustomed bulk. As things stand today I have included 816 letters (long and short), addressed to 206 correspondents. Some will come out before the finish, and I hope a

[1] The Eton name for roll-call.

few will be added, but that is more or less how the final thing will look. I was planning to stay here a full three weeks, but on the *eve* of my leaving I heard that the London Library rating-appeal has been put back to June 30, so I shall tearfully drive south on Tuesday June 24, for conferences etc.

10 June 1958   *Grundisburgh*

Positively celestial mountain book just arrived. I love it, although having a head which gets dizzy on a pair of household steps. But the pictures and descriptions of K2 etc *do something* to me that produces a delicious blend of exaltation and shuddering. It is like having the temperament of a poet with no poetical ability. I am a mute inglorious Whymper.

12 June 1958   *Grundisburgh*

Your letter arrived second post on Wednesday. I was beginning to think my long letter from the Chase had been too much for you. I cannot remember now what topics I brought up, but am sure they must have seemed very dull to you communing with Nature, far away on your Yorkshire wold.

Mr Melas is an example of donnish folly, viz the cryptic allusion. Why should I suppose that you, at least two generations later, should regard the Sherlock Holmes stories as we did in the Nineties? Mr Melas was the Greek Interpreter in the story so called and not a very good one. But will you in return tell me where to find Gibbon on the giraffe—of which I have some dim memory that I once read it, but no more.

Last week we dined with our Bishop and the talk turned to books, and he said he had recently much enjoyed, and had I read, *Old Men Forget*? He said his main impression was what a first-rate chap the author must have been. We saw eye to eye in this matter, and I nearly went on to say: 'But do you know the nephew?' What should I have got. The pursed lip, the raised eyebrow, the sniff, the 'Yes indeed I do'? One never knows; you may have stepped upon some episcopal toe in your time. No more for now, or I may miss the post which reaches you on Saturday.

17 June 1958

Your letter duly reached me on Saturday, but this, alas, cannot reach you before Thursday. My kindly farmer, who usually milks his cows up here and posts my letters on his way home, is away for three days' holiday at Morecambe, the cows are temporarily in the valley, and my delicious sloth is stronger than my very real desire to get your letter off on time. Tomorrow I plan to attend a cottage sale near Thirsk, and this will get posted on the way.

I'm sure I love the Sherlock Holmes stories as much as you do, but I certainly don't know them (or their characters' names) half as well. Funnily enough I have in this cottage copies of *The Sign of Four, A Study in Scarlet, The Memoirs,* and *The Hound of the Baskervilles*—all waiting to be re-read. So, alas, is *How Green*: will you ever forgive me if I don't read it this time? Just now I am in melancholy process of reading through the works of Lord Alfred Douglas: not a very admirable or likeable chap. Altogether I have done quite a lot of work on Oscar, though the end is not yet.

I hadn't time before I left London to look up Gibbon on the Giraffe, but will do so as soon as I get back—in a week's time, alas!—*Lente, lente, currite!*—and let you know. Meanwhile my faulty memory of Donald Somervell's excellent one is that the footnote starts: 'The tallest, gentlest and most useless of the larger mammals. *Camelopardus Maximus.* Little seen in Europe since the Revival of Learning...' That last phrase is superb, with its picture of herds of giraffes retreating from a platoon of greybearded scholars.

Did I tell you that my farmer and his family (and their helpless guests) all watched my TV appearance? Such is fame today, though the programme must have profoundly bored and bewildered them, poor things. They are the very nicest people I have ever met, totally unlettered but with superb tact, imagination and good manners.

The frightful new committee which I mentioned in my last letter is trying to create a huge new fund for the advancement and maintenance of literature, authors and the theatre. The money is to come (we hope) from a royalty of 1% on all out-of-copyright books, i.e. those whose authors have been dead more than fifty years. Several publishers have already agreed to pay such a royalty, and it seems *possible* that Stratford and the Old Vic would pay on performances of Shakespeare. At the first 'exploratory' meeting (a dinner-party given by the Society of Authors) Arthur Bryant and I were deputed to see whether the Pilgrim Trust would give the scheme its name and blessing. A.B. and I took Tommy Lascelles out to lunch, and thereafter wrote him a brief memorandum to show his fellow-trustees. They all seemed delighted with the idea, and I then saw Lord Kilmaine, the Secretary of the Trust, who was most encouraging. The Fund's first formal meeting took place at the Arts Council on June 5. Bryant couldn't come, and since I was almost the only person who knew what had happened so far, I was inveigled into the chair. The others present were Kilham Roberts (head of the Society of Authors), Sir William Williams (head of the Arts Council), Allen Lane (head of Penguin Books), Bob Lusty (head of the Hutchinson group of publishers), Rosamond Lehmann, Eric Linklater, Stephen Potter, Lionel Hale, Ivor Brown, and Herbert Agar. Directly I get back I have to see the P.T.'s Lawyers, and all round I can see a pile of work looming. Clearly it's an enormous mistake to take on *any* chairmanship, since one leads to another, and they are all unpaid (not even expenses). If only I could get Oscar to the printer, things would look a little clearer. Diana Cooper's second volume is awaiting my attention, and I shall certainly have to pay a brief visit to Chantilly in July. Up here I just don't think of any of these burdens, but simply laze and Oscarise and sleep and eat—the farmer's wife makes first-class bread and cakes and tarts, with which she is most liberal.

20 June 1958   *Grundisburgh*

What is your eye on in that cottage sale at Thirsk? Pamela would much like to know. She hasn't had much luck lately at sales. Chairs for which her limit is, say, £3.00 go for £17, and once at least the auctioneer ignored her bid and the thing went to the runner-up, an Ipswich dealer, with whom the auctioneer is said to be in unholy league. Like judgment, honesty is fled to brutish beasts. Not that they make much of judgment, if birds count as beasts. A small nameless bird has been in the summer-house for the last ten minutes; and it tries unceasingly to escape through a closed window, ignoring the wide-open door eighteen inches away.

I suppose you *must* read all through Alfred Douglas for O.W's sake. I always think of him as a pitiful figure, for can anything be more pitiful than tragedy without any touch of dignity. And the contrast between that really lovely youth of twenty and the seamed haggard face dominated by that dreadful white and bulbous nose (a really white nose I put it to you is worse than a red one, which, however ugly, is at least suggestive of one-time bonhomie and conviviality, however abused and prolonged). But perhaps A.D. did not see or feel the hideous gap between his promise and his performance. Though are not some of his sonnets very good and (of course) much under-rated? At one time he saw his life's object was:

> To fight with form, to wrestle and to rage
> Till at the last upon the conquered page
> The shadows of created Beauty fall.

Perhaps he thought he had achieved it. He and old Agate used to exchange a good deal of abusive—and amusing—wit from time to time. But I imagine he was pretty detestable most of his life. Poor chap, what could he expect, with that father?

Your whiff of the Camelopardus Maximus has whetted my appetite for the whole passage. What rich *private* enjoyment Gibbon must have got from demure irony. I always suspect there are many instances, especially in the notes, which have escaped notice.

I have just been at the Abbey School Malvern telling the Sixth Form about reading—my gist being largely that they should ignore all damning criticism of old or established authors but not the laudatory, and nearly all of both concerning contemporaries. And that few utterances written or spoken are more fatuous than 'Nobody can afford to miss . . .' and 'Nobody reads X (e.g. Tennyson, Brown-

84

ing, Meredith, Moore) now'. They were a delightful audience ('I dearly love a knot of little misses'[1]). A girls' school, where they don't play hockey and swear, is a very civilised community. Will *you* come and give away our prizes one day? A firm offer. Your journey will be paid for! You would enjoy it more than that awe-inspiring new committee you describe. Why *do* you do these things? From now on you must cultivate the habit of some medieval monastery, where the monks, when summoned by the Abbot to consider and discuss some new proposal, all fell asleep and only woke up when he paused, to say '*Namus, namus*' (i.e. 'we're agin it', short for *Damnamus*) and then fell asleep again. My uncle Edward delightfully likened the Eton staff to these monks, whenever he had some new plan. I don't believe you ever said '*Namus*' to any request (except perhaps to some gushing woman who wanted you to publish her book).

You have, with suspicious carefulness, taken no notice of my reference to your visit here and the possibility of its ever being repeated. I suspect it *is* one of the things to which your attitude is '*Namus*'.

Those serried ranks of booksellers, authors, publishers etc must be immensely hard to get moving: I must resign myself to getting a fortnightly postcard instead of a weekly letter. Meanwhile (1) Stay up north *quam diutissime* (2) Put letter to G.W.L. lower among priorities (3) Practise saying in a deep and throaty voice '*Namus, namus*' every morning (4) Eat plenty more of your farmer's wife's cakes etc.

Kisdon Lodge
Keld

23 June 58

Your letter hadn't arrived on Saturday—and I don't wonder, for mine can scarcely have reached you by then. Today I have not stirred from the hilltop, so I shall probably find your letter as I leave tomorrow. This I do with the utmost regret, especially as the weather has improved today, and the evening sun is streaming in on me as I write. The sale last Wednesday was great fun. It took place in a meadow in a little village near Thirsk (about fifty miles away) on the

[1] Doctor Johnson.

85

hottest and sunniest day of my holiday. By great good luck I secured a lovely grandfather clock for £1 (tell Pamela), made in Thirsk and I imagine always housed in the neighbourhood. It stood the journey well (first in the back of my sister's station waggon, and then in a trailer behind my farmer's tractor) and after some days of temperament and the insertion of a few wedges is now ticking away with lulling regularity. I also got an oak chest of drawers with seven drawers and very handsome for 30/-. Also a lovely picture of a sailing ship worked in wool. Such things are usually bought by dealers for several pounds, but this came at the end of the sale, and I got it for 3/-.

I still haven't read *Middlemarch* or *How Green*, being absorbed by Oscar in the daytime, and detective stories at night. I wish I could report Oscar as nearly ready for the printer, but in fact I fear he needs a lot more attention first. I now know so much more than I did when I started (though still not enough) that I keep coming on references in the early letters which now mean something and can be explained. I shall have to read through the whole thing again carefully and chronologically, then write the introductions to the nine parts into which I have divided the book, and try to worry out the more recondite footnotes while the printer is setting up the type—which will take some time. It was of course a crazy job to take on unless one could give one's whole time to it. One should be so soaked in the material that one knows immediately where something comes—and you know how little spare time I usually have. Up here I have been briefly able to concentrate on it, and so get right back into the picture. Luckily I am blessed with the gift of being able to put out of my mind anything that I don't immediately have to think about, so that while I've been here I simply haven't thought *at all* of the publishing business, the London Library, the Lit. Soc., or that new committee. On Wednesday morning, alas, they will all rush back at me, with an enormous pile of unanswered letters on my desk, a morning meeting at the L.L., an afternoon one with Counsel, and so on. Soon Long Leave will be on us, then a visit to Chantilly, but I'm hoping to be able to snatch a few more days up here later in the year. One of my difficulties is that I must most of the time have *all* the relevant Oscariana at hand, and this, together with the typescript of the letters, now fills two large cartons. Luckily my farmer is ready to transport anything up and down the hill on his tractor.

There are very few grouse about here this year, but I have seen some snipe, and today for the first time managed to identify one making that drumming noise high in the air. I have often before seen snipe, and heard the noise, but never before been able to bring them together. I haven't shaved since Wednesday last, or seen a paper since Friday's. I hate leaving this beautiful place, the silence, the wonderful air, the ticking grandfather and warm Aladdin lamp, the earth closet, the water fetched in buckets from a spring in the next field, with a high stone wall to climb in between. I have enough books and work here to last me for several months. Newspapers a day or two old, with time to read them slowly, I much prefer to the hurried glance before going downstairs to the office. 'If I ever become a rich man, Or if ever I grow to be old'[1], this is where I shall come. Forgive this elegiac note: my last evening here is always a moving and a mournful time. I realise how immensely lucky I am to have found anything so perfect, but that only makes leaving it the more distressing.

Write next to Bromsden, and on Sunday I will slide back into the accustomed rhythm, with details of my harassed return to the south. Now I must go outside and listen again to the curlews' mournful cry, which echoes my own. As Oscar wrote,

> He who lives more lives than one
> More deaths than one must die.

29 June 1958   Grundisburgh

Doctors tell one that for one's heart to miss an occasional beat is not serious, so our correspondence will not suffer. I think God did not mean you to write last week, because my letter had not reached you, and you had to write, so to speak, in vacuo. Correspondence means the exchange of ideas etc. Some are curiously bad at that and ignore all one's baits. Hester Alington, the very best of women, always thanked affectionately for a letter but made no further reference to it. One was always beginning again.

[1] Belloc, 'The South Country'.

Have you had a long enough holiday? I doubt it. I shall watch narrowly on July 8 to assure myself that you are refreshed in mind and body. We are green with jealousy over your grandfather, and have to be rather firm in resisting the temptation to hope that the time it keeps won't be all that perfect, just as one Forsyte could not help being pleased on hearing that a brother's indigestion lacked some of the mysterious twinges of his own. Bargains are evidently still to be found in the north, but don't forget that Pamela once got a small book-stand *free*—thrown in with something else she bought.

Oscar is becoming your old man of the sea, but I expect you wouldn't not have him on your back. The book should surely have a big sale. How annoying if the human race was wiped out before publication. From the Vansittart extract in the *Daily Telegraph* last Friday the genial Russians about now should be on the move.[1] Poor old Vansittart! How fatal in public life it is to prophesy woe, and then to be proved by events right, up to the hilt. But I suppose he did harp too much on one string. So did Jeremiah; so did Cassandra; so did Dean Inge—and what did *they* get out of it?

We have just had Bernard Fergusson here—to give away the prizes at Woodbridge and talk to the school about leadership, if you please, of all hackneyed speech-day topics. But he was quite excellent and got the perfect blend of *gravitas* and *levitas*, and the whole audience loved it. In proposing a vote of thanks I told them (what is true) that his survival in Burma was really a miracle, and likened the campaign to Camlan where only three of King Arthur's Knights were alive at the end, one because he was so strong that no one dared tackle him, no. 2 so beautiful that no one had the heart to hurt him, and no. 3 so hideous that no one would go near him. Do *you* ever give school prizes away? Beware of answering yes! Some public men are shameless. Lord Evershed, invited in October to come in the following July, answered (roughly) that though his court never *had* sat on a Saturday afternoon, there was no reason why it shouldn't, if it wanted to, and so with great regret etc etc. And I believe he is a very good chap. Old Lawrence, a Trinity oddity, refused a dinner-invitation sent in June

[1] The serialization of *The Mist Procession* (1958), the autobiography of the diplomat Lord Vansittart (1881–1957), who all through the 1930s had vainly predicted the German menace.

for the following January 27 on the ground that it was always in that week that he got one of his worst colds.

Your Yorkshire fastness does sound delicious—even the earth closet takes on a cosy friendliness in your description. How dreadful if someone discovered it. I never breathe a word of it. Some day you must read *How Green there*. It would fit—better than *Middlemarch*, which is more attuned to e.g. Woodbridge. Did you have that portentous rain on Thursday night? Almost a record here. For once E. and S.E. England got the worst. A niece of mine is here who lives mainly in Khartum, running the university. She left for leave in April when the thermometer stood at 112 in the shade, shortly after a day on which there were two inches of rain in an hour. All the Egyptians, she tells us, are extremely friendly to the English, that Nasser is not popular, that if we had gone through with the Suez affair, all would have been well, as the Arabs only respect success, etc, and that the Egyptian soldiers strongly resemble the swaggering Scotchman who, after expressing much desire for a battle, ran like a hare when one broke out, and protested, when turned back: 'Mon, they're no fechtin' up yon, they're killin' each ither.'

I am only just home after a visit to one of my girls' schools. The last fortnight in June is costive with prize-days, etc—and next week exam-papers start. I have about 1200, rather more than I desire or deserve and, my God, I shall be sick of adolescent outpourings on Shakespeare before August. You oughtn't really to write at all till *next* Saturday, but I suspect you will, and I shall answer—and I shall send *this* to Soho Square and catch you to-morrow, where alas, after Keld, you will feel your sole communion with nature is to 'watch that little tent of blue, which prisoners call the sky,'[1] if I quote correctly. Who the hell has got my *Ballad*?

29 June 1958   *Bromsden Farm*

This has been a summer's day, and nobody can believe it. I actually got too hot gardening and had to cool off in the shade. What next?

[1] From Oscar Wilde's *Ballad of Reading Gaol*.

My office desk I found piled high, but by Friday evening I was only six letters to the bad. I attended two meetings about the London Library's rating-appeal, which comes on tomorrow morning at 10.30 before the Lands Tribunal in Hanover Square. Both T.S.E. and I have to give evidence, though in fact everything depends on the persuasive oratory of our counsel, Mr Geoffrey Lawrence Q.C. He says the hearing may well last for two days or more, so I fear my correspondence will slip back again. I am going up to London after dinner tonight, so as to get some work done early tomorrow in the office.

I have now finished with the works of Alfred Douglas, thank goodness. Yes, some of his sonnets are indeed good, though not so good as he thought they were. Self-praise, like self-pity, tends to destroy sympathy; all the same:

> To clutch Life's hair, and thrust one naked phrase
> Like a lean knife between the ribs of Time.

are certainly remarkable lines. His tragedy was much longer and less dramatic than Oscar's. He had one son, now I believe in an asylum. I still haven't tracked down the Camelopard, and may have to apply to Donald S. for it.

Of course I'd love to pay you another visit at Grundisburgh, but I don't at the moment see when it is to be. July looks pretty full, and after that I know you are smothered in grandchildren. What about October? This is the one invitation to which in future I shall not, as instructed, answer '*Namus*'.

10.30 p.m. Soho Square

There's a lot to be said for travelling up on Sunday night, rather than Monday morning. There are fewer people on the train (and nobody I know), a smaller queue for taxis, and much less traffic in the streets. The flat seems rather stuffy after the country, but I have opened all the windows and hope for the best. Soon I must con over the evidence I have to give tomorrow: I purposely left it till late, so that it should be fresh in my mind: you shall have an account next week.

We shall have a full house in the country, with Adam home for Long Leave, Duff home from Oxford, and Bridget's young man on leave from the army. As long as I manage to avoid Henley Regatta I shall be content. For a fortnight the town is intolerable, with all possible prices raised—for regulars as well as visitors—you know, all those fat men in tiny pink caps. Why in rowing alone do the old hands have to turn up in fancy dress?

Peter F. is more than half way through his book about the siege of the foreign legations in Peking in 1900, so I should be able to bring it out fairly early next year. He says nobody will want to read it, but I hope he is wrong. About two fields away from Bromsden he has fixed up an automatic gun to keep the pigeons off the kale. Its regular detonations are not what I am used to in the North Riding. Now for my evidence.

2 July 1958   Grundisburgh

It is hardly within the bounds of reason, however charitable, that you should desire or deserve another lucubration (I never know what that word means, except that it is faintly derisive) from me, but I send this just to restore our epistolary rhythm, and you will find it in due course at Bromsden.

I see in today's *Daily Telegraph* that you are at this moment in the witness-box (under your full name, which I learn for the first time) with the hopes and good wishes of all good men behind you. I wish I could be optimistic about the result, but I have, like everybody else, become so used, in any and every such case, to see the worse cause vanquish the better that I am full of apprehension. And there is no greater offender than the law, since almost every judge rather sheepishly defends a manifestly unjust law by saying he has no power except to administer it. The oases of civilisation are daily more beset by the sandstorms of barbarism (to write, momentarily, like Vansittart). As I told one of my girls' schools last week, schools are once again, as in the middle-ages monasteries were, the last desperate strongholds of 'sweetness and light,' and warned them that when they go out into the world, they will find most of the standards they have learnt derided or ignored or even actively attacked. A.P.H. battles with fine wrath on your side in last week's *Punch*, but our world is no longer—if it ever was—governed by good sense and magnanimity, and the powers that be, i.e. the cheap Press and the Common Man, are impervious to ridicule.

Have you heard from Percy L. yet? His answer to my birthday letter came yesterday—he always takes some time—and I am sorry to see his eyes have gone back, and he can only dictate. I doubt if he will last much longer, though his letter is not too melancholy. He says his only occupations now are drinking and talking.

I have just begun Belloc's letters and find them rather disappointing. Too much politics and papistry. I read in the preface that H.B. regarded your uncle as the most intelligent man he knew. Why did I never know your uncle? Probably he would merely have thought me one of those pedagogues.

P.S. I see a scientist has said that beer, milk, tea, fried food, early marriage and celibacy all help cancer. And scientists expect us not to think them B.F.'s! *Zu Dienstag.*

5 *July 1958* *Bromsden Farm*

So glad you like the mountain book: its author[1] is a pet, and I only wish he could write something else. He has had the happy experience of being able always to earn his living by doing what he most enjoyed: after long years in the Indian Army (which were almost all spent surveying in the mountains) he was the first incumbent of the newly founded Chair of Geography at Oxford—a darlin' man if ever there was one.

Adam is home, very tall, spotty and cheerful, for Long Leave, and yesterday we celebrated his fifteenth birthday by giving him a croquet set (much coveted) and laying out a strenuous course in our meadow—which he will now have to mow when he wants a game! Did I tell you that Duff has bought half a car for £17.10.0? I haven't seen it yet, but it is said to be very old, very small, and extremely economical with petrol.

[1] Kenneth Mason.

92

I had a nice answer from P. Lubbock, very shakily written in pencil.

Sorry you don't like Belloc's letters. I can't help being prejudiced in their favour. I saw a lot of the old boy at Duff's and was very fond and admiring. I can hear his voice in his letters, but I don't think they gain from being read straight through, and are better if dipped into. Oscar's, on the contrary—but you have heard enough of this King Charles's head.

I can hear the distant explosions of the fireworks which signal the end of the Regatta, and am thankful I am not in a dripping punt beset with insects.

The Tribunal was exhausting but fun. It lasted four full days of legal time (10.30–4 with an hour off for lunch) and we probably shan't get the decision for at least a month. (In one way this is quite convenient, since we have the Annual General Meeting later this month, and we shall, Eliot and I, have quite enough to do explaining the raising of the subscription without having to debate the rating question as well.) Our counsel, Geoffrey Lawrence Q.C., was superb, both in his pleading and in his treatment of witnesses. The two opposing counsel seemed like cart-horses matched with a thorough-bred. (Incidentally, one of them, Patrick Browne, a very nice chap *and* a member of the Library!, was at Eton with me.) Lawrence made me the first witness, hoping that I might be able to knock the shine off the ball before Eliot came in. Somehow I scrambled through, but to read the verbatim shorthand account next day was highly chastening. 'Tell me, Mr Hart-Davis', said the rating authority's counsel, 'what is the touchstone by which you distinguish literature from other written matter?' 'How would you define a man of letters?' etc. It was definitely less nerve-racking than the TV Brains Trust, but one always had the feeling that every question concealed a trap. Eliot was terribly nervous, but warmed to his work and finished in fine fettle, rather sorry that he wasn't asked more. (I lunched with him and his wife on Monday and Tuesday. He was most genial and I got him to reminisce entertainingly.) Clearly the judge was entirely on our side, and it is simply a question of the law.

Very hot in the train yesterday, and unfortunately, as I was wearing braces, I could not doff my jacket. Why is it all right to reveal any garment and practically the whole human frame, but never braces? Very odd. *My* braces, at least, have nothing provocative or suggestive about them. Perhaps that elderly man, who finds women with one or no legs more erotically exciting than any others, could throw some light on the matter.

I wanted you to tell me more about Belloc, who from *all* accounts must have been the richest company. What I found disappointing in the letters was—after the politics, which fade away—the enormous amount of space given to descriptions of places he went to abroad. Perhaps many like them, but I always skip them, though, knowing about the writer, I read most of these. And I found the most interesting part of the book was the last, when he could no longer travel and his comments on men and things were full of stuff and had little or no topography. I met him only once at Mrs Cornish's, and of course he was great fun, and incidentally told us that his mother had seen Napoleon after his return from Elba and he looked *'un homme rompu'*.

I am temporarily deprived of the summer-house, as the garden is given over for the day to a platoon of the oldest and most shapeless women in Grundisburgh. How ruthless wives can be when bent upon good works. I shouldn't be in the least surprised to find that the summer-house has been 'tidied', i.e. everything put away in the wrong place or even destroyed ('You *can't* have wanted that filthy old ——' some age-old garment, gadget etc of one's special affection. What ass ever started the notion that women are the sentimental sex?).

I have frequently since seeing you pondered that question they put to you, viz How you distinguish 'literature' from other written matter. I think Housman would have said it was as unanswerable as he said was great poetry—as a rat to a dog. You know it when you meet it, but define it? No.

Lawyers' emphasis on *fact* often obscures *truth*, as it did when Edith Thompson was condemned, when that rather dreadful man Mr Justice Shearman actually interrupted her counsel's address to the jury to underline that they must think of nothing but the facts, and not try to weigh their possible meanings. Has any *good* judge worn a moustache as he did? Or run the hundred yards for Oxford? Sprinters always try to beat the pistol, therefore are essentially unscrupulous and unreliable. The brilliant A.W. Verrall totally failed as a barrister, because he saw through the case he was pleading as clearly as the one he was opposing, and his conscience would not let him conceal the fact. None the less barristers can be first-rate company—also judges, though I was too young to appreciate the wit and wisdom of Mr Justice Wills, who came to Hagley a few years before he made those deplorable observations to and on poor Oscar. I hate them when they moralise and tell the jury they are sure they view the fact that the woman in the dock slept with some man 'with the utmost detestation and horror'. I prefer the perfectly true comment of—who was it?— who when some teetotal ass said he would rather commit adultery than drink a glass of port said 'So would we all, my dear L., so would we all.'

I also wanted to hear you talk about T.S.E.'s reminiscences, in which no doubt D.H. Lawrence and Ezra Pound figured: I bet you got some good stuff—you being one of those to whom people like pouring out. Some day *you* will reminisce, but probably well after I have left for what optimists on patently inadequate grounds insist on calling a better world. I hope you can keep cool in your Soho Square eyrie— which I have never, even in winter, reached not out of breath and perspiring. Equally never have I regretted climbing the steep ascent to heaven. Mid peril toil and pain. Meanwhile cherish the idea of a midweek visit to Finndale in October—often the best of months. But I won't be a bore about it.

P.S. I thought your secretary charming!

13 July 1958   *Bromsden Farm*

Your letter arrived faithfully on Saturday morning, so after a few mishits our long rally is now decorously resumed. Before I forget it, the Gibbon reference is Vol I, Chap IV: the marginal heading reads:

'Commodus displays his skill in the amphitheatre'. Donald had slightly improved the footnote, which in fact reads thus:

> Commodus killed a camelopardalis or Giraffe (Dion. 1. lxxii. p. 1211.), the tallest, the most gentle, and the most useless of the large quadrupeds. This singular animal, a native only of the interior parts of Africa, has not been seen in Europe since the revival of letters; and though M. de Buffon (Hist. Naturelle, tom xiii) has endeavoured to describe, he has not ventured to delineate, the Giraffe.

I discovered that Donald has all his life been accumulating material for an *Anthology of Wit*, and I begged him to let me see some of it. He has a splendid sense of humour and considerable taste, so the result should be good.

I am now slowly, steadily and pleasurably reading straight through (some pages or poems each night in bed) the poetical works of Matthew Arnold, in search of quotations or references quoted by Oscar.

She whom you praised is not my secretary, but my assistant, right hand and great joy these twelve years past. You shall see and hear more of her in due time. Needless to say, your success with her was instantaneous and immense.

We have had a much too busy week-end, in the midst of gales, greyness and heavy rain. Duff and his girl came on Friday. Yesterday Comfort and I dined with the Osbert Lancasters and were persuaded to play bridge till 1. am (we won 2/- each!). This morning Bridget's young man arrived, Mrs and Master Lancaster brought Lucy Moorehead (Alan's wife) over for drinks, and Eric Linklater brought Adam, his own boy and a chauffeur from Eton. Ten to lunch, with no servants, puts a strain on cutlery, china, washers-up. Now they have mercifully all gone, except Bridget and her young man. Comfort retired to bed exhausted after tea. Duff is on his way to six weeks as junior reporter on the *Bolton Evening News*. Last Thursday, in a Junior League match at Eton, Adam took four wickets in four balls! He says the batsmen were useless, but since the last three were all clean bowled, he must at least have been accurate.

I have now got back to the ever-recurring situation in which I haven't room for a single book on any shelf here or in Soho Square. In 1961 Edmund Blunden is due to come home and remove his 7000 volumes from the flat, but what am I to do in the interim? Every day, almost, I acquire some book or books, all duplicates were given away long since, and I have seldom got rid of my only copy of anything without regretting it later. There is no such thing as *enough* books.

Do get H.E. Bates's latest novel (*The Darling Buds of May*) from the library. It made me laugh out loud several times, though I must warn you that Comfort could see nothing funny in it at all.

I must now rewrite someone's manuscript, and I don't feel at all inclined to. I wish more authors were literate and competent.

St Swithin [*15 July*] *1958*   *Grundisburgh*

Thank you for the Gibbon footnote—very rich. Is there any hope of D.S.'s anthology of wit appearing in my lifetime? Do persuade him—and press upon him what is the truth, that he has little to contend with. No one, to my mind, is more disappointing than Daniel George, who seems to have read everything, but I don't find much in his *Peck of Troubles*, *Alphabetical Order*, *Book of Anecdotes*, all being irritatingly just good enough for one to go on reading (which I do every morning in the smallest room) but little more. Though I grant you it is quite possible that, unknown to me, my perceptions and sense of humour are in decline. (Yesterday at a Woodbridge Governors' meeting the question was mooted of getting a retired beak to fill a desperate gap for one term, but he was turned down, because as one Governor said, 'Oh no he's not exactly gaga, but after all he is seventy-two'.)

I am *very* glad that you found no ghastly crisis when you got back on Tuesday after the dinner. I inherit an invincible pessimism, and often feel like James Forsyte who complained, at about my age, that 'the least thing worries me to death'. Luckily Pamela doesn't worry about the same things—or indeed about anything except what affects the family. I often admired the way you kept things going at your end of the table, when you must have been full of nagging wonder as to what it was all about. But that charming lady looked fully

97

equal to the task of ministering angel. I should love to hear all about her; I never saw a face with a livelier understanding.

I didn't know O.W. was fond of Matthew Arnold's poetry. Why have Sitwells etc such a down on him? Percy Lubbock always objected to 'the *vasty* hall of death' in 'Requiescat'. And will 'Self-schooled, self-scanned' etc do in the Shakespeare sonnet? Leavis objects to 'footsteps' in the sonnet, maintaining that footsteps imply movement, which in a mountain is absurd (surely hypercritical?). My *bête noire* is 'Who prop, thou ask'st, in these bad days, my mind?' which challenges Browning's 'Irks care the cropful bird' in 'Rabbi Ben Ezra'. *Per contra* 'Thyrsis' and 'The Scholar Gypsy' are utterly lovely, and why the hell, when I *could* learn, didn't I learn them by heart? And I hope never to read Sohrab's death without that tingle behind the eyeballs, because then I shall be dead in any sense that matters. I rather wish he hadn't given us that simile of Rustum eyeing S. much as a rich lady in bed eyes the 'slavey' (1890) who comes to lay her fire, because surely it diminishes instead of heightening the incident, like the comparison I came across not long ago of the sound of the sea to the swish of feminine skirts, which is to me a good many poles away from

> Black leagues of forest roaring like the sea
> And far lands dim with rain[1]

describing (I think) the view from Luther's Wartburg. I suspect that M.A.'s whiskers and pontifications have a way of inflaming antagonism. Anyway I always resent Dame Sitwell's pedestalling by many, especially when they speak of her facial *beauty*, as to which I content myself with Petrarch's observation about his housekeeper: 'If Helen had looked like her, Troy would still be standing.'

Your *ten* to lunch gives me a headache. On your rest-day too! But how like you are to Florence Nightingale: 'Rest! Rest! Have we not all eternity to rest in?' But is rest restful if you never wake? Socrates said nothing was more enjoyable than dreamless sleep. But not, surely, till you wake up? One often agrees with Macaulay, who thought many of S's dialectical victories were too easy. Perhaps they have often had it out in Elysium.

[1] Quotation untraced.

98

Your book problem sounds alarming. How like you to house 7000 volumes for someone else. I agree about weeding out. I did that—900 books—when I left Eton for here, and have continually missed any number of them, though they seemed the obvious choice for expulsion at the time. Some were left in Warre House library, but I doubt if any were among the spoils collected by that thief yesterday. I always wondered more thieves did not take advantage of summer afternoons. I always warned boys not to leave money in their clothes. A few heeded the advice but one who brilliantly hid his money in his books was so pleased with his brilliance that he told all his friends about it—and a fortnight later it all vanished. There is always a good deal of thieving, and it is practically impossible to detect, especially as most boys cannot quite remember how much they had. A mad world, i.e. good preparation for the adult one.

20 July 1958   *Bromsden Farm*

It is late at night, and I fear you won't get much of a letter to-day. I always leave Sunday evening, the last of my week-end, free for writing to you, and if anything intervenes there is no time left. This time it was my daughter's second *crise de nerfs*. She has been perfectly happy while her young man has been home on leave, but this evening, as his departure approached, she became very emotional and over-wrought. After Comfort had driven him off to Reading, the poor child broke down, and I had to spend an hour trying to comfort and calm her. Just as her mother did twenty-five years ago, she worries terribly about dying and not believing in God. I tried to persuade her that most people go through something of the same sort, and that when she is happily married and having children she'll be too busy to spend time brooding. She has got a job on the *Farmer's Weekly* in Fleet Street, which starts on August 18, but somehow we must try to fill in her time busily till then—not very easy at a moment's notice, with our own time so occupied. I feel terribly inadequate and ineffectual.

Directly Comfort got back from Reading we had to dispose of a wasps' nest with cyanide: it is in a particularly difficult place, under a concrete path, and I fear we may have muffed it. What next?

Your excellent letter welcomed me on Friday evening. Daniel George is an old friend of mine, but much reading has completely destroyed what powers of selection he ever had, poor chap. His anthologies are mostly deserts of disappointment. One day soon, when I have more time, you shall have a whole letter about the lady you met in my flat—Ruth is her name—and it will all be terribly private and revealing. Meanwhile I am half-way through 'Balder Dead'—not a very enlivening piece, but there are better to come.

Alas, except for the gleaning of a handful of dates, Oscar stands where he stood when I left Yorkshire, and I have now decided that on the four weekday mornings in London I will get up an hour earlier (6.30 instead of 7.30) and devote those extra hours unbrokenly to O.W. I will report progress, if any.

Last week was packed with committees, including that proposed new Fund, which has now been provisionally called the British Trust for Literature and the Arts, God help it. Next Thursday T.S.E. and I must face the assembled members of the London Library at the Annual General Meeting: we had a brief rehearsal last week.

Diana Cooper came in, looking younger and lovelier than ever. She brought a second draft of her second volume, but then took away the third section of it, to be added to, so I can't really get going yet.

All last week the so-called Soho Fair was in operation, with the square made noisy till midnight by the Salvation Army, two or three skiffle groups, thousands of strollers and streams of blocked and hooting drivers. Meanwhile marines and parachutes are piling into Armageddon and Nasser's smile broadens. Pay no attention, my dear George. As you say, we can do nothing, so enjoy your summer-house, and next week I'll try to send you a more interesting letter. I must revert to my old plan of beginning it on Saturday. If only we had any sort of a gardener to do some of the cultivating for us!

24 July 1958   *Grundisburgh*

You have all my sympathy—and so has the young lady. Foolish grown-ups (of whom there are far too many) always talk as if the sorrows of the young are light and transient, and of course to hindsight they may be—like most things—but they are devilish heavy at the time, for the young can't see the silver lining—indeed have insufficient experience to know that there always is one, and *time* weighs so crushingly at that age: 'the years like great black oxen tread the world'.[1] And how disgusting is the discovery that all those damned old saws are true—about work blunting the edge of sorrow, and *tout passe* and the rest of them. The best of all is my old friend Charles Fisher's advice to a hesitating bridge-player (often told to you before): 'Play the card next your thumb.' It is much better advice for life than for bridge. And once you said (kindly) that I never talked like a beak—to which I rejoin sarcastically 'Oh don't I!'

I often find it hard to see why people *should* believe in God, as I once said to Hester Alington. Her answer was that He certainly did make it very difficult, and at such moments one *mustn't worry* but go desperately on—Charles Fisher's line in fact. Much harm—especially to the young—is done by pious folk who pretend that it is all clear and easy and comfy—but as our common friend Carlyle said 'With stupidity and sound digestion a man may front much'.

There is something cheering about your failure with the wasps' nest. That again isn't nearly as easy as one is led to suppose, especially when wasps regard prussic acid as thoroughly toothsome food, as the wasps at Harlech did. Perhaps Celtic wasps are different. Only one year have we had many here, and then a neighbour took forty nests without any visible diminution in the number that made a wasp-line for our jam.

My *internal* pessimism is black and immovable—not mere funk, because I should not greatly mind if I passed away tomorrow, but at the strong possibility that Macbeth was perfectly right in calling life a tale told by an idiot etc. What, except luck, is to prevent three hundred years of painfully acquired civilisation from going up in smoke? But this is vain talk, because a genuine pessimist wouldn't enjoy as I do 'books, and my food, and summer rain'[2] and getting your letters, and writing to you, and dining at the Lit. Soc.—and a day like this, blue and white and fresh etc.

I shall love to hear all about the lady Ruth—as always about

[1] W.B. Yeats, *The Countess Cathleen*.
[2] Stevenson, 'The Celestial Surgeon'.

anything to do with you—and no ex-housemaster, unless he is a fool, is bad at preserving secrets.

'Balder Dead', I remember, tempted one in years gone by to substitute another monosyllable with the same initial. Surely there is nothing in it that could have appealed to Oscar? *I am pro tem* getting up at 6.30 for two hours' paper-marking before breakfast. It is the best time of day, I find.

This is all very small beer, but exam-marking is mentally debilitating. You will be pleased to hear that the Wykehamist entries for the Tennyson paper did contemptibly, and so I said in my report. Westonbirt *per contra* scored very heavily. One boy chose the Lotus-Eaters as his favourite on the grounds of its verbal music—and then produced several lines from a different poem. All the beaks had told their pupils to mention T's onomatopoeia, but unfortunately omitted to tell them how to spell it; one boy wrote it as three separate words. There are some dreadful little beaks about.

Why are you not a life-peer?

27 July 1958   *Bromsden Farm*

Your comments on my daughter's troubles may be beakish, but they are certainly wise, and had you not been so far away (luckily for you) I might have asked you to talk to her: other people's advice is always more acceptable than that of parents. However, the child is apparently recovered and has gone to friends in Wales for the weekend. We find the elder children's comings and goings, with or without friends and always without adequate warning, lead to chronic instability in the larder, which is either empty or laden with uneaten and rotting food. Oh well—you know it all.

My remarks about the wasps must have misled you, for they perished to a wasp!

I like to think that you too have been getting up at 6.30. I did so all last week, finding that first uninterrupted hour a splendid one for work, but disgusted to discover how little I accomplished. Nevertheless the feeling that Oscar is moving, however slowly, is very encouraging, and I shall carry on with the plan.

Last week was a busy one. On Monday I had another meeting with the Queen's solicitor (Sir Leslie Farrer) about that new Trust. On Tuesday I attended a luncheon party in a private room at the Savoy given by W.H. Smith to discuss an annual Literary Prize which they are planning to give. I sat agreeably between Harold Nicolson and Jimmy Smith. Veronica Wedgwood was there and told me that after Lady Rhondda's death it was discovered that she had always run *Time and Tide* on a private account, which was frozen directly she died, so that all the cheques sent to last week's contributors bounced! Nobody yet knows how much the old girl left, or what will happen to the paper. Immediately after lunch I dashed back to the office and conducted a meeting about the Dickens Letters which lasted from 3 till 7. Straight on to a meeting of my bibliographical dining club at the Garrick, where a bookseller friend Percy Muir told me that recently a French bookseller friend of his came over to London and rang Percy up in the country to ask him to lunch in London. Percy explained that he couldn't because it was the day of his village fête. Asked what this meant, Percy described the stalls, bowling for a pig etc, to which the Frenchman replied: '*Ah, oui, en France on appelle ça un garden party.*'

On Wednesday I spent most of the morning going through the proofs of Stephen Potter's new (and ostensibly funny) book with him—an exhausting job. In the evening Comfort arrived for two days' holiday in London. We had an excellent Soho dinner and went to a delightful French musical called *Irma La Douce*, all about sex.

On Thursday I lunched at the Garrick with one of the directors of Macmillan's, who formally invited me, on behalf of the firm, the family and the executors, to write the biography of Charles Morgan. After some discussion I went so far as to say that I would *consider* the possibility on condition that I could take all the papers home, that I had a completely free hand, without family vetoes, that there were no fixed dates for beginning or ending the book (goodness knows when I could start or how long it would take) and (most important of all) that they succeed in finding some way of paying £500 a year for three years, either to my two sons or to Eton and Oxford, in the form of covenants or a trust fund, so that I pay no tax on it. I thought this would put paid to the invitation, but my friend took everything in his stride, and promised to consult lawyers and accountants. Certainly such an arrangement would take a load of worry off me, but then the book would have to be written! It wouldn't be half as rich and amusing as Hugh: there isn't the same material: but it would be an immense challenge, to which all my literary longings might well respond. We shall see.

After this momentous lunch I hurried to the London Library for the Annual General Meeting, which was attended by 150 or more members. T.S.E. led off mellifluously, and then we swapped chairs, and for almost an hour and a half I stood up answering questions—an exhausting process, and for the first time in my life I had recourse to the water on the table. However, all went well in the end, all resolutions were carried, and the subscription was raised from six guineas to ten. The rating verdict is to be delivered next Tuesday at 2.30: I shall attend the court to hear it.

Then, still Thursday, I took Comfort to a cocktail party given by Patrick Browne (our O.E. opponent in the rating-appeal) and on to a long exciting film about the war in the Western Desert called *Ice Cold in Alex*. We both enjoyed it, but I was all in when we got back to the flat.

Except for Boothby, the new Life Peers are a pretty dim lot, and the whole thing seems to me quite pointless.

Do you know the novels of Rumer Godden? Many of them are excellent, and I recommend the latest, *The Greengage Summer*: if you like that I'll tell you which others to try.

At any moment I am to meet an American journalist, aged ninety-nine, who interviewed Oscar in the Middle West in 1882: he's sure to be gaga, but one never knows.

31 July 1958   *Grundisburgh*

I am black with sympathetic rage[1], though I suspect you expected it. I did, merely seeing the thing from outside and knowing that in these squalid times when financial interests are opposing those that are clearly civilised, the former always win. All good men know what

[1] At the failure of the London Library appeal.

ought to be done and I am sure the P.M. is among them. But if he proposes to take the burden off the London Library all the asses opposite will at once object 'then why not off the Hoxton Lending Library?' Damn them all! The invariable outcome of this conflict is one of the proofs that we are in for a new Dark Age.

> The signal-fires of warning
> They blaze, but none regard;
> And on through night to morning
> The world runs ruinward.[1]

But no more of that; I suspect that you are just as impatient of my gloom as my family are. And Cassandra was murdered, and no doubt Jeremiah was too, though history is silent on the matter. A large percentage of old men tend, as the years pass, more and more to resemble James Forsyte: how good Galsworthy was in that tale, though it is practically blasphemy to say so nowadays. Mere photography they sneer. Well I prefer a good photograph to a portrait in which all the tones and colours are largely arbitrary. Does anyone really think that in fifty years the *Saga* won't be valued more highly than e.g. *Mrs Dalloway*? Bah!. *The Man of Property* was one of the books set in the Certificate exam, and I have just been reading a good deal of callow and mainly second-hand judgments on the Forsytes. It is the literary criticisms, never the factual answers, which make one almost suicidal with boredom and irritation—and knowing that 2/20 is really the right mark for practically all and that one must not give it. Anyway I am nearly through now, and have not committed suicide yet—even after perusing the script of Miss Betjeman (daughter of John?) who wrote *forty-eight* sides on her five answers, not solely through that cerebral diarrhoea which she shares with nearly all schoolgirls in the G.C.E., but from having so enormous a handwriting that three and sometimes two words a line affronted one's eye. And all the candidates at her school (St Mary's Wantage) had the same sky-sign writing, and their bundle of eighteen scripts felt and looked as if it contained at least forty. I will send you a specimen page if I can.

'Chronic instability in the larder.' A pleasing phrase. Don't I

[1] A.E. Housman, *More Poems*, XLIII.

know it! The only answer is a permanent ham in the fridge, for, as C.M. Wells always says, 'All hams are good, though great hams are very rare; there was that one at Bembridge in 1899, and Allcock's at Aberdovey in 1904 and . . .'. They totted up to about eight in all. Incidentally C.M.W. invariably calls Allcock '*Nil Nisi*' or sometimes 'Nothing But', having in his make-up an engagingly fourth-form strand, the other strands being great, but I suppose not imaginative, scholarship and a profound knowledge of moths, wine, and salmon-fishing—plus of course cricket and football, though he rarely speaks of either, except that when primed with Hermitage he will tell a first-rate story or two about Tom Wass or Abel, or even tell you of his best innings, viz nine runs on a ruined and crumbling pitch, in the dark, against Richardson and Lockwood—and of course no protector. 'I needn't have had a bat; I was hit all over from chin to heel, but I didn't get out that night. I was bowled first ball next day.' By Tom Richardson, whose genial way it was to say as his victim passed him pavilion-wards: 'Best one I've bowled this year, sir.' All old cricketers of any aesthetic sense will tell you that Tom R bowling in 1894–8 was the finest sight in the world. And he committed suicide—like Shrewsbury, Stoddart, Albert Trott, A.E. Relf and many others. I wonder why. 'Sir, you *may* wonder.' As so often, Dr Johnson provides the only answer.

Did you, do you, have the same matutinal technique as mine? Up at 6.30, cold sponge of face, brew a potkin of tea, work two hours, then bath, dress, breakfast? And have you noticed how often the mornings, 6.30–8.30, have been bright and sunny, whatever horrors may follow? I am sorry about Peter's hay, I really am. It is the shadow over so many of my summers—the sight of ruined or spoilt harvests, hay or corn. So far, not much damage has happened in Suffolk—we get much less rain than you do, and only a few fields between here and Ipswich are tousled—just as if they hadn't brushed their hair—not laid flat. Nature is a tremendous ass, besides being quite inartistic, as O.W. said.

I haven't read a single novel by Godden—in truth hadn't even heard of him!—and I find to my shame that the Ipswich library is full of them—so I have taken out two, *The House by the Sea* and *The City and the Wave*. Are they what you recommend? Let me know, because in spite of your morbid taste for Brussels sprouts, I still have confidence in your judgment.

That is *most* interesting about you and Charles M. But have you, shall you ever have, the time? It will be grand if it comes off, because of course you ought to be writing. Though C.M. must be less fun to write about than H.W. There will be a lot of reading to be done too, including those rebarbative novels—not that I did not enjoy one or two very much. He seems to have been a curiously unpopular man (that appeals to you, I know) and I suppose conceited. Still, his comments on life and letters were very often, *me judice*, of first-class value. He was probably great fun when tight. But was he ever tight? Anyhow, good luck to you. But a' God's name don't fill your plate too full. I look forward to hearing how it all goes.

It is a gorgeous day here, and shortly I leave the summer-house for lunch, where I shall have beans and bacon (the *de rigueur* dish at all Worcestershire *archery* meetings in the early Nineties. Have you kept up your archery, as Roger Ascham insisted?) and raspberries and cream, and anyone who wants a better lunch than that can whistle for it—he won't get it.

(After lunch)

Just what I expected. I can just tolerate your liking for sprouts, but if you said you *didn't* like the broad bean, the matter would take a graver turn. It is true Pamela is *not* sound on this matter, but of course there is the compensation that thereby *I* get more of them. And what is your attitude about spinach? I used to hate it but don't now. All depends on the cooking, and with *cream*! Don't I recall that that was one of the items on old Heythorp's dinner? The book is indoors. It was nice to find that you were far from being averse to gastronomy.

4 August 1958   *Bromsden Farm*

I am so geared to the two-day week-end that a three-day one throws me out: by messing about at the beginning I end by achieving less than in the ordinary two days. I didn't write last night because, knowing I had today up my sleeve, I was finishing the typescript of

107

Peter's new book, *The Siege at Peking*, which he unexpectedly brought on Saturday, eager for an immediate (and reassuring) verdict. This I was luckily able to give, for I found the story absorbing and excellently told. I doubt whether many younger than you, except for a few sinologues, know anything at all of the Siege of the Legations—I certainly didn't—and he has told it without tedium anywhere. Today I have been struggling with a huge book on Havelock Ellis (the centenary of his birth falls on 2 February 59) by my old friend Arthur Calder-Marshall.

Comfort and Adam have just (8.45 pm) returned exhausted from a regatta. Adam won nothing, though he got into one final and one semi-final. He says the prizes were rotten anyhow—'useless things like ashtrays'. Once again he missed a Distinction in Trials by 43 marks, but secured the Science Prize (ugh!) for C. Next half he tackles the G.C.E. Will you correct any of his papers? I fancy he won't make much showing in English.

I see Cattley is dead: I never knew him to speak to, but didn't much like what I heard about him, though Duff found him helpful in the School Library. I'm sure he was a suppressed paederast—how say you?

Do you realise that your last splendid letter was six quarto pages long? You must have been delirious with relief after correcting all those frightful essays. The Betjemans live at Wantage, so clearly the young elephantographer is our Mr B's daughter.

My 6.30 a.m. ritual is simpler than yours. There is only an hour for work, since I have to start the day proper at 7.30, so I sit straight down to it, without wash or tea, and stumble on till they ring the Angelus in St Patrick's church across the square—and that naturally is the moment when I have just, at last, got something moving.

We all went to the Lands Tribunal to hear the old fool deliver his judgment, which he read from a typescript, haltingly and with a thick but soft brogue which made hearing difficult. This appeal has cost the Library well over £2000, and I can't think there's much point in our spending even more to hear the same miserable points of law argued before three judges in the Court of Appeal: however we are to have a meeting with Lawrence next week, at which all will be decided. I expect you saw that excellent leader in *The Times*: it was written by A.P. Ryan, who told me next day that he knows both the P.M. and the Chancellor are concerned at the plight of the Library, and that was why he mentioned them so pointedly. The subsequent letters were all much to the point. I think the next move is a public appeal for money (letter in *The Times*): apart from the legal costs, we now owe the Revenue some £12,000 of arrears, incurred while our appeals have dragged along. E.M. Forster (now seventy-nine) wrote a charming letter, offering a donation of sixty guineas.

It also looks, alas, as if that other Trust is going to materialise: the Pilgrim Trust have voted up to £500 for its foundation expenses, and Tommy Lascelles told me privily on the telephone that, when the new Trust is in being, the P.T. will almost certainly make another 'substantial' grant if asked. I see more work and committees looming.

Rumer Godden is a woman, but the two books you mention are by her sister and quite outside my recommendation.

Of course I like broad beans: in fact I like almost all food except various branches of offal—and I might even like them if I didn't know what they were. I love liver and kidneys, so why should I be repelled by the thought of heart, head, brains and trotters? I particularly like spinach in all its manifestations.

Last Friday I hired a car and drove to Roehampton, where I had a brief interview with the Roman Catholic Archbishop of Southern Rhodesia. How do you explain that, my dear Holmes? During the week I also went to a theatre, and dined out three times—once at Greenwich.

Now I must scramble out 250 words on my author 'Elephant Bill' who died last week. And there are 'blurbs' to be written for the catalogue, and Havelock Ellis is still lingering in his twenties. Next week, as I always hope, you shall get something worth reading.

7 August 1958   *Grundisburgh*

Put in the way you do, i.e. six quarto pages, it is clearly well beyond a joke, elephantography in fact—a beautiful word. My old friend Tom Cattley never wrote more than a side and a half octavo for the simple reason, which he often gave, that he had nothing at all in his head; he had plenty thirty years ago, but even then he was no great talker, and his normal temperature, literally, was 92, which may account for a lot. You are quite right; like many bachelor beaks—many of them excellent beaks—he was a sublimated homosexual, the adjective, or rather participle, being just as certain as the noun. He was perhaps a little too frank in his preference for bright boys of fourteen to all boys, bright or not, of eighteen. The result of which was that he didn't make much of his house, and his old boys had little feeling for him.

I am glad Peter's Peking book looks promising. I remember all the fuss half a century ago but none of the details. In those happy days we knew we were secure enough, and anything that dimly affected our interests could be put right by a couple of English gunboats just showing themselves. And not only were we much happier, but everyone else was too. I have read a few of the articles in Peter's last book and found them very lively, e.g. his career in the O.T.C. at Eton. Lately in the *Spectator* he has struck me as a little tired, but my impression may be wrong. What on earth are *you* doing with Havelock Ellis? Not that I know anything of him but a few pages of some immensely serious, and important, and unreadable tome on sexual aberrations, but though I am sure the subject has the most absorbing and hilarious possibilities, somehow I went no further. Was he a very good man? Malcolm Muggeridge says somewhere, when asked (probably by Kingsmill) if he would have liked to be Shelley, that he 'would rather be Streicher or even Havelock Ellis', but I don't know why. You will be able to tell me.

A science prize sounds very impressive. I never got within sight of one. I once won a history prize, and still have the Globe *Boswell* Arthur Benson gave me—a better prize than the good conduct prize I won in 1895 at Evelyn's, which was called *Among the Holy Places* with a lot of steel-engravings of the dullest imaginable places in Palestine. *But* it was bound in tree-calf, so, like any other thirteen-year old, I treasured it as a thing of beauty. I may see Adam's Eng. Lit. papers next December; one can never be sure. He will pass all right.

So far *all* the letters I have seen about the London Library have been on your side. What about that one which seemed to make it clear that the letter of the law was *not* binding on the Tribunal, however much the Chairman seemed to think it was. Mind you badger the P.M. about it. Even now the right thing does occasionally happen.

How the devil is one to know that the Christian name Rumer is feminine? It isn't a name at all. And you didn't tell me which books of Rumer I should read. I didn't make much of her sister's two books, but there is a whole shelf of Goddens in the library, and they can't all be by her sister.

I am glad you are sound on beans. I don't think I have tasted trotters or head (calf's?). Brains I rather like in small quantities. You are not, I hope, repelled by sweetbread. Your gastronomic tastes are as catholic as were old Saintsbury's literary ones. He must have been before your day, but no doubt you know some polymath, though in these hurrying times the breed must be rarer. Are you going over to Rome—or emigrating to Southern Rhodesia? What did that cryptic sentence mean? How, when your diary, i.e. letters to me, is published, will the editor explain it? I think of interpolating a malicious note to the effect that you had been much impressed by the miracles of St Januarius. Did you know that Thomas More was canonised only recently, the long delay being because Catholics resented his light-hearted remarks on the scaffold. Like the Germans in 1914, who said the English were worthless and frivolous people because they sang 'Tipperary' before battle.

I have been reading Hardy's life by his widow—very interesting, though she misses numberless opportunities of being more interesting. If only it had been written by Hugh Walpole's biographer! One gets very fond of the old chap, so calm and wise and unassuming. Is E. Blunden's life of him good? I don't think I have read it.

10 *August 1958*   *Bromsden Farm*

What shall I answer first? Havelock Ellis was an immensely handsome but impotent ninny, who wrote many books in dull and often clumsy English. Because of his impotence, shyness, high squeaky voice etc, he accepted as normal *all* forms of sexual aberration and, as you know, wrote a multi-volumed work on them. This was prosecuted and banned in England: the attendant publicity caused all the sexual misfits of the world to write to Ellis, and he gradually became their prophet, healer and guide. He married a Lesbian who gradually went off her head. He lived to be eighty. There's much more to him than that, but maybe you'll read the biography next year: it is very frank.

Duff has been awarded a 'major County Scholarship'—size as yet unknown. Perhaps I told you this last week. Anyhow Duff celebrated by taking all ten wickets for 29 in a Bank Holiday match in Wales!

We're no forrader with the London Library, since our Counsel was away all last week, sitting as Recorder of Chichester.

Rumer Godden's best books are *Black Narcissus*, *A Fugue in Time*, *An Episode of Sparrows*, *The River* and the last one, *The Greengage Summer*. If you find nothing in any of these I absolve you from further effort.

I love sweetbread: I wonder who brilliantly coined that name to obscure the physiological truth?

I journeyed to see that Archbishop to ask him to release Christopher Devlin (now a Jesuit missionary in Southern Rhodesia) so that he can come home for a year or two and write *the* biography of Gerard Manley Hopkins for the Oxford University Press. My friend Humphry House had written a lot of the biography when he died, and as his literary executor I am anxious that his work should not be wasted. The Archbishop was wearing lovely purple socks. He told me a great deal about his difficulties in S. Rhodesia, but listened sympathetically to my plea, and said he certainly would not stand in the way of the plan. The next move is with the Jesuits, to whom I have reported. It would be a great relief to get rid of this responsibility.

Those two volumes were not in fact written by Mrs Hardy, but by old T.H. himself. All she did was to put them together. E.B.'s book on T.H. is wayward in construction but full of curious information and critical acumen.

Last week began, mercifully, on Tuesday, when an old friend, Douglas Grant (a Scot, now Prof of Eng. Lit. at Toronto) came for the night on his way back to Canada. I took him to dine at the Travellers' (the Garrick being shut for holidays) and after dinner we sat with

Alan Pryce-Jones and Tony Powell. Alan was most amusing about a phenomenal fortune-teller he recently consulted. Without knowing even Alan's name this chap told him that he'd had an uncle who committed suicide (which happened twenty years ago) and other astonishing exactitudes. Then he gave the chap three letters in separate, blank, envelopes. Without opening them the chap described the writers with extraordinary skill.

On Wednesday I lunched with James Laver and his wife (very old friends) in their beautiful new flat in the Boltons. Next to me was Harriet Cohen, a wreck of a woman, full of stories of Sibelius, Paderewski, Elgar, Arnold Bennett, all of whom thought her the cat's whiskers, as no doubt she was. That evening I dined with a Canadian woman-professor from the West Indies, who is editing Coleridge's *The Friend*. Next day lunch with a Swiss professor from Geneva who has just published a thesis on *George Moore et La France*. Then visits from an Englishman called Cavaliero, who has been teaching in Malta, and a French professor from Lille who is compiling a bibliography of Beckford. Babel, my dear George, from which I was quite glad to escape to a meeting at the Arts Council about that new Trust. A.P.H. has now joined the party (of which I am still reluctantly in the chair) and he suggested calling it the Phoenix Trust, which we may well do if it's possible.

I didn't much like what little I knew of Brendan Bracken, and in the only near-business relation we had he carted me good and proper. Louis Golding[1] I first met at the Drinkwaters' in 1930. Then he was a brilliant talker, but the success of *Magnolia Street* turned his head and he became a bore. I once incurred his wrath by telling a mutual friend, with some reason, that I didn't consider Louis a suitable person to go to a boys' camp.

University Arms Hotel
Cambridge

13 August 1958

If the H. Ellis biography has much in it like the brilliant (and revealing) vignette of him in your letter, it will be a best-seller. 'A

[1] He and Bracken had recently died.

handsome but impotent ninny' ought to be copyright. I shall certainly read the biography.

I suppose old Hardy wasn't enough of an egoist to write good autobiography; and possibly he didn't think anything said by Shaw and Galsworthy at lunch was worth recording. I enjoyed E. Blunden's book greatly (just read it; didn't know it was here), his judgments are never superficial or commonplace. And I am now in the middle of *The Dynasts*, last read at Cambridge I think. It is tremendous. I should have thought even the critics of the day could have seen that.

That fortune-teller sounds most impressive—no chance, I assume, of collusion or preparation. All worlds on either side of death will be open to us some day, which may be the Almighty's way of dealing with the menace of over-population of the earth (if indeed He cares twopence about the earth—you see the impact of *The Dynasts*!). What He clearly is *not* bothering about is the Grundisburgh harvest; the last week has been almost entirely fine but for *just* enough rain every twenty-four hours to stop any harvest work. As an old farmer said to me grimly last week 'Thirty minutes' rain may easily cost a farmer £300'. Why don't we buy *all* our cereals and devote ourselves to supplying the world with meat? Don't answer; of course there is a snag somewhere.

An old pupil, Rex Whitworth, has just written the life of some great but unknown general.[1] Harold Nicolson gave it quite a good review in the *Observer*. But had H.N. his tongue in his cheek when he said R.W. had the graceful style one would expect from an ex-president of 'Pop'? Or does he think 'Pop' is what it was in old Gladstone's day? I have known many presidents who were practically incapable of speech. (*I* was once president—and did one good thing, viz got Alec Cadogan in while still in a scug cap. There had been growing up a belief that some colour was essential to membership—like that adolescent 'Philatelic' at Harrow.)

I never met Brendan B. But his utterances on and to the Governing Bodies Association committee seemed to me very apt and refreshing, though undiplomatically expressed. 'The whole plan, to my judgment, is completely imbecile' was one of the most recent—and I am bound to say an opinion I was strongly inclined to agree with.

[1] *Field Marshal Earl Ligonier* (1958).

Dr John Murray is another who makes it quite clear that he considers nearly all proposals about education to be off the target. He is one of those trenchant blends of Scottish and Oxford. I first met him in Charles Fisher's rooms (*circa* 1906) where, when asked his opinion of William Temple's *Christian Philosophy*, he put the book in its place as being by a man who was 'neither a Christian nor a philosopher'.

I imagine B.B. could be pretty awful. One can't tell much from obituaries. Oliver Baldwin was full of silliness, egotism, *un*-divine discontent, contempt for others (and of course for authority, discipline, tradition etc).[1] He was at Macnaghten's (who Barrie said was one of the best men he had ever met) and, like other failure Etonians, made no effort to get the good out of the place, but expected everything to be done *for* him, and never stopped picking holes and grizzling. Latterly, they tell me, he was addicted to the bottle, and that he was homo, but I know nothing of that. His fellow-soldiers found him so intolerable that whatever course might be going which took a subaltern away from his regiment for some weeks, O.B. was always sent on it, not, as no doubt his aunts thought, because of his mental brilliance. But he must have had *some* good stuff in him, though he never really gave it a chance. What a mess a little folly and conceit can make of a man's life.

I like your discreet and demure remark about Louis Golding and the boys' camp. I have forgotten *Magnolia Street*. Can a writer make a fortune now as he used to, e.g. *If Winter Comes, Economic Consequences of the Peace, How Green was my Valley* etc? George Trevelyan told Claude Elliott that his *Social History* sold I don't know how many copies but brought him only £3000. The trend, I suppose, when half England belongs to a party which frankly hates anyone to be prosperous by his own efforts and not by their damned enactments.

I have brought away with me *Black Narcissus* and *A Fugue in Time* to read in the intervals of evaluating the portentous outpourings of Miss Betjeman.

Looked in at Heffer's Bookshop. It is a *very* swell affair compared with what it was in my day. The man *we* knew as Young Heffer in 1903 and congratulated, to his obvious pleasure, on his really extraordinary resemblance to W.B. Yeats, died a few years ago. He was

[1] Elder son of the Prime Minister. He had just died.

very absurd but cannot have been at all a fool as it was in his day the shop went ahead by leaps and bounds. Monty James used to complain of his prices for secondhand books and often got the book he wanted from old David's stall for a—comparative—song.

I am always particularly delighted at seeing a gummed-up letter of yours, for it generally means that you have reopened it to add a juicy tidbit, and this last one is no exception. I loved your praise of *The Dynasts*, which I am sure is T.H.'s masterpiece.

I never knew Oliver Baldwin, and never heard a good word said of him: your remark about 'courses' in the Army brought it all back to me: one could often keep an undesirable officer almost permanently away on some course or other: a messing course was considered the nadir. I was lucky and spent only one week on a course in five years: it was on Aircraft Recognition, and took place in a desolate mansion outside Dorking. I found Macaulay's *History* in its library and read him delightedly each evening after our nasty dinner. At the end of the week I could distinguish almost any plane from any angle, but since they mostly became obsolete in a matter of months, *cui bono*?

I think it's still possible for a writer to make a fortune out of one book, but it more usually comes from one play or one film.

Last week was comparatively peaceful, since I had reserved two days for visiting the Arthur Ransomes in Lancashire; they couldn't have me, and I spent one afternoon in the B.M., and one in the London Library, footnote-hunting for Oscar.

I had another meeting with Geoffrey Lawrence, at which we decided to carry the London Library's case on to the Court of Appeal (though this is secret until the committee ratifies the decision on September 9). I'm sure this is the right thing to do, for reasons too complicated for enclosure here, but to be told you when we meet.

Did I tell you that my secretary (who had only been with me three months and wasn't very good) never returned from the August Bank Holiday? Her father rang up next day to say she had collapsed under the strain, and for the past fortnight I have been struggling with half-witted and ignorant temporaries. Yesterday I engaged a seemingly charming and well-qualified girl, who will report for duty when I get back on September 4. The nuisance of having—for the third time in a year—to explain everybody's name and address etc etc is scarcely supportable.

And now, as promised, and very much for your eye alone, I shall briefly tell you about my darling Ruth. She is a little older than I am, her maiden name was Ware, and she was brought up in Herefordshire, where her father was a choleric and impoverished man of leisure who captained the county in the Minor Counties championship. When she was nineteen she went up to London and got a job with a Jewish printer called Oliver Simon, a very good and successful typographer and printer of fine editions. He fell in love with her, proposed, and out of a mixture of being flattered and feeling grownup she accepted him. She was never in the least in love with him: he had a fearful inferiority complex and a nervous grin: his mother was a Rothenstein (sister of Will) and they all came from Bradford. They had two children, who are charming. The marriage staggered on unhappily.

I must now switch to Comfort. She is one of the (I suspect) many women whose sex instincts are in fact wholly directed to the production of children, and when their quiver is full they want no more (as they say in the courts) intercourse. So it was with her: when we married in 1933 she was passionate and gay, but after Adam's conception in 1942 she had had enough. I bore this enforced chastity uneasily for four years: if I had been a person who could flit from flower to flower, that might have provided a solution: but I am not: sex to me is indissolubly linked with love. And then in 1946 I met Ruth, and we fell in love like steel-filings rushing to a magnet. It was touch and go whether we didn't elope immediately, but somehow we held on, for our families' sake. I told Comfort about it, and she took it wonderfully, saying she was rather relieved on the sexual side, but hoped I wouldn't break up the family. I said I wouldn't. Ruth told her husband, who preferred to play the ostrich and go on pretending he knew nothing. Soon after this I got Ruth into my business, where she has been my prop and right hand ever since. For twelve years now we have been lovers in every sense, always blissfully happy together, with a complete unity of interests and of stillness. We are together in the office, in my flat whenever possible, and best of all in Yorkshire. We first visited that neighbourhood in 1947, and have been thereabouts every year since, but it wasn't till 1954 that we found the ruined cottage which we have restored and christened Kisdon Lodge. It had had sheep in it for fifty years, so in its new incarnation it is our creation, our child—the one place we can be quite alone.

I would have told you all this years ago, but first I thought you might be shocked, and then the opportunity never seemed to come. Two years ago Ruth's husband died, which made her life much easier. Now her children have left home, and one is married.

Sometimes we wonder whether our love has been fostered by all our difficulties, and then we think that perhaps it must be very strong to surmount so much. What the end will be I don't know, but on Tuesday we set off for another blessed fortnight. I wrote most of *Hugh Walpole* in Yorkshire, with R. typing each page as I finished it, and criticising brilliantly. Comfort is so used to the set-up that it is seldom mentioned. Sometimes she is unhappy, I fear, but I can find no better solution.

20 August 1958   *University Arms Hotel*

I am much honoured and touched by the story you tell in your last. It is, you know, something like an idyll—like the Book of Ruth! I mean of course objectively, because to you it is much more than that. Nothing was ever truer than *Amor vincit omnia* (as Chaucer's Prioress, in whose company I have been for a week, wore on her brooch) and both *Amor* and *vincit* have a score of meanings, from the depths to the heights—as indeed *omnia* does too. There really is something triumphant in what you tell me and in the way you have handled an immeasurably difficult situation—made so by the Immanent Will, which so often and so disastrously allows the union between this man and that woman, which seemed so promising, to be harmed, and it may be ruined, by deep and unforseen and unmendable discrepancies. Shocked!! I can't think you really thought I might be that. (Though I dislike those—often young women—who proclaim that they are 'unshockable'.) But I only by what strikes me forcibly as vulgar or mean or cruel, none of which elements remotely enter the love-story of Rupert and Ruth. Please let me meet her again some day soon—by which date you will (probably) have been able to convince her that I am less old and hidebound and slow-witted than I look—or at least that all the good wishes my heart holds for you shall always include her too.

The 'awarding' is nearly over, and I return home on Thursday. This hotel is comfortable, and to me there are few purer pleasures than living off the fat of the land for several days at someone else's expense. It is of course far too hot, as there are many Americans here, and I have for *five* nights slept under a sheet and nought else. Have you ever noticed how curiously ugly all middle-aged women who frequent hotels are? One exception here—a young Greek maiden who my susceptible colleagues insist must have been in Homer's mind when he imagined Nausicaa. The other women at her table must be the spit of the Queen of the Laestrygonians, whom he described in one unforgettable vivid line, viz: 'She was as large as a mountain, and when they saw her, they hated her.'

Drawbacks? (1) My pillow is too bulky, and I wake with a stiff neck. (2) The man next door snores—one of those reverberating snores like thunder among the hills. (3) The wine-waiter has bubukles on his nose, and my erudite confrères address him as Bardolph. (4) I left my sponge in the bathroom, and it has gone. I think of putting up a notice like that one at the Athenaeum 'Will the clergy-man who stole my umbrella kindly return it. This club consists half of gentlemen and half of clergymen, and it is clear that no gentleman would steal an umbrella.' For 'clergyman' read in this instance 'American.'

I am sorry L.A.G. Strong is dead: I met him once and liked him. He married Brinton's second daughter, a nice girl. Wasn't he rather a good story-teller?

I have to be very tactful and reticent these days, as you will under-stand when I tell you that the livelier of my colleagues thinks *The Dynasts* 'dull stuff', *The Irish R.M.* moderately funny, Carlyle and Meredith intolerable, H. James an old humbug, has never heard of *Earlham*—and hates porridge. *Per contra* he thinks Max B. the greatest writer that ever lived and Tommy Beecham the greatest conductor. Another, when D.H. Lawrence is denigrated, behaves rather like Dr Arnold when St Paul was by someone put above St John. 'He burst into tears and begged that the subject might never again be mentioned in his presence'—so Arthur Benson tells it.

Kisdon Lodge

Keld

25 August 1958

You've no idea what pleasure your letter gave us both. I knew you'd see the point, but you did so in a particularly wholehearted and delightful way. Bless you. I fancy the period during which I thought you might be shocked must have been brief, and after that I hesitated for fear of appearing unnecessarily disloyal to Comfort. She is a wholly *good* person—no vice in her at all, unselfish, uncomplaining, hard-working, but also now utterly unsentimental, with her deeper feelings so submerged as to be unguessable. Mercifully this teaching occupies and to a certain extent satisfies her. Enough of that.

This place is indeed for us the Earthly Paradise. Except for our beloved farmer who comes up the hill each evening to milk his cows, bringing our letters and yesterday's papers, we are completely by ourselves, in the most beautiful place imaginable, without machines or noise of any kind. I can't remember how much I've told you about the cottage (I think if you looked back at my old letters you'd find I'd never lied about the situation here, but simply prevaricated by avoiding mention of Ruth). Anyhow it consists of two rooms, one above the other, each with a tiny room opening off it. The bedroom is wide and low, with a miraculous view, and is furnished (as is the sitting-room) entirely from local sales. (I first thought of bringing *your* clock here, but it suited the flat so well that I had to leave it there, and now we have our splendid grandfather here.) The sitting-room also contains two comfortable arm-chairs, four other chairs, a wide kitchen table, and a superb desk-bookcase-chest-of-drawers (£1 at a sale). A splendid old range-fire downstairs, and a little coal one upstairs, which we light every night, for the luxury and pure pleasure of it. The tiny downstairs room is a combined pantry-kitchen-larder, in which we had a sink installed. All the water we fetch in buckets from a spring in the next field. We wash in a basin by the fire.

The cottage is in a green field and surrounded by others, with the wild fell starting one field above. Outside we have a coal-shed and E.C., with flagged paths leading to them. When we first arrived, these paths were buried under a fifty-year growth of turf, and it was the greatest fun unearthing them. All the buildings are made of local grey stone, as are the walls between fields, and all the farmhouses in the dale. We also have a porch with an outer front door. This acts as a wind-break, and contains a stone bench and our garden chairs and table. We eat out whenever it's nice enough—which hasn't been often this past week. In fact the rain, which looks like ruining the farmers by leaving bumper crops of hay to rot ungathered, has proved a blessing to poor old Oscar and his editor. I am going through all the letters and notes chronologically, preparing them for the printer, and Ruth is retyping each batch of notes as I finish it. So far I have done three and a quarter of the nine parts, and the possibility of concentrating on the book, with *no* interruptions, makes all the difference. Ruth is also staining the bedroom floor, painting the E.C. door etc, so we are busy at something all the time. Thursday is my (fifty-first) birthday, and we shall celebrate by going to a sale in a nearby village.

Duff writes in jubilation to say that his piece about his trip to West Africa on a cargo boat has been accepted by *Blackwood's*. No word from Comfort and Adam in Scotland, but I expect they'll write for my birthday.

I loved your account of the Cambridge hotel. Whenever I travel at the firm's expense I always enjoy the luxuries enormously, but I'm completely happy only *here*, where everything is slow and simple and primitive. From the bookshelf *How Green* looks reproachfully down, but, at risk of your taking umbrage, I am ignoring its blandishments and sticking to Oscar: this is my one chance of getting a clear run at him.

When we have to go shopping—usually to Hawes in Wensleydale, eight miles away over a steep pass—we pack all our purchases into haversacks and carry them up the hill. It's a precipitous twenty-minute climb up a rough track: only a tractor or a jeep can manage it on wheels. We have Ruth's little car here, a tiny Renault, which we leave by the road at the bottom. Write here this week, and then alas to Bromsden. We plan to drive south on Wednesday September 3. It takes a good eight hours, but we are now so used to it that we take it easy and don't let it tire us unduly. Ruth is longing to see you again: perhaps before the October Lit. Soc.? I had known L.A.G. Strong for twenty-five years and liked him very much. Not a wildly exciting chap, but genuine, generous, businesslike and kind. I think he was a good storyteller, but I suspect that, like so many, he exhausted all he had to say quite early on, but couldn't stop writing. Latterly I saw him always at the Royal Literary Fund meetings. Are you swarming with grandchildren? I only hope the summer-house is inviolate.

27 August 1958   *Grundisburgh*

Good! Do you know this correspondence has got so woven into the texture of my life that I was quite depressed at Tuesday not fulfilling its normal role of red-letter day of the week. And when the first post on Wednesday could produce nothing but a note from my banker denying the possession of a share certificate which I distinctly remember sending him, I very nearly phoned crossly to my Cambridge hotel saying they hadn't posted a most important letter I put in their box last week. I inherit an abiding pessimism about such (and other) things from my father. And somehow his defence, viz that if you always expect the worst, all the surprises you get in life are pleasant ones, like all other philosophical theories, ought to be more reassuring than it is. One or two things said by old James Forsyte always remind me of him, e.g. J.F.'s gloom about his cellar after his death: his excellent claret 'would be spoilt or drunk, he shouldn't wonder'. Surely that 'or drunk' is a delicious touch. Not that my father ever took his wine seriously—or anybody else's. I never remember the Hagley claret having the chill taken off it, and I am sure he meant eulogy when he said of our extravagantly insipid port that 'it would do nobody any harm'. Like so many of that generation he got his wine from some old friend on the verge of bankruptcy. Old Austen-Leigh of Eton similarly used to produce a wine which Walter Durnford said tasted like corked quinine. The beaks of the Nineties didn't know much about teaching, but by gum they had character. There are fewer such every year in every walk of life. And anyone of my age understands less and less what is going on. I humbly bought a paperback novel recently of which *eight* million copies have been sold, and beyond a certain rude vigour could see little or nothing in it. *God's Little Acre*[1] it was called. I found no character of the smallest interest. That is always happening to me. But I liked the two Rumer Goddens you mentioned, especially *Black Narcissus*. She has a great feeling for houses and their personalities. I shall embark on others of hers, when the flow of exam-papers from Barbados ceases, i.e. in another ten days or so—and then I have papers to set for next year. August and September are my (only) working months.

Kisdon Lodge as described by you makes my mouth water, but I want a little pen-picture of the 'miraculous' view. Is it moor and fen or crag and torrent? And what in the way of *trees*—of which, like a fool, I learnt nothing when I was young, and now when it is too late I love them increasingly, as that old ruffian Bismarck did, though I don't yet, as he did, like them much better than human beings. Of course he knew mainly Germans.

At Cambridge I won a bet of a million pounds. A dogmatic exam-colleague, with whom I saw the *Titanic* film, said that the tune of 'Nearer My God to Thee' was by Sullivan. I said it wasn't, and when he said 'What will you bet!' I said 'A million pounds', being really quite sure, but not really wanting to take the pound off him that I know he would have bet (an excellent but cocksure fellow). Of course it is by Dykes, as so many of those honeyed tunes are which we all pretend to be superior to, but really enjoy. I was once nearly complained of at Eton when in 'Lead Kindly Light' my spirited shot at a high E in the tenor part didn't quite make it, and the soulless beak in desk resented the sympathetic but undeniably hearty laughter of my neighbours. Luckily my tutor was Arthur Benson.

Your Duff is clearly marked out for a littérateur. Don't let him write like Amis, Leavis, Hovis or anyone called Wilson. All your offspring are bursting with brains, as one might expect. Have they their father's awe-inspiring energy too? Very doubtful. Who has?

[1] By Erskine Caldwell.

28 August

You will be sorry to hear that I have discovered a clear case of cribbing in two Certificate papers from British Guiana. My reporting of it to H.Q. will probably lead to war, or at least a demand for independence. The prize up to date is divided between Macbeth to the ghost 'Never shake thy curly head at me' and on the same occasion, 'Thou canst not say it was me who done it'. Another bright lad wrote that Lady M. said that if she had a child like M. she would 'pluck my nibble (sic) from his boneless gums'.

You must some day read *How Green* at Kisdon Lodge. It is made for it. Does your Ruth know it? Because if it isn't a *beautiful* book— an adjective *never* to be used unless one is sure of one's ground—I will become a Trappist monk and live in perfect silence on beans.

I look forward greatly to seeing Ruth (cheek!) again. You have no doubt warned her that retired schoolmasters are a pretty uninteresting lot, but I am encouraged by the thought that she is sure to like the people *you* like. And sometimes I feel defiant, like the Night Watchman[1] (I quote from memory) 'Lots o' people have made the mistake of thinking I was stupider than I was'—pause, then 'stupider than what I looked'—another pause, then 'stupider than what they thought I looked'. A divine man. And his name was George!

Kisdon Lodge
Keld

31 August 1958

Your tale of a blank Tuesday was so pitiful that somehow I must try and get this to you on time. If I give it to my farmer tonight, and he remembers to post it, all should be well. I am sitting on the flagstones outside the cottage door in the *sun*, which has shone deliciously yesterday and today. Sunday or no Sunday, I can see farmers and their wives and families haymaking in a dozen fields far away—but you want the view described, and I should have to be a combination of Ruskin and Wordsworth to do it any kind of justice.

Swaledale is a broad green valley running pretty well east and west for some thirty miles, from Richmond to Keld, which is the end

[1] The narrator in many of the short stories of W.W. Jacobs.

of Swaledale proper, or rather its beginning, for it is here that the River Swale first takes shape and name, fed by many mountain streams and waterfalls of great beauty. As one drives up the dale from Richmond the scenery grows gradually wilder, and here there are only very green grass fields up to where the brown-green of the fells begins towards the top of the surrounding hills. The cottage is high on one side of this wide green valley, 1600 feet above the road, on which even the twice-daily bus and an occasional lorry 'show scarce so gross as beetles'.[1] Behind us, one big field away, the fell begins. We can see as many as a dozen scattered farms, all built of the same local stone as the field-dividing walls. Cattle and sheep are the farmers' livelihood. The sheep are on the fells except in the depth of winter. A proportion of each farmer's fields is permanent pasture, and the rest kept for the hay on which the animals live in the winter. The only change ever in the look of the fields is their turning various shades of yellow-green as the hay ripens and is cut. The word 'fields' needs qualifying, since few of them are flat and many precipitous: their contours and varieties on the opposite hillside are a constant source of joy, particularly when the evening shadows deepen the ghylls and hollows with mystery and beauty. We are some way above the tree-line, and all the hilltops which stretch one beyond another in all four directions are bare and noble. Some way below us, straight down, there is a charming wood of ash and birch and hazel, but that is invisible from here. Along the road are to be seen occasional tall elms and other umbrageous trees. The tiny village of Keld can just be seen to our right at the bottom. Straight ahead the furthest range to be seen (about four away) is in Westmorland, near Kirkby Stephen.

Yesterday, for shopping, we drove north, over the most desolate and beautiful moors imaginable, to Barnard Castle on the Tees, and home by Richmond. Both B.C. and R. are charming towns. Have you a good map of the neighbourhood?

As it is Sunday, Ruth is frying us some sausages, bacon, tomatoes and potatoes for lunch. Usually we have a cold lunch, and always boiled eggs for our supper. The farmer's wife bakes us endless delicious cakes etc.

[1] *King Lear*, Act IV, Scene 6.

Later. The clouds have now rolled up, and I am continuing this indoors, while Ruth re-plasters the inside of our little built-in cupboard (the cottage walls are at least three foot thick).

I am sure your opinion of *God's Little Acre* would be mine, and that the eight million are fools. A sale of that size should have made you suspicious.

Ruth is thrilled by your messages and longs to write to you herself, but I have restrained her: *someone* must do the manual work. How nice to find you quoting the Night Watchman: I was brought up on him, and have most of the books, but haven't looked at them for ages. I had forgotten that his name was George.

Every day here I have worked at Oscar, and am now on the sixth of the nine parts. Here are a few of his jokes, from the time when he was reviewing books for the *Pall Mall Gazette*:

Andiatorocté is the title of a volume of poems by the Rev. Clarence Walworth, of Albany, N.Y. It is a word borrowed from the Indians, and should, we think, be returned to them as soon as possible.

K.E.V.'s little volume is a series of poems on the Saints. Each poem is preceded by a brief biography of the Saint it celebrates—which is a very necessary precaution, as few of them ever existed . . . Such lines as those on St Stephen may be said to add another horror to martyrdom. Still it is a thoroughly well-intentioned book and eminently suitable for invalids.

Judges, like the criminal classes, have their lighter moments, and it was probably in one of his happiest and, certainly, in one of his most careless moods that Mr Justice Denman conceived the idea of putting the early history of Rome into doggerel verse for the benefit of a little boy of the name of Jack. . . . If Jack goes to the bad, Mr Justice Denman will have much to answer for.

Perhaps you knew them already. None of them comes into my book, but nevertheless I shall be surprised if the massive volume does not amuse, move and delight you. I wonder how long it will be before I am able to enjoy it objectively, without thought of dating or cross-reference: years, I expect.

If tomorrow is fine and sunny we are planning to drive forty miles to Morecambe or its attendant watering-place Grange-over-Sands, and bathe in the sea. We have never been to either place, and we have a great affection for such North-Country holiday resorts, provided they don't lose their heads like Blackpool. Tuesday will be Oscar here, and the sadness of packing the cottage up for the winter; and on Wednesday we shall drive weeping south. I shudder at the thought of my office desk piled two-foot-deep in letters and manuscripts demanding attention. My new secretary reports for duty on Thursday: I hope to goodness she's efficient.

Ruth has arranged lovely bouquets of wildflowers all over the cottage—she always does—and they will have to be sadly committed to the flames before we leave. I've had a cheerful letter from Comfort in Scotland, where the weather seems to have been better than here. Write to Bromsden, and from among the litter of unpaid bills and uncut grass I will answer.

4 September 1958   *Grundisburgh*

I have got your picture of Swaledale (a delicious name). Excellent! Ruskin would have had at least half-a-dozen lines of blank verse. The K.L. view seems to have everything—in water and hill, and far horizons, and all the colours there are, shifting with the movement of sun and clouds—not out of range, I hope, of nice farm-noises and sheepbells, but no hedge-crickets, I suppose, or redbreast whistling from a garden-croft. This is the time of year, when, believe it or not, the robin comes and sits on the mowing-machine as I mow (but I don't do much mowing now). Ornithologists say that it is the Nazi of the small bird world, a ruthless bully and monstrously selfish. Nature is no sentimentalist, and didn't mind giving the little villain what a grandchild calls that lovely 'orange chest'.

Now, my dear Rupert, perpend. The next Lit. Soc. is on October 14. I stay with my daughter Diana for it. She is here now and wants you to dine on *either* the 15th or the 16th and of course your lady-wife too if available, but I think you said she never is in mid-week. Pamela too almost certainly won't be there. I know your soul is entirely above such things, but you will get a very good dinner and as good a cigar as Havana can put out when on its day. The fact that you will have seen me on the 14th and heard all my conversation, though slightly daunting I admit, must not put you off. Remember your Horace: '*Nihil est ab omni parte beatum*' or, *anglice*, every silver lining has its cloud. But Diana and her good man much want to meet you (neither has *any* intention of writing a book).

You have never told me whether you read in bed. Probably not, as you must always be exhausted by 12.0. But let me tell you that as a bedside book Jacobs's omnibus volumes (there are two) are unsurpassed. Each story is of the right length, and you fall asleep chuckling, which is better than any barbiturate. *The Irish R.M.* is of course another. And—as who knows better than you—stuff as good as that does not get staled by age. So many people *tick* books off like American tourists in Rome.

I am glad to hear Oscar goes well. I like the three gems you send. So many writers since (e.g. Guedalla) have attempted his brand of wit that it seems to me quite likely that our sillier critics may be deceived into thinking that anyone can bring it off, that it is *vieux jeu* etc. But surely the book must be a best-seller? Do you know at all when it will be out? Don't wait until the tastes of the common man (damn his bleary and myopic eyes) have infected all readers. And a' God's name don't forget I am 75⅔.

Morecambe I saw once on a Bank Holiday—an obviously lovely spot made into a small hell by *homo sapiens* in astronomical numbers and holiday mood. I fear that you may not have found it much better than Blackpool, which is simply and frankly HELL. Tuppy and I once visited it in August. You literally couldn't see any sand, there was so solid a crowd on it; and there were some six mechanical bands along the front playing fortissimo different tunes. The silver lining to the nuclear cloud sent over England by the Chinese will be that nothing will be left of Blackpool, and beyond that colossal wreck only will 'the lone and level sands stretch far away'.[1]

P.S. I don't believe Sonia C's story[2] of that game with King Edward— sliding bread and butter pieces, butter downwards, down his trousers

[1] Shelley, 'Ozymandias'.
[2] From *Edwardian Daughter* (1958) by Sonia Cubitt, née Keppel.

—not once but often. I mean, he may have been a fool about many things, but surely not about trousers?

Here I am again, back to the treadmill, the noise, the interruptions —and the sweet routine of writing to you on Sunday evening. Thursday was fine and sunny for our long drive: we left at noon and reached Soho Square at 9.30 p.m. London seemed—indeed was— terribly noisy and stuffy after our cool and silent mountain-top. Moreover, as you will have read, the next day (Friday) was a London record for heat and humidity: I was in the Henley train when the thunderstorm broke. Here everything is drenched and dripping, and our lawn is rather like William Plomer's. He wrote the other day from his Sussex bungalow: 'Our lawnette, when stepped upon, closes over the ankles with a noise like gargling, and squirts jets of water up one's leg.' Comfort says the kitchen garden is full of interesting pond-life, never seen there before—but we have masses of ripe and ripening *strawberries*! Apparently a late variety and most acceptable, since we haven't a single plum, and the remaining apples are steadily being beaten from the trees. Too wet for mowing, thank goodness, and I have pulled Oscar on to 1898.

You ask about farm-noises at Kisdon Lodge. On still days one can hear lowing, bleating and barking from the dale and the opposite slope, and on still nights the rushing of the river below. In August the immediate noises (curlew, lark, plover, grouse) are far fewer than in June, but there were still some. Did I tell you that on one of our last days we picked a jam-jar-full of wild raspberries just down the hill? Lots of harebells still, and wild geranium, loosestrife, ragwort etc, with heather, bilberries and rowan berries—oh I am so homesick for it all, and shall remain so until next June.

I sent you a postcard this morning, saying I'd love to dine with Diana on October 15: I shall much look forward to the evening. And you'll be at Soho Square at six on the 14th, won't you, to see Ruth again.

Yes, I always read in bed, but usually sleep swiftly overtakes me.

Detective stories I generally read, but I see that it's time W.W. Jacobs had a turn. There are some dozen volumes of his in my bedroom here, so that is easily arranged. But I am still in course of reading through *Aurora Leigh* and Matthew Arnold and Oscar's other favourites, in the hopes of running to earth a few more of his quotations, so my bedside table is piled high.

Oh yes—our drive to the sea was a great success. We reached Morecambe about 1. pm, the high tide was slapping the orange-peel up against the foot of the promenade, and we immediately saw that bathing there was not for us. So we bought a picnic lunch and drove on another twenty miles to Grange-over-Sands, on the other side of the bay. It's a wholly charming little place, like a bit of Cheltenham set down between hills and sea. We had a delicious swim off some rocks, ate our lunch, and drove home *via* Kendal, where we had tea and visited the tiny secondhand bookshop. The sun shone intermittently all day, and strongly in the evening, so that our drive home, through Sedbergh and Wensleydale, was beautiful beyond words. We shall go to Grange again one day.

Comfort came back cheerful and sunburnt from Scotland; Adam returns on Tuesday; Duff has retired to a caravan in Wales to work for Greats. His County Scholarship is for £200 a year: isn't it splendid! Particularly since the Charles Morgan project has now evaporated. His widow has decided that she doesn't want any mention of his love-affairs, and wants to postpone the biography for twenty years. This seems rather hard on Charles, since by then most of the people who knew him will be dead, and I can't imagine why this decision wasn't reached before they asked me to write the book. However, except financially, I'm rather relieved, and perhaps I'll find something better to do instead. They say (Macmillan's) that they're thinking of bringing out a volume of Charles's letters.[1]

My office desk is piled high with letters from everyone I've ever heard of, all waiting to be answered. My new secretary seems calm and efficient, so by the end of next week I should be up to date. Next Tuesday the London Library committee meet, I hope to endorse my intention of taking our case to the Court of Appeal: you shall have a

[1] *Selected Letters of Charles Morgan*, edited with a memoir by Eiluned Lewis (1967).

full report next Sunday. Later this month I have to fulfil an old engagement to speak at the Library Association's dinner at Brighton. To my horror I have just discovered that it's white tie and decorations, which will mean an expensive visit to Moss Bros, since my old tail coat and other accoutrements are all too old, tight and shabby. What a nuisance!

Now I must advance into 1899, and then spend a few minutes with the Night Watchman.

10 September 1958   *Grundisburgh*

Excellent! October 15. You have probably had the invitation by now. Diana is generally pretty quick off the mark. I don't know who she is going to get. Probably someone they think you don't know, and whom it will turn out you have known for years. On the 14th Alexander (I forget whether D. goes too) will be back from India, after a fortnight's stay there, and what we hope will be a successful effort to save India from bankruptcy.

I feel deeply for you—leaving Keld and arriving in London with its (almost) billion mud-coloured inhabitants. I like W. Plomer's description of his lawnette under water uttering the sound which must have begotten the Suffolk word 'stolchy' for muddy. Your *strawberries* fill me with envy. Have they *any* flavour? (cattish!) I also envy you your Kisdon noises. Once we could counter with a watch of nightingales ('ollerin away all night' as a disgusted rustic put it), but building operations have ousted them, and now the bulbul is as rare as the hoopoe.

Aurora Leigh I read at Cambridge but can't remember a word of it. Arnold Bennett, in one of those *Evening Standard* articles bringing culture to *hoi polloi*, recommended it, and that old ass Ruskin said it was 'the greatest poem in the English language'. Perhaps you will tell me you agree—even after coming across the passage in which 'daunting' rhymes with 'mountain'. Did Oscar really read it? It is very unlike *Reading Gaol*.

All my papers from Barbados have now arrived, and I shall be shot of them in three days. How intolerably *wordy* young women are on paper; they keep on saying that someone is brave and courageous,

131

or humble and modest. But they *absorb* the set book like sponges, and would score full marks if they could write English. And they are always capable of such things as I got this morning: 'Lady Macbeth said she knew what it was to snatch her baby from her boneless gums and dash it on the ground.' And of course *all* say that Macbeth was 'very annoyed' to see the ghost (or 'goast'; after all we have 'toast') in his chair. They have all been told to quote Goethe; and so they do, but under some pseudonym like 'Geotha' which puts that majestic old goose among the Anglo-Saxons with Hroswitha etc.

You keep a brave face about Morecambe, but admit you drove on for twenty miles. I was at Grange once with Tuppy and recollect nothing beyond that he had a row—as nearly always—with the station-master, and that a man asked if he might watch us playing billiards on the hotel table; I made a break of six and he departed, obviously murmuring *Nunc dimittis*.

I am humbly but testily re-reading *Emma*. You always deride my habit of re-reading stuff to which I have been allergic, and I think it is fairly absurd. But so many good men and so many too many even better women do go on so about the woman Austen—and as Tolstoy said about lovers of Shakespeare, I can only conclude that the 'Janeites' are all mad. I am half-way through, and send you an interim report, viz that the conversations in the book fall mainly under two heads, i.e. Mrs Dale,[1] and passages to be put into Latin Prose. Mr Woodhouse ('Oh my dear, *deliciously* amusing!') hits exactly the same note every time he comes in, and the boringness of Miss Bates is positively overwhelming. No more o' that i' God's name.

Poor old Percy Lubbock is profoundly melancholy, longing to die, and ill with what sounds like dropsy (do they *tap* one for anything else?). Eupeptic women—relatives, I gather—think he should be bearing up better, as a man of philosophy and character, but the alliance of old age, illness, loneliness, and blindness is a formidable one. He is, too, a very bad patient, rebellious and wilful, and women always disapprove of that. An otherwise very sensible one was *shocked* when I quoted from a letter of Housman's how after some dinner-party, 'I ran up the stairs to my rooms, as usual, hoping to die at the top'.

[1] *Mrs Dale's Diary* was a long-running radio serial.

It may be the Indian summer of the last few days, or it may be the
H. bomb, but the fact remains that for supper this evening I had a
large plateful of big, ripe, tasty strawberries—and the three others
had large platefuls too. I hate to go on bragging like this, but I can't
get over the phenomenon myself. If we have much more of this
weather I shall have to cultivate the art of writing to you on my knee
in the garden, for this week-end it has been difficult to stay indoors.
I managed to finish the text of Oscar outside, and now there are only
my introductions to be written, and some hundred and twenty
lacunae in the notes to be filled.

Diana was indeed prompt with her invitation, and I no less with
my grateful acceptance. She said that if they weren't back from India
in time, you would entertain me. I see that Humphrey's second book
is out: have you read it?

What about the airmen who breakfasted this morning in Hong
Kong and had tea in London? My only reaction is to rush back to
Kisdon, where everything moves at a primeval pace.

Down here I now have *Many Cargoes*[1] by my bed, and read one
story a night, with much pleasure: do you remember the skipper who
loved doctoring and making a 'prognotice'? *Aurora Leigh* also keeps
going: Oscar, like you, read it as an undergraduate, but now, instead
of scourging yourself or otherwise mortifying the flesh, you force
yourself to re-read *Emma*—well, well!

By dint of talking very firmly—and very *loud*—for half an hour,
I managed to persuade the London Library committee (of which
fewer than half turned up) to endorse my plan for carrying our appeal
to the Court of Appeal. Roger, Harold Nicolson and old John Hugh-
Smith had previously agreed to oppose me, but Roger and Harold
allowed themselves to be persuaded, and no doubt Hugh-Smith
would have been too, had he not been too deaf to catch a word that
anyone said. This left him in a puzzled minority of one, wondering
what had happened to his allies. Did you see that Brendan Bracken
left £1000 to the Library? And the same to the Royal Literary Fund.

On Friday we had our half-yearly sales conference, at which for

[1] By W.W. Jacobs.

two long hours I harangued the assembled 'travellers' on the merits of the firm's autumn books. Luckily I was feeling quite brisk, and they seemed reasonably impressed. I still haven't started work on Diana Cooper's second volume, but must do soon. On Thursday Adam is coming up to London for the night. Each holidays he comes for a good dinner and a play: goodness knows what I'll take him to.

I spoke to T.S.E. on the telephone last week. He seemed pleased with his play's[1] reception in Edinburgh: packed houses and arguments between critics. It opens in London on the 25th, the eve of his seventieth birthday. On the great day itself Ruth and I are bidden to the Eliots' flat for drinks. You shall hear all about it. We saw a lot of them during the last London Library appeal, and have grown very attached to them.

I am toying with the idea of compiling (when Oscar is finally polished off) an iconography or *catalogue raisonnée* of Max's drawings. Such a thing is badly needed, since there's no way of finding out how many there are, or where. There would be no money at all in it; in fact the job would get pretty close to that 'pure scholarship' which is its own reward. And it would be essential to obtain Lady B's full co-operation and goodwill. Even now I amuse myself, between sleeping and waking, by trying to decide how such a compilation would be best arranged: chronologically would clearly be best, but as many of the drawings are undated, that presents difficulties. The ones reproduced in books or listed in exhibition-catalogues would be comparatively easy, but even then their present whereabouts would take some finding. The Ashmolean at Oxford has a fine collection— but I am drooling on, it is midnight, your patience is running out, and I have to catch the 8.45 train in the morning. So the last section of Sheet Four, must, I fear, remain unutterably blank.

17 September 1958   *Grundisburgh*

The family holidays here are just ending and P. and I return to our normal Darby and Joan existence. Last Sunday we filled three pews in the parish church, which made a considerable sensation among the

[1] *The Elder Statesman.*

134

worshippers. An elderly parson, known to be pretty gaga, was so staggered that he prayed for the Duke of Wales and Elizabeth the Queen Edinburgh, and later gave out that there would be no Communion service on the 58th of the month. You will enjoy grandchildren. The discovery, when they get to about eight or ten, that to them grandfather is an amiable and quite harmless old fuddy-duddy soon ceases to have any sting in it.

Did you get that thunder-plump on the very evening after you finished your letter glorifying the weather and positively swanking about your strawberries. I wish I could raise you, as they say in poker: the best example of the successful counter—stop me if I have told you—was when our Vice-Provost Warre-Cornish went to London to attend a Sotheby auction at which a copy of the Mazarin Bible was to be sold. In the bus was a fellow-librarian from Cambridge who called out with a genial sneer 'Come to bid for the M.B., I suppose?' 'No thanks', said old Cornish; 'I've got a better one at home.' Isn't the copy in the College Library actually the best or at any rate one of them? You probably know. Rather pleasant to be able to make an answer which no other man in the whole world could truthfully make. I don't know how Eton got it. Stolen, perhaps, by Nicholas Udall, the Headmaster who stole the college plate, was homosexual, went to gaol, and on coming out was made Headmaster of Westminster. Those were the days!

I have finished *Emma*. The second half is better than the first, but much of the dialogue nearly kills me with its insipidity—yet the David Cecils would see in it irony so delicate as to escape myopic eyes and coarse tastes like mine.

I saw you got your way over the London Library in spite of John Hugh-Smith's opposition. He is a rum old bird. I have known him since 1892 at prep school, and he was in Arthur Benson's house at Eton, and at Trinity. We always quarrelled, and are now bosoms, when we meet, i.e. about every five years. He was at Diana's pre-wedding party last year, his chest so heavily equipped with gadgets as to resemble the engine-room of a submarine; but he paid little attention to it and heard practically nothing that was said to him—or else, which is equally likely, heard it but paid no attention. He is a relative of Pamela's and greeted her with the breezy question 'Are all you girls still alive?', the youngest of the girls being over fifty. Luckily they all are alive; not that he would have turned a hair whatever the answer, which I don't think he waited for. I remember him asking Arthur Benson at Boys' Dinner 'Sir, would you take orders if you were in the running for the headmastership?' to which the reply was 'My dear John, that is the kind of question that should never be asked.' Was J.H-S. abashed? He was not.

I am glad you have resumed W.W.J., the perfect bedside literature; it must be good for any man to fall asleep gently grinning. I remember the doctoring skipper—and the patient who had paralysis but, after a dose or two of the mate's medicine, leapt out of bed, and ran up the rigging like a cat. W.W.J. has the same absolute rightness of touch in words as P.G. Wodehouse and Misses Somerville and Ross. And do you know there *are* people, I have met them, who see nothing in any of them, just as some morons, believe it or not, can't see that J. Austen is on the same level as Shakespeare.

What rot that the C. Morgan life has fallen through—though it might well have over-burdened you, but the *catalogue raisonnée* of M.B. would surely give you plenty of fun. I did not realise his drawings were so much all over the place.

I have a small literary job in prospect! Dick Routh[1] has undertaken a *small* dictionary of national biography, no doubt for the rising generation of readers who couldn't tackle the large one, and he wants me to do some of the men of letters—about 600 words each. I think it might be quite a nice little bread-and-butter job. I shan't be expected to throw new light on anyone or anything.

21 September 1958   *Bromsden Farm*

Those lists which each spring and autumn reach you looking so fresh, and occasionally tempting, are always a source of the utmost mortification. Each time I am *sure* that there will be *no* books for the next list: then at the last moment I manage to scrape together a sufficiency, but by the time I have written or rewritten those frightful 'blurbs' I am so sick of them all that I can barely stand

[1] Eton master.

hearing them mentioned. Some weeks pass, and then the finished article always surprises me by being much less awful than I remembered. And so it goes on, and goodness knows what will be in the spring list!

Tiresome though it may be, I can't resist telling you that on Friday Comfort picked *three hundred* ripe strawberries (she got so bored with it that she counted them to keep herself amused) and another basketful today: we just eat and eat and wonder.

Your job for Routh sounds rather amusing: let me know which literary blokes you have to tackle.

Adam came up to London on Thursday: I gave him an excellent dinner and took him to quite a good murder play. Next day I gave him ten shillings and told him to amuse himself. It was his first day alone in London, and he managed very well, travelling by underground, getting himself lunch and tea, visiting three museums and three newsreel cinemas!

On Friday evening I stayed up to attend the annual dinner of the book-publishers' 'travellers', where I was the guest of my London representative. The dinner itself (in the Connaught Rooms) was very good, but the proceedings lasted from 6.15 till 10.45, and there were 450 men with all the chairs and tables very close together. Two powerful singers performed and there were speeches—the chief one by Sir Vivian Fuchs. He was interesting about Antarctica, but went on a little too long. He started well, after a tumultuous welcome, by saying he felt like the man who went to have a medical examination for an insurance policy. When it was over he asked 'How am I standing, doctor?' And the doctor answered: 'I really don't know: it's a miracle.' One of the chaps at my table asked me if I knew what the Leaning Tower of Pisa said to Big Ben—'I've got the inclination if you've got the time'—which I liked very much.

Did I tell you that next Thursday I have to make a speech at the annual dinner of the Library Association at Brighton? It will mean hiring a tail coat from Moss Bros and spending the night at Brighton, where they have booked me a room at the Grand Hotel. I think I am responding to the toast of 'Literature', but nobody seems very sure. The excellent Librarian of West Sussex (who operates at Chichester) has recently taken Orders and is now also curate of Bosham (the legendary scene of Canute's experiment). Do you think that, on the analogy of the Squarson, I'd be justified in referring to him as a Librarson?

I haven't read any of the manuscripts I brought down for the week-end, and several female novelists will soon be growing restive. Diana Cooper is getting back (from Greece) to Chantilly early in October, and if I have got her next book in shape by then, I may have to go over for a day or two. You can imagine how frustrating all this is, when I am so longing to polish off Oscar: there just aren't enough hours in the day, and in London I am still getting up at 6.30.

24/25 September 1958   *Grundisburgh*

How my mouth waters at the prospect of Max's cartoons, even more than at your three hundred strawberries. How can such things be? I should like to say with conviction, as old Johnson did on one occasion: 'Sir, you must not tell this story again; you cannot think what a poor figure you make in telling it'. But somehow I find myself forced to believe it. I am interested that Comfort finds counting a palliative of boredom—because that is the only way I can get through doing four hundred strokes of the hand-pump which empties the flooded cellar. There is an electric pump, but in Suffolk whenever there is a thunderstorm all electricity is cut off and the pump doesn't work. I find the best method is to count *one* 10 times, two ditto and so on. I used to recite *Paradise Lost*, but it slowed down the pumping.

When I have finished setting papers I shall embark, six hundred words apiece, on George Herbert, Herrick, Heywood, Surrey and Hakluyt for Routh. I shall enjoy doing 'em, but I don't suppose they will be up to much.

Those dinners can be very long—songs and speeches and a com-median were the order of one devastating evening in Ipswich some years ago—the centenary of some Ipswich cricket club—from 7 to 11. The *va et vient* was incessant, but I sat solidly through the four hours to the astonishment of my leaky neighbours. It is one of my few accomplishments, but not, I fear, one that will be mentioned in my obituary, still less on my tombstone. I like Fuchs's story of the man insuring his life. I have had only one examination and had some pleasure in writing down that I had had two operations, viz cholecystotomy and cholecystectomy. The doctor professed astonishment, clearly underrating the pedant's penchant for outlandish Greek derivations. There is sometimes a wild beauty about scientific terms. Tennyson would have loved 'dextro-mendelic-laevomenthelesta', and anyone but a zoologist hugs himself with delight before that repulsive toad-like monstrosity at South Kensington whose name simply is *squatina, squatina, squatina*. Did you ever get far enough in maths to tackle problems about the behaviour of 'a perfectly rough insect'? Though of course, as Winston, *aetat* ten, found out, it is just as absurd that *mensa* should have a vocative.

I much regret never seeing the *Manchester Guardian*, and should be very grateful for any plums you cull from it. Is Roger in it every week? I heard from him a day or two ago. He seems in good fettle but is afraid he may not be much at the Lit. Soc. this autumn as he is 'deep in the pocket of Lord Beaverbrook', whatever that may mean. He professes to be thinking as tenderly of Chiang as Mr Gladstone did of the Bulgars; and apparently backs Mr Dulles's sabre-rattling. What odd mental pictures we have of ourselves, none surely odder than Roger seeing himself as Horatius Cocles.

I am not sure about 'Librarson'. Isn't it rather too near 'Abhorson', a name of dreadful note?[1] Some names get right into one's midriff. I always had a horror of Mr Murdstone in *David Copperfield* quite apart from what he did.

28 September 1958   *Bromsden Farm*

Once again the Gibbon quotation[2] brought down the house and redeemed my speech from total banality. I have now worked it off on the Antiquarian Booksellers and the Library Association, so don't see much chance of using it again on this side of the tomb—or the Atlantic. The Brighton affair was ineffably tedious: a mediocre and protracted dinner with insufficient liquor (during the W.C. interval

[1] The executioner in *Measure for Measure*.
[2] About the Emperor Gordian. See Vol II of these Letters, pp 94–97.

before the speeches I nipped out to the bar for an extra brandy), and five speeches (two of them by gigantic women) before mine. After having to hire a tail coat for the occasion, my mortification was completed that morning by T.S.E. (bless him) ringing up and offering me and Ruth two tickets for his first night that night. Next day (Friday) R and I attended his birthday party at 6 p.m. Only twelve people, with champagne and birthday-cake, and all his presents laid out on a table. I lit the cake and told him he must blow all the candles out with one breath, which he meekly knelt down and did. I instigated Epstein (who was nothing loth) to propose his health, and when we had all drunk it, T.S.E. said, very simply and with evident truth: 'This is the happiest birthday I've ever had.' Both Ruth and I have come to love him dearly: he is so affectionate, simple and modest, and in private his sense of humour is fine. We gave him a little old silver snuffbox and a specially bound copy (all leather and gilt edges) of the Symposium about him.

Yesterday (Saturday) I drove seventy miles to an enchanting little church at Fisherton-de-la-Mere, near Salisbury, for the memorial service to my lifetime friend Edie Nicholson (widow of the painter). It was at 3.15, and realising that Siegfried Sassoon lives only five miles away, I boldly invited myself to lunch with him. (Although we have corresponded for many years, and have numberless mutual friends, particularly E. Blunden, we had never met before.) He lives quite alone with a housekeeper in a huge and lovely Georgian house, set in a vast park, nobly timbered and surrounded by miles of wall. The spreading lawns are all long grass, except for an area next to the house. The drive is overgrown and inaccessible, so I had to leave my car by some long stables and approach the house through a shrubbery. Inside, one huge room opening into another, one after the other, all with fine books and pictures. In the hall S.S.'s bat and pads proudly displayed, for though well over seventy he still makes some runs. He is thin, tallish, good looking with a large but not noticeably Jewish nose: a tonsure-sized bald patch covered by profuse and only slightly grey hair from in front. Dressed in flannel trousers, dark blue blazer and loosish collar. Although he complained of lumbago, he rushed about speedily. He was neurotically nervous to begin with, and didn't look at me for almost an hour. He gave me a glass of sherry, said he never drank in the middle of the day, and asked whether I could manage half a bottle of claret. I said yes, and he bustled off to the cellar and returned with a half-bottle of Beycheville 1933—terrifically good—with which I washed down some fine roast duck. We talked nineteen to the dozen, about Oscar and Max (whom he knew well: he has six or seven drawings), Edmund B., Nicholson, Gosse etc. Gosse, he told me, though perfectly normal in every other way, had what can only be described as a passion for S.S.'s uncle Hamo Thornycroft, the sculptor. When someone asked Lytton Strachey whether Gosse was homosexual, L.S. said—wait for it—'No, but he's Hamo-sexual', which I thought rather good. Eventually I had to tear myself away, for fear of missing the memorial service altogether. I truly believe S.S. enjoyed the visit as much as I did—which was immensely. At any rate he begged me to return as soon as possible, for as long as possible, but goodness knows when I'll have the time. He confessed to being terribly lonely, especially in the winter.

Do let me see your potted biographies when they're done. I once asked G.M. Young how to pronounce Hakluyt. He said: 'Hacklewit, of course: it's an old Devon name'. So there!

Peter has finished his book on the Boxer Rebellion, and I shall send it to the printer this week. He flew up to Scotland the other day to shoot with Gavin Astor and the P.M. He said the air was black with grouse, and the P.M. shot well. Their best day was 160 brace. Next Tuesday I am to dine with the Priestleys—and for supper tonight I had a soup-plate piled high with fresh strawberries and cream!

1 October 1958   *Grundisburgh*

I am glad to hear the Gibbon did its customary job. Even at the M.C.C. annual dinner I had to stop while they laughed—when I was halfway through the next sentence. They see the length of a ball quicker than the point of a joke. Apropos of cricket, I was browsing in an *Ego* last night and found that C.B. Fry's order of merit over the ages was Ranji, W.G., Trumper, Bradman, Hobbs, on which I make two comments (1) How can anyone be *above* W.G. or Hobbs, or alternatively, as the lawyers say, how could either have done more than he did? and (2) Ranji and Fry always over-estimated each other, both apparently blind to the stark fact that each was found wanting in too many Test matches, which after all is *the* test of the *whole* cricketer—body, mind, and heart. C.B.F., for so clever a man, was very inaccurate; he never, e.g., remembered that Lockwood and Richardson were at their best together in very few matches, as in R's *great* years, 1895-6-7, L. was sunk in whisky, and when he revived—in 1898—R. was going downhill. But in the 1898 Surrey v Yorkshire, when Y. got out twice under 180 (my *Wisdens* are in New Zealand) on a plumb pitch George Hirst told me he 'reckoned it was the best bowling he ever had to face—no rest at either end'. Those lists in order of merit are silly; there are too many candidates. It is a case of 'there is no measuring the precedence between a louse and a flea' at the other end of the scale. But how bored you must be with all this. It is one of my bonnet's bees. Sorry.

As to the T.S.E. symposium I don't really feel that I have the shadow of a right to your generosity because, much though I liked him at the Lit. Soc. dinner, I have never been a fan, my line about his poetry always having been that of the old Scotch peasant-woman who, after praising a sermon, and being asked if she had understood it, replied 'Wad I hae the presoomption?' And the fans (like J. Austen's) irritate me when they ecstasize over the '*poetry*' of some line in e.g. *The Cocktail Party* like 'She will be coming later'. But don't let that make you think for a moment that I don't know he is a great man. The trouble is no doubt—and many must feel it besides me—that if one's tastes were mainly formed before 1914, one is bound to be, as regards modern writing, in a fine chaotic bewilderment in 1958. It was a pity too that even before 1914 the veins in all the arts were really worked out—poetry, music, painting—all were at a lowish ebb. I hope matrimony won't prevent T.S.E. coming to the Lit. Soc.

Your account of Siegfried S. is very interesting—and sad too. *Why* is he so lonely? He must have any number of friends, and is there no wife and family, and is he bereft of employment and no longer interested in the passing show? Perhaps like old Carlyle he has lost faith in both God and man—which anyone may well have done.

Gosse! Hamo!! *Pauvre humanité!* I appreciate your editorial touch, keeping the Strachey jest till one turned the page. Is *anyone* in the clear once and for all? Shall we one day have spicy hints about Mr Gladstone *vis-à-vis* Randolph Churchill? *Infandum!* But the trend in plays and novels seems almost all one way now. Last week I read *Cat on a Hot Tin Roof*. Perhaps it is better on the stage, but it is poor reading, though it fulfilled its bedtime function, viz sending me happily to sleep. When up and awake I am re-reading *Hamlet*, full of the views about him of Rebecca West and Señor Madariaga, which I doubt not you know. They completely upset the age-old view of him as a gentle weak-willed visionary. Surely the actual evidence for their view is very strong, and how does the Bradleys' and Dover Wilsons' belief in his lovableness and high-mindedness square with 'I'll lug the guts' etc? It is all very strange. I wonder old Agate didn't spot it. He would have welcomed the idea that Ophelia was no innocent.

Thank you for 'Hacklewit'. I shall certainly use it and will send you the potted life. I can't see your heartbeat quickening over it.

Yes, Roger in the Beaver's camp is very odd. Liberal principles and Tory cash, is it a case of?—with the usual result. I don't in the least know how deep his Liberal roots are; sometimes I think he regards them (and himself holding them) as a great joke, and enjoys keeping everyone guessing. The dear man, as far as I can see, affects to be pro-Chiang in the far east. I am sure that on the Judgment Day we shall find R. watching the proceedings with a gentle and appreciative smile, and even then won't definitely know whether he is moved, or amused, or apprehensive or what. He is writing a Penguin about Liberalism and tells me his main trouble is to understand on Tuesday what he wrote on Monday. It must hamper progress a good deal!

By the way I did old Agate an injustice. He did see the ugly side of *Hamlet*, and complained that it was often so much cut about that it didn't emerge. I should like to have seen Irving.

5 October 1958   *Bromsden Farm*

I completely agree about the inanity of trying to arrange cricketers of different periods in any sort of order of merit—or poets, musicians, actors or novelists either—and it is a sure sign of poverty of thought when a critic can praise one performer only by running down another. We shall never know whether Irving was a greater actor than Garrick, and who cares? Let Trumper and W.G. sleep in peace with their deathless and unclassifiable fame.

Siegfried has always been neurotic and homosexual: the first war shattered him beyond recall. In middle life he married Hester Gatty and had a son called George. The marriage held together precariously for some years, and then Hester left. Siegfried was pathologically affected by this, and for some time refused to speak to even his oldest friends unless they promised never to see or communicate with Hester again. E. Blunden for one refused to comply (he didn't particularly want to see her, but was sorry for her and refused to be dictated to). After some years S. took him back to favour. Now Hester lives in Scotland, George is a married scientist with no literary interests, and Siegfried is an ageing ghost in a huge disintegrating frame. When occasionally he stirs outside it and meets congenial people he enjoys it enormously, but for the most part his neurosis makes him play the hermit, writing occasional poetry and prose. He has always been well enough off. One of the best of his later poems was written on the birth of his son: here it is:

MEETING AND PARTING

My self reborn, I look into your eyes;
While you, unknowing, look your first time on me.
Thus will *you* stand when life within me dies,
And you, full knowing, my parting presence see.

Alone I stand before my new-born son;
Alone he lies before me, doomed to live.
Beloved, when I am dying and all is done,
Look on my face and say that you forgive.

Do get his *Collected Poems* if you haven't got them. He's a very fine poet—and crystal-clear always.

When I was a student at the Old Vic Ernest Milton played Hamlet, not perhaps according to the latest views of today, but in a frankly *sinister* way (nothing lovable or sunny about it), which seemed to fit the words very well. I always love seeing parts played in totally different ways. Sybil Thorndike played St Joan (as Shaw meant) as a bumptious North Country lass: Madame Pitoeff as a tortured mouse. This altered the whole emphasis of the play but didn't spoil it—which proves the play's worth, to my mind.

My dinner with the Priestleys was agreeable—excellent food and the great man amusingly mellow. The other guests were Leonard Russell (Literary Editor of the *Sunday Times*), his wife Dilys Powell, and a television producer called Grace Wyndham-Goldie.

On Friday I took my French novelist Maurice Druon to the Tower of London, which has a place in his next historical novel. The Resident Governor, Brigadier Wieler, to whom I had written, received us with sherry and much courtesy, and for an hour and a half we were immersed in armour, dungeons, executions and escapes. I always find the place most moving and exciting. Do you? My Frenchman adored every moment.

Alas, the strawberries are now under water, but Duff ate a plateful on October 1. Thank goodness this house is not in a valley: we've water enough as it is. Celia Fleming put all their clocks *on* an hour last night, so they have been in great confusion all today.

8 October 1958   *Grundisburgh*

That is sad news of Siegfried S.—such a good poet, I agree. 'Meeting and Parting' has real quality. And how nice it is to *understand* at once. It is not only the poets of our day who baffle me, but isn't a great deal of the prose also very cryptic? I mean, in the *New Statesman* review of your T.S.E. symposium, what the hell does K.E. Gransden mean in his first sentence by saying T.S.E.'s play 'seems to have divided the admirers from the Myras?' I suppose the itch to be smart and up to date is irresistible. I hate it.

According to Madariaga, Kean and Lamb were mainly responsible for the sentimental view of Hamlet, and the Bradleys and Dover Wilsons have stressed the 'lovable' note in our day. Did the Trees and Victorians generally cut out the 'I'll lug the guts' etc and muffle H's frank murder of Rosencrantz and Guildenstern and, what when once

145

pointed out seems obvious, viz that Ophelia isn't at all shocked by the shocking things he says to her. Have you ever drawn T.S.E. on these and cognate things?

That is very interesting about *St Joan*. I only saw Sybil T. and I expect would have scouted the notion that Joan could be played differently—and even now I don't see how a 'tortured mouse' (your words) could have led the French into battle. Some critics today run down the play, for which I hope they will in the next world be particularly damned. And I see that K. Tynan not only accuses T.S.E. of sentimentality in his last play, but derides anything to do with Christianity or even religion as if it were beneath the respect of any intelligent man in 1958. But you know, this won't do. A man may have no religion himself, but if his opinions on life and literature and serious drama are to appear in print, he must show that he understands what religion has meant and means to many, or his judgements will be essentially shallow. Wasn't this the central vacuum which made many of Lytton Strachey's character-studies inadequate and even trivial? He had no idea what religion was supposed to be about. But they tell me K. Tynan is very fine. I never see the *Observer*, but even before I knew Ivor Brown I resented his being ousted to make room for a callow young smarty—who incidentally was largely responsible for boosting *Look Back in Anger*.

The Tower is a tremendous place. My ideas of it were gained from Harrison Ainsworth and I can never see it except as profoundly grim. Do you remember Macaulay's fine paragraph beginning 'There is indeed no sadder spot on earth than that little chapel' (quoted from memory—as one might say poured from a vessel full of holes)?

11 October 1958   *Bromsden Farm*

Mark the date, for this morning we removed the nets from the strawberry-beds, which are still covered with fruit and *flowers*. I write this not in vaunting vein but as a scientific Selbornian fact. A good bonfire is going in the orchard, but the B.B.C. prophesies rain, and no doubt this idiotic moon-rocket will further disturb the already chaotic atmosphere.

146

Sunday noon

For some unexplained reason I had a splitting headache all yesterday. Nevertheless I was determined to finish the proofs of Mary Lutyens's youthful autobiography,[1] and they kept me up till 1. am. I then slept for *nine* hours, and woke with my headache as before—isn't it tiresome.

You're right about the poor quality of much of today's prose: smartness is all. I imagine 'Myras' was a reference to a skit on T.S.E. called *The Sweeniad*, recently published, and written by some dim Cambridge don masquerading as 'Myra Buttle'.

Next time you catch T.S.E. at the Lit. Soc. you must tackle him on *Hamlet*. The traditional answers to your questions are (1) Ophelia was too innocent and silly to understand most of what Hamlet said to her. (2) R. and G. were spying on Hamlet and deserved to be murdered. (3) When you have just killed the wrong man by mistake, such words as 'lug the guts' might be said by anyone, and H had never respected Polonius anyhow.

Siegfried has now asked me to be one of his literary executors, along with E. Blunden and G. Keynes. Apparently he has voluminous diaries, which he thinks I'm just the chap to edit! Might be most amusing.

Peggy's play *Shadow of Heroes*[2] is terrifyingly good, gripping one all through and leaving one limp and gasping. Brilliantly produced and acted, whatever the smarties say (I have just seen the Sunday papers).

19 October 1958   *Bromsden Farm*

I'm sorry, but this pleasurable habit has overcome our neutrality pact, and in any case this won't be more than an interim scrap. I am staving off a cold or chill (which latterly I have successfully avoided), so do not feel any too bright. Also cows keep breaking into the garden, playing havoc with lawn and bed, and have to be ejected.

Tell Pamela that if her other two daughters are as beautiful and attractive as the two I've seen, I begin to understand why they have

[1] *To be Young* (1958).
[2] By Robert Ardrey, about the abortive Hungarian revolution of 1956.

been kept away from me all this time—I am distracted enough as it is.

Needless to say, *you* were a *succès fou* with Ruth the other evening, and she wished I had done quite a bit more telephoning!

It was nice coming on you in Foyle's, which I pass through often. If one has the patience their open shelves of secondhand books are often rewarding, since they've no idea what they've got. Nowadays most booksellers know only too well.

I have just finished the new Graham Greene ('Grim Grin' he is called in France), which I enjoyed lightly.[1] He is by now a very practised hand. I have begun Wheeler-Bennett[2] (I thought his wife charming) and there are other books piled up waiting.

If only someone would leave me a Cézanne, I would gratefully retire from publishing and London. Then your weekly letter might be longer—and even duller!

23 October 1958   *Grundisburgh*

I very nearly did the same—and regret I didn't—and wrote to you last week in spite of our compact; I ought to have known that you would. Then we should have been like Charles Lamb and his friend who agreed overnight to give up snuff, threw their boxes out of window, and met each other searching for the boxes early next morning. Sorry about that chill. Coming soon after that headache—might not Nature be saying 'Hi, push some of that pile off your plate'? Not that I know a thing about it, and regard as a fool and a bore anyone, not a doctor, who gives me medical advice, as no doubt you do too. But I don't like hearing you are not right on top of the world—the world is grim enough even when one is.

Cows—yes we have suffered from them in the same way. Not only do they muck up lawns and barriers, but nothing contents them but the best, e.g. they eat the heart out of every lettuce and leave the rest. The only silver lining is that a cow cannot help uttering a low but penetrating 'moo' of satisfaction when it finds something really toothsome, and at one time I could pick this up immediately from the

[1] *Our Man In Havana* (1958).
[2] *King George VI: his Life and Reign* (1958), by John W. Wheeler-Bennett.

148

summer-house and rushed out in time to limit the damage. Now we are encircled in barbed wire, and they have to confine their destructive activities to gnawing the bark off any tree that is clearly one of the best of its kind. Damn them—though I must say I do like milk, cream, butter and beef (less than mutton, however; are you with me here? Undercut I grant you, but not topside).

You made a bullseye with Diana, as I knew you would. She and A. agreed afterwards that it was one of their best dinner-parties. What excellent value Wheeler-Bennett is! He said in the heat of the moment that he intended to come more often to the Lit. Soc. dinners. Peter F. was *excellent* company on my left. I must say they are most enjoyable evenings and I can never thank you enough for getting me into them. And to top all there is that golden hour in your flat before the Lit. Soc. To hear that your Ruth was not bored with me goes straight to my heart and to the tips of my ears which have tingled ever since. And I thought their tingling days were over. But I *will* make a riposte to her benediction—a riposte which I suspect you may easily think intolerably impertinent, and she too, which if so you must keep it hermetically from her, and here it is—that after meeting her twice, I should quite truly and definitely have thought less highly of you if you hadn't fallen in love with her! Does that make you think me an intolerable bounder? Probably. Call up all the excuses you can, the chief one being that charm plus and intelligence plus are a very rare blend in Suffolk—or indeed in any county.

Talking of bounders, I got, after we met at Foyle's, the *Life and Adventures of Frank Harris*. It originally appeared as *Life and Loves* and was instantly banned, so I suppose, though the Elek people don't say so, that it has been expurgated. I found the book very disappointing —partly because of the boredom of the never-ending catalogue of his own achievements—invariably triumphant—and partly through a pervading suspicion that half his tales were not true. But mainly because it just isn't good enough. Few of the character-drawings seemed to me good, and few of his judgments on men and things have much weight or wit. I suppose he was before your day, but surely O.W. and M.B. and George Moore must have had a pretty clear notion that he was *the* man of four leters, if ever there was one. Or was Alfred Douglas his superior?

149

I like 'Grim-Grin'. The French always know exactly where the nail's head is. '*J'aime Berlin*' for Chamberlain when kow-towing to Hitler, and their faulting the education of the P. of W. and the late King as having 'too much Hansell (their tutor) and not enough Gretel'. Hansell, I believe, was the worthiest, and stupidest, and primmest of prep-school beaks. I remember enjoying *The Quiet American* and will get hold of this latest.

Did I tell you that I went to two horror films in London to see if their blurbs were right in promising that my hair would behave like quills upon the fretful porpentine? Alas, at one I fell asleep, and my only reaction on a close view of the faceless man was to think how nice it would be if far more people *were* faceless. I forget exactly why he was, but perhaps the fact that he was buried with Pompeii, when Vesuvius erupted, is a satisfactory explanation. I am looking out for a Cézanne for you.

26 October 1958   *Bromsden Farm*

Diana Cooper, back in England for a week, is going to ring me up tomorrow, expecting me to have got her next volume into shape—and I am only about two thirds of the way through. Since I have had the typescript for the best part of two months, always deferring it in favour of something more pressing, I now feel bad and guilty about it. The fact that Diana would never dream of blaming me only makes it worse. So I must work hard and late tonight, and in the morning train, and tomorrow night in the flat. You've no idea how the very sight of a thick bundle of typescript depresses me. Which shows that I wasn't cut out for a publisher, for your born one is forever cheerful and expectant.

In bed I have been reading with great joy Eric Linklater's new novel *Position at Noon*. It's a delightful *tour de force*, which should immediately be added to your library list. I keep thinking that if some of the young men could write half as well, they might be a good deal less angry. Let me know if you agree.

My cold was overpowering last Monday night—catarrh everywhere, all teeth aching, little sleep—but thereafter retreated, and in three days was gone, leaving me more outraged than hurt, and so many more hours behindhand with my work. Of course you're right about there being too much on my plate, but it's almost impossible to remedy, except by renouncing the plate altogether—which reminds me, I am much too fat, know by experience that I feel better mentally and physically when I'm thinner (or at any rate lighter), and shall arrange a week of starvation as soon as may be (an excellent reason for refusing all engagements). Sorry to be so self-centred.

Another cow broke into the garden, and, when pursued, cleared the fence into the field like a gazelle. Truly I hate animals, and should loathe to turn and live with them. Beef or mutton? I've never thought to compare them like that, and don't know the answer.

When I read Ruth your winged words about her she will blush with pleasure, and I shall have great difficulty in restraining her from writing you a love letter!

The only point of Frank Harris's so-called autobiography was its persistent obscenity, all of which was removed for the London edition, leaving only his lies and slipshod prose. I could have told you not to waste your money on it, but perhaps you hoped that, like the horror films, it might stand your hair on end. I can't help applauding your questing spirit, even when it leads you to sleep uncomfortably in the London Pavilion rather than peacefully at home.

This afternoon Duff drove over from Oxford, bringing a powerful friend, and between them they dug a good stretch of the kitchen garden. Duff has been put in charge of all the arrangements for the Worcester College Commem Ball next June. These include purchasing £800 worth of champagne, and I only pray that neither his thirst nor his arithmetic betrays him. I imagine he does little work.

Last week Adam wrote from Eton: 'We were taken to a film called *The Snows of Kilimanjaro*. It had nothing to do with snow or Kilimanjaro, and was j. hopeless.' So much for Hemingway!

Needless to say, Oscar's final touches are again postponed until I can cope with them, and meanwhile two new caches of letters have come to light, both small but I hope interesting: I haven't seen them yet.

Waiting to be read I have *Kitchener, Sir Charles Dilke, The Abbey Theatre, The Oxford Book of Irish Verse* and goodness knows what. I should love a year's solid reading—partly planned and partly way-ward. I keep taking down unread books from my own shelves, reading a chapter or two with immense pleasure, and then having to put them back, so as to correct some infernal author's typescript. You must forgive the complaining egotism of this letter: perhaps next week will show some improvement. On All Saints Day E. Blunden will be sixty-two: I have just sent him a brief birthday note. It will be a great day when he takes his 7000 books away from Soho Square, bless him.

30 October 1958   *Grundisburgh*

Your pulse I hope has by now pretty well returned to normal, now that John XXIII sits in the seat of St Peter. I haven't really followed the vicissitudes, and am still slightly hazy about that childish business with the smoke. In fact let me be quite frank and admit that the organs of human utterance are too frail to describe my lack of interest in papal affairs. And as (to me) the only duller thing I can think of is the motor-show, you will realise that the morning paper does not detain me long just now.

Local affairs are rather pressing at the moment. Yesterday I had, as President of the Ipswich Gilbert and Sullivan Society, to welcome the Mayor and escort him to his seat to see and hear *The Gondoliers*. I am sure now that I never wish to see another G. and S. opera. To *hear* eight or ten tunes out of each, yes, but the humour is all evaporated by now out of all those songs one really knows by heart. The incurably Victorian prose dialogue is dead. Some say the tunes are too, but they are not to me, and not for another decade shall I leave off singing e.g. 'Take a pair of sparkling eyes' in my bath.

You are oddly flat about beef and mutton. Did you never know the agonising choice put before you in the pre-war Simpson's—saddle of mutton or beef steak, both perfect of their kind? I have always thought of you as one who, as Johnson put it, 'minded his belly very carefully', and you have always, thank you, told me the menu at your Lucullan banquets. But perhaps I should have spotted that you are not in a gastronomic mood from your complaint that your belly is

152

too large—which I have never noticed. I used to be able to lose one and a half stone in a summer holiday, having what they call a very rapid metabolism, and for years now I have had practically no breakfast—except away from home when I positively revel in egg and bacon.

Then—more local stuff—this evening I have to be Question-master at a clerical brains-trust in the village hall. I have looked through the questions, and shall find it rather hard to avoid a certain ribaldry. The questions are rather like those that Man Friday put to Robinson C.—and completely stumped him. You remember? 'Does God like the Devil?' 'No, he hates him.' 'But God can do anything?' 'Yes, certainly.' 'Then why doesn't God kill the Devil?' Why indeed? I expect I shall put my foot in it by betraying that I think either the lay question or the clerical answer ridiculous. We shall see.

An *entrancing* Max Beerbohm book has arrived[1]—a lovely thing to have, bless you. Caricature now is so often merely slightly rude portraiture, but M.B. knew all about it, e.g. the A.B. Walkley with his cerebral dropsy—a critic whom I am always on the verge of finding intolerable—so cultured and dogmatic and Oxonian and Jane Austenian. But I am quite prepared to be told I am wrong.

I say these young Oxonians! We had plenty of baby-rows at C. and O. half-a-century ago, but they didn't hit the headlines. Why are rowing-men always quarrelling? Perhaps because nobody *really* knows how to row, how to teach one man to row, and *a fortiori* how to teach eight men. Tuppy once picked up a little manual of rowing in Spottiswoode's, and was delighted by the first sentence he saw, in heavy print: 'Remember the oar is put into the water with the feet.' I treasure an exhortation I once heard of Jelly Churchill's describing some movement of the hands: 'It is like passing someone a plate of hot foup (you remember his lisp). It is hot, so you want to get rid of it quickly, and it is foup, so you don't want to fpill it.' Bobby Bourne says it is an excellently vivid and apt simile for that particular movement. The towing-path at Eton was full of human nature. Marsden, his eyes on his crew, bicycling into and out of the river, wet through but making no pause in his objurgations. Brinton, furlongs distant (he couldn't bicycle), crying in the wailing tones of some sea-bird

[1] *Max's Nineties* (1958).

'Try to row well; try to row well'. I once told Havvy[1] that all coaching consisted of was to shout in a furious voice, 'Three, you're late'. After an interval while his laughter was quenched in asthma, he said 'You might well do worse. Three always *is* late'.

How boring you must be finding all this. The family was in the news yesterday. Thomas Lyttelton winning the Steeplechase once again, and Humphrey fined for speeding. I shall be in to-morrow for blasphemy. Look out for it. The last batch of Brains Trust questions has just come in; they contain 'How did Methuselah manage to live so long?' and—rather with an air of *that* will make 'em sit up—'How does the panel square the account of Creation in *Genesis* with Darwin?'

I have just begun *George VI*. Wheeler-Bennett must be an unfathomable mine of learning. One has the impression that there can be nothing more to discover. What a tiresome father George V must have been—so rigid and cross and humourless; and if Hansell knew his job the princes must have spotted quite soon that their august father did not know that 'me' is the accusative of 'I'. But perhaps Hansell didn't know it either. *Dilke* I have on my list. When I was young there was a sort of 'Oh no, we never mention him' aroma about his name, and an intriguing legend that he went to bed with two women at once. I wonder if Roy Jenkins's book throws light on this. The lady (one of the two?) in the case I gather ended as a(n) R.C. of exceptional piety. Like a boy in my house who, after many warnings, was pushed out after getting drunk in Camp, and is now in a French monastery—the apple of the Abbot's eye. Who derides the usefulness of a classical education even when it stops short at *oratio obliqua*?

Does it do anything to allay your restiveness to be told that I constantly hear your praises sung—as publisher, chairman, speaker, public-spirited citizen, *bon viveur*, biographer, conversationalist—a much more comprehensive list than in the ode to Mr Pecksniff which eulogised him as 'architect, artist, and man'. Probably, like Carlyle, when told of his fame, you will grumpily reply you would much rather have a plate of porridge.

I insist on sending my love to Ruth. Somehow I don't think it will turn her head, if you pass it on. The looking-glass doesn't lie—nor the birth-certificate.

[1] R.S. de Haviland, former Eton master.

I always particularly enjoy your items of local news, and this latest crop prompts me to confess to you (possibly not for the first time) that I have never in my life witnessed a Gilbert and Sullivan opera. Some day I suppose I must, just in case they proved to be my favourite fare. If such an opportunity arose, which would you advise me to tackle first?

If I were given that Simpsonian choice between beef and mutton, I should decide by the look of the individual joints—which must show that I am, as they now say, ambivalent in this important matter. If you insisted on an immediate and binding decision here and now, I should plump for beef as the safer bet, remembering tough and undercooked mutton from schooldays. Are you answered now?

Glad you like the Max book: I find A.B. Walkley agreeable in small doses, and have several of his books. Dear old Katie Lewis, who is eighty and daughter to the first Sir George Lewis (portrayed by Max), says she knew every one of the subjects of the cartoons, except Edward Martyn and Henry Harland, of whom she had never heard. One, as you know, was George Moore's friend and butt, the other editor of the *Yellow Book*.

I'd love to watch you coping with your Brains Trust, and all those naughty questions about Mr Darwin. But next Friday it would be your turn to laugh, for on that evening I am condemned to be the Guest of Honour at the annual gathering of the Robert Louis Stevenson Society, in some temperance building off the Tottenham Court Road. I'm told the attendance will be scanty, and mostly old ladies, but one or two will know *everything* about R.L.S., and who am I to invade their idolatry? What on earth can I say? And when find time even to think about it? Oscar's remarks on R.L.S. in the letters were few and mostly derogatory, but I might make something of O's life-long dislike of Sidney Colvin: he surely is fair game. But even those references must be looked up. Why on earth did I agree to go? It was, as Henry James said of his *T.L.S.* article, 'an insensate step'.

Which reminds me that last Wednesday, on a glorious golden-sunny autumn day, Ruth and I drove down to the Sussex home of an old friend of H.J.'s, the American actress and novelist Elizabeth

Robins. She died in 1952, aged ninety, and her lovely fifteenth-century farmhouse is now a fabulously comfortable rest-home for worn-out professional women. But in a bungalow hard by lives E.R.'s old friend and executrix, Octavia Wilberforce, a delightful retired doctor in her late sixties. She gave us a delicious fricassee of chicken and lemon sponge, and produced ten letters and two telegrams from Oscar to E.R., which she allowed us to take away and copy. She has an enormous shed stuffed with E.R.'s books, letters and papers, including letters from Henry James, Shaw, Ibsen and goodness knows who. I could have spent a fortnight there blissfully. It's a goldmine for some researcher, and I think the old lady is slightly bewildered by her responsibility, and was clearly delighted to talk to two people who knew about E.R. and her friends. She particularly took to Ruth, as who would not. Your message shall be passed on.

As for all those flattering things you report hearing about me, I would indeed prefer a plate of Swaledale porridge, but in the meantime one can't help feeling both gratified and grateful. Now I must review four detective stories and finish correcting the Havelock Ellis proofs before going to bed.

5 November 1958   *Grundisburgh*

Business before pleasure: I shall be at the Lit. Soc. Tuesday. But what a silly heading—I shall be at your Dickens door at 6. pm, expecting for the nth time that the bell-pull will come away in my hand. Don't ever get it replaced, at any rate before it perishes thus.

Gilbert and Sullivan. No, I think you were of the generation which began to turn up its nose at the operettas. Humphrey, who likes any amount of good stuff that is not jazz or modern, can't bear them; he was the first I ever heard who definitely said it' was possible for music to have *too much tune*. Moreover all the G. and S. harmonies are obvious and *vieux jeu*. In fact he looks on them as many, not wholly silly, do on those who in the twentieth century were still following the Tennyson formula, if so it can be called. He thinks as little of my riposte that 'Take a pair of sparkling eyes' will continue to be sung in baths and never Vaughan Williams or Bartok as your modern painter does of the objection to his work that no one wants to hang it on his walls. So the eternal argument goes on, to and fro. If you ever do come across G. and S. I would recommend as your first *Iolanthe* (2) *Patience* (or even first for an Oscar Wilde expert) (3) *Mikado*. These, *me judice*, have the best tunes and G's best wit.

There was an element of comedy about the Grundisburgh Brains Trust. There were rather too many questions and a few were omitted which in my opinion and Pamela's were not of general interest or importance. I boiled one or two together and in the end only two were left out. Both had been sent in by our Rector! He rather stuffily wanted to know why, and I answered with truth and nothing but the truth that they were not on my paper, leaving him under the impression that somehow the slip on which he wrote them had gone astray. One question was why in the Communion epistle and gospel are now separated by a hymn, and the other was why do the R.C.s celebrate a different number of Sundays after Whitsun than does the C. of E. The panel had no idea that they did—and if you can think of a topic more completely empty of interest or moment I should like to hear it.

The flaw of course of all such affairs is that there are no atheists, or even agnostics, in the audience. I always hope to hear asked—Why are so many churchy people conspicuously uncharitable, censorious and narrow-minded? and How is it that, as we see so often, it is perfectly possible for a man to be upright, just, charitable, magnanimous etc without any religion at all, e.g. old Judge Holmes?

Please tell me on Tuesday *all* about your R.L.S. occasion, because I scent a bouquet of richly absurd possibilities. I hope you may have said what I have always wanted to, that I like everything about R.L.S. except his more affectionate admirers (the same feeling so many of us have about Lamb and I have too about J. Austen). And of course many of his detractors, though I suspect many of these are really objecting more to the *Schwärmerei* about him in the Nineties. Do you see that a Penguin history of Victorian Literature has come out, mainly compiled (according to the *T.L.S.*) by members of one university and five at least from one college. The quotations show pretty clearly that the articles about Arnold, Tennyson etc are by members of Downing College, damn their horrid, spiky, little dry souls. As for *that man*,[1] he should be put on a desert island with Edith Summerskill, Barbara Castle, and Beatrice Webb; that must surely be *one* of the many kinds of hell a resourceful deity has devised.

I wonder why O.W. disliked R.L.S. Too hearty perhaps. Was it he who said that he understood R.L.S. had written a book about his Travels in the Cevennes with Sidney Colvin? It sounds like him.

P.S. Will you give away the prizes at the Abbey School (girls) Malvern on June 5? It *would* be fun!

Saturday night, 8 November 1958   *Bromsden Farm*

I didn't come down here till this morning, having been delayed in London by the Robert Louis Stevenson Society. The whole evening was richly comic, and at the same time rather touching. I enclose the programme, so that you can briefly survey the full horror. It took place in two small rooms of some sort of students' club connected with London University. There were twenty-eight people present, mostly elderly ladies and old men with deaf-aids. I and the President (a nice Yorkshire novelist called Lettice Cooper) had comfortable chairs behind a table, but most of the audience were on hard wooden collapsibles. Soon after the President had begun her introductory remarks a late-coming old lady slipped in and sat on one of these, which collapsed completely, precipitating her onto the floor. She was patched up, and the fun went on. The two musicians were determined ladies of uncertain age with short grey hair. Miss Somebody, in particular, attacked the piano with gusto, as if to make sure she got full value out of each note. Never has a previous announcement of composer and piece been more necessary. The young lady from Samoa was rather beautiful in a husky Polynesian way, with long black shining pigtails, and a pink chrysanthemum over one ear. Forewarned of her approach, I greeted her with some lines of verse written by R.L.S. for an earlier Samoan beauty. My half-hour of random jaw and readings from letters (Oscar and Henry James) seemed adequate—at least they took it in silence, and no one else fell off their chair. At the end I had to ask these poor old creatures to stand for a minute in solemn silence to

[1] F.R. Leavis.

158

the Immortal Memory, after which Miss Reeves sang 'Under the wide and starry sky' rather well, and we adjourned for sausage-rolls, sandwiches, cake, coffee and fruit—all good and plentiful, but difficult to handle standing up and besieged by old ladies longing to explain their or their families' long-connection with R.L.S. Then Miss Somebody got going again, and I thought of

> The Abbé Liszt
> Hit the piano with his fist.[1]

Then Miss Reeves sang 'Home, Sweet Home', almost everyone made a speech, thanking everyone else, and I walked home exhausted. It lasted two and a half hours (outrunning the programme) and they were all as nice as could be.

Sunday noon

It is, as you know, Long Leave. Adam is home, also the Linklater boy, also Bridget. Duff and his girl are driving over from Oxford for tea, so Comfort is busy roasting and baking.

Duff seems to be rather good at the Field Game these days: any-how he scored all the six points by which a scratch beat the School the other day! Did I tell you that he has had a short story accepted by a magazine called *Argosy*?

I can't, alas, give away your prizes on June 5. My escape to York-shire is delayed only by the necessity of appearing at Eton on the Fourth, and I plan to rush north on the 5th or 6th. So sorry.

I went on Thursday to the opening party for Bumpus's new book-shop, and talked to Somerset Maugham (more malicious and saurian than ever), Epstein, Arthur Ransome, H.E. Bates, Ian Fleming, Frank Swinnerton (with whom I was photographed), C.P. Snow, and a mass of publishers. E.M. Forster made quite a good little speech.

On Monday Comfort came to London for *her* half-term holiday. We dined excellently at the Garrick with my sister (oysters, roast pheasant, ice-cream) and went to T.S.E.'s play *The Elder Statesman*. I was prepared for the worst, but it bettered expectation. I don't think the old pet will ever be a dramatist, and the flat pseudo-verse in which these plays are written destroys naturalism without putting

[1] From E.C. Bentley's *Biography for Beginners* (1905).

anything practical in its place. This play is tolerably acted, and there are a few good scenes and remarks, but that's all. On Monday the stalls were more than half empty, so I fear the play's days are numbered.

My friend Michael Howard, who is Lecturer in Military History at King's College, London, has just sent me the manuscript of his long-awaited history of the Franco-Prussian War. It is enormously bulky, and he wants my detailed opinion of it, being prepared, he says, to rewrite it entirely if I so advise! God knows when I shall be able to get down to it. Just now I'm correcting the proofs of a book about W.B. Yeats and reading the manuscript of a children's book. When shall I be able either to finish Oscar or to read anything for pure pleasure?

67 Chelsea Square
London, S.W.3

13 November 1958

I hesitate to interrupt your meditations about obscenity which I see you have been in the middle of. 'Something will come of this', said Mr Tappertit, 'I hope it mayn't be human gore'.[1] That ridiculous existing law about 'those whose minds are open to such influences' has had too long a run; I am always surprised to see how respectfully lawyers and others treat it. Because all the expression I have quoted really means is 'the entire human race'. But lawyers are strange creatures. When some perfectly understandable case comes up, e.g. a man has run off with a married woman, some asinine old judge will always say that he knows the jury one and all regard the man with the utmost horror. Bilge, my dear Rupert. I didn't often attend the divorce court, but I can remember noticing the jury faintly licking their lips as they gazed at some attractive and erring lady in the witness-box. They were *not* regarding her with horror. Why, by the way is Divorce coupled with Admiralty in the law-court? I must ask Somervell that at the Lit. Soc. I remember that old bore Lord Phillimore judging a case where a barge had run into a pier, and it came up that the mate had seen, some time before, what was going

[1] *Barnaby Rudge*, chapter 4.

to happen, but had kept his mouth shut (the reason being that he was not on 'speakers' with his captain). Old P. could not understand it, and eventually asked the mate—a morose and inarticulate man— 'But, witness, could you not have said to him "You goose, you goose, can you not see that a collision is imminent"?' When several of the words were explained to the man, he grunted that no, he could not have said any such thing, and we had no difficulty in believing him. Phillimore was an ultra-refined old scholar. What was that epigram about Nature making 'a brace of Phillimores' when she wanted to make two bores, and ending 'But Nature herself would yield the ghost, if asked to make a Phillimost.' Something of that sort, but I have garbled it, like Goldsmith.

We had Agnews and Cadogans to dinner yesterday: Geoffrey Agnew most affable, but, alas, my old fag and friend Alec Cadogan! Well I suppose the diplomatic iron has entered his soul, and all conversational topics are handled as if the other participants were Gromyko and Molotov. He *is* now the man in the iron mask, and poor Pamela found him heavy going. It may not be all Gromyko's fault because the Lady Theodosia C. (straight out of Trollope) might dry up the genial current of anyone's soul. She never drew breath. I hardly heard a word she said. She heard hardly a word I said, and those she did hear she ignored. Exhausting. Literally the opposite pole as a companion to your Ruth. Joan and Philip Astley blew in for an hour at 6. She spoke with marked affection of Ruth—as indeed how should she not? Philip was up to me in 1910 when he had the looks of the young Alfred Douglas. He hasn't them now, but is a very pleasant fellow.

We lunched with the Homes (she was Elizabeth Alington) at the House of Lords. The dowager Duchess of Devonshire was of the party ('Mowcher' Cecil) one of the nicest creatures in the world. They were all very funny about the recently-made peeresses; only one apparently much addition to the oratorical strength of the House of Lords, and of one all one old peer could find to say after long contemplation was that she had a very good neck for an axe.[1]

[1] Lord Ballantrae tells me that the old peer was his uncle Patrick, eighth Earl of Glasgow, a retired captain, R.N. On the first day of the peeresses' admission he met two of them in the corridor and said 'As you may know, I

Roger came to tea—full of demure and sometimes salacious mischief. As you saw at the dinner he was mainly closeted with Jo Grimond. He tells me, with no sign of anything but amusement, that he is in the Beaver's black books for an observation made—of all incongruous occasions—at some Jane Austen ceremony, which an amiable journalist dug out and sent to the B. who got chapter and verse from Roger and then wrote to R that he found the remark 'most offensive'. I can't remember what it was, but it was roughly on the lines that he would as soon expect fairness in the *Daily Express* as he would a clean shirt on a cow.

16 November 1958   *Bromsden Farm*

Pausing for a moment in my meditations on Obscenity, I must admire your daughter's crested writing-paper. Is the bird a *Hood*ed Crow? And why is it leaning on the admiral's anchor? Presumably to get its second wind (*ventis secundis*), though I can't make out why this is in the ablative plural—or isn't it? Did I ever tell you of the flustered Coldstream guardsman who was asked by the R.S.M. what the regimental motto was. '*Nulli secundus*, sir.' 'And what does it mean?' 'Better than nothing, sir.' He was despatched to the guardroom at the double.

I thought you were in particularly good form last week, and only hope I didn't appear as dim as I was feeling. Nor did matters improve later, for on Wednesday night I was obliged to sit up playing bridge with the Gollanczes till 1. am, and was not at my best for darling old Rose Macaulay's memorial service on Thursday morning. There I saw many friends, including Vita Nicolson (Sackville-West) who scarcely ever comes to London. Harold told me he hadn't heard a word of the excellent address (they were rather far back in the

---

fought hard to prevent the admission of ladies to the House, but now you are here may I be among the first to welcome you?' As he passed on the ladies heard him say to a companion in his best quarterdeck voice: 'Did you see Lady Ravensdale? My God, what a neck for the block!' Lady Ravensdale (Lord Curzon's eldest daughter) took this as a great compliment and was delighted.

church) and soon after it started Vita thought Harold was going to cough and forced a cough-lozenge into his mouth. This went straight down the wrong way, so the old pet had a miserable time.

Betjeman, unusually neat in a tail-coat, read the lesson very well—from *The Wisdom of Solomon*. Can you explain the meaning of 'run to and fro like sparks among the stubble'? And is it not rather hard on the beloved dead that we should pray for light perpetual to shine on them? Russian prisons contain few worse tortures.

However, the whole service was good and fitting, though it contained rather too much unaccompanied choral singing for my taste. Outside afterwards Betjeman rather spoiled his effect by wearing a battered brown round pork-pie hat, which combined with the tail-coat to give an effect of the Crazy Gang.

Divorce in the courts is coupled not only with Admiralty, but with Probate as well. 'If Probate be the price of Admiralty, Lord God, we ha' paid in full.'[1]

Your Agnew-Cadogan party sounded a little heavy. Why on earth did they give C. the O.M.? I only wish I could come next week when you asked me, if only to tell Pamela a few jokes after her ordeal. But no—I shall go further, and most certainly fare worse.

Have you been sneaking out to any more horror films?

Which reminds me, Peter thought Cuthbert was a trifle tight at the end of dinner: is it conceivable? When I told Tommy that Cuthbert was complaining because there were no announcements, Tommy said: 'Let's announce that Cuthbert has been expelled from the club.' But I discouraged him.

Did you catch James Laver's recital of the Americans' new name for the White House? The Tomb of the Wellknown Soldier. Not bad?

Tomorrow I have to lunch with several hundred chartered accountants—can you imagine?

Our Obscenity Bill may have another chance this week, and again on November 28. Did you ever read A.P.H.'s book *The Ayes Have It*? It's a full account of all he went through before his marriage bill went through. Interesting and most relevant to our attempts today. Our leading light in the House is Roy Jenkins, who wrote the Dilke biography—a most charming and able chap.

[1] See Kipling, 'The Song of the Dead'.

Needless to say, Fred *did* ask the H.M. whether Adam could come up for our silver wedding dinner, but surprisingly enough the H.M. approved, so he will come up for the evening, and the family will be complete. Somehow my old father must be coped with: I shudder at the thought of the expense.

19 November 1958   *67 Chelsea Square*

Are family crests generally intelligible? The crow and anchor above seem to me on the same level of incongruity as the goat and compasses or the dog and duck. And you may well ask—Why *'ventis secundis'*. There cannot be more than one fortunate wind at a time. I like *'Nulli secundus'*, the pendant to which is perhaps *'pax in bello'* which some genius of fourteen translated 'freedom from indigestion'. Old Inge had a good collection of such howlers, and made a pretty penny out of printing extracts from his commonplace book in the *Evening Standard*. I remember a good one—not a howler—viz that the great Moltke was only seen to laugh twice in his life, once when they told him his mother-in-law was dead, and once when he heard that the Swedes regarded Stockholm as a fortress. Grim!

I share your bewilderment as to why being like sparks among the stubble should be thought the height of human felicity. But the Bible can be very odd. I remember some paper of Lytton Strachey's at Cambridge in which that humorous and slightly lavatorial mind pointed out that the promise that 'out of their bellies shall rivers of water flow' was a blessing that was not confined to the elect. The sort of joke the undergraduate loves—and the undergraduate that survives in the septuagenarian!

I have seen no more horror films, but had a good day at the Queen's Bench yesterday; the case began at 10.30 and ended at 4 and though, like almost all judges, old Hilbery deliberately mumbled, both counsel and witnesses spoke up. One old woman had run over another on a Zebra crossing and the whole crux really was—was the inability of the victim to work as well as she had caused by the accident, or by her age and rheumatic condition (she was sixty-eight). She claimed two years' salary and got a year and a half's. I was glad that only one witness said zĕbra. The judge rather pointedly said zēbra.

Cuthbert was, I think, intoxicated by the exuberance of *my* verbosity rather than by those admirable vintages. He groused a little, if you please, at there being so *much* food! What he will say, soon, at light perpetual shining upon him one trembles to think.

We go home to-morrow, fog permitting; I have a school G.B. meeting at Ipswich at 2.30. I doubt if I shall make it. We have had a good ten days with four dinner-parties. Edward Ford told us all about his tutoring of King Farouk—*not* a success, largely because H.M. was firmly convinced that he had been told to spy on him. The king was covered with scent and rings and adiposity. How would he have done as Jelly's pupil?

How did your meal with the chartered accountants go off? Did you make an easy joke about the superiority of gastronomic double entry over economic ditto? Or perhaps there were no speeches. My Old Boy begins to cast its shadow. I grow too old for the Mr Chips rôle.

23 *November 1958*   *Bromsden Farm*

I like to think that you can't construe *Ventis Secundis* either. My family motto, which I am pretty sure was annexed by my grandfather (he compiled an almost entirely apocryphal family history), is *Dum Spiro Spero*, which strikes me as more dogged than hopeful. What is yours?

We are full of hopes for our obscenity Bill (this is our—the committee's—third one). Much depends on whether next Friday it gets a second reading 'on the nod', i.e. without debate or division. If it does it goes to Standing Committee (how tiring it sounds) and has a good chance of getting through.

My lunch with four hundred chartered accountants was pretty good hell: most of my conversation was with a slick Old Harrovian who is apparently making a fortune by retailing refrigerated pig on the Persian Gulf. Since, he explained at some length, pig is tabu for Mahommedans, all the European troops, engineers etc were screaming for sausages, pork and bacon until he stepped in with his refrigerators. What next?

Yesterday Comfort and I drove to Oxford and lunched very agreeably with Donald Somervell in his rooms in All Souls. The only other guest was Patricia Hambleden, the nicest of women. Do you know her? Daughter of Lord Pembroke, widow of the last Lord H, Lady in Waiting to the Queen Mother. Afterwards I spent a happy hour book-hunting in Blackwell's, and then we gathered for tea in Duff's sumptuous rooms in Worcester. A boil on his arm had prevented his playing rugger, and he regaled us with cream buns and other fanciful cakes. At five we went to the first house of Celia Johnson's new play, which is on its way to London—an agreeable light comedy which we all enjoyed.

To-day we planted a hundred daffodils and narcissi in the orchard, in the distant hope that Spring will one day return. The myth of Proserpine must surely have originated in one of these northern fog-bound lands, and not in the perpetual sunshine of Greece.

The family dinner-party for our silver wedding on Tuesday is beginning to loom portentously. My old father is equal to at least four wet blankets, and now Comfort has invited her mother, with whom I am barely on speaking terms, to come for a preliminary drink. Why did I ever suggest it? Why was I ever married at all?

Also I have just realised that I have failed to book a luncheon-table anywhere for St Andrew's Day next Saturday. Patricia Hambleden is taking her boy to lunch at London Airport, and if all else fails I dare say I shall do the same. My true motto is: 'If it isn't one thing, it's another!'.

This evening I heard on the radio of a teddy boy who went to a barber's. 'Short back and sides?' asked the barber. 'No', said the teddy boy; 'just change the oil.'

I went last week to a literary cocktail party at John Lehmann's. I abominate such gatherings, but couldn't get out of this one, and it was better than most: champagne to drink and just enough room to move. My old friend William Plomer told me he is writing the libretto for Benjamin Britten's new opera—all about a tortured boy in mediaeval Japan. Anywhere for a lark, I suppose.

Ruth was quite unhappy at your being so long in London without her seeing more of you, but I told her you were fully occupied with horror films and dinner-parties.

The shadow of my old boy dinner (next Wednesday) is deepening. I always dislike it in prospect and like it in retrospect—one of those anfractuosities of the human mind I suppose. Our family crest is a Moor's head and the motto is '*Ung Dieu, ung Roy*', *ung* being, they tell me, old French for '*un*'. The resources of the English language are inadequate to depict the entire irrelevance of both. My great-great-grandfather was Governor of Jamaica; I had a great uncle who was very possibly eaten by cannibals. I know of no other connection with the colour-bar. As for the motto, it is a fine defiant gesture to nothing in particular, like many another: isn't yours a shout from some heroic last ditch? It has more blood in it than ours, and has also that pleasant English trait which Chesterton noted as part of Joe Chamberlain's appeal, i.e. the impression of a superb rearguard fight against enormous odds, when he really had all the big battalions behind him.

Talking of Joe C. I am immersed in the strange Dilke story—surely one of the oddest ever. To begin with, was there ever a drabber, duller-looking Don Juan in the whole history of romance? And what a mask those great beards were. The eyes need the mouth to complete an expression, and one can't see what Tennyson, Browning, Morris, Doughty, Tolstoy etc were *really* like. Though one knows that when Browning did shave his off, Mrs B. exclaimed 'It must be grown again this minute'. And I think it was FitzGerald who somewhere found fault with Tennyson's mouth. Dilke's face is as blank as a London fog, and I put it to you that a man who wanted—and got—*two* women in his bed must have had a fine extravagance in his make-up, and surely showed it in his face if anyone had ever been allowed to see more of it. I haven't really got to Mrs Crawford yet, who apparently ended as a saint, but never said another word about D.

Tell me all about your family party. My interest is not wholly benevolent, because from what you have let drop I scent amusing possibilities with a touch of *contretemps* about them. 'Why was I ever married at all?' is a question that I suspect all husbands have at times asked, and the question is not always rhetorical, just as Chesterton said that every thoughtful man has at one time or another thought of suicide. C.M. Wells, that whimsical man, used to maintain that the only thing that stopped him from seriously contemplating it was the difficulty of disposing of his corpse, and the awful bore it would be to those who found it. That difficulty keeps murders down to some extent (one Deeming solved it for a good many years, by burying wife after wife in his cement kitchen floor. Monty James, who had a macabre strain in his humour, used to say D's motto must have been 'Marry in haste, and cement at leisure').

30 November 1958   *Bromsden Farm*

I shall think of you on Wednesday, wishing I was one of your Old Boys. I always enjoyed our dinners, at which my Uncle Duff was easily the best speaker, but they died with dear old Jelly. *Ung Dieu, Ung Roy*, you know.

Yesterday was our most painless St Andrew's Day so far. Having no need to wade through mud and fog to those infinitely tedious games, we picked Adam up and took him straight to London Airport, where (amid a mass of Etonians and parents) we had an excellent lunch. The restaurant has one glass side, through which as one eats one can watch Viscounts loading and taking off for all parts of Europe. After that, with the utmost scuggery, we sat in a nice warm cinema in Slough (poorish films) until it was time for Lock-Up and tea in Adam's room. The poor child is in the middle of his G.C.E., for which he has to do *nineteen* papers. I wonder if his English ones will fall to you—or do they keep you off the Etonians, judging you no better than an Australian umpire? Certainly if I had to mark W.S. Maugham's last book I shouldn't give it more than half-marks for style and English. Those drab, broken-backed sentences (with so little behind them) might have been written by a foreign governess who had learned English entirely from books. Clearly W.S.M. has absolutely *no* ear for prose-rhythms, and very little eye, for much of it *looks* so awful. However, he's eighty-three, and a G.O.M., and he has asked me to lunch at the Dorchester next Thursday, so mum's the word.

As you say, Dilke proves—if proof were needed—that Don Juan and Adonis are two quite different people. Perhaps one could write an

essay showing that the greatest womanisers have always been ugly—
Casanova certainly was, but Byron must have been handsome before
he got too fat (doubtless his lameness was a great attraction).

The silver wedding party went off much better than I had expected. Preliminary glasses of champagne were drunk in the Lit. Soc.'s
sherry-room. Apart from the family (ten strong), Peter, my mother-
in-law, her semi-paralysed son, and the Hamish Hamiltons looked in.
My father tottered in for dinner, and by putting the girls (Comfort,
Bridget and my two nieces) beside him in relays, I managed to keep
him in good humour throughout. We ate smoked salmon, roast
pheasant and ice-meringue with hot chestnut sauce. The same wines
that satisfy the Lit. Soc. My brother-in-law proposed our health
graciously, and the bill came to more than £30.

Luckily next day I earned £21 by speaking for forty minutes to
some seventy members of the Book Society. A rambling jaw went
down quite well, but in the ensuing conversazione (with drinks) I was
relentlessly pursued by a coal-black, soft-spoken Nigerian, who
threatens to send me a mass of his short stories.

The silver wedding celebration made my darling Ruth very unhappy. Although it had no significance, and changed nothing, it's
easy to see how the reaffirmation of the tie that prevents my marrying
her upset her. I think she's all right now, but her misery made me feel
miserable too. As I have quoted before, 'He who lives more lives than
one . . .'

3 Wyndham House
Sloane Square

4 December 1958

As always, I enjoyed the Old Boy Dinner last night. They were
very welcoming, and all looked to me very much as they did in
Remove, what they had lost in hair being made up in waist. One—
now was it Geoffrey Davson, i.e. Anthony Glyn?—said he knew you,
and did he say you or maybe only Heinemann's were moving to new
premises? Can I face ringing a bell that does *not* come out in my hand?
I dislike old things changing.

Yes, Casanova, John Wilkes, H.G. Wells—all ugly men. George
Moore? but how far *was* he a Don Juan, for didn't some lady say he

was one who 'told but didn't kiss'? A few of the Byron pictures hint at charm, which all said was overwhelming, and he said himself that it was always the women who made the first advances to him and not *vice versa*. Who knows the truth? It will be most annoying if after all there isn't a next world where we may get the answers to all such problems—the *Marie Celeste*, Bacon and Shakespeare, the Wallace murder, the Baccarat case etc.

Your silver wedding party was a tremendous affair, though I don't *like* to think of that £30 gone west, even though much came quickly back from the Book Society; still I expect you gave a lot of pleasure.

Poor Ruth. How invincibly vulnerable is deep love. That Wilde stanza you quote is always persistently relevant—and there are those, e.g. the old Wykehamist Wavell, who said the *Ballad* was 'insincere'! We must remember that a common Wykehamist trait is to suspect the sincerity of all non-Wykehamists.

7 December 1958   *Bromsden Farm*

This afternoon I interrupted my labours on Diana's proofs to spend three solid hours going through Peter's with him, so you will understand if my usual epistolary waffle degenerates into proof-corrector's symbols. So many thousands of hours have I spent on such thankless work that I can scarcely read *any* book without whipping out my pencil and marking the solecisms, tautologies and plain errors.

Had I applied this treatment to Somerset Maugham's latest, the margins would have been black with glosses. However, at luncheon on Thursday he was at his mellowest. He hates women, and their presence always brings out his adder's tongue: on Thursday there was nobody except himself, his male secretary, John Sparrow and myself. He always has the same suite at the Dorchester on the fourth floor, overlooking the park, and the huge sitting-room is furnished with his own books, pictures, Epstein's bust of him, etc—all of which the hotel stores when he is away. Luncheon is served there by a bevy of waiters. We had Martinis, a sort of Scotch egg cooked with cheese, a tremendously good and authentic mixed grill, fresh peaches and ice-cream, washed down by copious Hock, with brandy and coffee to follow. All excellent, and of course I never stopped talking. W.S.M.'s stammer is as bad as ever, but now when he can't get the word out he snaps his fingers in a tiresome way, which he never used to do. When he first met Sparrow (not very long ago) he believed that everyone called him Johnny—and he still does, though no one else ever has. I almost did too, to keep him company. (When I was twenty, my father had a dotty old chauffeur who always called me and my sister Mr Rudolph and Miss Dreary—her name is Deirdre. We missed the moment for putting him right, and all the rest of the time he was with us we called each other by these names in his presence, to reassure him.) T.S.E. and his wife had visited W.S.M., who commented with pleasure on their evident happiness. Usually it is unhappiness and other negative states that he stresses, so I took this as a sign of grace. W.S.M. said that when he booked a passage to Yokohama for October 1959, the people gave him a look as much as to say 'Poor old josser, he'll be dead long before then.' He was wearing a purple-and-black smoking jacket, which he said belonged to his secretary. He is clearly determined to outlive Winston: what a job the obituary-editors will have if they die on the same day!

Write to Soho Square this week, if possible, so that your letter reaches me on Friday morning, when I set off in luxury (first all the way) for Chantilly. I'll write to you from there, and post it when I get back to London on Monday evening, so it may be later than usual at Grundisburgh.

The Lit. Soc. will be pale and quiet without you. Lockhart looms, but as I shall have come almost straight from Twickenham, we can talk about rugger, in which he is interested. Ruth and I have been to every University Match since 1947, and always enjoy this annual treat, whatever the game is like.

It probably was Davson (Glyn) who said he knew me. Heinemann's are indeed moving—to a new, inadequate and traffic-blocked house in the heart of Mayfair, but I hope to answer your ineffectual bell-pulling in Soho Square for the next thirteen years. Then my lease runs out, and I shall, God willing, write to you from some snug retreat in the North Riding.

The American hospitals are too good: they always get Dulles better.

You are in Henry James's predicament—who, whenever he read a novel by another, rewrote it in his mind throughout. I do the same with many a sermon I hear—generally in the way of supplying an obvious and relevant quotation. Clerical ignorance of literature seems very common now. Our man here—he came only eight months ago—goes to another extreme. Last Sunday he referred to Karl Barth and the Orphic myth, without any explanation of either. Meanwhile half the unmarried young women are with child, and many of the marriages precede or follow the arrival of the firstborn by a matter of a few weeks or even days. Not necessarily as a sequel to the Orphic myth, as none of them comes to church. And after all East Anglia has always been noted for the trial trip before marriage, as in old days husbands, especially farmers, liked to know they would have families before committing themselves.

I stayed a night recently with S.C. Roberts at Cambridge, who showed me a copy of Raleigh's *Six Essays on Johnson* that had belonged to Max Beerbohm. Some pencillings of his (very few beyond markings) were in it. He put more than one query opposite R's saying J. did not fear death, only Boswell on death, and to J's remark that 'Great people do not like to have their mouths stopped' M.B. had added 'especially by a man with his mouth full'. (Who by the way is J.G. Cozzens who, according to Colin Wilson in a monthly magazine, is 'in every way a much greater writer than Max Beerbohm'? 'In every way' is surely a little excessive.)

Pamela says the 27th will do very nicely for our annual luncheon—always one of the lights in the darkness of the dead vast in middle of the winter. Exam-papers have been coming in a steady dribble. I am just finishing the Shakespeare papers. And I declare to you, Rupert Hart-Davis, that *except for some of the poetry* greater drivel than *The Merchant of Venice* has rarely been written. I mean all the *gup* about its drama and characterisation etc. I feel sure S. meant Shylock to be a figure of hatred and derision, and was so bad a dramatist that he just didn't see that to make all the men-Christians sh-ts, and Jessica a heartless little bitch, and to give Shylock a gift of magnificent speech simply didn't make sense, but was bound to arouse admiration and sympathy. I don't believe he cared twopence about his plots or characters; he *did* care about words, and had the most overwhelming command of them that ever was. And now tell me I am an ass and simply don't understand. But when I retort that Tolstoy and I see eye to eye in this, what do you say then? That we are both asses? Perhaps you are right.

I am glad about Soho Square—though at eighty-eight shall I be able to make your stairs? Your lease will still have a few months to run. Never have a lift. Don't have that jagged tooth under your stair-rail removed or that hidden step on the top flight made visible, I *like* these things. And when I arrive panting and—only temporarily —speechless, let me always find you and Ruth *exactly* the same as ever. I may die there, as Housman always hoped to after scaling the stairs to his rooms in Whewell's Court. I *should* like that, but it might bore you.

Château de St Firmin
Vineuil
Oise

14 December 1958

Your letter arrived just as I was leaving for Victoria, and I enjoyed it in the train to Dover. My journey was enjoyably uneventful. Over the usual delicious lunch on the French train (hors d'oeuvres, fish, steak, cheese, sweet, half a bottle of Meursault, coffee and a liqueur) I chummed up to a limited extent with a pale-faced chap who turned out to be Peter Smithers, Conservative M.P. for Winchester. Then, back in my carriage, I was relentlessly talked to by a ravaged-looking female American television operative, and by the time I had moved my watch on an hour for French time we were at the Gare du Nord, where Diana was waiting with the car. Since then I have stirred out of the house only once—for a brief shopping expedition to Chantilly. Otherwise it has been sessions of proof-correction punctuated by huge and delicious meals. The cook (an English pansy, heavily made up) has been ill in bed, and *all* the work of the house has been done by a splendid Italian girl called Lucia. No one here but Diana and her secretary Norah, who was Duff's secretary. This afternoon Cynthia

Jebb, wife of Sir Gladwyn, drove out from Paris to talk about a carpet. Tomorrow I leave Paris at mid-day by the Golden Arrow. I find it refreshing to spend even a few days among quite different scenes, sounds, tastes and smells.

You ask about J. G. Cozzens. He is a pretentious American novelist of extreme volubility. His latest tome (*By Love Possessed*) has been widely acclaimed as the 'Great American Novel', so long awaited. Like those endlessly ponderous novels by Theodore Dreiser, *B.L.P.* consists of long discourses on business, sociology etc, interspersed with lubricious sex-scenes, to keep the reader going. You have been warned! Mr Cozzens is not worthy to sharpen Max's pencils.

I assure you, my dear George, that to a man who once spent several weeks holding a spear (pike or halberd) at the back of the stage on which *The Merchant of Venice* was regularly performed—to such a wretch you need say nothing of the play's shortcomings. Those interminable casket scenes—oh heaven! I'm sure you're right, and Shylock took control of his creator. I hate to agree with you *and* Tolstoy, but for once I must.

Last Monday Ruth and I journeyed to Stratford-atte-Bow (no distance on the underground: only three stops after Liverpool Street) and there paid our first visit to the Theatre Royal. It is an exquisite eighteenth-century theatre, quite unspoilt: even the bar is contemporary. The play was *The Hostage* by Brendan Behan, the Borstal boy —an extremely amusing charade with songs and tragic interludes, set in a Dublin tenement and impossible to describe. Very Irish, very fast, very gay. Some good jokes: 'What is an Anglo-Irishman?' 'A Protestant with a horse'. We enjoyed it no end.

On Thursday I lunched with Mrs Ian Fleming (née Charteris, then Lady O'Neill, then Lady Rothermere, now Mrs F). She has long been a close friend of Mr Gaitskell, and at luncheon were two of his henchman—Tom Driberg and Woodrow Wyatt. To balance them were Lady Violet Bonham-Carter (in splendid form after her world tour) and the Austrian Ambassador, who was grateful at being remembered ('No one ever recognises me'). I was between Lady Glenconner and Elizabeth Montagu, both charming. Excellent food and drink: why can I have been asked?

Next week will be much occupied with the presentation of the

Duff Cooper prize to Betjeman by Princess Margaret. You shall hear about it next Sunday. And on Tuesday an American friend is taking me to the new musical, *West Side Story*. How I do gad about! And how I'd love to get away from it all. It's usually people in the whirlpool who hate missing things: people who are happily occupied elsewhere just don't bother. Or is that wishful thinking? Anyhow it's difficult enough to arrange one's own life without trying to advise others. Now it's time for another smashing meal, and then more proofs. I shall post this on the white cliffs of Dover.

18 December 1958   *Grundisburgh*

How good you are on J.G. Cozzens. I remember now I saw reviews of that portentous book, and resolved comfortably that I need not read it. I suppose all America is lapping it up. And I get a clear little vignette of you in France. You must by now be a fully-equipped gourmet, and I follow your banquets with watering mouth. Were you, in fairly early youth, allowed to choose your favourite dishes on your birthday? A good old Victorian habit. How loftily you will smile on hearing that my choice was mince and egg and what is called summer pudding—bread soaked in some kind of fruit-juice, with of course lashings of cream. One day they sent up custard instead of cream; I never thought the same of grown-ups for years afterwards, and doubt if I don't still feel the same now (we had mince and egg and rice-pudding at lunch today—both first-rate!).

Yes, you *do* gad about. I often wish I had half your complaint, but I don't know. I should get exhausted long before you do. Fancy those innocent Yanks having in their charter 'the pursuit of happiness' as one of man's legitimate aims. Don't he wish he may get it! And who ever has? (Small point—I hope you *always* alter '*Whatever* do you mean?' to '*What ever* do you mean?' *Quodcunque* is not an interrogative.)

175

Bridget and Adam will be here to welcome you, but I think Duff will be away. Adam won the Junior Chess Cup at Eton: he says it's the size of an egg-cup, but I say a cup's a cup for a' that. Perhaps next year he'll win the School cup, which I believe is one of the biggest in the school. We shan't, I gather, know about his G.C.E. for some weeks.

I ate so much in France (3 lbs gain in weight) that I strong-mindedly resolved to eschew the smashing lunch on the return train —only to discover at the Gare du Nord that my seat was in the Pullman to which lunch is brought, so of course I succumbed and ate my way deliciously through hors d'oeuvres, a whole fried sole, superb veal, *petit suisse*, ice and coffee, washed down by a half-bottle of excellent wine. A brandy-and-soda on the boat, followed by tea on the English train, kept me going to London. Next day I was taken by an American friend to the terrific new musical, *West Side Story*. It is *Romeo and Juliet* transposed to juvenile delinquents in New York, and the music is loud enough to blow one's head open. The dancing is superb, and the whole thing most effective. We were in the sixth row of the stalls, and next to us was a party containing the P.M. and the U.S. Ambassador, with their wives. When the P.M. came back to his seat after the interval, the whole house cheered him. He was clearly delighted.

On Thursday, after much fuss and many arrangements, the Duff Cooper Prize was presented to Betjeman by Princess Margaret, to whom I completely lost my heart. My dear George, she is exquisitely beautiful, very small and neat and shapely, with a lovely skin and staggering blue eyes. I shook hands with her coming and going, and couldn't take my eyes off her in between. All her photographs belie her. Much champagne was drunk, and Diana was pleased.

There was *no* irony in my remark about the Lit. Soc. Martin Charteris's charming wife, whom I met for the first time the other day, said she always looks forward to the Lit. Soc. dinners, both be-cause Martin enjoys them so, and because he retails to her all the jokes and sayings (whose? must be yours!) afterwards.

My Christmas shopping looks like being left till Christmas Eve, as usual. How cumulatively tiresome it all is. I already have almost three hundred cards.

I expect you noticed that the Government, terrified of losing East Harrow because of A.P.H.'s intervention there, gave time last week for a debate on Obscenity. Our fear now is that by the time they have finished with our Bill it will be emasculated beyond usefulness, but we still hope. The situation is complicated by the imminent publication here of a book called *Lolita*, which is clearly indecent. Although many hope that its publisher (Weidenfeld) will go to gaol, we don't want to argue our Bill under this shadow.

(University Arms Hotel, Cambridge)
Angelo's, Eton College, Windsor

31 December 1958

I hope you did not think our visit ended rather curtly on Saturday. But with that conjugal sixth sense that even the most unimaginative can acquire (though many don't) I could see that Pamela was fighting an uphill battle against a germ of short-lived but active malignity, which has decimated Eton since Boxing Day; and in fact she did go straight to bed as soon as she got home and missed the evening at Rose's, where Humphrey was (and it tests the utmost efforts of any germ to make her do that). All the sufferers in several different families here are comically insistent that Xmas diet had nothing whatever to do with it, but of course they convince nobody (like the Chinese proverb 'A man with a red nose *may* not drink, but nobody believes it'). It is just one of those things. She would have loved to prolong our visit to you *quam diutissime*, and so would I.

I saw a good deal about *Lolita* in the Sunday papers. When will its fate be decided? I am not sure if I wholly trust Bob Boothby's judgement on pornography, but perhaps he sways many votes. Still, if Boswell's *London Journal* passed muster, it is hard to see where the line is to be drawn.

Do you know Robert Graves? I know nothing of his poetry, but always find his prose second-rate. In his last bookmaking he records a broadcast pulling to bits Milton's 'L'Allegro'. It appears his daughter aged thirteen asked him if it wasn't 'rather confused'. He read it and in the face of scores of better men down the centuries he corroborates his daughter's opinion. A silly man, surely? There are too many about.

I found still going strong the man at Jefferies (now Thomas) who first cut my hair thirty-nine years ago. But my world thins. I told him I intended to call on Mr X. 'Oh he died three weeks ago.' 'Oh dear, then I shall go and see Mr Y.' 'He is being buried this afternoon.' Grim.

N.B. *All* the six great frosts since 1908 have begun round about Jan 20. *Verb. sap.* We leave here on the 9th, i.e. the day of the great snowfall of 1959.

4 January 1959

My dear George

It is past eleven p.m. There is snow outside. Russian projectiles are 'orbiting' in a sinister way round every heavenly body. I am behindhand with everything. Our cricketers are a laughing-stock. Our Foreign Secretary has lost his tonsils. There is no health in us.

Your Christmas visit was a joy, though I was much concerned for Pamela. It was heroic of her to come at all, bless her. I saw Diana and Alexander[1] at Philip Astley's memorial service. I am so sad for Joan and the little boy: they were a very happy family, and Philip adored the child.

So glad you're enjoying those Cardus pieces: all my solicitude in cutting out and sticking in, more than twenty years ago, is now amply rewarded. Would that we had Gubby Allen and other 'good Free Forester stuff' in Australia now! I should certainly bring in Trueman, Swetman and Dexter—and cable to that oily Archbishop, asking for a special dispensation by which D. Sheppard could be despatched by rocket.

I am halfway through a borrowed copy of *Lolita* and must finish by Wednesday, when the Herbert Committee meets to consider it and Mr R. A. Butler.[2] I fear that between the two of them our poor old Bill may founder. So far I should say *Lolita*'s literary value was negligible, and its pornographic level high. It is about *nothing* but a middle-aged man's lust for a twelve-year old girl (who had already lost her virginity to the farmer's boy and is quite ready for her elderly lover). No detail is omitted, all told with relish, and in so far as the book

---

[1] George's daughter and son-in-law.

[2] Under the auspices of the Society of Authors A.P. (Sir Alan) Herbert had organised a committee to draft a suggested Bill to improve the law on Obscenity. R.A. Butler was Home Secretary.

might well suggest to children that sex begins at eleven, I think it should not appear. Did you see that rhyme in one of the weeklies?

> Goldilocks, Goldilocks, wilt thou be mine,
> Although I am ninety, and thou art but nine.

Robert Graves I have known slightly, on and off, for many years. Not an attractive personality. Some of his poems are very good: most of his voluminous prose I haven't read, but sensible people have spoken well of *I Claudius* and others of his historical works. Poets can never live on their poetry, and if they are unwilling to work except with the pen, they are forced to try some sort of prose—Masefield adventure stories for boys and others, the Sitwells all sorts of travel and *belles lettres,* and so on. Graves has tried most things, and generally earned a good living thereby.

I have just realised that perhaps this will reach you on your birthday. Very many happy returns, and may your seventy-seventh year be blessed. As a child you must have missed many presents by your birthday's proximity to your Saviour's. My Bridget's is on the 13th and she seldom gets much, poor lamb.

On Tuesday I am going to resume my plan of getting up at 6.30 and devoting an hour to Oscar before my bath. Without some such pressure the great mass of typescript will never get to the printer, and I am fast forgetting all I ever knew about the subject.

You will soon be getting the first of my 1959 books, which appear on January 30: altogether twenty-four books are due to appear between now and the end of June—too many for my peace of mind.

Today we drove to the Cotswolds to lunch with Comfort's stepmother. Blue skies, bright sun, beauty all the way—and now the wireless warns of fog and frost.

Adam was much taken with you, and I think was much flattered at being allowed a brief *tête-à-tête* with the great man.

Yours ever
Rupert

8 January 1959

My dear Rupert

'Behindhand with everything' is the kind of message found pinned to the coat of a suicide. *Don't do it*—or perhaps at Xmas it is nearly universal. I should be too, but luckily for all concerned I am on the shelf—or almost, as I have at least a month of exceptionally tedious and exacting work, co-ordinating the papers and marking of nine separate boards, and stating what marks the board I am on (Oxford and Cambridge) would have given. We, let me tell you, are the only remotely civilised examiners, i.e. we do *not* think that the object of reading *Macbeth* or Tennyson is solely to acquire two or three hundred isolated *facts*. All the others do, and their instructions to examiners cover five closely typed pages, the reading of which I find literally nauseating, and when pedants like me say 'literally' they mean 'literally'.

We go back to Grundisburgh to-morrow, and I *know* our journey will be in snow and/or over ice. *Marquez mes mots*. Why does one find every winter fouler than the last? And how often the *laudator temporis acti* is right. Perhaps not for wage-earners, though they don't seem all that happy. We get back to Faust, who could never be got to admit contentment whatever they gave him. And you remember the shoe-black passage in *Sartor*.[1] Did you, by the way, notice how *one* of the

[1] 'Will the whole Finance Ministers and Upholsterers and Confectioners of modern Europe undertake, in joint-stock company, to make one Shoeblack HAPPY? They cannot accomplish it, above an hour or two: for the Shoeblack also has a Soul quite other than his Stomach; and would require, if you consider it, for his permanent satisfaction and saturation, simply this allotment, no more, and no less: *God's infinite Universe altogether to himself*, therein to enjoy infinitely, and fill every wish as fast as it rose. Oceans of Hochheimer, a Throat like that of Ophiuchus: speak not of them; to the infinite Shoeblack they are as nothing. No sooner is your ocean filled, than he grumbles that it might have been of better vintage. Try him with half of a Universe, of an Omnipotence, he sets to quarrelling with the proprietor of the other half, and declares himself the most maltreated of men. Always there is a black spot in our sunshine: it is even, as I said, the *Shadow of Ourselves*.'

(Carlyle, *Sartor Resartus*, book 2, chapter ix)

two possible theories about how the world began (in the final Reith lecture), i.e. that there is *no* beginning or end, takes us straight to Vaughan's:

> I saw Eternity the other night
> Like a great ring of pure and endless light.

Science limps after the poets for all the massive conceit with which it stiffens its votaries.

Pamela was herself again after twenty-six hours. She would have cried off any other lunch, though unlike so many wives she is not of the 'crying-off' kind. And my daughter Helena and her man Peter Lawrence empower me to urge you to call on them when you come to see Adam. I want you to meet all my daughters, because I think you would like them and I know they would like you. Adam is about a year junior to Aubrey Lawrence and they haven't really met. But Aubrey has a not very clear-cut tale of Adam always failing in construe up to Colquhoun and then getting a Distinction in Trials. The best kind of score *me judice*.

How right you are about birthdays in January. A pencil left over from Xmas, or a small bottle of scent, if you please, are about all one can expect. How did you remember mine? I was born three days after Lord Attlee and no doubt a star danced that week.

Adam was entirely easy to talk to—how should his father's son not be? I don't think I often find Wilde's advice very useful. 'Talk to all women as if you were in love with them, and all men as if bored.' Or have I got it wrong?

I have to-day had a letter from him you call 'that oily Archbishop'. I know him only as a first-rate Chairman and a genial chap. He does laugh a good deal and press photographers always catch him at the zenith of a guffaw, all molars and uvula. A pity. Did Archbishop Laud ever smile? Not that he had much to smile at.

I am coming to the Lit. Soc. on Tuesday and will be straining at your doorbell round about 6. Will your lovely Ruth be there? *Hoffentlich!* Jonah is coming; I have just had a good letter from him—from Alnwick where they have had a week of blue skies and sun, which is quite another pair of shoes from the Thames Valley or Cambridge.

Yours ever

G.W.L.

I am most distressed by Elisabeth Beerbohm's death. She was angelic to me, and one side of her sharply divided nature was warm and cherishing. Certainly she made Max's last five years a paradise for him, but at his death her occupation was gone, and I fear she has been lonely and miserable ever since. Lately she seemed to withdraw more and more into herself, clutching Max and all his works to her, so that it became almost impossible to make any business arrangement with her. Poor darling, I grieve for her, and for her macabre end. Apparently the doctor says she must have died instantly—from a heart attack in her bath—but wasn't found for something like a week!

Goodness knows what will now happen to all the Maxiana, the copyrights etc. On Monday I shall ring up Max's lawyers and find out whether they have Elisabeth's will. As I think I told you, I have long had in mind as many as five or six more Max books, which may now become possible if there are reasonable executors.[1] Today I rang up S.C. Roberts, and he is writing something about Elisabeth for Monday's *Times*.

I wonder what sort of journey home you had. Here there is snow everywhere, but the roads are mainly clear. The cold is bitter and I hug the library fire. Unfortunately at midnight I have to drive to Henley to fetch Adam and some young friends from a dance: the friends have to be distributed all round the countryside.

I love to think that Henry Vaughan was three centuries ahead of the Reith lecturer. What or who do you imagine T.S.E. is foreshadowing in like manner?

I had a charming note from the P.M.,[2] saying that he hasn't been to the Lit. Soc. for years, sees no likelihood of coming, and suggests resigning. Tommy proposes to make him an honorary member, which will create a vacancy and start up the cumbersome electoral machinery next autumn. I think I shall put up Roy Jenkins, the Labour M.P. who wrote the Dilke book, if I can find a seconder. He's very nice, intelligent and friendly.

[1] So far I have produced only five: *Letters to Reggie Turner* (1964), *More Theatres* (1969), *Last Theatres* (1970), *A Peep into the Past and other prose pieces* (1972), and *A Catalogue of the Caricatures* (1972).

[2] Harold Macmillan.

Adam, believe it or not, is *making* a wireless set out of a thousand particles of metal! I am astounded that a child of mine should be capable of doing such a thing: my own mechanical skill *just* enables me to switch a set on and off. But I suppose it's no more extraordinary than that *your* son should be the world's leading jazz trumpeter. Certainly the inborn belief that one's children will be recognisable chips off the old block dies hard.

I am in the middle of reading a huge biography of the American dramatist Eugene O'Neill, which has been offered to me. It's extremely interesting, but so long that it will probably have to be priced beyond all sales. It is called *The Curse of the Misbegotten*.

On Friday I slogged out to Putney to lunch with Arthur Ransome and his wife. A.R. was in bed with a bad back, and after lunch we gathered round his bed with a nice young man called John Bell (my co-executor) while Arthur read his will aloud to us. I hope to goodness he lives for ages: he is seventy-five next week.

I was glad to see the authorities included my three candidates in this Test team, though so far Dexter hasn't done much to justify himself.

You will be eagerly awaited at six on Tuesday. The house is full of painters, so your difficulties in gaining admittance will be greater than ever.

I am truly in despair about Oscar: he was so nearly finished last September, and now he slips steadily backward, as other tasks accumulate and my memory softens like melting butter. One difficulty is that this final stage can be completed only in Soho Square, where all the reference and other relevant books are housed.

Now I must return to *The Misbegotten* until it's time to fetch the children: the house never felt warmer.

15 January 1959   *Grundisburgh*

There is nothing new to say about the Lit. Soc. evening, any more than there is about our creation, preservation and all the blessings of this life, which the clergy tell us we ought to give thanks for every day. Your patience—haven't I reason to know it?—is great, but I suppose falls short of the divine, and if I said all I think about you and Ruth and the repast and the company on those celestial Tuesdays, you couldn't help being bored. The hour beforehand in your room sends me to the gathering as mellow as Eric Linklater, but from a different cause; as Arnold Bennett puts it somewhere 'not intoxicated but inclined to take a much more favourable view of the world than it really deserves'. I don't quote accurately but you see the gist.

I was in a good environment—the President, Ivor Brown, and Wheeler-Bennett, whose reception of stories about Hitler and Co which he had been familiar with for years was mere perfection—and I *never* exaggerate. Tommy Lascelles is full of flavour and quality; the only drawback to him is that he will depart so early, and Tim takes him, and I accompany them, Diana living only a hundred yards away. And what a succulent party I left at the end of the table, preparing like the Doctor to fold your hands and have your talk out, R.H-D. especially seeing through all things with his half-shut eyes, as Pope rather optimistically said coffee made the politician do.[1]

Did I tell you that Ivor B, bless him, is going to give away the prizes at the Abbey School on June 5? It is a great weight off my mind. I wrote to seven people without success. What an ass I was not to think of I.B. before; but the luck evens out in the end, as I really think he is the best of the bunch, and I am pretty sure they know it at the Abbey.

I become more like Mr Pooter every day. Believe it or not, we had nearly got to Tommy Lascelles's dwelling when I remembered I had left my bag in the porter's lodge at the Garrick, and the celestial Tim took me back without a murmur.

I returned home this morning—dense fog up to Witham, and then bright sunshine. But the damnable cold has come back, and every grain of the snow that fell last Friday is still there and makes the lawn look like somebody's boothole. Did Peter F. motor home last night? The genial blend of fog and ice has something Dantesque about it.

I see the Russians promise us several men on the moon in a few years' time and some even on Jupiter. That planet they tell me is almost as hot as the sun, so I think Khrusch and Co must be a little optimistic. Anyway I hope they all go there and find they have left

[1] *The Rape of the Lock*, Canto IV.

their refrigerators behind. The moon and its minerals are shortly to be 'exploited'. *Homo sapiens* is a stuffy little fellow, don't you think?

I am expecting great fun with Havelock Ellis,[1] moving about in surely a very strange world. E.g. on pp 20, 21 I somehow miss the full beauty that H.E. sees in all that maternal micturition. And yet he *was* a Victorian. But the necessary adjustments in the point of view would not have been easy for the Worcestershire mind in the mid-nineties.

I have not yet heard what happened today at Sydney, but I felt very contemptuous at breakfast, on reading that as soon as May and Cowdrey struck, Benaud shut the game up for a draw. I simply don't recognise that as the way to play cricket, and can't remember any players before Hutton thinking it was. It is largely the fault of the cricket journalists that everything has got so distorted. I don't yet (3.30 p.m. Thursday) know yesterday's score. May has that mark of the great batsman, of making runs when he is out of form and touch. C.B. Fry's view was that 'we can all make runs when we are fit and seeing the ball', but Ranji could get a hundred v. Briggs and Mold on a lively wicket, when suffering from 'bronchitis, indigestion and *corns*' (a nice anticlimax)—which of course I have told you before, but you *may* have forgotten.

I see my cousin Molly Stanley is dead—one of those really staggering heroines. Fifty years ago she was permanently paralysed below the waist by a hunting accident (her first remark when she became conscious was 'Do take my foot away from my neck, it looks so silly'). She survived, crippled, for half a century, had a family and was never depressed or impatient or out of pain. There must be *something* after death for human beings like that.

P.S. Your Ruth is a lovely thing—body, mind and spirit, and if you or she think that is cheek on my part I can't help it. I had to say it; one must recognise and hail really fine things when one meets them: so there (second time).

---

[1] The biography by Arthur Calder-Marshall.

Yesterday evening, just after the thaw set in, I was summoned by loud cries to the nursery, where Adam, shining with pride, switched on his home-made radio, and through the shrill scream of atmospherics we could distinctly make out a prim Third Programme talk on African Art. I am more than ever astounded at the boy's skill. In his spare time he has fixed up a bird-table outside this window, and I have happily wasted time watching blue-tits, robins, wagtails and the bully blackbird. Comfort says if I watched long enough I should see a nut-hatch—but should I know it if I did?

I thought you were in particularly good form last Tuesday, and so did Ruth. I'm not sure I shall repeat your glowing words to her, for fear of turning her head, but they certainly lifted up my heart on a cold manuscript-ridden Saturday morning—bless you.

Tomorrow night, the last of the holidays, I am taking Adam to *Macbeth* at the Old Vic: the last time I saw the play was with Edmund Blunden at Stratford twenty-five years ago, and I'm looking forward to fresh beauties revealed—as they usually are.

On Friday my telephone-girl (who is very pretty but almost half-witted) got my Paddington taxi ten minutes too soon. I was still signing letters, so told her to make love to the driver till I was ready. She asked him in, and on the way to the station he described the scene with true Cockney wit:

'She said: "The boss says I'm to make love to you till he's ready," but I said: "I'm too old for all that. What I used to do all night now takes me all night to do." '

Here he paused, then said musingly:

'I should say she's a simple girl—the sort you could send out for a pint of pigeon's milk.'

Apparently he had called her attention to the fact that some of the new paint in the front office had been put on back to front, and she was duly impressed.

Yesterday I actually managed to put in a couple of hours on poor old Oscar. Apart from completing the notes and writing my introductions, all the numberless corrections have got to be transferred to the top copy of the typescript for the printer. This is comparatively automatic work, requiring no books or preparation, so that one can do it piecemeal. Unfortunately Diana Cooper's and Peter's page-proofs are coming in simultaneously next week, so I shall be busier than ever, especially as I have to make Diana's index.

There still seems to be no trace of Elisabeth Beerbohm's having made a will, so all depends on her sister. Tomorrow I am lunching at the Athenaeum with S.C. Roberts to discuss this and other matters. I believe he is to be the next speaker at the Johnson Club (on March 10): if so we must attend. I hear that Prof. Sutherland resigned after that filthy meal in the Garret, but now the Cheshire Cheese is doing well.

I have been bidden to a feast at King's on March 14 as the Provost's guest, and shall certainly go. It's very nice of him to ask me. I shall probably stay with Humphry House's widow, unless, as seems possible, she is even then having her gall-bladder removed, poor lamb. On March 18 I have promised to address the assembled book-collectors of Manchester: 'it was an insensate step'.

Yesterday I read the whole of a novel which I've just had translated from the French. It's called *The Lion*[1] and I think you'll like it, for most of the characters are wild animals. There's another about Alexander the Great, which I should have read weeks ago—oh dear, where is the time?

All this is while I read two or three detective stories a week (in bed), but I fear my source may soon dry up, since *Time and Tide* is clearly on its last legs. I shall miss this solace after a steady supply for fifteen years. And to think that the vast majority of the world's population never reads a book of any kind! They don't, you know, however much we may kid ourselves. Thank heaven I don't have to be one of them!

23 January 1959   *Grundisburgh*

This really *must* be a scrap and no mistake, as this filthy job of investigating the exam-papers and scripts of other boards is laborious beyond words. As a rival to the business of looking in a dark room for a black hat which isn't there, I confidently put up marking a closely

[1] By Joseph Kessel.

written answer of three sides to a question on a 500-page book which one read over fifty years ago. And what old Pardon[1] once described as 'touching the confines of lunacy' (the actions of the selection committee of 1909) would equally apply to the well-meaning organisers having obliterated all the marks and underlinings of the original examiners (and sometimes a line or two of the answer as well). So I am rather up against it, and they want all the stuff by the end of the month, damn them. I need hardly say that in the paper on the *Midsummer Night's Dream* searching questions are asked about the plot and the characters and none about the poetry, though everyone except an Eng. Lit. examiner knows that 1 and 2 are absurd, and 3 is incomparable. Enough!

The young are marvellous. Adam's radio! Did old Fred Coleridge stimulate that? *He* doesn't know a radio from a rabbit, any more than I do. And I still gnash my teeth over my fatuous ignorance of trees and birds. My old father should have mildly bribed us in the holidays to acquire the elements of country life. Bribery is a very important part of holiday education, but that generation didn't know it.

Oh! these cricketers! strains, fractures, sorenesses, belly-aches (literal and metaphorical) after every match, and nobody knows why. The return of Lindwall is interesting. But the *Times* man was wrong about one thing. He wasn't the fastest: Miller's fast one was quicker. How do I know? Sir Hutton told me—at the same meal at which he said apropos of Ramadhin that it was awkward playing a bowler when you didn't know which way the ball would turn on pitching, but still more awkward when the bowler didn't know either.

That is a very good conversation between your telephone girl and the taximan. We once had a man-cook, retired seaman, who described our half-witted boot-boy as 'put in with the bread and taken out with the cakes'. 'The sort you could send out for a pint of pigeon's milk' is infinitely subtle. Falstaff might have said it.

I was immensely interested in the Havelock Ellis life—but rather strongly nauseated by him. Surely his kind of sexual contact is the one most hated by women, and didn't I once read a French novel all about that? I was interested to see that Inge greatly admired him but couldn't do with his most famous work—wouldn't have it in his

[1] Sydney Pardon, writer on cricket.

house in fact. H.E.'s marriage is an extraordinary story, crammed with oddity and a good deal of heroism. He is one of those—rather like old Carlyle—whose defects one thinks one could easily avoid and whose virtues one couldn't get within a mile of. They were a rum lot —James Hinton, a most sinister man; and Olive Schreiner!

You will like Noel Annan. Give him my regards. I met him at the Founder's feast two years ago. The youngest head of a college that ever was; I realised at the dinner that he might easily have been in my house—awful! (Do you know the right collective noun—e.g. a pride of lions—for heads of colleges? *A lack of principals*; and for wing-commanders? *A flush of W.C.s.* Neither of them mine.) I look forward to *The Lion*. (How, pray, am I henceforth to clothe my naked greed in decent garb, now that you have exposed my camouflage to the delight and gentle mockery of Ruth?)

I have just re-read *Jane Eyre*, *Oliver Twist*, *The Warden* and *Cranford*. I will *not* read *Hard Times* or *Redgauntlet*.

26 January 1959   *Bromsden Farm*

We are a preoccupied pair: you with your examination-papers, and I with a streaming, stupefying cold which fell upon me yesterday morning and is still in full flow. I can keep only one eye open at a time, my head feels like cotton wool, and I fear your ration of correspondence this week will be both exiguous and dreary. After my seven-years' immunity from colds this one (my second of the winter) finds me outraged and full of self-pity—the least attractive, surely, of all attitudes.

No nuthatches have come to cheer me, unless my rheumy eyes mistook them for sparrows. All the same, the bird-table is a great delight.

Adam is back at Eton, with his wireless, watching the floods creeping up South Meadow and wondering how far they will have to get before the whole Coleridge contingent is sent home. Did that ever happen in your day? I remember devoutly praying that it would in mine.

Adam and I both hugely enjoyed the Old Vic *Macbeth*. An actor called Michael Hordern played Macbeth better than I have ever seen him played before (Gielgud was a disaster in the part), the others were adequate, the production was good, and every one of the matchless words clearly audible. Beatrix Lehmann's Lady Macbeth was not a success, except in the sleep-walking scene which she did beautifully. Earlier she trembled on the edge of comic parody, but it's a terribly difficult part for any actress.

The Havelock Ellis book (out next Friday) looks like getting a lot of reviews, and perhaps sales as well. Have you read *To be Young*[1] (which I should have sent you)? Raymond Mortimer rang up to say he likes it enormously and will review it next Sunday. I have just read Peter's book for the *fourth* time (the final proofs) and still think it extremely good and interesting. He and Tommy are having a splendid correspondence about the Lit. Soc.'s electoral procedure. Tommy says he welcomes new members he didn't know before: 'I prefer the buggers I don't know to those I do.' The debate continues.

As you may have seen, our poor old Obscenity Bill got its second reading (for the second time) on Friday, and A.P. Herbert has retired from East Harrow.[2] This was settled at a meeting of the Herbert Committee in the Savile Club on Friday afternoon. We have now pretty well reached the limit of compromise, and if in Committee the Government try to emasculate the Bill further, we shall withdraw it and start again. That idiotic and gratuitous letter in *The Times* about *Lolita* on the very day the Bill was coming up is considered deliberate sabotage, particularly since two of the signatories are on the main Herbert Committee, and a few days earlier had agreed that for the moment the less said about *Lolita* the better.

A.P.H. was in splendid form on Friday, and when I got home I took down his *Misleading Cases* (untouched these many years) and was delighted to find how amusing and well written they are. Clearly one shouldn't read the book straight through, but I recommend one or two taken at bedtime.

I will allow you to leave *Hard Times* on the shelf, but I beg you to reconsider your harsh decision about *Redgauntlet*. It is almost my

[1] By Mary Lutyens.
[2] Where he had threatened to stand as an Independent at a by-election and, if elected, to bulldoze his own Obscenity Bill through the House, as he had his Divorce Bill.

favourite of all that noble band, and I think perhaps you have forgotten it. Or have you only an edition in very small print? If so I shall be tempted to forget my principles and lend you my first edition, in which the words on each page are so few and so well set out that they practically read themselves. The early nineteenth century was the peak-time for novel-printing, and most later novelists (e.g. Dickens and Thackeray) suffered from huge, crowded, eye-straining pages. The only things worse than too-long lines are very short ones printed in double-column like a newspaper. Nowadays the fearful cost of paper and everything else compels one to get as many words into each page as one decently can.

Comfort has just brought me some hot whisky-and-lemon, which, combined with the pleasure of writing to you, seems to have staunched my cold for the moment. Luckily I have no engagements till Tuesday, when I lunch with the Governor of Lloyd's, an old army friend.

30 January 1959   *Grundisburgh*

> He nothing common did or mean
> Upon that memorable scene,
> But with his keener eye
> The axe's edge did try.[1]

No doubt you have already drunk to the memory of the royal martyr?

I am very sorry about that cold, and so is Pamela, but she always maintains that the more streaming, the sooner gone. So I am in hopes that when you get this your nose will be as quiescent, your eye as dry and clear, and your voice as bell-like as they normally are. I recognise and hail the note of outrage in your reporting on it, because I too never get a cold and protest to high heaven when I do. But according to our local chemist, they are on the point of discovering the preventative, in fact he thinks *he* has. He is not wholly unlike Uncle Ponderevo in *Tono-Bungay*.[2]

[1] Andrew Marvell, 'An Horatian Ode upon Cromwell's return from Ireland'. King Charles I was beheaded on 30 January 1649.
[2] By H.G. Wells.

I fear Adam has watched the anti-cyclone with fading hopes: the floods must be falling visibly. But I fear, in any case, South Lawn is rarely or never flooded—certainly not as soon as Warre House or its neighbour. The unsportsmanlike architect built it on piles, and even in 1947 (when the water to be disposed of was three-and-a-half times greater than in the great flood of 1894) South Lawn, like Satan, stood like a tower 'proudly eminent'. I missed 1894 by one year, but we had fine skating at Evelyn's over the fields and fallows; some old boys skated from Eton to Evelyn's (near Uxbridge). Those were the days.

Macbeth. You make my mouth water. Of course Gielgud wouldn't do; whoever cast him for it must have been a fool. Do you know the enclosed sentence of Masefield's? Anyway you won't mind being reminded of it.

Let your Macbeth be chosen for the nervy, fiery beauty of his power. He must have tense intelligence, a swift leaping, lovely body, and a voice able to exalt and to blast. Let him not play the earlier scenes like a moody traitor, but like Lucifer, star of the morning. Let him not play the later scenes like a hangman who has taken to drink, but like an angel who has fallen.

[John Masefield, *A Macbeth Production*, 1945]

I like to remember how when Bourchier in the part charged every word, look, movement, with sinister and even appalling significance, C.E. Montague observed that even murder wasn't as serious as all that. As to Lady M., who ever really played her right throughout? I never saw the great Ellen, but I cannot believe she did, for all her magnificence. The first thing she was was *lovable*—surely the last Lady M was? To avoid caricature, hasn't the actress got to do that hardest of all things, viz. *under*play verbally and vocally, and at the same time give an appalling impression of malevolent strength and determination behind every word, and who the devil can do that? Rosalind, late Countess of Carlisle, perhaps.[1] She had no imagination, but then neither had Lady M. (You remember the admirable Bradley on 'What, in our house?')[2] How good to hear that audibility is coming

[1] See note p. 103.
[2] *Shakespearean Tragedy* by A.C. Bradley (1904), p. 369.

back to the stage. Just when senescence began to slow my ears, audibility was regarded as 'ham', and how old Agate raged! He, by the way, always maintained that Macbeth was a far harder part than Lear, the blend of murderer and poet being beyond human scope. I wonder.

I look forward to the Havelock reviews. You make no comment on my rather prim reactions, but is it any good pretending one *wasn't* born in January 1883? I expect both you and Ruth must sometimes think me an old granny—as in fact I am when I hear or read emphatic eulogies of the Osbornes, the Amises, the cats on hot tin roofs etc. But you often reassure me by sharing my opinions, and if Ruth's perception is not as swift and winged and straight to the central gold as an arrow, well then mine must be as wide of the target as was the Lord Lieutenant of Worcestershire who opened the County Archery meeting at Hagley in 1890 with a shot which missed the entire target and the protective canvas behind it, and hit a cow in the backside some eighty yards away.

But now for bell, book, and candle, which you were going to get anyway. I read *one* chapter of *Redgauntlet* which answered one of the questions in an exam-paper, thought it excellent and made a note of R. for my next bedside book. I had so totally forgotten it that I am not even sure I *did* read it, and I was vaguely classing it with *Castle Dangerous* etc. when I foolishly condemned it to you (G.K. Chesterton: 'We all have a profound and manly dislike for the book we have not read').

To be Young is my next venture (with *Redgauntlet*! I generally have two going at once). It was in your last batch of generosity.

That is a deliciously characteristic remark of Tommy Lascelles, and how well one knows what he means. How pleasant and satisfactory it is that people should be different; they apparently won't be much longer.

Years ago some foul boy borrowed and never returned my *Misleading Cases*. I loved it—as I do *Topsy* as well. His pen is quite unerring in these regions. Is *M.C.* still in print? Or to be found in the Charing Cross Road?

What did I read recently about a scandalous pub in Soho Square where things are done you'd not believe in Soho Square on Xmas eve? You have kept strangely silent about this. Perhaps you are a director.

If it isn't one thing it's another. Diana's proofs have so occupied my week-end that it is now past bedtime on Sunday night, and not a line written to you. Nor have I any events to retail. That cold proved to be one of the most virulent I've ever encountered, and I was compelled to spend the first half of last week in bed in the flat, streaming from nose and eyes, unable to read and very sorry for myself. Darling Ruth nursed me so devotedly that she inevitably caught the cold, so when I got up I put her to bed and nursed her. Now we are both quite recovered. All my 'engagements' had to be cancelled, including the luncheon with the Chairman (not Governor, as I said last week) of Lloyd's.

Adam reported every inch of the Eton floods with scientific objectivity—2 ft 6 below the '47 mark, three yards from Fred's boys'-entrance, his garden-seats floating away, swans on South Meadow. He has 'done something fatal' to his wireless, but is confident of its resurrection. He has been made captain of the house Junior League soccer side (some new-fangled innovation) and since they won their first match 11–0 his hopes are high. I sent him that *admirable* bit of Masefield. I agree with every word of it, and the actor we saw didn't fall far short of M.'s ideal. When Oscar saw Irving and Ellen Terry at the Lyceum in 1888 he wrote: 'Judging from the banquet, Lady Macbeth seems an economical housekeeper and evidently patronises local industries for her husband's clothes and the servants' liveries, but she takes care to do all her own shopping in Byzantium.' Can't you *see* the whole production?

Neither Ruth nor I ever for a moment think of you as 'an old granny'. On the contrary, we marvel at your easy acceptance of modern lapses and intransigence.

Thank goodness you're weakening about *Redgauntlet*, which I *know* you'll love. *Castle Dangerous* was the pitiable production of a worn-out, dying man.

My books did well to-day—two long leading reviews in each of the two important papers. I'm particularly pleased about *To be Young*: the author is so charming.

I must try and find you a copy of *Misleading Cases*. When I read in

195

the papers of the gang-wars, stabbings, strip-tease and general de-bauchery, with which Soho is clearly riddled, I marvel that I have lived in the heart of it for eight and a half years without a glimpse of any such activities. I suppose you might say the same about incest and scoutmastery in Suffolk, which no doubt are reported each week in the *News of the World*. To the pure, my dear George, all things are reported.

Six winter aconites are bravely flowering in the garden. Perhaps spring isn't so far behind. Don't you agree that the *first* flowers of the year are much the most exciting, surprising one each time? But there are in fact at least two more hellish months ahead of us. The London air last week was disgusting, and I was thankful to miss so much of it by being in bed. I do hope you'll nevertheless be able to get to the next Lit. Soc. dinner on Tuesday week. Now the iron tongue of midnight has tolled goodness knows what, and I must to bed. Perhaps I'll have more to tell you next week. Let's hope so!

4 February 1959 (Thomas Carlyle died 4 February 1881)   *Grundisburgh*

You shouldn't do it really. The idea of starting your letter to me *after* midnight, weak and flat after the worst of colds. How can you not resent my existence at such a moment? Be *very* careful now; the east wind is abroad in the land like Bright's angel of death, and there is that familiar February phenomenon of the thermometer saying the temperature is 40° and the tips of one's ears and nose saying it is 20°.

I enjoyed *To be Young*, especially the first part, which is wonderfully vivid, and never flags, though I for one find it very hard to see how she does it—style or character or both, I suppose. But my sympathies with these Theosophists are as imperfect as Lamb's with Quakers, and somehow I can't quite do with Bishop Leadbeater. I forget what happened in the matter of homo-scandal, of which he apparently got cleared. But I put it to you that strong suspicions in that province are nearly always justified. Or was that only in the past? I mean against men like Helbert of West Downs or 'Sligger'[1] of Balliol, who had immense influence with the young, there was never a whisper. Perhaps there would be nowadays. I suppose the oddly frequent allusions to

[1] Nickname of F.F. Urquhart.

water-closetry in Mary L's book merely show she was her father's daughter. I remember him bubbling over with some such anecdote at Provost Quickswood's table. It was *not* a success.

I have had a nice little local *row*! Asked to contribute to a leaving-present for a Woodbridge parson—unwillingly sent cheque for £1—not acknowledged—wrote fortnight after to ask had it arrived—no answer—wrote to protest about discourtesy—organiser offended—and asked didn't I know that cheques need not be acknowledged nowadays—wrote glacially commenting on organisers regarding a contribution to a gift in same light as payment of tradesman's bill. No answer. There isn't one of course, but alas, he has my £1. Bad manners make me positively waspish, nothing much else does. The organiser said he was not in the habit of being discourteous. I ought to have answered as Gussie Fink-Nottle did when old Tom Travers said he had never talked nonsense. 'Then, for a beginner, you do it dashed well.'[1]

How right you are about the year's first flowers. And what about

> The full-throated daffodils
> Our trumpeters in gold
> Call resurrection from the ground
> And bid the year be bold.[2]

I quote this every year. Forgive me. It usually comes in March.

7 February 1959   *Bromsden Farm*

I shall post this tomorrow, to make sure of catching you. Adam reports abortive skating on flooded football-fields, but has now retired with flu, after his side had won their second *soccer* match 23-0. His G.C.E. marks seem to me very good, but perhaps it's just parental pride. Latin 95% and 85%, Greek 78% and 70%, French 81%, Maths 95%, 96%, 88% and 93%, Physics 92% and 83%—and so on, surely Fred should be pleased? Like you, I have never taken much interest in professional soccer, and haven't watched a game since goodness knows when.

[1] P.G. Wodehouse, *Right Ho, Jeeves*, chapter 17.
[2] C. Day-Lewis, *From Feathers to Iron*, section 14.

So glad you enjoyed *To be Young*: it continues to receive excellent reviews, and the author is transported with joy. How can any sane person have taken those preposterous Theosophists seriously? Clearly Mrs Besant had a terrific personality, but Leadbeater and the rest were appalling. I know nothing of Helbert of West Downs, but Sligger I knew at Balliol and very much disliked. A purring old doctored tom-cat, who gave lemonade-parties at which he stroked the knees of rugger-blues—ugh! I've never seen a more completely homosexual man, though for all I know he may have sublimated his horrid passion with mountaineering and hair-shirts.

Yesterday Jonah brought me the typescript of his new book, which is delightfully entitled *I Forgot to Tell You*. I must read it before Monday. Also a chunk of the first volume of Stephen Potter's autobiography, which, like all his manuscripts, is a mass of dirty bits of paper, vilely typed, corrected in illegible biro, episodic and half-revised. My patience with authors diminishes rapidly.

I loved hearing of your row about the parson's leaving-present: if you'd been a little quicker you could have stopped your cheque. As I have often said to you before, and shall often say again, the older I get, the more important do good manners seem to me.

Later. I've now read Jonah's first fifty pages—with great pleasure. The book consists of a number of chapters, unconnected one with another, each containing a reminiscence which he forgot to include in his three previous volumes. Without their previous publication and success, this would scarcely stand on its own, but as a pendant and epilogue it should do well. I am touching up his spelling, punctuation, and occasionally grammar, as I go along—which necessarily slows me up. I never cease to wonder at the inability of so many otherwise-intelligent people to spell, remember the look of words and names, or look them up.

A neighbour who came to lunch today aroused my envy by telling me that her bird-table (a mile from here) is regularly visited by cross-bills! Have you ever seen one? She says they like pine-needles, which she has nearby and I lack. I must import some.

As the weeks pass and Oscar lies unfinished, I despair of ever completing the task. It begins to look as though R's and my Yorkshire holiday in June will have to be devoted to the job. Last June we expected to be correcting the proofs in a year's time! The publishing business and my other London activities have grown to be so multifarious that I have *no* spare time left.

After good-nighting you, Roger, Betjeman and I drifted into a neighbouring pub where hoi polloi were in force. We were the only men wearing hats and they came in for a good deal of derision—J.B's rightly, for it was almost non-existent in depth, and sat on the noble brow like the crest of a waxwing (do you have them in Oxon? One appeared in the garden here a week ago). But a sozzled Canadian made a dead set at me, on the ground mainly that I didn't know the right way of wearing a Hamburg, as he called it. So I had to ask him to show me the right way. He put it on and was not the first man to find that his head went very little of the way towards filling it. He returned it, hiccuping that I had the largest head not only in England but in France too. It was all very inconsequential and odd. Tommy Lascelles would not have been amused.

Suffolk is silent and windless and drab under a sky of apparently eternal sepia. There were two men in my carriage who talked a little rugger-shop. I think they were ex-blues. I felt no urge to stroke their knees even if they hadn't been heavily ulstered. There was also a very plain elderly lady who smeared and powdered herself *twice* between Liverpool Street and Colchester. At the end she gazed long at her handiwork in her glass and, like the Creator at the end of the sixth day, saw that it was good. I could have told her different, as Sir W. Robertson used to say to the cabinet.

Adam's soccer side is surely making history. Are you sure it isn't rugger? I see Eton is taking the game very seriously and shouldn't wonder if the Field Game is on its way out, but like cricket—and of course Charles II—will probably be an unconscionable time a-dying. Adam's G.C.E. marks are quite outstanding—not a weak spot anywhere. I suppose he is doomed to science—the first leading scientist perhaps to blend science and the arts.

Crossbills are unknown to me (not that that is odd) but also I believe unknown in Suffolk. Starlings are the devil; I was pleased to read that for some forgotten reason hundreds or even thousands of them died recently. Pigeons are a foul nuisance too in these parts. Do you see eye to eye with those who say *all* things are sent for our good? Our rector is one of them. H.G. Wells has a fine indictment of this optimism in *The Undying Fire*. He makes it very hard to maintain one's affection for the liver-fluke, which, in the delicious words of Mrs Cadogan[1], 'plays tallywack and tandem' with one's liver.

Pamela is sitting at the rector's feet listening to his lenten address —not because she wants to, but to swell his meagre audience. Last night she attended the Youth Club, merely because the good woman who runs it said no adult ever came. To-morrow we both go to hear a lecture on leprosy for a more mundane reason, viz. I have a morbid interest in leprosy (another of God's ultimate blessings?) ever since reading about Damien. His life—with a good deal of skipping and editing, made a good Sunday Private—with of course Stevenson's famous outburst of fury to end with. Do you remember that awful word of his describing what it must have been like living with lepers and, whenever there was a knock at the door, not knowing what kind of 'butt-end' of humanity would enter?[2]

I must go to bed and start on *Redgauntlet*. I must also tell you that on re-reading your last it is clear that your sentence about Sligger will have to go in my book. Posterity shall not be deprived of 'a purring old doctored tom-cat' down to 'mountaineering and hair-shirts'. Dons and beaks and scoutmasters are always suspect unless—and this is the wry and rather dreadful truth—they deliberately restrict their *good* feelings for youth from developing to the full—they go too near the edge to escape the prurient insinuations which we all enjoy harbouring.

[1] The housekeeper in *The Experiences of an Irish R.M.* by E.Œ. Somerville and Martin Ross (1899).

[2] Father Joseph Damien, a Belgian missionary (1840–1889), spent his last sixteen years tending the lepers on Molokai Island in the South Pacific and eventually died of leprosy. Robert Louis Stevenson's scathing Open Letter to a Presbyterian clergyman who had traduced Damien's memory was published in 1890.

Your unedifying visit to the pub reminds me of the Chinese proverb: 'The Dragon in Shallow Waters became the Butt of Shrimps.'
Changing Hamburg hats with drunken Canadians indeed! What
would your fellow-examiners say? In future I shall have to make sure
that Tim drives you straight home, and no larking about! I walked
back to Soho Square through the serried ranks of tarts shrilly discussing Mr Butler, Sir John Wolfenden and the musical glasses. Either
because of them, or because I'm not used to so much wine and company, I scarcely slept at all that night. The most tiresome thing about
insomnia is that if one *knew* one was going to be awake for three hours,
one could get up and do three hours' useful work. As it is, one tosses
and turns, hoping to drop off again, neither asleep or awake. However,
it doesn't often happen to me nowadays, thank heaven.

How was your lecture on leprosy? In my salad-days I took part in
a three-hour variety performance at the leper colony in Essex (the
only one in this country, I believe). We had fully rehearsed a three-act
comedy (two men, two women) called *The Mollusc,* but at the last
minute the mother of one of the girls refused to let her go, for fear of
catching leprosy. So we collected another couple of chaps (including a
pianist) and did our best. We were housed and fed (for the evening)
in a bungalow so drenched with disinfectant that one could scarcely
get one's breath, and we performed in a decent-sized hall with a
proper stage at one end. If our planned programme had gone through
we should have been protected from seeing our audience by foot-
lights. As it was, all the lights were on, and although it was encouraging to see the lepers' pleasure, their appearance was most distressing.
I remember in particular a grizzled old sea-captain and a little girl of
nine or so. My dear friend Charlie Marford, the Cockney actor who
had arranged the whole thing, was indefatigable and full of resource.
We acted scenes from Shakespeare (Dogberry and the Watch, Shylock
and Tubal etc), sang songs, went through the motions of dancing, and
racked our brains for other stunts. I read aloud the whole of Oscar's
story 'The Happy Prince', and Charlie did lightning sketches of don-
keys which, when turned upside down, proved to be caricatures of
Lloyd George. It was all most exhausting, and strangely moving: all

those doomed and mutilated people apparently so simply delighted. That was in 1928: nowadays I expect they have television and such diversions.

I can't remember what I wrote last week about the Wilde letters, but it seems to have misled you. 98% of the work is *done*, but I can't send the manuscript to the printer without the final 2%, and that simply can't be done at odd moments. It needs a clear fortnight, with no other work, and all the O.W. reference books (which are at Soho Square) around me. Even if I waited for June in Swaledale, it would mean carting dozens of books, and all the manuscript, along. But how am I to find the time before then? Every evening I spend dining out puts my publishing work further in arrears: it's endlessly tiresome.

I sent Ruth a Valentine on Thursday—the first I have ever dispatched. She was much pleased. She is my prop and joy.

19 February 1959   *Grundisburgh*

How pithy Chinese sayings always are! Geoffrey Madan unearthed a good many, but there was a strong suspicion among his friends that he invented quite a lot of them. I like 'A man with a red nose may not drink, but nobody thinks so' and 'Better the chill blast of winter than the hot breath of a pursuing elephant'.

Insomnia can be the devil. I have had a bout or two, but none since breathing the narcotic air of Suffolk. I remember finding Horder's counsel good, viz 'One can do with very little sleep. Lie quite still and don't toss about or worry; then you will get plenty of rest: it's worry that does the harm'. Nice and dull and obvious and hard to follow, like all the best advice.

The leprosy lecture was dreadfully tame—no 'butt-ends' of humanity, only a few men who had a few what looked like water-blisters of the most domestic variety. Practically all the slides were of scenery. There are more flowers and sunshine in Sarawak than in Suffolk. It seems that leprosy is on the point of being 100% curable, though it will always take a goodish time. I am afraid Gehazi leaving Elisha's presence 'a leper white as snow' is mere rhetoric. The whiteness of a leper is like that of a white elephant, i.e. a lot of greyish scruffiness looking like patches of dust. Not for a moment did poor Gehazi resemble the Warre House double cherry-tree in April, which had the whiteness of snow and then some. I should like Housman to have seen it.

Apropos of him the Headmaster of Bromsgrove wants a column on H. for the *Bromsgrovian*, as March 29 is the centenary of H's birth. Oh yes I told you. And the *admirable* John Carter says he will do it—on condition that the Headmaster will lend him the *Bromsgrovian* of 1877 for the Housman exhibition from August to Michaelmas which J.C. is organising. It has some rare early work of H's in it—which I have no doubt the old curmudgeon refused to do anything about subsequently if anyone asked about it. A perfectly fair bargain of J.C.'s I think. I hope there isn't some grim Housmanly embargo on any such transaction at Bromsgrove. But the Headmaster tells me that there is no evidence that H. had the smallest affection for his old school, though I suppose they must have taught him pretty well. Perhaps he was like Osbert Sitwell whose education in *Who's Who* is entered as 'in the holidays from Eton'.

It is delightfully characteristic that you should have entertained lepers in your youth—and from what you say of their appearance, it must have been before sulphonal had been discovered. In about 1904 Downing College (Leavis's) with its lovely grounds and shortage of students, where 'every prospect pleases and only man is vile',[1] was the butt of much crude wit. One term instead of its usual terminal intake of two black men and no other, the rumour went round that *one* white freshman had come. Two days later the rumour was corrected; the white man was really a negro with leprosy. Weren't we mad wags in 1904?

I still haven't got on to *Redgauntlet*, held up recently by the charming Cecilia Ridley—a very good lass.[2] I am glad to see that amid the chorus of praise for Miss Lutyens, Brother Leadbeater gets a poorish press. I hope you share my admiration and liking for old Lincoln,

[1] Bishop Heber (1783–1826), 'From Greenland's Icy Mountains'.

[2] *Cecilia:* the Life and Letters of Cecilia Ridley, 1819–1845, edited by Viscountess Ridley (1958).

whose health you drank last week. That delightfully earthy coarseness of his! Only Churchill of our P.M.'s could have defended in the cabinet some unexpectedly large expenditure with 'Gentlemen, you can't manure a ten-acre field with a fart'. Mr Gladstone? *Infandum!* But L. was as good a man as Mr G.

Tell me something brilliant to say about Herrick, on whom I am writing for Dick Routh's Junior National Biography. He wrote over twelve hundred lyrics. Too many, some immensely bad. But then he suddenly produces 'Here a little child I stand, Heaving up my either hand' which is simply and easily delicious. He seems to have paid about as much attention to the civil war etc as Jane Austen did to the Napoleonic. Similarly future editors of *your* letters will comment on your lack of apparent interest in the hydrogen bomb. Very unlike Cicero's letters—and very much less boring.

22 February 1959   *Bromsden Farm*

I go further than you, and assume that *all* 'Chinese proverbs' originated in the western world. I'm particularly fond of 'Ask the young: they know everything.' When I was young I took this literally, and gracefully accepted it as a tribute to the clear-eyed omniscience of youth. Now that I have grown-up children I see that the saying is wholly ironical.

So glad John Carter turned up trumps. I suppose Laurence Housman's death will entail another piece in the *Bromsgrovian*. L.H. was a tiresome old cissy (Hugh Walpole once told me L.H. had got into trouble for picking up a boy in a public lavatory—not, I should have thought, a highly romantic trysting-place), and he made a frightful hash of A.E.H.'s remains. I always think A.E.H. himself was largely to blame: he had the greatest contempt for L.H. and his works, and yet left him to decide what unpublished material should be printed. Most of L.H.'s many books are dim and dated, but some of his little plays have life in them, and in one called *Echo de Paris* he wonderfully recaptured (so responsible witnesses affirm) Oscar's conversation in 1899–1900. I used to see L.H. sometimes when I worked for Cape, who latterly published him.

I can see that you are funking *Redgauntlet*: be brave and jump in: you won't want to come out, I promise you. Yes, Lincoln was a splendid man: I must read more about him. The Gettysburg address is pretty good by any standards, isn't it?

Your saying that my letters are 'very much less boring' than Cicero's, though flattering, is not wholly reassuring. Admittedly there are widely differing degrees of boredom—but I accept the remark as a slip of the biro.

I can't help you with Herrick. Veronica Wedgwood has three good pages on him in her excellent little book *Seventeenth-Century Literature* (O.U.P. 1950), from which I learn that 'during the whole of the eighteenth century he (R.H.) was wholly forgotten and he had to wait for rediscovery until Maitland's edition of his work in 1825.' (If I had published the book I should have made her avoid the juxtaposition of 'whole' and 'wholly', but let that pass.) Which only goes to prove what old Edward Garnett used to say of literary reputation: 'Don't worry: everything finds its own level in the end.' V.W. writes: 'His particular talent, which could so well express the transient sweetness of a summer frolic or the crackling warmth of a winter festival, may speak an *envoi* to the whole [there she is again!] bright gathering of writers who were travelling so fast, with their country, into the bleak season of civil war.' Do what you can with that.

One day I dined with my old (prep-school) friend Wyndham Ketton-Cremer. He is writing a book about Felbrigg, his lovely Norfolk home, and he wants me to publish it for him. It is likely to be his best book and I am pleased.

Adam's soccer side last week won 27–0. He assures me it really is *soccer*. Duff promises to bring a team of stalwart diggers over from Oxford, and Comfort has promised them each three and sixpence an hour—we may be ruined.

Today was *warm* and *sunny*. Comfort gardened herself to a standstill, and I did a little work myself, besides sitting in the sun trying to wield the Sunday papers. Peter walked over and went through his finally revised proofs. His mother-in-law is now pretty well moribund in his house, which is rather a bore for him.

From inscriptions on the Great Wall of China

(1) The Three Good Things:
    (a) Certainty held in Reserve.
    (b) Unexpected Praise from an Artist.
    (c) Discovery of Nobility in Oneself.

(2) The Three Bad Things:
    (a) Unworthiness crowned.
    (b) Unconscious Infraction of the Laws of Behaviour.
    (c) Friendly Condescension of the Imperfectly Educated.

Plausible inventions if spurious?

The omniscience of the young—yes. Old Henry Jackson told us he had heard W.H. Thompson, the Master of Trinity, at a College meeting say to a young Fellow: 'We are none of us infallible, not even the youngest', which if you ever come across you will always find ascribed to Jowett. It puzzles me that W.H.T., the grimmest, and Aldis Wright, the second grimmest of men should both have been great friends of FitzGerald, surely the ungrimmest of men. I like to remember that some spirited undergraduates once pushed a sheep into A.W.'s room at Trinity. The sheep was all against it, and there was a good deal of scuffling before entry was effected. A.W. was sitting on a hard straight-backed chair with his top-hat on (he was said to wear it in bed) and there followed this faultlessly simple dialogue: 'What's this, what's this?' 'A sheep, sir,' and the door banged. Did you know that no smell has such stamina as a sheep's, especially if it is frightened? Old Aldis's room was uninhabitable for days. A ridiculous old pedant.

I didn't know that Laurence Housman was a queer too. (Leo Pavia had the same penchant for romance in a lavatory.) Gow[1] disliked him a good deal, and says he was very tiresome and untrustworthy over A.E.H.'s manuscript poems. A. and L. must have been vinegar and oil. Affable guests at Trinity frequently ruined their chances of a pleasant dinner by congratulating A. on something that in fact was the work

[1] A.S.F. Gow, Eton master and later Fellow of Trinity College, Cambridge.

of L. On such occasions A. spoke no word for the rest of the evening. No one ever mistook him for Old King Cole. Where can one find L.H.'s *Echo de Paris*? I have only his *Victoria Regina* plays, many of which are excellent.

My biro did not slip. My saying about your letters and Cicero's was one of those humorous touches whose point is in meiosis, or if you prefer it litotes, the classic example of which is the young lady's remark that Niagara was a pretty sight. Tuppy Headlam was fond of employing it, but it often misses fire in unskilled hands. But as a matter of fact some of Cicero's letters are very well, though letters about contemporary politics are—to me—unfailingly tedious, e.g. many of Horace Walpole's, though one mustn't say so.

Thank you for V. Wedgwood on Herrick. I found—and incorporated—a good sentence of Edward Thomas, viz 'There is no greater proof of the power of style than in the survival of the work of this trivial vicar'. He was a rum 'un sometimes, viz in his bland assurance to God that He will get no harm from his lewder poems. The eighteenth century of course thought that pompous platitudinarians like Akenside (or Lyttelton!) were better poets.

I have met Ketton-Cremer—one of our East Anglian worthies—and liked him. Didn't he write something good about Gray not long ago? And isn't he a member of the Johnson Club, or was he once there as a guest? At the next meeting C. Hollis will be my neighbour, and I expect Roberts will be worth listening to. I have a horrid feeling that the Secretary may suggest that it is time I wrote another paper. I shall resist stoutly, having no real excuse. It is no good pleading old age, as I rather think that only you and Hollis are younger. Do they ever elect a new member, or does the wraith of old Chapman[1] still bar the way like the angel at the gate of Eden? New blood is wanted as much as in English cricket; it may be that both are moribund—which I must tell you I am rather feeling myself after a G.B. meeting of Woodridge School. And I have a touch of lumbago. To-morrow (when I post this) I go to the memorial service to my cousin Stephen who began life in the Navy and ended as a managing director of the Army & Navy Stores, which sounds somehow incongruous. No odder perhaps than General Birdwood who became Master of Peterhouse, or, vice versa

[1] R.W. Chapman, Johnsonian scholar and editor of Jane Austen.

Freyberg who I believe was a dentist. Not that many a dentist does not deserve the V.C.

You did not, I hope, miss the mention of that vicar who wants flogging back in the penal code for young delinquents. His parish, believe it or not, is Much Birch near Hereford. How delighted the boys at Eton were when Jackie Chute, whom they liked (rightly) but thought a bit of an ass (also rightly), became rector of Piddlehinton.

Where is that tremendous epitaph on the grave of a child that died as soon as it was born?

> When th' archangels trump shall blow,
> And souls to bodies join,
> Many will wish their lives below
> Had been as short as mine.

P.S. Love to Ruth.

1 March 1959   *Bromsden Farm*

I have often vowed never again to publish any book that I can't read in the original—i.e. in French or English. The people whose opinions one is forced to follow on other languages are often would-be translators in need of work and money, so that one can't wholly trust them. But then I remember that far my biggest seller was a German book—*Seven Years in Tibet*—and then I weaken and let through some horror. (Years ago I published a book on Yugoslavia which had clearly been written by the Godfrey Winn of Sweden—ugh!). The more factual such a book is, the safer: directly one ventures into 'works of art', real or intended, they are apt to suffer a hideous sea-change. All this is by way of preamble to the announcement that I have spent *all* today and yesterday reading the translation of a 750-page German autobiography, for which I have already paid the translator £600.[1] It's rather a good and interesting book, but far, *far* too long, and will clearly have to be so expensive that no-one will buy it—oh dear, it has quite flattened me out. In fact I probably thought it better than it is because I was able to read much of it sitting on the lawn in my shirt-

[1] *The Owl of Minerva* by Gustav Regler (1959).

208

sleeves. I thought of you in your summer-house and hoped you were sunbound too. All our yellow crocuses have rushed into bloom, and every bird was singing.

Adam's soccer-side must have slacked off last week, for their winning margins were only 6–0, 6–0, and 9–0. They have now scored 90 goals in seven games and are, understandably, top of the League. Apparently the four top sides now play it off in semi-finals and final—it sounds a funny arrangement to me.

I loved your Great Wall of China sayings: did you make them up? The first one reminds me of Yeats's lines:

> Be secret and exult,
> Because of all things known
> This is most difficult.

I quote from memory, since it is late and I have no time to browse happily through W.B.Y. I'll try and find you a copy of *Echo de Paris* on my Berwick Market stall or elsewhere. You emerged triumphant from your Ciceronian comparison, and my umbrage is reduced.

Ketton-Cremer is once again President of the Johnson Club, so you'll see him on March 10. I wish I was going to be with you, but the Lit. Soc. is apt to get into a tangle without its shepherd.

On Tuesday last Ruth and I went to Elisabeth Beerbohm's funeral service at Golders Green. I had stupidly not realised it would be a Jewish service and so had no hat to keep on. We hid behind a pillar, and afterwards Jonah was bragging a bit because of his battered old Homberg. S.C. Roberts (wearing an even older one) gave an excellent address, and so did Dr Garten, the German master at Westminster. Next day I spent the evening with E's sister and brother-in-law near Swiss Cottage. They are German–Jewish refugees: he a lawyer and she a librarian. They gave me Rhine wine, biscuits spread with various excellent condiments, coffee, sweets and a small cigar, and couldn't have been nicer. They're both highly intelligent and may well be easier to deal with than E, since they have no emotional undertones in discussing Max and his works. One day I lunched with the Birkenheads, one with the directors of W.H. Smith, one with thirty-four other men (including Sir William Haley, the Dean of St Paul's, the Swedish Ambassador and Uncle T. Cobbleigh) in the holy of holies at

Lloyd's (grub and company both A.1.). The new Chairman, Tony Grover, was an army friend of mine. I also went to a theatre, to a cocktail party, and dined with Eric Linklater—a week so busy that I staggered down here exhausted on Friday.

Have you yet summoned up courage to tackle *Redgauntlet*? I shall certainly get the new biography of Ethel Smyth, whom I knew slightly in 1930–31—a splendid old creature.

Goodnight, dear George.

5 *March 1959*   *London*

Damn! This will be a miserable letter. Rule 1 in correspondence is—have the letter you are answering before you. Well that is my invariable practice. Your letter duly arrived on Saturday, just as we were about to set off hither. I read it once (i.e. with two more perusals to follow) and then, if you please, left it behind. And, my memory having long gone with the wind, I cannot properly answer it.

I don't like London—too many people and not enough of them nice to look at, or to listen to, and *all* with vile manners as soon as they are at the steering-wheel of a car. Every human being is said to have a soul—but in the tube at the rush hour??

Tell me *exactly* two things. *A Taste of Honey*.[1] Alan Dent condemns it heartily, and half the rest of the critics condemn *him* for doing so. It sounds muck, but what do *you* think? And I see Wilfred Feinburgh's book has been boosted through five editions already.[2] Is it any good, or is my suspicion well-founded that a great number of people buy and read a book *solely* because the Press convinces them that all the Joneses are reading it? Few statements irritate me more than 'this is a book which no one can afford to miss', the unwritten end of which is 'or the Joneses will despise you'. What bilge it all is!

To-morrow I lunch with the Archbishop, the G.B.A. committee being the guests of the Mercers' Company (perhaps 'at the same table

[1] A play of low life in Salford by the nineteen-year-old Shelagh Delaney, recently transferred to the West End from the Theatre Royal. I later saw it in New York and enjoyed it very much.
[2] *No Love For Johnnie*.

as the A.' would more exactly tell the truth, but he is a genial old bird, and at our last meeting accused me afterwards of scowling at him when he was speaking. Archbishop Laud would not have noticed if anyone had scowled at him—or cared), and to-morrow evening my brother has a party. A distinguished civil servant called Sedgwick will be there—a grandson I fancy of the old geologist Adam S. of Cambridge.

Those Chinese sayings are from Geoffrey Madan's collection.[1] I don't *think* he invented them, but wouldn't have put it past him. Next week I will send you another little handful. He had a sharp eye for anything in any way apt, culled from any quarter, e.g. an Underground notice 'Stand on the right and let the rest pass you'—as good as many axioms from the New Testament.

I got a nice dry grin from the Eton Rambler fixtures etc, just arrived. From last year's record two adjacent entries:

	No. of innings	highest score	total	average
R.P. Fleming	1	0	0	0
P.D. Hart-Davis	1	0	0	0

(I won't swear to the last two columns)

My lumbago is on the way out; but I now have a slight pain in the place occupied, I believe, by my liver. I suspect cirrhosis. Watch the paper for bulletins. But Amsler[2] once said in his blunt way 'You're like all perfectly healthy men; your skin itches a little after a midge-bite, and you think you've got leprosy.'

I must stop. Next week I will say all I *meant* to say to-day. I hope the Johnson dinner won't be too dreary. Good old Jonah is coming as a guest.

P.S. My brother told me this advice from a doctor 'Take things more easily,' adding what the doctor did not say—'as the psychiatrist said to a kleptomaniac.'

[1] *Livre Sans Nom*, five anonymous pamphlets (1929–1933).
[2] Eton doctor.

I don't think you missed much by leaving my last letter behind: I'm sure there was nothing in it, and you did beautifully without. I bet you aren't in your summer-house today. Here the North Wind howls and I stoke up the library fire: last week-end, as I thought at the time, was a dream.

Idiotically I have only just realised (or remembered) that you were part-editor of *An Eton Poetry Book*. It came out during my last year at Eton, I bought it immediately, learnt most of it by heart and have treasured it ever since. My children have enjoyed it too, and the volume has a comfortably worn look. I don't suppose I had opened it for twenty years until for no conscious reason I took it down yesterday. I had remembered it as solely Alington's work, so your name on the title-page was a lovely surprise, and I'm delighted to find that I think the book just as excellent as I thought it in 1925. There can never have been a better anthology for stirring boys' enthusiasm: the selections first-class, and so well printed and arranged. Thank you, dear George, for the pleasure you gave me long ago and yesterday. Was the book a big seller? It should have been. And is it out of print now? I hope not.

Last week I spent the best part of two days with my German auto-biographer, and despite my general antipathy to Germans I came to like him very much. He has a splendid sense of humour, and his life story is amazing. I persuaded him to cut thousands of words out of the book, which will be a help.

The only way I could answer your question about *A Taste of Honey* would be by going to see the damned thing—from which I recoil. The same goes for the Feinburgh book, which I'm sure is rubbish: surely we get enough about the lower ranks of the Labour Party in the newspapers? Stop worrying about them both: you are in no remotest danger of ossifying mentally. What you say of literary fashion and 'keeping up with the Joneses' is partly true in this country, and wholly so in America. Once when I was there, the two books which were in everyone's drawing-room (mostly unopened) were *The Waves* by Virginia Woolf and a book called *How to Win Friends and Influence People*. It seemed to me inconceivable that *anyone* could enjoy them *both*, and I'm sure they were simply social assets. However, it doesn't much matter if a good book is bought for the wrong reasons. The author has earned royalties, and the chances are that eventually many of the copies will fall into appreciative hands. The great tragedy is when a first-rate book doesn't sell at all, for then there are no copies to fall into anyone's hands. The only thing in favour of 'remaindering' unsold books is that the copies are at least circulating rather than rotting in the publisher's warehouse.

Do send me some more Madaniana. After his death I went laboriously into the question of publishing a book of them, chosen by John Sparrow, but G.M.'s widow proved more intransigent than eight prima donnas, so I retired gracefully.

Peter Green (a very intelligent young man) sent me a proof of his life of Kenneth Grahame, which I am half-way through. K.G. I find both pathetic and distasteful: I'd be amused to know your reaction.

The Obscenity committee met last week, with A.P.H. in great form. I dined one night at the Athenaeum with Wyndham Ketton-Cremer, and lunched another day with Ronald Searle, whom I found as charming as his drawings have always seemed to me revolting—which is to say, exceedingly. (Sorry about that sentence.) He is a great Max fan, and we talked mostly of him.

Peter is now thinking (Ssh! it's a secret, so keep it dark) of writing a book about Younghusband's expedition to Lhasa in 1903–04. I think only one participant (F.M. Bailey) still survives.

And now I must write some notes on a delicious little bombshell of a book about Dickens and his actress-mistress, of which you shall hear more anon.[1] Tomorrow will start off dismally with another funeral at Golders Green—that of the wife of Jonathan Cape's partner, who was also my partner from 1932 to 1940. I only hope I shall be buried in Swaledale with a few villagers following the coffin. Golders Green gives me the creeps—Jewish or otherwise.

[1] *Dickens Incognito* by Felix Aylmer (1959).

There was a good gathering to hear Roberts who was entertaining on 'Estimate' Brown[1] of whom I knew exactly as much as the Corinthians knew about the Holy Ghost. We dined in much too small a room in the Cheshire Cheese after picking our squalid way past spittoons and fag-ends. It is all rather a hugger-mugger affair (especially compared with the Lit. Soc.). *After* the meal had begun the secretary tried to make me propose the health of the guests. I stoutly resisted, and he pushed it onto a pink and portly man, called Butler, unknown to me, who did it admirably. Jonah was there, guest of Ketton-Cremer, but I saw very little of him. Another guest was that distinguished invalid, John Hayward, whom I expect you know. How *did* he get that really horrifying lip (lower)? One feels that *some*thing could and should have been done about it. De Beer,[2] Basil Willey,[3] old Uncle L.F. Powell[4] and all were there, but I seem to be able to *name* fewer of them every time. The summer meeting is to be at Brighthelmstone, and a member volunteered to read a paper with suspicious celerity, for are not those who *want* to read papers rarely among the good ones?

How kind you are about the *Eton Poetry Book*. It is, I think, out of print now, and never had very much of a sale. Macmillan's didn't do much about it and always maintained that its title was against it, but Cyril Alington insisted on it. It is true the relevance of it is not very clear. My copy always opens at 'Little Orphant Annie' which I tried to eliminate, but Cyril was mysteriously keen on it. One or two reviews rightly derided it, but mostly such reviews as the book got were quite cordial. One infuriated me. I did practically all of the stuff about the poems and poets, and some ass regretted that readers should be 'told what to think about them'. As no doubt you (and everyone else with eyes) saw, the main gist was to record what *had* been thought or said about them, very often inviting readers to differ, e.g Coleridge (was it?) saying that Blanco White's sonnet was 'the finest and most

[1] John Brown, Scottish clergyman and poet (1715–1766) published *An Estimate of the Manners and Principles of the Times* in 1757.

[2] Esmond de Beer (b. 1895), editor of Evelyn's Diary and Locke's Correspondence.

[3] Professor of English Literature at Cambridge and author (1897–1979).

[4] Johnsonian scholar and editor (1881–1975).

grandly conceived'—I think I quote right—'in the language'.[1] Surely *very* high among rules for critics is 'Never use superlatives'.

I will send you some more of Madan next week. His widow shilly-shallied endlessly about his book, of which several copies were distributed among his friends. I didn't get one, and wasn't of the inner circle. A remark of mine, however, *is* in the book—ascribed to Gaillard Lapsley, that admirable U.S.A. Trinity don who invariably embarrassed one with his ultra-perfect manners. You remember Michael Finsbury, who dressed too much like a wedding-guest to be quite a gentleman.[2]

I had a pleasant little chat with the Archbishop last week. He was most genial; in fact if you described us as 'buddies,' nobody could cavil. The Mercers' Hall where we lunched was rebuilt last year and must have cost an astronomical sum—so vast that the Insurance policy on it forbids any smoking. And at the general meeting after a lunch at which Lucullus would have opened his eyes (and, of course, his mouth) I always look forward to 'abstract my mind and think of Tom Thumb'[3] and enjoying a Monte Cristo cigar out of my opulent son-in-law's Xmas box. But I enjoyed the masterly chairmanship of the Archbishop. They tell me he can be very ratty if opposed, but I have never seen it.

I hope you told Virginia Woolf about *The Waves* being on the same table as *How to Win Friends etc*. Would she have laughed or not? You never can tell with the *genus irritabile*. (What, by the way, has happened to Leonard Merrick and his books—invariably praised by the critics and quite or nearly unread by the public? I cannot recollect ever reading one.)

Tell me all about the Lit. Soc. (including the food of course). It is much better fun—and cheaper!—than the Johnson dinner, and one rarely sees a spittoon, or hears one being used.

[1] Joseph Blanco White (1775–1841), an Irish–Spanish theological writer, composed one sonnet in 1825 called 'Night and Death', the only thing he is remembered for.

[2] In Stevenson's *The Wrong Box*, chapter 8.

[3] 'When Charles Fox said something to me once about Catiline's Conspiracy, I withdrew my attention and thought about Tom Thumb.' (Doctor Johnson)

Kenneth Grahame. I shall read his life. A pitiable man apparently, but who can say those three books are anything but delicious, one would say the work of a serene and delightful man. I always liked *The Golden Age* and *Dream Days* better than *The Wind in the Willows*. As for e.g. 'The Reluctant Dragon' tale—but what did I say about superlatives? But dash it all, what else can one use about, say, the talk between St George and the Dragon before the fight—St G. indicating a spot on the vast body which he could safely prod with his spear, and the dragon demurring, as it was a ticklish place and it would never do if he laughed during the battle. I look forward to reading the Dickens book. The scabrous and salacious old Agate used to aver that D. 'tumbled' half the women he met and all the housemaids—but it may have been wishful thinking.

Of course you must be buried in Swaledale—but not yet, please.

Did I ever read you my poem in which Golders Green was mentioned? My only poem in print!

15 March 1959   *36 Soho Square*

Sunday is much the pleasantest—or least disagreeable—day in London: little noise or traffic and fewer of those hideous people that so displease you. I got back from Cambridge at lunch-time and went to the nearest Lyons (usually jostling with people), where I consumed a (believe it or not) Wimpy Cheeseburger, some coffee and a strawberry ice. The W.C. was composed of a hot bun containing a hamburger, onion and cheese—much better than it sounds. Here (No 36) I found your letter, which had just missed me on Friday, when I caught the 4.30 train from Liverpool Street. Geoffrey Keynes met me at Cambridge and drove me out to his house at Brinkley (about thirteen miles). It's a pleasant Jane Austenish house with three acres of garden. They (G. and Mrs G., who was a Darwin, sister of Sir Charles and of Gwen Raverat, cousin of Bernard, grand-daughter of *The Origin of Species*) gave me a huge dinner, after which we sat in G's incredible library and he showed me rarity after rarity: goodness knows what his books are worth. I got to bed exhausted at midnight. On Saturday morning G. drove me back to Cambridge, where I lunched in Trinity

Hall with Graham Storey, who is editing the Dickens letters for me. Oh yes—before that Geoffrey took me for a walk by the Backs, over King's Bridge where the crocuses carpeted the ground in full bloom. We penetrated the dim religious light of King's Chapel, and G. thoroughly enjoyed showing me everything. Did you know that Maynard Keynes, by wise speculation, doubled King's income and then left them all his books and pictures as well as half a million in cash? Geoffrey had to sign a cheque for £243,000 in favour of the Revenue for death duties!

In the afternoon Storey drove me to Madeline House's, where I talked for an hour before taking a taxi back to the Provost's Lodge at King's. My fellow-guests were Lord Bridges (charming and very young for his age) and a couple called Wollheim (he a philosophy don at London University). I slept in Noel's study (very comfortable) and while we were changing for dinner all the lights fused. Nothing daunted, we joined another 150 chaps and consumed the enclosed delectable dinner. I sat on the Provost's right(!!). On my other side was Maurice Hill, a delightful geo-physicist and nephew of Geoffrey Keynes. Afterwards the whole gathering adjourned to the Lodge, where I managed to sober up on four tumblers of orangeade. I talked to many, known and unknown, among them Leslie Hotson, Dadie Rylands, E.M. Forster (rather deaf now in a crowd but otherwise unaged) and a young don called Michael Jaffé, who insisted that when he was an undergraduate (some ten years ago) I had given one of the only three tolerable talks to some literary society in Cambridge. Even if he was confusing me with someone else (as I assured him) this was agreeably gratifying. I got to bed by 1 a.m., and was brought my breakfast in bed, with the *Observer*, at 9. And so back to London. I had a long talk with Noel about Adam's future, and am more than ever inclined to think he should go to Cambridge (i.e. King's) rather than Oxford. Noel says they are most anxious to get more scientists from Eton, and he (Adam) should be able to get some sort of scholarship or grant. What do you think?

John Hayward has some sort of progressive muscular atrophy, about which nothing can be done: he's certainly not a pretty sight, poor chap. I read some Leonard Merrick years ago, and thought him NO GOOD: perhaps that's why he never sold.

217

Please produce your poem on Golders Green as soon as possible. And pray for me on Wednesday evening, when in a hostelry called the Nag's Head I have to address the assembled Book-Collectors of Manchester. Afterwards I stay the night with Phoebe Hesketh near Bolton. WHAT can I say to the brutes? I can't use the Emperor Gordian every time—oh dear![1]

19 March 1959   *Grundisburgh*

Of course it was bound to come, and I am back again in the armchair and inflicting upon you—now what would Henry James have called the Biro? (It would have been a good question for my Extra Studies in old days. I wish I had kept the five 'Little Jack Horners' rewritten in the style of Pope which led the chairman of Cammell Laird —a civilised business-man, financier etc—to say, after reading twenty specimens, that if any of these five wanted a start in C.L. they should have it). Of course you remember H.J.'s apologies for his typewriter— never called a typewriter but such things as 'this graceless mechanism', 'this bleak legibility' etc. The thermometer is on the wrong side of 40°, and hare or venison could be preserved for days in the summer house without any danger of approaching that height of ripeness which Dr Johnson would have found superlatively toothsome.

I am disgusted at your not getting my last letter by the first post on Friday. It was posted in *London* on Thursday afternoon, in Northumberland Avenue, just outside the Royal Empire Society (but on the very next day there was a man chiselling away changing Empire to Commonwealth. Deplorable! 'Empire' and 'Imperial' are fine words, Commonwealth isn't). I suppose postmen are as slack about 'service' as other nationalised workers. They used not to be.

I read in yesterday's *Times* that there is quite likely to be a printers'

---

[1] 'Twenty-two acknowledged concubines and a library of 62,000 volumes attested the variety of his inclinations, and from the productions which he left behind him it appears that the former as well as the latter were designed for use rather than for ostentation.' (Gibbon on the Emperor Gordian)

strike. Do you know about that; and how does it hit publishers? The last one was just before our correspondence began. How hateful these strikes are. I don't believe e.g. German workers have this brutal indifference to national interests. And I see some genial chap wants the Burnham scale to plump for a 20% increase in teachers' salaries next October. That would mean goodbye to many independent schools.

Your last letter gave me an odd turn, for the first line I happened to read was 'The W.C. was composed of a hot bun'. This, I thought, must be *Alice in Wonderland* brought up to date. No novel or story in 1959 but must mention the W.C., and made of a bun is just what it might have been in the White Rabbit's house. I have never heard of a Wimpy Cheeseburger. I shall look out for it. And strawberry ice! Your time at Cambridge sounds pleasant. The Backs perhaps you saw about a month too early. I remember days when no comment was possible beyond 'By Gum!' Maynard Keynes, I always heard, so manipulated the King's money that from having been about the poorest college, financially, he made it the richest. And the queer thing is that his first essays in speculation were completely unsuccessful. Did you know him? Very courteous and kind, and with a mind of frankly terrifying swiftness in ordinary talk. What talk I had with him, you will be surprised to hear, was never about finance. His death, like Temple's, was infuriatingly untimely. Did King's Chapel impress you? Surely yes. Gow told me that Lovell of Queen's, Oxford, some sort of expert on buildings, and clearly looking at architecture as Leavis looks at literature, on entering King's Chapel, looked at the roof and murmured 'Bestial'.

I was talking to the Leys School intelligentsia on Monday and, *inter alia*, derided the Leavis view—not mentioning his name. I must tell Ivor Brown that nothing delighted them more than his version of the Lord's prayer rendered into a blend of civil service and commercial English. 'That our daily intake of cereal filler be not in short supply' is nauseatingly good.

Roger enjoyed his Lit. Soc. dinner between as he put it 'Fergusson (merry) and Sargent (polished).' Your fare was better than the Cheshire Cheese bully beef. Your King's menu is mouth-watering too —the hand of Keynes is visible in the left-hand [wine] column. Oscar

Browning and Walter Headlam had to put up with the sort of beverage that Uncle Pentstemon ('uttering a kind of large hiccup') derided as 'grocer's stuff'.[1] H.G.W. describing a plebeian wedding-breakfast was flawless in humour and perception.

You are right about Lord Bridges. Is Wollheim the author of a belittling view of Walter Bagehot, whom everyone else praises very highly, and did you like him? His review of the book gave the impression that he would be surprised to find Wollheim wrong in any way. G.M. Young puts B. at the very top of the Victorians. Michael Jaffé is an amiable fellow, some say a little too anxious to please. But what harm in that, when so many are the reverse? Dadie Rylands, I hope, is well and happy, but why is he not writing anything these days? Up to the neck in dramatics I suspect. He was a grand audience in A and B extra studies and is particularly pleasant to meet. It is a pity he can't or won't write letters. Arthur Benson made the same complaint when D.R. was an undergraduate. E.M. Forster I never knew. I wish I had.

Surely you would do well to send Adam to King's. I hear very well of it nowadays under its youthful Provost. I don't believe you could do better, though of course my knowledge of Oxford is scanty.

Another handful of Chinese sayings:

The Three Rare Things
(Sights of the Kingfisher)

1) Clear memory of Romantic conversation.
2) The meeting of Great Equals.
3) Unremarked abbreviation of Pious Exercises.*

*(This beats me, but it has a mysterious charm)

The Three Foolish Things
(Spring Lambs)

1) Deep sleep in an Unknown House.
2) Setting to sea in a Borrowed Junk.
3) Not to lag behind when the Elephant approaches a New Bridge.

[1] In *The History of Mr Polly* by H.G. Wells.

Are you *sure* I haven't sent you my one printed poem—to Plum Warner? I told it to Ivor Brown who smiled—not unkindly—and then gave full and accurate information to Tommy Lascelles and me about Golder.

P.S. I am deep in *Redgauntlet*. Very good but I do sometimes murmur 'Get *on*, get *on*, old dear.'

22 *March 1959*   *Bromsden Farm*

So far, thank goodness, I know nothing of a printers' strike, but anything that would slow down the flood of unnecessary books and give me a few free days for Oscar would be most welcome. I loved the new lot of 'Chinese sayings'. You certainly haven't ever sent me your poem, so please do. You sound rather half-hearted about my beloved *Redgauntlet*: I must read it again myself—but when?

Last week was somewhat interrupted by my journeying on Wednesday to Manchester to be the guest of honour at the annual dinner of the Manchester Society of Book-Collectors. I had relied on the four-hour train-journey to compose my speech, but a resolutely affable chemical engineer from Macclesfield insisted on talking most of the way, and I arrived with only a few notes scribbled on a small piece of paper. It was very hot in the upper room at the Old Nag's Head and I had *two* stout table-legs where my knees should have been. I was between the President, an H.M.I. who recently published a bibliography of Chesterton, and his wife, who won my heart by immediately saying she hated Manchester and hankered for her home in the south. The dinner was plain but adequate, my speech neither, but once again I got away with the Emperor Gordian—God bless you! Then *four* people made speeches saying what a splendid chap I was, and the party broke up into general conversation. They were all very friendly and appreciative and I was glad I'd gone. Then Phoebe Hesketh drove me to her home near Bolton, and next morning we walked on the moors and flushed three curlew (or curlews?) before I caught the London train at Wigan. On it I had the best train-lunch I've ever had in this country—but that was nothing to the superb dinner I consumed that evening (menu enclosed). It may not read interestingly, but every drop and morsel were quite first-class. It was the dinner given by my father's stockbroking firm to celebrate his retirement after sixty years. Everybody, I think, had been dreading it for weeks, but (as so often in meetings with my father) your cousin Oliver saved the day with his eupeptic humour and made the whole thing a great success. I told him my father had got his doctor to give him some sort of stimulant to get him through the evening, and as soon as Oliver saw the old boy he said: 'Hullo, Richard, I hear they've given you a subcutaneous injection of Bollinger 49'—which delighted the old fellow. I sat between Anthony (Lyttelton, of course) and my cousin Ian Cameron, well away from my father's business contemporaries, several of whom (particularly Alfred Wagg) looked as though they'd been exhumed for the evening. But they were all charming, and the whole occasion was rather touching. Goodness knows what the old boy will do with his time now. For years I suspect that he has been nothing but a nuisance in the office, but the effort of getting there and back occupied most of his day.

Adam reports that his boys'-maid has got her own television set, and he wonders whether the Welfare State hasn't gone a little too far. His side is now in the final of the Junior Soccer League. Their semi-final score of 4–0 was rather a come-down.

On Thursday, as perhaps I told you, Ruth is flying to Italy to spend a fortnight with her daughter. My horror of aeroplanes greatly adds to my reluctance to be without her so long, and she's not tremendously keen on it herself. The post to and from Italy is incredibly bad. Oh well, I shall try to catch up with my work while she's away.

I invested a small sum on Oscar Wilde in the National, but he fell at the fourth fence.

25 March 1959   *Grundisburgh*

Odd! Whenever I get a letter from you in which you say you are practically down and out, smothered with work and fatigue, I know that it is going to be a particularly good one. Rather like Brahms, who wrote to someone that he had 'had to insert' into his violin concerto

222

'a feeble slow movement'—and proceeded to charm everybody (except E.M. Forster) with the most delicious thing in the world. And Kipling's 'Recessional' was retrieved from the waste-paper basket wherein he had chucked it as not up to much.

No, I did enjoy *Redgauntlet*, but now and then got impatient with the conversation, almost every item of which resembled a passage to be put into Latin Prose. I know I should be made of sterner stuff. You clearly had a great success at Manchester. I have long adopted the plan of pleading deafness to a garrulous fellow-traveller, in fact I have always disliked talking in the train to anyone—sometimes breaking my rule when there are only two of us in the carriage. What *did* you have to say to the chemical engineer? Was your talk of hydrogen and litmus paper? I am glad the Emperor Gordian came in useful again. My brother who is always speechifying to audiences interested in iron and steel, and extolling the advantages of co-operation, also has a winner (I think I found it in some digest in a dentist's waiting-room). An advertisement: 'Communist with own knife and fork would like to meet Communist with own steak-and-kidney pie.' And he often uses Walter Hagen's remark on the *first* tee of the *first* round of the open championship 'Well, boys, who's going to be second?' And then did actually proceed to win it. Positively Miltonic!

Curlew I am sure is right as against curlews. I always liked Mr Squeers's saying 'twenty pound', and in fact, as often as not, my father did. Is that singular used now for anything but fish? 'Trouts' would ensure blackballing at any club. Shall I try it at the Lit. Soc?

I send you the menu of C.M. Wells's birthday dinner (*aetat* eighty-eight, and he looks about fifty-six). The Burgundy he took two sips of and said 'A little disappointing. It is good but I expected it to be superb.' John Christie[1] was there. He has let his white hair grow and now has a strong resemblance to Thackeray, with a hint of Luxmoore, with neither of whom he has an iota in common. Plum Warner wasn't there, on, I fear, the slightly risible grounds that after dark he is afraid of being either run over or coshed. And yet half-a-century ago he stood up to Ernest Jones like a man—the man even W.G. admitted was 'fast', which adjective he wouldn't wholly allow to Richardson,

[1] Eccentric millionaire (1882–1962). For some years a master at Eton. Founded the Glyndebourne Music Festival on his own estate 1934.

if you please. C.B. Fry said Jones was too quick to hook even when he pitched half way. Wells in 1901 had Woodcock on his MCC side v Eton. I made 22 against him—nearly all through the slips. I played at his first delivery as it plopped into the wicket-keeper's hands. Wells reminded me that as his side came onto the field, Woodcock, knowing that schoolboys had never seen anyone nearly as fast, said to him, 'Shall I slip 'em down, sir?' and got the reply 'What do you mean? Bowl your ordinary stuff.'

I hope old Alfred Wagg is well. He left Benson's before I arrived, and I met him only half a dozen times, but what a kind and friendly fellow he always was. I suppose he was at Eton with your father.

You are not, I presume, listening to some rather dreary reminiscences of Galsworthy, who does not sound a very lively companion—so buttoned-up, and serious and habit-ridden. Still he created old Heythorp—who would have derided him vigorously! Match me that marvel. How the young moderns despise him, and how little they ultimately matter. I read that Malcolm Muggeridge likens Macmillan in Russia to a character out of the Forsyte Saga, by which, no doubt, he means the lowest depth of outmoded futility (would Galsworthy have been amused by the lady who said she had recently seen a comedy—Gallstones by Milesworthy? I am afraid not).

I am pretty sure my Xmas letter to Percy Lubbock at Lerici never reached him. He hasn't answered, but I fear he is in a poorish way—quite blind now, and immensely fat, and sad, a good deal, apparently, sponged on by various young men. And villas are springing up all round Gli Scafari, though as to that blindness must be a boon.

I enclose my doggerel. Few people realise how easy that sort of stuff is to write. One idea and a handful of words that rhyme is all that is wanted. And the result imposes on dear simpletons like P.F.W. who actually wrote 'What a brain is yours!'
P.S. I agree with you (and Winston) about aeroplanes, and try to re-assure myself by remembering the milkman's reply to a complaint that one day his milk was sour. 'Think, lady, on how many days it *isn't* sour.'

To P.F.W. on his birthday, shortly after the practice had started of naming streets, courts etc after well-known Londoners.

Why some names entirely perish
Like stones in the depth of the sea,
While others we honour and cherish,
Has always caused wonder to me.
For instance, does anyone hold a-
-n idea (I've forgotten it clean)
Of who in the wide world was Golder
Who made that unpopular Green?
Opinion grows daily that Potter
Whose Bar's in the county of Herts,
Was in truth a good deal of a rotter,
Of wholly contemptible parts.
But I think that one might have been fonder
Of him—though not quite as a friend—
Than that lumpish nonentity Ponder,
Who is known far and wide for his End.
Far and wide? I can see you are grinning
And think my veracity's small,
For of Ponder, his end or beginning,
We frankly know nothing at all.
And so with them all; it is really
An incontrovertible fact
That of none is known, dimly or clearly,
A single word, thought, look, or act.
Oblivion scatters her poppy,
But for reasons quite obvious to all
They've resolved this old custom to copy,
And glorify street, court and hall
Throughout London—the names that adorn her
Strike a note that will never be dumb,
For among them rings out that of Warner
Known—and loved—the world over as Plum.

Easter Day, 29 March 1959   *Bromsden Farm*

These four days have come as a blessed respite, and today it has
been too wet for anything but the library fire. Each night I catch up

hours of lost sleep, and am generally so relaxed that I am almost comatose. I've even brought down my Oscar Wilde footnotes, so that I can remember what they're all about, and maybe take up the task in London next week. We have no children here, so peace reigns. Adam's team won the Soccer final 5–0, and their total score for eleven games is 118–0. He says the cup is the second smallest in the school, the smallest being the Junior Chess Cup, which he won last half.

I loved your poem, and don't wonder old Plum was pleased. Many thanks for the excellent Communist-with-own-knife-and-fork joke, which I shall salt away to astonish some other collection of credulous provincials.

My darling Ruth flew off to Milan on Thursday, and will be away for a fortnight. The light grows dim while she's away, but I shall use the time to try and get all my publishing work up to date. She has been taken to Florence for Easter, and just as I was imagining her sightseeing in brilliant sunshine, I heard on the radio that in Rome the Pope gave his blessing in pouring rain. Contrariwise, my sister reports on the telephone from Argyllshire that they've had a lovely sunny day. Thank God we weren't marching from Aldermaston!

The C.M.W. menu is almost Galsworthian in its superb simplicity, and I like the club's having printed even the date in French. I only hope I shall be enjoying Burgundy at eighty-eight. My father at eighty confines himself to whisky and kümmel in very large and frequent doses.

I have been finishing *Heroes and Hero-Worship*, begun many months ago, and have specially enjoyed all the stuff about Cromwell in the last chapter. I think it will have to be *The French Revolution* next.

I expect you saw that our Obscenity Bill got surprisingly well through its Standing Committee. Next week the Herbert Committee meets to discuss tactics for the last lap—Report and Third Reading (the Lords are considered a pushover, if you'll forgive the phrase).

I'm also enjoying the new biography of Ethel Smyth.[1] Her friend the Empress Eugénie invariably referred to the Franco-Prussian War and the overthrow of the Second Empire simply as '*les événements*', which is almost Dickensian in its charm.

---

[1] By Christopher St John (1959).

Next Friday is said to be Neville Cardus's seventieth birthday (though in his autobiography I'm pretty sure he says he was born in 1890) and a big luncheon is to be given him in the restaurant of the Festival Hall. I have subscribed and shall go.

Monday morning

The sun is shining, but black clouds loom. I have been lingering deliciously over my coffee, toast and marmalade, unable to put down *The French Revolution*. What a magnificent opening, with every stop pulled out and sounding. I care not whether the history is exact and rejoice in the book as literature—surely the greatest piece of sustained rhetoric in the language. When did you last read it? I can't wait to go on, but the garden is calling, and I am in the middle of relaying a brick path—a soothing therapeutic task which I enjoy. Occasionally Fleming rides by on a foaming horse, otherwise nothing intrudes on the rustic solitude. And mercifully I have a great ability to dismiss from my mind the worries of tomorrow—the hideous pile of letters on my office desk, no Ruth to guide me, the telephone, the printers' delays and all the rest of it. I imagine you in your summer-house, perhaps with some of your countless descendants sporting round you. I heard Humphrey's band on the radio the other day, but alas it is not my cup of tea. The problem of the generations is too great. But there are plenty of other things to enjoy, if only one had the time.

1 April 1959   *Grundisburgh*

'Comatose'! Nirvana—that is the right holiday aim. It is all piling up nutriment, like the camel's hump—or is that a legend from Pliny or Herodotus, or the Rev. Wood[1], one of whom records that the lion's hatred for the hyena is such that if their skins are hung near each other, 'the lion's skin will immediately fall away'? Anyway I hope you are now entirely rested and dealing with that ghastly pile that confronted you yesterday (Host pressing eminent lawyer to have another drink and at last lawyer: 'Well thank you, yes; I shall find a huge pile

[1] The Rev. John George Wood (1827–1889), voluminous writer of popular natural history.

of letters to answer when I get home.' Host: 'But how will another drink help you to answer them?' L. 'It won't—but it will help to create that state of mind in which I don't care whether they are answered or not.').

I knew you would appreciate the C.M.W. menu. He always had three gastronomic *bêtes noires*, i.e. sherry or cocktail, soup, and sweet. I agree with him to a great extent—though I have come across some very affable soups in my day. And at lunch, of course, a currant-and-raspberry tart, a blackberry fool, a jam omelette, a treacle-pudding—well dash it all. Before we go a step further, I must know whether you are with me so far. There are others too. Which would *you* choose for your last lunch before execution?

I am delighted by your liking for Carlyle. He has always been a favourite of mine, though I have latterly kept quiet about him; so many find him rebarbative and don't recognise power when they meet it ('*Une des plus grandes preuves de médiocrité, c'est de ne pas savoir reconnaître la supériorité là où elle se trouve*'—another of Geoffrey Madan's, written apparently by one J.B. Say, whoever he may have been).[1] Scene after scene in *The F.R.* will—literally—raise your pulse and your rate of breathing. Quite wrong of course for any prose to do so, according to Maugham and Murry *et les autres*. I have been reading lately in bed a good deal of G.M. Young (given, I need hardly say, by R.H-D) and thought repeatedly how wise and perceptive he is. He never lets one down with a shallow or petulant prejudice. What confidence a man gives you who is always out to see the good in writers and men generally, and does very little indeed of that eternal and tedious hole-picking.

Give my regards to Neville Cardus if you have speech with him. I had a good crack with him once, and we began a little correspondence, but it soon became clear he didn't want to keep it up and it lapsed. Someone warned me that he takes up new friends and drops them with equal speed, which may well be, without damning him overmuch. Anyway, a man who wrote those cricket-books—the early ones especially—is sure at least of *my* lasting goodwill.

I envy your Gladstonian power of detachment. I imagine most or all of our great men have had it—Wellington, Churchill etc. Arthur

[1] Jean Baptiste Say (1767–1832), French political economist.

Benson once asked old Gladstone if he didn't often lie awake and wonder whether some great decision he had just made was right or not, and got the astonished answer (in broad Lancashire) 'No! Where would be the use of thaat?' I always cherish the memory of Winston in 1940, handed a bankrupt situation by Neville Chamberlain and going off to bed, where he slept eight good hours. Whereas *I* lie awake half the night if a pipe freezes. And there are fussier folk than I, e.g. the elderly spinster who slept no wink till (at 4 a.m.) she decided on the name for the new kitten—i.e. 'Kitty'. Or if you think that is spurious, I can beat it with almost any example from the spinstery of Grundisburgh.

I read this morning of a bridge-game at some swell club yesterday where each player held a complete suit—the odds against which are about a quadrillion to one. Pity it happened on April 1, if they really want to be believed.

I share your taste in the matter of Humphrey's music; but all our values are hurrying down the drain. I went to *The Reluctant Debutante* yesterday. They tell me the play was better than the film; the film seemed to me sheer drivel with some smartish backchat, most of which I did not quite catch. But does London really flock to a play in which the point is that a dance-band drummer is a Spanish prince incognito? And Humphrey points out that the difficulty nowadays would be to find a drummer who was a drummer and not a royalty.

I sympathise about Ruth's absence. To point out what fun it will be when she returns is the lunatic's reason for beating his head against the wall—so nice when I stop. But that is all the consolation I can give you—beyond of course the old couplet from Stephen Hawes about the longe day.[1]

5 *April 1959*   *Bromsden Farm*

At last I have seen a real live nuthatch! After tea today it came several times to the bird-table and ate greedily. A neat and pretty little bird, the shape of a kingfisher, with a long beak, a pink chest,

[1] For though the daye be never so longe,
At last the bells ringeth to evensonge.

229

and a black back as sleek as a seal's. I think the blue-tits disapprove, for one of them did a turn of sentry-go on the table for some time afterwards.

Adam arrived covered with glory. This was his first half as a specialist, and he got a Distinction in Trials, and also the Trials Prize (top of the B Science specialists). This being his third Distinction, he got an extra pound for that! He's not sixteen till July. I opened one of our three bottles of champagne to celebrate his achievements, and all ranks lapped it gratefully up. Duff has mown all the grass, and the croquet season opened to-day. Daffodils are pouring out all round. I expect you've been in your summer-house.

I entirely agree with you (and disagree with C.M.W.) about sweets, and also soups. I can't decide what sweet I'd choose for my last meal—probably apple tart in the end, though I'm very partial to rich concoctions of chestnut purée.

My liking for *The French Revolution* continues, though I haven't got a great deal further, since I purposely left it here, so as to concentrate on other things in London. I have a delightful second edition in three volumes (1839), with an attractive small page: all the one-volume editions are in such tiny print. So you've been re-reading G.M. Young. Poor old boy, it isn't whisky but melancholia that has got him down. He has to have a male nurse in All Souls, and I think Sparrow and the other birds would be much relieved if they could ship the old polymath off to a nursing home—or even to Paradise—for he is a great nuisance to them.

I've always noticed that when cinema-avoiders *do* go to a film, they always choose a rotten one. I could have told you to avoid *The Reluctant Debutante* at all costs. I managed to sit through the play (because Celia Johnson was in it) but that was enough. Also Rex Harrison is just about my least favourite actor. Next time you must ask my advice.

Last week in London was a short one after the holiday, but Ruth's absence made it seem long and empty. (She returns, thank heaven, next Friday. I rang her up in Milan and she's all right, if a trifle home-sick.) I went to one unremarkable dinner-party, but mostly worked in the flat. On Friday I attended Cardus's seventieth birthday lunch. It was held in the deserted restaurant of the Festival Hall, and, though those facing the huge windows had a lovely wide view of the river (did you know that the clock on top of the Shell building is known as Big Benzine?) the others (of whom I was one) might have been in any provincial hotel out of season. Forty-seven people turned up, and during the preliminary drinks I had some talk with Ivor Brown (nice as ever but even more liberally spread with scurf, cigarette-ash and shaving-soap than usual), Lady Violet Bonham-Carter (who I think must have strayed in from some other function, since she clearly had no connection with this one), John Arlott and others. The only other cricketer present was John Woodcock, the Cricket Correspondent of *The Times*, but just as I was about to question him about Australia, we were summoned to lunch. I was between an immensely vivacious lady pianist and the No 2. music critic of the *Daily Telegraph*, a pleasant-spoken young man with an Old Wykhamist tie and eyes almost touching (each other, not the tie). Most of the other guests were musicians or critics, with Arthur Bliss and Moiseiwitsch at the top table. It was rather fun, and surprisingly easy, fitting the odd faces to the still odder names which I have so long passed quickly by in newspapers. The genial little foreigner with black hairs growing on the top of his nose could only be Mosco Carner, and naturally the tall bearded Levantine was Felix Aprahamian of the *Sunday Times*, the balding intellectual Desmond Shawe-Taylor, and so on. Malcolm Sargent made a suitable speech and Neville responded. Then some tributes from absent friends were read out—from Ernest Newman, Bruno Walter, etc, and that was that. I think Neville was delighted with it all. He looks just the same as he did twenty-five years ago. The lunch itself was eatable rather than memorable.

Tonight I must review five thrillers, and read (much of it for the third time, and it doesn't grow on me) the latest manuscript of three quarters of the first volume of Stephen Potter's autobiography. Before condemning the vanity of authors (as I do every day) one should re-flect that it is pretty well all they have to sustain them in their lonely task, and that it is present in the great no less than in the minor scribes.

On May 9 I have agreed to take part in another W.H. Smith 'brains trust'—chiefly because it's at Giggleswick School, which I'd love to see. Wasn't Agate there, or do I dream? Anyhow it's in *Yorkshire*, whither, two months today, I shall be blissfully hurrying. You've no idea how, all through the year, Ruth and I dream and scheme in preparation for this brief respite. But then I suppose most people have no such solace.

9 *April 1959*   *Grundisburgh*

Cold apple-tart I hope, and then I am with you. George Wyndham practically sacked his cook if she ever sent it up hot. But the practical Pamela says that it is very rare to find cold pastry that is not heavy on the tummy, and she may be right. My view is that of the late Mr Justice Day[1]: 'My stomach has got to take what I give it.'

Please give Adam warm congratulations from me. You must be immensely proud of him. And how nice to think that with such a father he will never be one of those philistine scientists. I like the picture of the H-D family quaffing champagne over an intellectual triumph. Usually the magnum is brought out to celebrate a spillikins victory or such-like (what a solemn fuss they make now about table-tennis, and I see a young lady has marched out on finding that her 'sandwich' racquet was forbidden. Is that the racquet with a thin rubber sheet between two of cork? And why forbidden?).

You will have passed by now the lovely 'O evening sun of July' in *The French Revolution,* but you have some tremendous things to come. FitzGerald, whose favourite poet was Crabbe, and clearly found it uncomfortable to be roused, wrote in a letter of 'Carlyle's canvas waves', but surely the authentic sea is audible in the great passages. F. had a good deal of the old woman about him (not perhaps in *l'affaire* Posh[2]!) —easily shocked, e.g. by Hardy, George Eliot, and even Browning; and I gather the real Omar had a fine oriental salacity in many lines, expurgated by F. Did you see that long thing on *The Rubaiyat* in the *T.L.S.* in which the writer thanked heaven the Omar Khayyam Club had ceased to exist? But it met last fortnight and does so annually and flourishingly, as a correspondent last week pointed out. Surely the editor should have put a brief apology? I dined there once as a guest,

[1] Sir John Charles Frederic Sigismund Day (1826–1908), Judge in the Queen's Bench Division.

[2] Nickname of Joseph Fletcher, a Lowestoft fisherman to whom FitzGerald was much attached.

but the speeches were disappointing. Oscar Wilde's son was in the chair, and a voluble but unaware American guest made some observations about homosexuality. How cautious one has to be! Do you remember poor old Thackeray facetiously telling a man who had just made a balloon ascent that he couldn't imagine how anyone could do such a thing unless perhaps he was a dentist in ordinary life—and of course it turned out that the man *was*!

I *am* sorry about G.M. Young because I find his stuff immensely re-paying. His mere learning is surely quite staggering; and he some-times makes the characteristic All Souls error of over-rating his readers' knowledge and being teasingly allusive. But he has given me much enjoyment. Now for the Kenneth Grahame book, preparatory to which I have read *The Wind in the Willows*. There is *some* fun in it but much less than in e.g. 'The Reluctant Dragon'. I have a suspicion I shall resent young Peter Green, but maybe not: I look forward to hearing from you and Ruth at *6 p.m. next Tuesday* exactly what I ought to think. Will old Bernard Darwin by any chance be at the Lit. Soc? I should like another crack with him, though he writes better than he talks.

I am glad the Cardus lunch went well, though surely the cricket-world was poorly represented. Is my feeling correct that he is not altogether *persona grata* there? I could not help sending a word of good wishes to N.C., as one who loves his charm and skill with words (per-haps that was why Lady Violet was there?) and have spent an hour this morning re-discovering how unfadingly good *Good Days* and *A Cricketer's Book* are. I once tried to get N.C. made a member of the M.C.C. as the laureate of the game, but failed dismally.

Yes, old Agate was at Giggleswick. Tuppy always alleged that he knew a man called Wigglesworth who lived at Biggleswade and was educated at Giggleswick. But I don't think we believed him. I fancy the clientèle is mainly local.

11 April 1959   *Bromsden Farm*

I'm going to try and post this tomorrow, so as to make sure of your getting it before you leave for London. In fact you're lucky to get a letter at all, for on Wednesday morning I woke up with an incipient stye in my eye. It got steadily larger and more crippling, and on Thursday evening I sought out a doctor who gave me three kinds of penicillin (capsules, drops and ointment), which are just now beginning to take effect. As luck would have it, Wednesday and Thursday were two frantically busy days, so that by yesterday I was half-blind and wholly idiotic. Today I have solaced myself by watching the bird-table, where a *pair* of nuthatches have been regular visitors, among tits, chaffinches and robins. And *then,* to delight me, there arrived a spotted woodpecker—black-and-white with a pillar-box-red under-side to its tail. Much too big for the table, and immensely shy, constantly climbing up the stem and taking fright before it reached the top.

I'm happy to say my beloved Ruth got home safely last night, though I shan't see her till Monday. I told her my stye was psychosomatic and symbolised my tears at her absence.

On Tuesday, at the bibliographical dining club, I had some talk with Robert Birley and he convinced me that today *Oxford* is in fact the place to send a budding scientist, so, with a sigh of relief and a brief pang for the lost delights of King's, I switch my thoughts back where they belong. Birley was entirely human, forthcoming and *un*-shy, and I enjoyed seeing him. At dinner I sat him between Sparrow and John Hayward.

G.M. Young's assumption of knowledge in his reader I find almost as flattering as irritating. Sometimes I tried to make him explain an allusion for the benefit of the weaker vessels, but he invariably refused incredulously. Nowadays when most writing is directed at the semi-literate I respond to some sort of a challenge, though I shall never get anywhere near the standard of Macaulay's schoolboy. Sparrow told me the other day that G.M. is now pretty well gaga, which causes some confusion in hall and common room. Sparrow is his literary executor, and some years ago G.M. told him to destroy all unpublished writings. I doubt if there are many, but certainly G.M.'s letters should be preserved, and perhaps some published. I have quite a lot.

Jonah was seventy-four last Monday and was much pleased at my sending him a greetings telegram. He will be at the Lit. Soc., and his new book will soon be in proof.

One day I trekked again to Putney and had lunch by Arthur Ransome's bed in which the poor old boy has now been for four months. He's bored stiff, can't sleep and is often in pain: clearly my visits distract and amuse him, but the journey takes an hour each way (with a change and wait on the underground) so I don't go as often as I should.

The Obscenity committee on Thursday held what I hope may be one of its last meetings, for on April 24 our Bill (amended but not disastrously) comes up for Report and Third Reading.

Diana Cooper's second volume is ready and will go to you next week—in time to prevent your being tempted to read the extracts in the *Sunday Times*. Fleming's book comes out a month later. As far as possible we try to stagger the appearance of our more successful books.

The Budget leaves my withers unwrung: I suppose we're all fractionally better off, but it doesn't seem enough to get excited about. Beer I seldom drink, and a commercial-vehicle-chassis plays no part in my life—or yours. The printing strike looms distantly, but I lose no sleep on its account.

15 April 1959   *Grundisburgh*

Your birds, I think, make more of a show than ours do. But have you ever glimpsed a kingfisher? I have *once*, and never again, but once is enough to set one living in hope continuously. And—here is *my* bit of swagger—has your robin ever sat on your mowing-machine *as you mowed*?

Yes, but don't forget R. Birley is a fanatic Oxonian, and wouldn't even admit A.J.P. Taylor to be truculent, or Trevor-Roper conceited. But loth as I am to admit it, I do think O. has something which C. has not, apart from their respective curricula.

I go to Cambridge this afternoon to discuss the G.C.E.—and mainly to say without infuriating them why the other boards have a less civilised approach to examining in Eng. Lit. than the O. and C. which I represent. As it must involve my throwing buckets of doubt on the value of *any* examining on Eng. Lit. I shall, as you see, be treading on thin ice. But I am *always* aware of the wisdom of Jelly Churchill's saying that Eng. Lit. should certainly be taught in school, by those who knew *and loved* it, but never examined on.

Your account of G.M.Y. reminds me of an Eton occasion when the classical pundits, from Rawlins downwards, were puzzled by something in, I think, Tacitus, and someone suggested to Gow that he should put the question to Housman. Gow refused, on the grounds that H. would merely say that the meaning was obvious to the feeblest intellect—and never say what it was. The old curmudgeon!

Jonah was *delighted* by your birthday greetings. He really is rather a disarming old dear; he so loves being kindly treated. Ivor B. was excellent value, and so was Peter F.—an immensely likeable fellow—and no bores darkened the doors. Ivor B. maintained that N. Cardus is not so much deaf in the ordinary sense, but that as he never *has* listened to anything said to him, he now can't! Jonah, alas, was not greatly attracted by the Johnson Club, especially when I told him S.C. Roberts's paper was well above our average. We both agreed on the vast superiority of the Lit. Soc. evenings and also on the major reason, i.e. the greater intelligence, trouble, tact, humanity, spirituality, loving-kindness, and general qualities of body, soul and spirit of the Lit. Soc. Secretary.

Monday morning, 20 April 1959   *Bromsden Farm*

Alas, I must have got up too soon, for the flu counter-attacked savagely and I have been in bed all week-end. Still there, in fact, with some fever. Cannot read or write properly, but will send you a letter as soon as I can.

St George's Day [23 April] 1959   *Grundisburgh*

Stupid of me! Not that it would have made any difference (Ruth did not contradict me when I suggested that, like Winston and in fact all good men, you were a very bad patient!). But if you had used the word *flu* I would have told you what all doctors have said about the '59 germ, viz that it is in itself fairly mild, but convalescence from it is slow. Any number I have met complain that though soon past the worst, they feel second-rate for a longish time. Hope you have a good leech. Mine is a charming man, but I sometimes wonder if it is the *whole* duty of doctors to agree genially with the patient's diagnosis of his case. Still, as a body they have found out so much in the last thirty years as to make it certain that the earth will be intolerably full in twenty years time. Anyway so says Huxley in his revision of *Brave New World*, *not* a cheerful book! And fancy an accurate and literary scientist misquoting 'And *beer* do more than Milton can To justify God's ways to man.'[1] Do you know the worst misquote in the language? Andrew Lang in his History of English Literature (mercilessly trounced by Henry James) has 'All the charm of all the Muses, flowering often in some lonely wood'.[2] And wasn't he a friend of Tennyson's—who never forgave Sir William Harcourt for referring to his 'earliest pipe of half-awakened birds-eye'? Ivor Brown told me that C.E. Montague often misquoted, and defended himself on the ground that it was pedantry to verify by looking up. I don't agree, do you? The printed word should be as accurate as possible. *You* never pass a misquote in a proof I bet. Pamela is highly appreciative of Diana Cooper's second volume, though she found rather too much about *The Miracle*. I haven't read it yet, but start to-night.

My meeting at Cambridge over the G.C.E. went off all right, though a young bearded highbrow from the north objected to my saying that answers on poetry produced dictated judgments and second-hand raptures (which of course is luminously true, as Gore used to say). How common in matters educational, religious or political is high-minded cant! The young beardie maintained that it is not hard to teach the young how to enjoy poetry. Nor is it—if a teacher is *first-rate*. And how many first-rate teachers are there? I have met four in thirty-seven years—and none of them taught Eng. Lit., which is the hardest subject.

This is an interim report, so to say. More would bring the temperature up again. By the way Pamela, chuckling last night, proclaimed, what no one else has seen, a similarity between Diana Cooper

[1] It should be 'malt' (A.E. Housman, *A Shropshire Lad*, lxii).
[2] All the charm of all the Muses, often flowering in a lonely word.
(Tennyson, 'To Virgil')

and me! Only I fear in one respect, i.e. when Duff was late for something, she was convinced he was dead. I am exactly the same about her or indeed any of the family.

24 *April 1959*   *Bromsden Farm*

Delighted with your letter to-day. Still bedridden, feverish, unable to read, write or think. Perhaps *jaundice* now plays a part. If I could find the wall I'd turn my face to it like Mrs Dombey. Will write when I can.

28 *April 1959*   *Grundisburgh*

There is no evidence that anyone about to have jaundice regards a letter with anything but the same nausea which is instantly produced by the mere thought of eggs and bacon, fried sole, mushrooms on toast, cheese remmykin etc, but there is perhaps the faint chance that it might not.

You would, I think, be incredulous and amused to know how much I hate your being ill. I feel quite inclined to act as old Carlyle did—i.e. sent a bottle of Mrs C's medicine to an ailing friend, having no idea what it was supposed to cure, or what the friend had—an action which he somehow did not think incompatible with his conviction, communicated to a doctor, that a man might just as well pour his complaints into 'the long hairy ears of any jackass on the road' as into a doctor's.

But how is that immense pile accumulating on your desk to be dealt with? I don't suppose I could help, could I? I am at present engaged in writing brief biographies of more or less otiose people like Surrey and Langland and Lydgate. The last, if you please, they used confidently to class with Chaucer. I nearly misjudged Porson when he wrote of Southey's *Madoc* that 'it would be remembered when Homer and Virgil were forgotten', but he regained his pedestal with a bound by adding 'and not till then'.

The ink keeps on drying on this letter, because I am in the summer-house, there is a cherry-tree on my left front, an almond (or is it a prunus?) on my right ditto, and as you know, 'fifty years are little room'[1] to get the full benison of things in bloom; while the sun is out, what *is* there to do but just look? It has been a *good* April, i.e. plenty of rain and not too warm, so it won't upset the summer, or at least oughtn't to. The cuckoo appeared here on the same day as last year, i.e. Shakespeare's birthday—very tentative and his vocal chords clearly needing lubricating. But I suppose you with your nuthatches think very small beer of the cuckoo. Close to he is oddly rough; as the *Irish R.M.* ladies said: 'Not thus does the spirit-voice poise the twin notes in tireless mystery along the wooded shores of Connemara lake,' and even the jaundice-germ must admit, that is a lovely sentence, and Maugham and Murry and Dobrée and Leavis and Orwell (who thought the word 'loveliness' *mushy*) can go to hell. Can you face *music* in bed? It won't do you any harm to sleep as much as you can; you must have heavy arrears to make up.

I liked Diana Cooper's book, though not so much as the first volume chiefly because there are fewer letters from Duff. There are some good portraits in it, and Conrad Russell's letters are good value. He used to come to Tuppy's from time to time, and I loved his slow calm wisdom and humour. Tuppy took him once to dine with a bachelor colony, i.e. Chute, R.A. Young, and Sam Slater. Each came in separately and Conrad afterwards said there should have been some sort of warning, as a guest might easily have a weak heart. They were about as ugly a trio as you can imagine.

I say what an odd and brutal affair U.S.A. law is! That old Sacco and Vanzetti case was bad enough, and now I read that Leopold (who with Loeb murdered a boy for fun in 1924) after thirty years in prison, when his sentence came up for revision was sent back for twelve years. He made good in prison, and did a lot of good scientific work for the U.S.A. in the war. Where is the sense or humanity in that? He was nineteen at the time of the murder and in 1954 had done *twice* as long as an English life-sentence. I wonder what old Judge Wendell Holmes, the wisest of men, would have said.

[1] A.E. Housman, *A Shropshire Lad*, ii.

Now for Ethel Smyth. I have glanced at four pages, and on each there is a row with some very old friend. Why did V. Woolf say she couldn't write? A little occasional loose grammar doesn't mean you can't write, does it? Her two volumes of autobiography are (to me) immeasurably better reading than e.g. *The Waves*. I always, by the way, hated 'Lisl', and expect to hate her more. Nor could I ten years ago do with that fluffy-looking Brewster. E.S. herself I expect to like immensely, though I dare say she could infuriate. In 1879 she was furious with my Uncle Edward for upsetting the cream-jug over Lisl's black velvet dress, and merely saying, 'That's what comes of gesticulating.' Poor U.E. How should *he* know that cream-laid velvet is never the same again?

Shall you manage the Lit. Soc. in a fortnight? And if not how will it survive? If Bernard Fergusson is there let us ask him wasn't Wingate *quite* intolerable as a man. A general nearby says not only that he was, but that his Chindit ventures really achieved very little and used up a lot of men and money. I suppose orthodox soldiers do say that.

4 *May 1959*   *Grundisburgh*

This is far beyond a joke, even for Nature who loves over-doing things (e.g. drought, rainfall etc). Jaundice is one of her worst ploys— on and on, and human beings share the same pedestal of repulsiveness with steamed fish, which was for days all they allowed me. Not that one wants *anything* much. All summed up in that great sonnet's line 'With what I most enjoy contented least'.[1] The foul thing is just a poison envenoming one's whole body and mind. No chance, I fear, of seeing you at the Lit. Soc. next week. You must have got a very virulent germ at the start. I suppose the leeches do know something of flu by now, and jaundice too. Such ailments as I have are incurable but happily mild. Gow's Itch is one, and the other will shortly be in the manuals as Lyttelton's Finger-Tingle. Gow is an excellent friend to have, because *any* ache or pain one may start he has always had far worse for years and knows all the ropes.

[1] Shakespeare, Sonnet 29.

My letters can hardly help being very dull, because whatever live-liness they may ever have comes from the impact of yours; there is no spark from flint if there is no steel. You must say at once as soon as they show any tendency to turn the yellow ochre of your ailment to gamboge. Do you remember old Johnson's reply to Boswell's com-plaint that he did not write: 'Do not fancy that an intermission of writing is a decay of kindness. No man is always in a disposition to write; nor has any man at all times something to say.' What even his penetration did not reach to was the man who has nothing to say, but none the less writes, a less common breed perhaps than those who talk without anything to say, but equally calling for suppression. This is of course the age of jaw, and how it darkens counsel. Nothing can happen anywhere without a spate of comment, and when men like Rothermere and Cecil King are at the top, one knows that the com-ment will be framed to start more comment.

I have just heard from someone who has recently seen Percy Lubbock. He is almost quite blind and longing to be off; but he has a nice young intelligent Old Westminster boy who is a good reader, which makes a great difference to P. My informant, Wilfrid Blunt, says the young man is getting rather a bellyful of Henry James (*The Bostonians* mainly, I think. Is that one of the hard ones? I never read it) and also, inexplicably, Arthur Benson—some of his biographical sketches, no doubt. Not surely *The Upton Letters* etc which, in that nice French phrase, do not permit themselves to be read now. In fact their vogue was gone before he died in 1925. And I imagine E.F's novels and R.H's are as dead as A.C.B's. A very odd brotherhood, so clever, and humorous and self-conscious and ultimately rather futile. The old father must have been a terror, with his temper and insomnia, and intolerance and lack of humour, and religion.

I have just, by the way, finished Ethel Smyth's Life, with great enjoyment. Rather too much about her music and the fuss she kicked up about it, but that doesn't matter, and in all else the excessive old termagant is good fun to read about. The sequence in nearly all her personal contacts recurs regularly—*Schwärmerei*, rage and disagree-ment, estrangement. I agree with Julia Brewster—the wronged wife—who said 'One has to be very well, Ethel, to enjoy your company' (or words to that effect). It is interesting to read that Virginia Woolf

241

admired her writing (to E.S.) and ran it down to Lytton Strachey. I believe the explanation to be that L.S. was a man with whom communication was apt to have a contemptuous or denigratory tone, particularly about successful contemporaries. Not a really honest man, I put it to you. He admitted that he had no evidence for saying Dr Arnold's legs were rather too short. A small point no doubt, but *'ex pede Herculem.'*[1] But these Bloomsbury highbrows didn't really think any writing good but their own kind, did they?

I have just written brief biographies of Lydgate and Malory. L. is abysmal, M. is sometimes on the *Iliad* level. Why don't you bring out an abbreviated *Morte D'Arthur*? Perhaps it has been done. Do you know the 'Chapel Perilous' chapter? or 'Balin and Balan' or Lancelot's fight with 'Turquine'? The man—very likely without knowing it—was an *artist*.

10 May 1959   *Bromsden Farm*

I am so touched by the skill and fidelity with which you carry on the rally with no one on the other side of the net. Bless you—your letters are a great joy.

Alas, I am still in bed (three weeks yesterday) and still not fully *compos mentis*. Trying to concentrate for more than a minute or two makes me sweat and feel dizzy. But it's all getting better, and I am far less suicidal. For a fortnight the bemused contemplation of Death—or, as they say nowadays, Total Disengagement—was my constant habit.

Comfort said 'Why don't you read some of your beloved Scott?' But I could face nothing: even a glance through *The Times* reduced me almost to tears (the effort, I mean, not the contents). Now I have got as far as Dorothy Sayers, whose works I am *very slowly* re-reading with much pleasure.

Comfort has to be away teaching most of each weekday, and since there's no one else here she sent an S.O.S. to Ruth, who has been here for the inside of the past two weeks, and returns again this evening. The two of them get on well, so I am wonderfully looked after, and not separated from R.

[1] (We recognise) Hercules from his foot.

Adam has been made keeper of the Junior [cricket side]: when Duff was keeper they won the cup.

Goodness knows when I shall be up or back. We're (R and I) still hoping to take our Yorkshire holiday as planned—but I'll let you know.

In my next letter I'll answer all yours and try to provide better value. This is just to take you my love and tell you that I think I shall survive. The mainspring broke, but the repairers are good these days.

13 May 1959   *Grundisburgh*

Well at least you *are* on the mend, and the really pestilential period is over. Much sympathy was expressed for you at the Lit. Soc. No ailment gets a poorer press than jaundice. Tommy L. says he has had it three times. There was quite a good gathering, just over a dozen. I sat between Ivor Brown and Cuthbert, who was positively sunny. The sun of January rather than of June perhaps, but I am bound to say I found his talk of good astringent quality, and though his valuation of his fellow-men was a long way from being gushing, it was not indiscriminate.

We were in the small room, so there wasn't much *va et vient* afterwards. I had precisely the same conversation with Lockhart that I have had several times, every time in fact before. Luckily I cannot catch more than a word or two, so can simulate fresh interest fairly plausibly. The gist of it is that K.G. Macleod's heart is not what it was; that he is otherwise in good fettle; that with his ability he could have done great things, had he had to, or wanted to; that don't I think he was the greatest athlete ever. I say something about C.B. Fry, he burbles a long sentence of which I glean the gist to be that no, K.G. was the greatest, because he never trained or took any trouble. Here the good Ivor comes trenchantly in and says that is a point in K.G.'s *dis*favour, not the opposite. More burbling, happily *quite* inaudible. It is not you see a thrilling intercourse, but what can I do? I think he supposes that a former putter of the weight is neither able nor willing to talk of anything but the athletic prowess of half-a-century ago.

How immensely encouraging and civilised is what you tell me about Comfort and Ruth happily meeting—the kind of thing that renews one's faith in human nature, which is constantly in need of renewal in a world of politicians and press magnates. (You will not, please, omit to give R. my love.) I found Trollope was the first reading I could face without feeling sick. Tuppy once said a Trollope novel was the best reading in the train, because, *inter alia*, if the wind did blow over a few pages while you took a nap, it didn't matter; you just went on. What was the story about a man who couldn't stop reading a scabrous novel, but at the same time disapproved of it so strongly that he tore out each page when finished and threw it out of the carriage-window? The sort of thing Pepys or Boswell might have done.

In all the letters about Latin I have seen, no one has pointed out that the main reason for preferring Latin to, say, Russian is that half the English language comes from it. In that list of Headmasters in last week's *Sunday Times*, the canvas of the so-called public schools showed them pretty equally divided, roughly all the upper ten (snob!), Eton, Harrow, Winchester, Rugby, Marlborough etc were pro-compulsory Latin, and all the Worksops and Jerseys etc were anti. Not but what some of the stock claims for the study of Latin aren't pretty silly and indeed dishonest. Old A.B. Ramsay somehow managed to persuade himself that it was the *stupidest* boys who got most out of it, which, as the Euclid of my youth used to say, is absurd. But fancy talking of this to one with jaundice!

Roger F. and his wife have just been here—very good company. R. had to supply a brief biography of himself for the back of some Penguin; he will not, I gather, have put in such items as some do, viz Agatha Christie: 'I enjoy my food'—though that appears to be true enough, someone who met her recently reporting that she is enormous. R. is very bad for Pamela, as he often says that we ought all to spend much more money than we do—'every woman being at heart a rake'[1] so to speak. R. has just bought a silk umbrella for £8 odd. So have I—a cotton one costing £1. 15. 0. Do you think my wife is pleased? Not a bit of it—derisive! We took them over recently to see a water-mill of

[1] Pope, 'Epistle to a Lady'.

great age; recently vacated, but leaving on a shutter a number of sea-side picture-postcards which the last miller (obviously a lineal descendant of Chaucer's) had thought funny. So did R. He was particularly tickled by a rustic contemplating two huge show-potatoes labelled 'King Edwards' and saying 'Lummy!—I should have thought they were King Kongs.' It *is* good, as all the rustic was getting wrong was seeing the final 's' in each name as possessive—not plural.

I have read little since Ethel Smyth. I rather liked some quotations from Pfeiffer on old Maugham[1]; 'a good writer of the second rank' is surely right? And the judgment that M's view of life remains what it was at twenty-five is not amiss. And about his friends' visits: 'He looks forward so eagerly to their visits that by the time that they arrive he has had almost enough of them.' 'New friends give him more pleasure than old ones, for they are unexplored territory' was even more pithily put by Tommy L. 'That faint hostility which he calls tolerance.' Who is Pfeiffer?

Whit Monday, 18 May 1959   *Bromsden Farm*

Forgive the biro. I am writing in bed, though since last Wednesday I have been up for an increasing part of each day. That lovely weather was a great help, and I am gradually feeling less groggy and dotty. I sent for all the Wilde material, but haven't yet felt strong enough to tackle it.

Yesterday Comfort and Bridget drove over to Eton and took Adam to see the Duke of Edinburgh play polo in Windsor Park, which they all enjoyed greatly. Ruth and I stayed peacefully here by the fire. On Wednesday morning R. is going to drive me to the sea—probably Brighton or Worthing, where we plan to stay about a week. No rooms are booked, so perhaps you'd better write here, and I'll see that it's forwarded.

Now I'm going to re-read your last *five* letters, none of which has been answered, and will comment here and there.

Most of the time I just slept (one night delirious) and dozed. I had a small radio by the bed, but couldn't bear to have it on. Duff last

[1] *Somerset Maugham, a Candid Portrait* by Karl G. Pfeiffer (1959).

week made 65 not out in twenty minutes for Butterflies v. Worcester. He was dropped in the deep *eight* times (four times by the same chap), and two of the drops ricocheted over for sixes. Today he plays for Fleming v. Nettlebed, and so does Tim. I loved your description of the Lit. Soc.

Next week, stimulated by sea-air, I shall hope to send you a full-length letter. To-day even these two miserable sides make my head spin muzzily. Ruth sends her love—and so do I.

21 May 1959   *Grundisburgh*

What a time you have had! Delirium one night? Did you say the most awful things, as apparently one's subconscious self is a sort of Mr Hyde, and reduces Rabelais to whistle in the matter of vocabulary. Delirious vestal virgins pour out a stream of words they never knew—like the young lady late for dinner, as recorded by Cherry-Garrard illustrating the danger of too great innocence, which I would tell you, if I didn't suspect that I have done so already. Were you prayed for in Henley church? You would have been here; our rector prays for people without being asked to, and once did so for an elderly gentleman who was present, some alarmist villager having said two days before that 'poor Mr Barker had gone to hospital'. And so he had—to have an ingrowing toe-nail dealt with, or something equally un-lethal.

I hope you are past the steamed cod stage in the way of diet, and are on the way to old Heythorp's dinner (Oh no, no R in the month, so no oysters). But you will soon pick up at Brighthelmstone with your lovely companion. (How few people—or drugs!—are *both* tonic *and* sedative.)

I like your tale of Duff's innings on the loveliest cricket-ground in the world—Worcester College. My nephew Charles once hit a ball so far into a neighbouring wood there that it was no good attempting to find it, and no attempt was made. A man *did* go and look for a later hit, and after five minutes a party went out to look for *him*. Charles was a fine hitter and escaped the danger of being caught by an out-fielder by always carrying the lot. There is something majestic about being missed eight times—the sort of thing that used to happen whenever I watched my Junior—when they were in the field. Tuppy wouldn't, couldn't, watch his. He once told us why not. A and B were batting, C bowling. A hit a catch to short-leg (D) and didn't call, so B ran and arrived at A's ground. D missed the catch, but picked up and threw the ball—to the wrong end, where A and B were. B started back to his ground; the wicket-keeper (E) threw the ball to the bowler who broke the wicket when B was still yards away. But he couldn't be given out because there was no umpire, which nobody had noticed. Tuppy added or invented a good many more incidents, but the above ones are *true*. He was quite right—nothing is more degradingly futile than really bad cricket, to play or to watch. I don't mean not very skilful cricket, but cricket not seriously played. Do you know my old friend Harry Altham, the new M.C.C. president? A very good man, excellent cricketer in his day and full of commonsense—an oddly rare combination. He is one of the Governors of North Foreland Lodge girls' school where I (the Chairman) make a speech next week on their fiftieth anniversary. I am in labour with the speech now, but haven't got further than a striking parallel between the present head-mistress and Mad Margaret in *Ruddigore*. As the Bishop of Winchester is also giving an address, I am leaving most of the 'uplift' to him. These occasions are I suppose inevitable but they are none the less dreadful.

I am quite out of touch nowadays. I read *Punch*, *Spectator*, *New Statesman* every week, and I don't understand half what they are talking about, or their comments. So many of the reviewers and commentators seem to be intent on a sort of slick profundity. Perhaps they are all very young. I have just got from the library Swinnerton's last novel. Pamela has begun it and says it promises well. Diana last week left behind *Dunkerleys* by Howard Spring and I read it in bed—with enjoyment. It is full of people who are human. Do you put H.S. high? I am a genuine Blimp and ready at any moment to say out loud 'I must say I do like a good story', risking the acid query: 'Why must you say it?' And I am just about to write a thousand words on Chaucer after finishing five hundred on 'the moral' (and intolerable) Gower. I see no prospect of ever being strong enough to tackle Occleve.

I shall have to disgorge five guineas for the new *D.N.B.* volume just out. Do you ever contribute? I was once asked to—about Ranji—

but knowing nothing about his political career in India I declined. Probably I should have come under the lash of that old pedant (was it Churton Collins?) who found over a hundred errors in the first twenty pages of the volume he looked at.

Foully cold to-day. I doubt if you are bathing. Here we *always* begin May with a dazzling week, and follow it with a North Wind full of spikes, and lingering like an unloved guest. I am, so to speak, only just in the summer-house. The Yank family is ensconced over the old stables. Very friendly and happy. P. told them the orchard was the children's playground, but they never go near it, preferring the dusty little yard giving onto the road. I asked the four-year-old why they didn't go into the orchard and got the answer: 'There's chickens there; they might bite me.' Like giving a child a really fascinating toy. After two days it is again concentrating all its interest and affection on a faceless doll, or battered bar of wood, or tailless rocking-horse that doesn't rock.

Get well at once please, Rupert. Breathe deeply, eat heavily, sleep deeply, and don't dream of dizzying yourself with writing a long letter. Love to Ruth. I hope she rules the convalescent with a rod of iron—beautifully camouflaged in velvet.

25 May 1959   *Dudley Hotel, Hove*

Your splendid letter reached me this morning, and I read it aloud to Ruth on the promenade, to both our delights. The improvement in my health is startling. Last Wednesday Ruth drove me the ninety miles from Bromsden (in constant rain) and I was quite exhausted when we arrived. This hotel, though wildly expensive, is thoroughly comfortable, with masses of delicious food. We have a charming room on the top floor, with our own bathroom. The weather has steadily improved, and yesterday (a scorcher) we both *bathed*! The sea was *icy*, and we stayed in for seconds only. On Saturday we spent the afternoon watching Sussex v. Glos and were impressed by Parks, J. both as batsman and wicket-keeper: also by the batting of Lenham, a gainly young man with a fine free style. One of the umpires was Fagg, A., who, you will instantly recollect, is the only man to have scored two double centuries in the same first-class match.

I am allowed to eat anything, but forbidden alcohol for three months.

I don't think I've ever read anything of Howard Spring's. Life seemed too short. Nor have I ever contributed to the *D.N.B.*, though I suggested many revisions (which he made) in Michael Sadleir's article on Hugh Walpole (in this new volume) and in Harold Nicolson's article on my Uncle Duff (which will be in the next). Here I am slowly re-reading E. Blunden's *Cricket Country* with much enjoyment. You must have read it: do you remember the wonderful description of the household of the Hon William Somebody (the book is upstairs)? Answer this question.

On Thursday we shall reluctantly drive back to Bromsden, so write there, and I shall hope to answer in a letter of normal length.

Who would have believed that Dulles's death could cause all this brouhaha? Will the Court go into mourning when Selwyn Lloyd shuffles off this mortal coil?

27 *May 1959*   *Grundisburgh*

Good! But I am not surprised: I thought the presence of Ruth would do what no leech with his potions could manage. But no alcohol for three months is rather severe. I don't remember that twist of the rack when I had the damned thing. But as so often happens, one suspects that the faculty doesn't know all that about an ailment. Otherwise why should they differ so much as they do in the treatment? The doctor I had at Eton in the nineties had one treatment for practically everything, 'a hot bath and a hot drink and get to bed', and his patients did just as well as anybody else's. In those days we had 'growing pains' which ascended the hierarchy in succeeding years as rheumatism, lumbago, fibrositis and slipped disc without anyone discovering the cure for any of them.

Cricket Country of course I know, and possess, though where the heck it is now who can say? Books do hide themselves uncannily.

I wonder how old Ivor B. will do at Malvern. I have warned him of the twittering vapidities of the school play on the evening before. I suppose Salathiel Pavy[1] must have played Lady Macbeth and Desdemona adequately somehow, but girls playing men make me shudder. Their thin little voices! Sir Anthony Absolute I remember sounded like an angry starling. We shall see.

There was a lot of absurd fuss about Dulles. A year ago we all said (rightly) what a stubborn old nuisance he was, and now we slobber bibfuls about him. I am reading Gunther on *Inside Russia*. *Most* interesting. Not too much politics and economics, and what there is I skip. Do you realise there is *no* golf-course in all Russia, and that a hat costs £14 and boots £70?

Can you face the printed page yet? Pamela was a bit disappointed with F. Swinnerton. Too complicated, she said. I shall take it to Eton on Friday, my H.Q. for North Foreland Lodge on Saturday when I face the monstrous regiment of women. One story I shall tell which they will like. Do you know it? The girl who had the question 'Where are elephants found?' She had no idea, so wrote: 'Elephants are enormous and highly intelligent animals and are very seldom lost.' But I often suspect you know *all* my stories. How kind you are about them! Love to Ruth. Some things however well known and established must none the less always be expressed. Taking divine and other blessings for granted is one of humanity's worst stupidities.

29 *May 1959*   *Bromsden Farm*

I think the only way of sending you a full-length letter this week is to make it a serial and write a page a day. Ruth and I drove back from Brighton yesterday, your letter arrived punctually this morning, and then Ruth drove home to Hampstead. I miss her dreadfully, but we shall be reunited on Monday, and on Friday there are all the joys of our mountain-top before us. We bathed again on Wednesday: the

[1] Boy actor of Shakespeare's time. Ben Jonson's epitaph on him contained these lines:

> Years he number'd scarce thirteen
> When Fates turn'd cruel,
> Yet three fill'd zodiacs had he been
> The stage's jewel.

water, I daresay, was just as cold, but it didn't seem so, and I'm sure that after a week or so I should get quite used to it. We enjoyed the whole Brighton trip enormously—excellent hotel, wonderful weather, no hurry or stress or nuisance. Physically I feel fine (and am so sunburnt that no one will believe I've been ill), but mentally I'm still fairly woolly, and good for only the shortest spells of reading or writing. I have no doubt that this long and enforced rest-cure was badly needed.

Duff has just rung up cheerfully from Oxford. He and seven other drybobs (all members of the college rugger fifteen) managed to pass the necessary scrutiny and are rowing in Eights Week as Worcester IV. They scored a bump on each of the first two days, but are now in the exhausting position of sandwich-boat, having first to row through at the head of their own Division and then catch the tail-ender of the Division above. This looks like being beyond them, and on Saturday (Duff says) they may well get bumped themselves by B.N.C. IV. Have a look at Monday's *Times*.

As a result of our drives to and from Brighton (by different routes) I have firmly decided that I abominate all buildings erected since 1820, and particularly those of this century, ending up with rows of squalid little bungalows that look like insecure anchors for their clusters of television-masts. How comparatively charming and unspoilt the countryside must have been in your youth.

Yesterday Diana Cooper signed copies of her book at Hatchard's, and five hundred copies were sold! Apparently Evelyn Waugh escorted her there, extremely tipsy, and bullied everyone who came into the shop to buy a copy and get it signed! Now I shall relapse into coma and write more tomorrow.

Sunday evening

We were just sitting down to supper last night when Fred's Dame rang up to say that Adam had got a fast ball in the mouth while batting and had been taken to hospital. Later we got on to the hospital and learnt that he had lost one of his front teeth (he had particularly nice ones), poor lamb, and this morning he was reported otherwise all right, except for a bruised and swollen lip. As I have often said before, if it isn't one thing it's another! So far Adam's side have won all three of their Juniors, scoring altogether 460 for the loss of eight wickets: he seems destined to be involved in high scoring, and I only hope this accident won't affect his nerve.

3 June 1959   *Grundisburgh*

It looks as if, fundamentally, Nature or Fate has done you a good turn, viz in making you stay out substantially before you broke down from overwork, as you very well might have. And, dash it all, am I wrong in supposing that it wasn't all worth a week with Ruth? And your northern mountain-top just round the corner. I see it is to be un-settled to-morrow in the north and fine in the south—in fact I suspect a heat-wave, as there invariably is when I go a long train-journey with a heavy suitcase. Ivor B and I go to-morrow to Malvern. He sends me a mysterious postcard saying he will probably be joining my train at Evesham—where, if I remember rightly, it doesn't stop. I used—*aetat* thirteen—sometimes to watch the expresses thunder past Slough, and —I think—the South Wales expresses do ditto past Hagley, and merely swelled with pride when my father stopped our train from Eton at Hagley, which normally it ignored. He was a director of the G.W.R. and had a gold token on his watch-chain which enabled him to travel first-class, free, all over England.

North Foreland Lodge no longer plays cricket, and in the absence of Harry Altham I congratulated them on dropping it and likened women's cricket to what Dr Johnson said of women's preaching.[1] I am not sure they didn't think I was referring to Dr Hewlett Johnson,[2] and not Dr Samuel. The Olympic fencing champion was there, an N.F.L. old girl called Gillian Sheen. She is a professional dentist, and the N.F.L. fencing instructor gravely told me that the wrists which brought her fame in *l'escrime* must guarantee outstanding certainty and despatch among the molars and bicuspids.

I see Duff's pessimism about what would happen on Saturday was, alas, justified. A sandwich-boat has a hard time. My junior four at

[1] 'Sir, a woman's preaching is like a dog's walking on his hinder legs. It is not done well; but you are surprized to find it done at all.'

[2] Popularly known as the 'Red' Dean of Canterbury (1874–1966).

Eton was never as high as that; they had their work cut out usually to keep away from the Maidenhead pleasure-steamer. In a rowing manual I once glanced at I read that there are twenty-eight possible mistakes in putting the oar into the water, i.e. even more complicated than the golf-swing.

How right you are about the countryside. I remember how I used always to feast my thirteen–eighteen-year-old eyes on Oxford as the train approached it—and me a fanatic supporter of Cambridge—and it really is heart-rending to think what Oxford must have looked like a hundred years ago. What with the gasometers and Nuffield and the traffic, it is mere hell in August now.

I hope Diana Cooper's book is filling the firm's coffers. The reviews I have seen are good, though of course the *New Statesman*, *more suo*, has to have its little sneer. Who the devil is Eisenstein who gets a full page in the *T.L.S.*? Pryce-Jones seems to be deliberately making it less readable week by week. But John Carter was good on some egregious Yank professor who seems to have been tampering with Housman's text in a manner which would have burst H's gall-bladder. I cannot imagine what the man will say in reply.

I *am* sorry about Adam's front tooth. It is another black mark against a drought that school-cricket pitches are all horribly fiery, and the parched earth is sprinkled with front teeth. W.G's famous ball from the Australian Jones nearly did the same; after all the beard is only an inch or two away.

On Monday I go to Oxford (c/o R. Mynors Esq, 14A Merton St) and on Wednesday return here. Your address is locked in my bosom. I shall not be sorry to miss the Lit. Soc., *te absente*, and so avoid the censure of Sir Cuthbert.

8 June 1959   *Kisdon Lodge, Keld*

Although I'm writing this on Monday I fear it can't reach you till Wednesday—if then. Our faithful farmer will take it down the hill this evening and it should leave tomorrow. I'm addressing it to Grundisburgh for safety.

My three days in London last week seemed very hot, exhausting and *noisy* after my six weeks in the country. I played about in the office, saw as few people as possible, visited Arthur Ransome in hospital and dined quietly with my father at the St James's Club. There I saw Osbert Sitwell, terribly shaky now with *paralysis agitans* but still just able to eat and drink without help. I gossiped agreeably with him for a little.

The Fourth of June seemed endless. I borrowed my sister's car and at 11 a.m. picked up Alistair Cooke, Eric Linklater and wife, Duff and a girl. Mercifully no rain fell until the last half-hour of the Fireworks. Comfort brought a magnificent picnic of cold chicken and strawberries. Also a splendid new gadget (I think American), a bag which you can fill with ice and bottles. Adam, gap-toothed but cheerful, met us carrying his home-made radio, from which the Test Match commentary was issuing. Comfort took Alistair to see School Yard etc while I watched the cricket, and tried to avoid seeing too many friends, for I soon began to feel dizzy and tired. I did however see Jonah and Evy, John Carter, Peter F. and a few others. Another picnic for tea, more cricket-watching, then an excellent dinner at Monkey Island, though I began to long for an alcoholic restorative. Alistair never stopped talking for a second all day, which was an enormous help and enabled me to remain mum. By the time I had dropped them all and got back to Soho Square it was 1 a.m. and I was too worn out to sleep. However the thought of coming here sustained me through everything. On Friday Ruth and I lunched with my sister in Hampstead and then drove off happily. We had tea in Northampton and stayed the night at Bawtry, just south of Doncaster. That left only a hundred miles for Saturday, and we were in the cottage by 3 p.m., having been driven up the hill with our luggage by the farmer's son in his jeep. His wife had already swept and aired everything and lit a magnificent fire, so we settled in immediately. That night we slept eleven hours, and last night the same. The climate here is quite different from anywhere else. Ever since we arrived a gale has been blowing, with intermittent sun, and we are glad of a fire in the sitting-room all day. We also have a delicious one in the bedroom in the evening. The place is alive with curlews and larks and on the last stage of our drive, coming up the pass from Wensleydale, we saw our first blackcock—great excitement. I have brought the Eddie Marsh biography[1], and on the shelf *How Green was my Valley* awaits me. Otherwise it will be mostly Oscar.

If A.E.H. had destroyed all his scraps, drafts and manuscripts, instead of leaving them to his asinine brother Laurence (whom he despised), none of what Carter rightly complains about would have happened. I see P. Lubbock is eighty: I must write to him.

Ruth has arranged lovely bowls of kingcups and wild geraniums, the grandfather clock ticks peacefully, the wind howls outside, the view is unbelievably beautiful—we are in paradise.

10 June 1959 *Grundisburgh*

I returned here this morning and your letter arrived this evening— the posts of course being cleverly arranged so that one can't answer till the next day. You don't sound all that well yet, but I hope that a spell at Kisdon Lodge will so work that you tread the ling like a buck in spring.[2] Of course the Fourth of June has often reduced men of conspicuous eupepticity and vim to the last state of Augustus the chubby lad.[3] Not since I was a boy do I remember thinking it anything but a day of wrath. It does go on and on. The longest reach is between tea and dinner, or used to be; it was always then that the most boring Old Boys called and simply would *not* go. How would you feel now if a real bore appeared at 6.15 and cheerfully announced straight away that he 'needn't leave' till 8.15, as his party wouldn't be back till then? I gather they have restricted the number of firework-tickets so as to keep out those rowdies who used to turn up tight and throw things about. There is no human being I detest more than the fourth-rate Old Etonian. It was this kind of thing that put an end to Montem,[4] and I have often hoped that June 4 might go the same way. After all

[1] By Christopher Hassall (1959).
[2] Kipling, 'The Ballad of East and West'.
[3] After refusing food for four days:
      'He's like a little bit of thread;
      And on the fifth day he was—dead!'
   From *Struwwelpeter* (1847) by Heinrich Hofmann (1809–1894).
[4] An Eton festival which took place every year from 1561 to 1847.

why make such a fuss of George III? Where did I recently read a demure reference to the undoubted truth that the only Kings of England that were certifiable were the two with whom Eton is most closely connected?[1]

I have a fancy you had *How Green* last year, but never quite got to reading it. I hope you will. The Welsh idiom, to my ear and mind, is as entrancing as J. M. Synge's Irish. There are too some grand scenes and people. I fell without a struggle in love with Bronwen and have never fallen out.

Ivor Brown did very well at Malvern. In the train thither his external appearance was much as you describe. I noticed that his aquascutum (wholly superfluous as the day was hot) was frayed, and gaped in a good many places, but on speech-day he was in spotless dark blue, and they all thought his appearance was most distinguished (it *is* a good face don't you think?). His speech to school and parents was *excellent*; he did not depend as so many do on a handful of funny stories (there were one or two of course), but the serious passages were in exactly the right key, and so well phrased that every ear in the audience was alert: I think he enjoyed the whole thing; he was certainly given a very warm welcome by everyone, old and young.

The book I had with me on all these journeys (Bromsgrove at the week-end) was your uncle's *Talleyrand*. Has it ever been fully appreciated? It seems to me beautifully done. How did he thread his way through the hideous tangles of French Revolution intrigues? T. seems to me a really great man in many ways—so far-sighted and sure in all his counsel, which the little cad of a megalomaniac[2]—so like Adolf H. in many ways—after a time ignored. I am about half-way through.

On Monday my old pupil John Bayley and his wife Iris Murdoch came to dinner. I liked the tousled, heelless, ladder-stockinged little lady—crackling with intelligence but nothing at all of a prig; her only defect as a dinner-neighbour was a too low and rapid utterance. My daughters of course say their father is as deaf as a haddock, but it wasn't only that, as the other guests agreed about her inaudibility.

[1] Henry VI, who founded the school, and George III, who was born on the Fourth of June.
[2] Napoleon Bonaparte.

256

Douglas Veale, the ex-Registrar, claimed to be the only Certificate-examiner whose report had been quoted in *Punch*. He had referred to a 'howler' in a Latin Composition paper, and Graves or someone got hold of it. A boy putting into Latin 'the more I do something or other, so much the more wine I drink' wrote *'eo plum vinum bim'*. He is a charming man and lunched the Abbey School Governors royally—smoked salmon, roast duck, strawberries and cream, plus (or plum) a courtly and consequential hock, and a raffish, anecdotal brandy, to borrow from an old vintner's catalogue.

How right you are about A.E.H. and his folly in leaving his stuff to a brother whose brains he openly derided. Old Gow, who had *some* say, but not much, told me he had great trouble with Laurence, who had *no* discrimination, and A.E. knew it, but none the less left him to print what he thought good and burn the rest. As Gow acidly said, L. didn't know what *was* good. What I find annoying is that so little of A.E's admirable prose survived. He wasn't going to trust anyone with that; one lecture he actually tore into tiny fragments page by page, as he delivered it. The pedantic old churl didn't choose to leave behind him anything not perfect, and, despising the judgment of his fellow-men, he was unmoved by their praise. He was curiously humble about his English prose. All he said about such things as his superb address when George V visited Cambridge was 'It may have a certain amount of form and finish and perhaps a fake air of ease, but there is an awful history behind it.'

15 June 1959   *Kisdon Lodge, Keld*

Your spanking six-pager was brought up the hill by Mr Hutchinson, the faithful farmer, and has given much pleasure. A week here has made all the difference to my health, mental and physical, as I knew it would, and I now feel perfectly well, with another blessed fortnight stretching ahead. The browsing and sluicing might not be to your taste, but they suit us fine. Take yesterday for instance—a heavenly day with fourteen hours of continuous sunshine from a clear blue sky. We got up at 8 (an hour earlier than usual) and breakfasted behind the cottage on the eastern side. Two upright garden-chairs and a pretty portable table. Invariably our breakfast consists of cornflakes (which I never touch elsewhere) with brown sugar and fresh farmer's milk, bread, butter, marmalade and tea. Then I smoke one of the four pipes to which I ration myself each day—large ones, you know, stuffed with strong flake tobacco (Erinmore and Condor Sliced) which I smoke only here. Then, yesterday, we sat all the morning reading, sunbathing, and watching a pair of curlews keeping guard over four mobile babies in the grass. Lunch, also alfresco, consisted of a delicious veal, ham and egg pie which my sister had sent from some special place in Nottingham, with salad, followed by white peaches (from a tin) washed down with lemonade. By mid-afternoon the sun had moved over, so we shifted chairs and table to the front of the cottage, where we can contemplate the extravagantly beautiful view. Tea, out there, is all of the farmer's wife's baking—fruit-cake, shortbread and ginger-biscuits, all first-class. About seven we came in, lit the fire, and at 8 had our accustomed supper of boiled eggs, lemon-curd tart, bread and jam, fruit and Wensleydale cheese, with more tea. Then we draw up our armchairs to the fire and, with the Aladdin lamps on the table behind us, read and gossip till bedtime. I have been concentrating on Oscar, but have also re-read Evelyn Waugh's first book *Decline and Fall*, which is still very amusing, and am plodding through *Eddie Marsh*. I should say two hundred pages could have been cut with advantage. There's a lot of interesting background stuff, but one longs for a bit of foreground, which the impotent old ninny is too dim to provide. It's small beer in a gallon pot, but I shall persevere to the end. *How Green* still beckons from the shelf!

Reverting (as they say) for a moment to browsing, Ruth is always longing to cook elaborate meals, but I won't let her (though she's a wonderful cook) because I want her to have a proper holiday. I relent only on some Sundays, when we have hot meat and occasionally sausages.

So glad Ivor was a success at Malvern: I felt sure he would be. I agree about *Talleyrand*: for a first book it's an astonishing performance. I brought it to Jonathan Cape soon after I arrived there, and its great success did me a lot of good.

You will be pleased to hear that Oscar is at last on the move again, and by the time we leave here (alas!) on the 29th he should (E and O.E.) be ready for the printer. But what use is that, when every printer will be on strike? God knows how long it will last, but it's sure to cause a sickening hold-up in our business.

This morning I have, from the back window, been watching a wheatear feeding its young. I even photographed the operation, but Ruth says it won't come out because of the reflection of the window-pane. We shall see. At the moment R. is upstairs, giving the bedroom a vigorous spring-cleaning. We have fetched the water from the spring and washed up the breakfast things. It's a beautiful day, but so far with little sun, and our fire is already lit (I having cleared out yester-day's before breakfast). I tell you all these domestic details so that you can get some idea of our idyllic existence. Sometime between 5.30 and 7 this evening the farmer will come up to milk his cows, bringing us our letters and Saturday's papers, which we shall read after supper, taking the *Times* crossword in our stride. To-morrow we may possibly go shopping, as it's market day in Hawes, and if we get another scorcher like yesterday we shall drive to the east coast for a bathe—probably to a charming little Victorian watering-place called Saltburn-by-the-Sea, north of Whitby. We've been there once before. To our disappointment there haven't so far been any local sales, but we shall get the local paper this evening. Now I must turn again to Oscar, and soon it will be time for lunch.

18 June 1959   *Grundisburgh*

Lovely! Just what I wanted. I now have the picture of you both pretty clear, and only a snapshot of the countryside—which I don't suppose for a moment you have—is lacking the full-length. The brows-ing does sound just right; I assume you have your eye on the veal and ham pie's successor. Also that you are in the land of baps and ban-nocks, or failing them, what John Buncle called 'extraordinary bread and butter'. (It is much the most absurd book ever written.)[1] The

---

[1] *The Life of John Buncle, Esq.: containing various Observations and Reflections made in several parts of the World, and many Extraordinary Relations* (vol I 1756, vol II 1766) by Thomas Amory, an eccentric Unitarian who was married seven times and died in 1788, aged ninety-seven. Hazlitt called him 'the English Rabelais' and Leigh Hunt published extracts from his work in *A Book for a Corner* (1851), but all agree on his absurdity.

curlews were a nice touch. I hope you agree the ginger biscuits *must* be Huntley & Palmer's. They are Medes and Persians at my table and always have been. (No, I re-read and see that yours are home-made. That is all right, provided you give *no* encouragement to imposters like McVitie & Price.) But one does have shocks. I once met a man who *preferred* shredded marmalade to Cooper's—which is putting Eddie Marsh above Augustus the physically strong, who reverberates through Carlyle's Frederic (always so called). Your supper is the very spit of ours pretty well every Sunday.

That you *still* haven't begun *How Green* cries to Heaven. I suspect you know you won't be able to put it down if you start. Perhaps you will when I tell you emphatically that Ruth is in it all right—not of course the only book where she is.

Granny Gow has just been here for a long week-end, rather too long! He is very infirm and can't do practically anything for himself. And daily becomes more inaudible—he just can't be bothered to speak up.

We have reached the strike season. Already four or five in progress. There is nothing which shows up the folly of *homo sapiens* more clearly. How shall you fill your working hours? What about that book you ought to be writing? Have you dipped into the new *D.N.B.*? It is much less impersonal than the old ones, and Leslie Stephen's motto 'No Flowers' is fairly often ignored. So far it has not had a very good press. There was a silly slating by R.H.S. Crossman in last week's *New Statesman*—so smug and cocksure and Wykehamist—complaining that craftsmen and socialists in industry were inadequately treated. Is the *D.N.B.* meant to be a history of the times? He admits that there have been very few outstanding socialists. I cannot see that Maxton and Ellen Wilkinson are very poorly handled. What, after all, did they *do*?

I am lost in admiration of anyone who does the crossword 'in his/her stride'. I never do it, partly because I don't as often as not understand the clue. I never was the smallest use at any kind of puzzle. Monty James always had a huge jigsaw going; it made me tired to look at it.

I heard from Percy Lubbock to-day—quite a cheerful letter to my surprise. He seems to have plenty of company, and I gather friends played up well for his birthday. That *T.L.S.* man hinted there might be too much Pater in his style. I don't see it. I am not well seen in Pater, but seem to remember that his self-consciousness was nearly always perceptible, and I see no sign of it in *Earlham*. I confess I found P.L's *Edith Wharton* hard going, but largely because I disliked her so much. I suspect Henry James was much tried by her. Gow hates H.J., particularly *The Turn of the Screw*, which he calls an 'obscene' book. And one can't call him exactly prim. I suspect it frightened him, as it well might. Butterwick began it and didn't dare go on. But he always had the liver of a chicken, though a good man at Sotheby's. The book that terrified *me* sixty years ago was *Dracula* and I believe still would; and I didn't much want to read *Uncle Silas*[1] in bed. I once read at Eton a ghost story called 'Thurnley Abbey' to a lot of boys in a room lit by one candle. Some were very pallid when the lights went on. Do you know it?[2]

Eighty-three in the shade! 'Rich and deep was the day, gathering its power, bending its great energy to ripen the teeming garden' (*Earlham*, of course).

Good to hear you are *well* at last. But how could you *not* be with that nurse?

22 June 1959   *Kisdon Lodge, Keld*

I meant to devote all yesterday to my blest pair of sirens, George and Oscar, but the unbroken sunshine of the longest day kept me outside, where there was just enough breeze to make writing tiresome. So I fear this will be a day late.

So glad you approve of our feeding arrangements. When I get back I shall hope to send you some snapshots of our miraculous countryside, but they are difficult to take: we are so perched up that the perspectives go awry and spaciousness becomes a huddle. Still, we are persevering with Ruth's new camera.

---

[1] By Sheridan Le Fanu (1814–1873). Published in 1864.
[2] By Perceval Landon (1869–1927). Published in his *Raw Edges* (1908) and reprinted in *The Supernatural Omnibus*, ed. Montague Summers (1931).

On Saturday night our farmer cut the hay in the fields before and behind us, so now instead of waving flowers and grasses we are surrounded by the delicious smell of new-mown hay, freshened this morning by some heavy rain which fell in the night.

Granny Gow sounds an intolerable visitor: thank God we haven't got him here! In fact we want no visitors at all, and even resent a passing hiker miles away. I completely agree about R.H.S. Crossman, though maybe he does you good by releasing a flow of adrenalin into the blood-stream.

Have I never before mentioned crossword puzzles? I'm sure I must have, for they are almost the only things I am (through long practice) extremely good at. I began doing them when I was at Eton, which is also when *they* began, and have done *The Times* one pretty well ever since (it used to be difficult to get hold of when I was a private soldier in barracks in the Blitz). Normally in Soho Square Ruth and I do *The Times* one in ten minutes or so during our morning coffee. I also do the *New Statesman* and *Spectator* (have won thirty shillings' worth of book tokens this year so far), the *Observer* (Ximenes) and the *Sunday Times* (Mephisto), but the best of all is the *Listener*, which is often most ingenious and amusing (occasionally it becomes mathematical and I retire). Luckily Ruth shares this passion, as she does everything else. We both love jigsaws too, but they take up too much time and space.

On Saturday, a perfect summer's day, we drove twenty-three miles across the moors to Barnard Castle, where we shopped. Then on to a sale in the Temperance Hall of a nearby village. We stayed only for the china and oddments, which took one and a half hours, and bought three plates, part of a charming tea-set, an engaging toast-rack and two lovely coloured lithographs in maple-wood frames—all needed and suitable here—for a total cost of 14/9. (There is another, nearer, sale on Thursday.) We drove home through Teesdale (which you would think beautiful if you hadn't seen Swaledale) and over the moors again to Brough on the edge of Westmorland.

I haven't shaved for over a fortnight, but alas the growth is slow, and I still look more unshaven than bearded. What there is is a pepper-and-salt mess, though Ruth sweetly says it's getting golden in the sunshine. I long to see what the finished effect is like, but in another week it will all have to come off. Have you ever grown a beard? It's delightful not having to shave I find.

I see much more Henry James than Pater in Percy Lubbock's style, and I never got right through *The Region Cloud*[1]—did you? I too loved *Dracula* in my youth, and at home I have a fine first edition (quite a rare book): I must try it again. *Uncle Silas* I have never tried.

Yesterday, when I meant to be writing to you, I finished *Eddie Marsh*. I think you'd better put it on your library list. It *is* too long, and E.M. is more pathetic than heroic, but there are lots of good jokes and stories in it, and it's generally entertaining. Quite a lot of Winston. The account of Rupert Brooke's last days and death is graphic and moving.

Ruth has gone out to pick wildflowers, which she arranges in heavenly little bunches all over the cottage. You've no idea how pretty cotton-grass can look. The orchids are over, but any amount of other things are in flower.

We might possibly come up here again for a week or two in August, if I have the face to absent myself even *more* from the office. The strike has pretty well brought work there to a standstill, they tell me, and I see one optimist forecasts that it may last for *ten* weeks!

Ruth has just come back with masses of orchids (not over at all!), wild geranium, sorrel, vetches, grasses and bluebells. She sends you her best love and says she particularly enjoys the flattering references to her in your letters.

25 June 1959   *Grundisburgh*

I returned this morning from my girls' school, where every year I behave for two days exactly like that hearty old horror Mr Chips. The dreadful thing is that I much enjoy it, for, like the dear Doctor, I dearly love a knot of little misses. I have two granddaughters there— fourteen and eleven, who luckily don't take after their grandfather in looks, and are great fun. The headmistress has a touch of genius. She once got a lot of small girls to write down anything they thought or

[1] Percy Lubbock's only novel.

wondered about the headmistress's ways, and more than one apparently asked 'Why, when short skirts are the fashion, does Miss X always wear long ones?' She laughed delightedly and said: 'But don't you realise that I have such hideous ankles'—i.e. she has like Monty James so much natural dignity that she never has to stand on it. The assistant mistresses are always the slightly disheartening element in a girls' school. Why must so many of them be so *anaemic*?

I return to a garden the colour of the Sahara, or at least the Gobi desert—and in Hampshire yesterday there was half-an-inch of rain and all the madder-browns were emerald-green in twelve minutes. What does 'madder' mean? and, if it comes to that, why crimson *lake*, burnt *siena*, and yellow *ochre*? As far as I remember, crimson lake had the nicest taste, and gamboge—why *gamboge*?—the nastiest, perhaps because so much yellow comes from arsenic. Every hour or two the fire-warning goes, as some heath catches fire from a cigarette-end, or even from the rays of the sun concentrated through a lemonade-bottle. The Lord Cranworth, who knows our climate intimately, says it may not rain till October—as in 1921 when the barley was eighteen inches high. Couldn't you *bottle* some of your new-mown-hay fragrance and send it here?

No, Granny Gow would *not* do at Kisdon, though you would enjoy his dry flavour in the right surrounding. After all, even Housman produced a silvery laugh after punishing the Trinity port laid down in Edward FitzGerald's time. A tight smile was all I ever saw. And how right you are on the flow of adrenalin. The health I have is largely due to Leavis and Amis and Osborne and the *New Statesman*, and the umpire who gave me out in a critical school-match at Eton.

My respect for you and Ruth, which might have been thought incapable of increase, approaches the region of awe at what you tell me of your crossword powers. It is tremendous. I can't believe it is only practice. There is native genius in it somewhere. Ximenes! A friend staying here once took fourteen minutes to get *one* word—and that turned out to be wrong. Will you do the *Times* one in my presence one day? I shall feel like E.V. Lucas watching Cinquevalli[1], i.e. seeing things done which he *knew* to be impossible.

---

[1] The great juggler. See volume one of these letters.

I saw Harry Altham yesterday—actually cheerful about modern cricket! There were 32,000 spectators at Lord's on Saturday. I said—following an august example—'What went they out for to see?'[1] The answer was not John the Baptist but May and Cowdrey. To which *I* reply: 'That is not enough; in my day there were at least twelve to see, in a Test Match, perhaps more.' But H.A. is famous for euphoria and eupepsia (and eugenics too; he has a *cold* bath every morning, and when I asked him if he bathed in the Serpentine in January, his negative was not emphatic. But in spite of these drawbacks, he really is the nicest man you could want).

Pamela's mouth watered at your sale exploits, and mine did and does at the name Swaledale. It *must* be lovely, isn't it? Or is it like the Black Country where the names Daisy Bank, Cradley Heath, Windson Green have been given to a series of down-at-heel slums and slag-heaps (not that the names approach the broad and opulent majesty of Swaledale. I like writing it and rolling it round the tongue).

Yes, *The Region Cloud* is unreadable. I don't think I ever arrived at any notion of what it was supposed to be about. You *must* read *Uncle Silas* at night, by the light of one candle, preferably with a wind moaning round the house. I notice a suspicious silence about *How Green*. How well I know that state of affairs. Have I praised it too much? That fatal treatment has kept me off any number of books, e.g. Damon Runyon and Thurber.

I grew a beard in Greece in 1912. It was *red* and far from popular. No one ever said anything as nice about it as Ruth did about yours. But then—no, better not. I shall say it some day when she isn't by!

29 June 1959   *Kisdon Lodge, Keld*

We have stolen two more days here, and will now drive south on Wednesday morning. My colleagues report a complete stoppage on account of the printing strike, the redecoration of my flat (bathroom and kitchen) won't be ready till Wednesday, and Oscar was within two days of being ready for the printer. Luckily to-day and yesterday have been cool and wet, so I am full steam ahead with him, and by Wednes-

[1] *Matthew*, 11, viii.

day he will be printer-worthy. There are still a great many missing notes, dates etc, which I hope to gather while the type is being set up —and it's possible that a few new letters may turn up—but the major work is done, and the relief enormous. While we've been here I've transferred thousands of corrections (on 850 letters and 1600 footnotes) to the top (printer's) copy, so now we have a complete duplicate of everything. *Laus Deo!*

While I am writing this, Ruth is engaged, three foot away, on a fascinating task. We have a little folding card-table, which is useful indoors and out. Its green baize top was full of holes and very shabby, so we cut it off and bought some new scarlet plastic material which has to be ironed on (through brown paper) with a hot iron. We have a splendid iron, given us by our farmer's wife (who is now all-electric): it consists of an ordinary iron-shaped container and handle, inside which one puts a chunk of iron, heated red-hot in the heart of the fire. Irons in the fire at last! R. has now done the top of the table beautifully, and is struggling to iron the edges at the side and underneath.

For lunch we had lettuce sandwiches, Wensleydale cheese, apple pie and stewed gooseberries. My beard has another day to live: R is now rather taken with it, saying I look like a sea-captain. A suitable photograph will be taken.

I wish you could see the great stretches of green which sweep away from us on every side, topped by the heather-covered fells. No Gobi-colour here. (By the way, Peter F. told me long ago that the word Gobi means Desert, so Gobi Desert is a tautology: I love pointing out such pedantries to one who enjoys them.)

Next time I visit you I will do *The Times* crossword in your presence: it's sure to be an especially difficult one, and I shall be humbled.

We went to another sale last Thursday—an enchanting one out of doors in a little village. We bought (for a total of 24/9) a coloured china rolling-pin, a very pretty candlestick, two sweeping-brushes, a double saucepan, a first-class Aladdin lamp with shade (one of ours was a bit dicky), and a lovely glass plate engraved with dates etc of the 1887 Jubilee. This last will probably come to Soho Square and be proudly shown to you.

Ruth has triumphantly finished ironing the table, which looks splendid.

I'm not sure whether you realise that Keld and Kisdon are in fact *in* Swaledale, which stretches from here to Richmond, without benefit of railway. It is far the loveliest of the Dales: I'd love you to see it, but we could get you up here only in a jeep or Land-rover.

Next week-end is Long Leave, *and* Henley Regatta, *and* Adam's sixteenth birthday. All he wants, he says, is a new slide-rule, which he must choose himself.

Duff is going to Greece with David Caccia (Harold's son), but I don't know what he's going to use for money.

Ruth is now settled by the fire with a book from the cottage library —*Hetty Wesley* by Q. We have a fine run of Nelson's admirable seven-pennies—much better print and binding than our vaunted Penguins. My reading has lately been all Oscar, except for a chapter or two of *The French Revolution* at bedtime. I am still only just over half-way through, and Dogleech Marat is scarcely on the scene.

On the table is an exquisite bowl of wild roses, which R. picked yesterday in the rain. Both the last two nights we have slept for *ten* hours! I send all these details so that you can a little picture the scene. As I finish each section of Oscar, R. reads it through to see what I have missed; she also types many new notes, which I cut out and stick into the bulging folders. No one else will ever know *quite* how much work has been involved.

The drive on Wednesday—a melancholy business—will take us eight or nine hours, and we shall hope to start about mid-day, after packing up and stowing away everything here. Two days in the office, and then Bromsden Farm, where I shall eagerly expect your letter. Comfort reports a garden as parched as yours, and there will be almost a month's accumulation of bills and other horrors to tackle. I take it you will be at the July Lit. Soc.—and beforehand in my attic? It's the last dinner before October, and somehow I shall have to get through it on barley-water. Up here we never drink any alcohol anyhow, so the prohibition is no trouble. Now I must polish off Oscar, and then it will be tea-time, and then we shall cross two fields to fetch a pint of fresh milk and this morning's post, including Saturday's newspapers. It's a perfect life for us.

Write to me, as Oscar says, when you have something better to do.

Thank you for your note about Gobi. Why is nearly all the information one picks up inaccurate? Only recently someone (R. Mortimer?) applied that lovely sentence of Gibbon's 'Twenty-two acknowledged concubines . . .' to Commodus instead of Gordian. Cousin Oliver reported his father's eulogy of *W.G*'s neck. Well I don't suppose the doctor's rivalled driven snow, but in sober fact the remark was made about E.M's.[1] When a fourth leader repeated the canard I wrote a brief correction which they have ignored. Housman always maintained that a love of truth was the rarest of human virtues. I am much enjoying Peter's Boxer book.[2] It surely deserves the good reviews it is getting. And your uncle's *Talleyrand* greatly impressed me. How *did* he find time to acquire that mass of facts, sift them and present them with a confident lucidity which makes the book delightful reading?

How grumpy you must be feeling, having exchanged Swaledale for Soho Square (*I* feel grumpy in sympathy!) where I suppose all is in a sort of chaotic idleness. The lay view, at any rate in Suffolk, is that workers who strike for a huge advance when their wages are already much higher than most people's, must be in the wrong. The man Briginshaw's face has the same stolid and irascible mulishness as that of 'Terrible Ted' Hill of the Boilermakers. But I understand very little of what goes on. Nobody seems to share (e.g.) my bewilderment at Cousins and his damned union solemnly pontificating about nuclear bombs. They can of course give their opinions as individual voters, but why as an industrial body? Especially when one knows that not one in twenty has given more thought to the pros and cons than I have to gynaecology—not so much in fact.

I remember the 1887 jubilee (*aetat* four), or rather I remember two things about it (a) that I contributed a spadeful to the planting of the Hagley Jubilee oak, and (b) that I was shortly afterwards sick—thus contradicting the common fancy that one always remembers pleasant and forgets unpleasant things; for I have no recollection of the delectable comestibles that had that lamentable result.

---

[1] E.M. Grace, brother of W.G. and like him a famous cricketer.
[2] *The Siege at Peking* by Peter Fleming (1959).

Christopher Hollis came here to give away the Woodbridge prizes. He did it very well in a crackling voice, though stressing rather unnecessarily at one point that all his audience, old and young, were born in sin. I don't think Woodbridge parents hold any such view. They look rather what one of the old Forsytes termed a 'rum-ti-too' lot, resembling in fact to my eye the sort of crowd one sees in January in a bargain basement. If you say that merely shows I have a good deal of 'snob' in me, I cordially agree with you. But there it is.

I hope you didn't miss that review (some good man, but gosh! my memory in 1959!) in which a good deal of praise of the E. Marsh book was tempered by a remark that it compared unfavourably with the Life of Hugh Walpole. This is not *nearly* well enough known. However, you can say with Landor: 'I shall dine late but . . .'[1] Readers' tastes are unpredictable and who knows that better than you? Surely Oscar W. will bring the shekels pouring in. I am full of excitement about it.

I remember reading *Hetty Wesley* years ago and have a vague memory of an iron upbringing—e.g. flogged for crying after a flogging, surely a good example of the vicious circle (the best example perhaps is that of the man whose soup was so hot that he sweated into it, and it increased in such heat and quantity that he sweated even more. Not a very delicate instance perhaps but cogent). The 'dog-leech' episode I remember as wonderfully vivid, in his 'slipper-bath' whatever that may be. How sporadic and local your uncle shows the 'Terror' to have been, daily life in most places going on much as usual. Perhaps all revolutions are like that. Marat I imagine as largely lunatic. Does Belloc write of him at all—as he did, splendidly, about Robespierre— 'a man all convictions and emptiness, too passionless to change, too iterant to be an artist, too tenacious to enliven folly with dramatic art, or to save it by flashes of its relation to wisdom.' Isn't that pretty good? (but I wish I was *quite* sure what he means by 'iterant').

Not much of a day—hot sun and wind, a poor combination rivalling, no doubt feebly, the Gobi Gobi. Swaledale is the place. Your little saga of it—last four letters—is full of music, say Beethoven's

---

[1] '. . . the dining-room will be well lighted, the guests few and select.' To which more than a century later W.B. Yeats added, in 'To a Young Beauty':

> And I may dine at journey's end
> With Landor and with Donne.

'Pastoral', and Ruth stars it like that lovely air that recurs throughout the second movement (do you boggle at 'stars'? I mean it as Conrad uses it 'the channel glittered like a blue mantle shot with gold, and starred by the silver of the capping seas'), and though you use practically no adjectives her presence graces every little picture you paint. What fun—and frequent pain of course—it must be to be an artist!

P.S. Have just acquired an Irish linen jacket. Pamela says she has waited forty years to see me well-dressed.

It is ten p.m. and I have just come back from driving Adam to Eton —a long stream of almost motionless cars most of the way—after what must be the sunniest and hottest Long Leave for many a year. I have been in the garden, exiguously dressed, catching up on four weeks' worth of everything. All now happily disposed of, thank goodness.

Those last two stolen days in Swaledale advanced Oscar most satisfactorily: two pouring days of rain, on which I copied and composed while Ruth checked and typed beside me. And then on our last day the sun returned, and we went for a last lingering walk along the top of Kisdon: soft turf studded with wild thyme and many other flowers, curlew calling, an occasional grouse or hare. That evening the farmer took down the hill in his jeep (with the milking pails etc) four large parcels of books and typescripts, and in the morning we got up at 8.30. Packing up the cottage and stowing everything away took $2\frac{1}{2}$ hours, and then we walked sadly down the hill laden with haversacks and carrier-bags. The drive to London (265 miles) took us nine hours, including substantial halts for picnic lunch and tea. As usual London seemed stifling, ugly, crowded, and above all *noisy*. Soho Square, which nine years ago was delightfully quiet at night, is now pandemonium until 1 a.m. at earliest.

I love your liking all the Kisdon details (the snapshots should be ready tomorrow), and if Ruth shines through them like a star, that is exactly what she does in my life. When the time came, on the last evening, for the beard to be removed, R. became quite sentimental about it. Incidentally I had a fiendish time getting it off.

Fleming's book is selling splendidly, but we shall run out of stock if the strike goes on more than another fortnight. Briginshaw (as you unerringly sensed) and his union NATSOPA (which, by the way, my daughter was forced to join when she went to the *Farmers' Weekly*) are easily the worst of the lot. That union contains all the *un*skilled workers in the various trades—hewers of paper and drawers of ink—and they are constantly trying to get as much money as the skilled men. The only advantage of the strike is that no proofs can arrive to demand my attention, and in a few days my desk should be clear.

Only yesterday did I see that review which praised my book at the expense of E. *Marsh* (it was by Angus Wilson)—very gratifying, I must say.

Adam's side is in the semi-finals of the Junior, and their hopes are high. The only year Fred won the cup was when Duff was captain of the side! At the end of the half Fred is moving to the new house, which seems to be slap in the middle of Judy's Passage. Goodness knows how one will approach it with car and luggage. It has central heating, Adam says. His new (temporary) tooth is so lifelike that I couldn't tell which it was.

On Friday night we all went to an excellent entertainment in the grounds of our neighbours the Brunners (Lady B. is Laurence Irving's sister); with lights, recorded music and voices they told the story of a tragic pair who were imprisoned in the tower there for the murder of Sir Thomas Overbury. All very well done, and *delicious* sandwiches (some of creamed haddock, some of chicken and mushrooms) obtainable from stalls manned by devoted women slaving for the Village Hall.

I see that Suffolk is beset with heath-fires: I hope they're well away from Grundisburgh: I don't want you singed.

Oh yes—among the massed correspondence here I found a rebate note saying the Inland Revenue owe me £193!! Another Eton half assured. I go from hand to mouth.

9 July 1959   *Grundisburgh*

It is quite infuriating but I cannot manage the Lit. Soc. on Tuesday. Those bovine and malignant G.C.E. authorities have piled on to me a

271

great mass of scripts—far more than they had led me to expect—and no more time in which to get them marked. So I simply cannot spare a day and a half while they silt up. I was greatly looking forward to it, and especially to a good crack with you. Really the cussedness of things!

London, poor you, must be quite ghastly in this heat; and any thought of Briginshaw must damp your forehead. It does mine here! I like, or rather I don't like, the simple reactions of him, Cousins and their kidney. 'We don't like arbitration because the case for a strike is always so weak that the arbitration invariably goes against us.' Damn them all.

Good news about Adam's tooth. In old days it would have been dead white, i.e. matching no tooth that ever was; in still older ones the gap would have been irreparable. And just think what dentistry must have been in Dr Johnson's day.

I am writing a life of Shakespeare in 1500 words for Dick Routh's wildly improbable biographical dictionary. I don't find it very easy. Until I really began to poke about I hadn't realised how very few facts about him are really known. The point I have arrived at combines the convictions that W.S. of Stratford couldn't have written the plays, and that no one else could have. You may remember that old Agate, after toying with the Baconian theory, came, characteristically, to the conclusion that S. wrote the bulk of every play but that he was Bacon's 'fancy boy' and his patron put in numerous odd bits here and there. But does that really hold more water than any other theory? It is interesting to find that Masefield found in the Stratford bust 'a man with much vitality of mind' and that the Droeshout portrait, which most people find frankly doughy, shows 'a face of delicate sensitiveness'. Isn't this wishful thinking? I shall of course give Tolstoy's opinion; after reading all the plays some seven times he says that the universal admiration of the poet proves the world to be mad.

I much enjoyed Peter's book. He gives the whole Boxer affair the right tone of fundamental absurdity punctuated with horror. I love the explanation of the rebels always firing high as they thought the higher the rifles' sights were set, the more potent the shot. I hope the six hundred millions of them are equally childish now. There are grim possibilities about a people who don't value individual life waking up to the truth that collectively they can overwhelm the rest of the world.

Yes, I remember, it was Angus Wilson, one of those (to me) immensely clever and entirely unreadable novelists—but evidently a first-class critic. The Library is being very dilatory about the Marsh book, but it doesn't much matter as I spend much time daily getting up the answers to the G.C.E. papers next week. Many of the questions are much too hard for sixteen-year-olds, viz 'What does *Pilgrim's Progress* gain by being in the form of an allegory?' (Don't breathe this to anyone! The paper is to be done next Wednesday.) And now candidates like John Betjeman's daughter will turn out a brilliant answer of breath-taking fulness. I often find that several candidates are both cleverer and more learned than I am. I except the Barbados boy who wrote 'Wellington was the French general who helped Nelson to defeat Napoleon at Trafalgar Square.' And I did *not* invent that.

Adam appears to be always leading his side to a crushing victory, whatever the game. He should be comfortable in the new house—overlooking my old garden. In 1895 at Benson's we had one bathroom, candles, no heating, but a very large number of cockroaches. One always appeared whenever I had a bath.

How long did your beard get? Could you curl it? I remember the agony of removal. I believe there is a convenient technique, but never knew it. And isn't your skin very tender underneath? We are of course really *meant* to be bearded.

12 July 1959   *Bromsden Farm*

It's very sad that I shan't see you on Tuesday, and Ruth will be as disappointed as I am. Never mind—we must look forward to October. Meanwhile, here to divert you, are a few wholly inadequate photographs of Kisdon. Next time we shall try to take some that will give you a better impression. Be an angel and let me have them all back. I can't tell you how I yearn for that company and landscape. If I hadn't all these children and other responsibilities, I should leave London and publishing, fame and fortune, and fly to Swaledale. 'Dark and true and tender is the North.'[1] However, things are as they are, and for the nonce I must hang on, hoping for a few more blessed days in August. Anyhow the piloting of Oscar through the press will take a full year. I am even now drafting the introduction and am truly on the last lap, though I keep on finding hideous mistakes. Ruth says this is bound to happen in so large an undertaking and I mustn't worry: we shall pick up all the errors in the proofs: I hope she's right.

Last week in London was too much of a good thing, and on Wednesday night I lay sleepless and gasping on my bed, with all doors and windows fixed open to admit the roar of engines and the cries of roysterers. Now it is mercifully cooler after much thunder and rain, and I hope it will keep so while you correct those numberless papers and write your life of Shakespeare on a threepenny-bit.

Certainly the Lit. Soc. wouldn't have been much fun last week. Next Sunday I'll report on Tuesday's dinner. I don't in the least mind my liquor-prohibition, but it makes other people's drinking seem unduly protracted and boring, and I can quite see why teetotallers so easily turn into prigs.

On Thursday I lunched with T.S.E. to discuss the London Library, whose A.G.M. is on Tuesday. He was suffering a little from shortness of breath, but was most genial and charming. I am quite devoted to him: he is a saintly character but entirely human, with an unexpected sense of humour. He explained gravely and sadly that his false teeth didn't allow him to eat his favourite raspberries in public. I have always preferred older people to those of my own age or younger, and I dread the time when I am left the oldest.

I fear Adam isn't as good at cricket as Duff was, and he got no further than the XXII. But luckily Adam has a happy accepting temperament and doesn't worry about such things.

I am *still* reading *The French Revolution*, and have now reached Part 3: *The Guillotine*. I keep that here, and in London am reading a huge tome called *La Jeunesse d'André Gide*, which is surprisingly interesting, and right in the Oscar period.

I wish I liked Lord Birkett. He is that frightful thing, a professional after-dinner speaker, full of smug clichés. He is much disliked by his brother-judges. Perhaps he'll be able to get some sense into these

[1] Tennyson, *The Princess*.

274

bloody printers. Meanwhile all is at a total standstill, and I have almost caught up with my arrears of correspondence. Some say that when the strike is over, all the printers will take their fortnight's holiday, but I find this hard to believe. They'll surely be short of money for one thing.

15 July 1959   *Grundisburgh*

Snapshots returned, with many thanks. Interesting to see that Nature meant you to be a blend of Ezra Pound and the late Kaiser Wilhelm II. I get a delightful impression of Swaledale and your 'settled low content' which is Orlando's fantastic phrase for a pleasant humble abode. All the candidates write practically the same answers about *As You Like it*. The teaching of Eng. Lit. is now dreadfully competent as regards attaining a decent pass-mark, and beyond that very prosaic and boring. The fact is that teaching in Eng. Lit., to be any *real* good, demands a spark, and sparks are just as rare in Academe as anywhere else. But there is definitely something charming about these snapshots coming while I am at this play, for there is a congruity between Swaledale and the forest of Arden. I am not *quite* sure whether to see you as Jaques (you are looking *very* thoughtful), Orlando, or the Duke. There is no difficulty at all about Rosalind. You know, my dear Rupert, the Swan of Avon frankly maddens me at times. I have had to look into *Much Ado* again. Do *you* find Beatrice the last word in charm? I don't believe it. I am sure Ruth never tricks and twirls the language about like that! It is S. the *poet* who appeals to me; the dramatist is so wildly silly sometimes—simply could not be bothered; e.g. in *As You Like It* Orlando not recognising Rosalind in the forest, and the fantastic pairing off of Oliver and Celia. Apropos of the former, some great detective once said that anyone could disguise his or her face, but the voice was very difficult and the walk still more so. It was this last, wasn't it, that dished Miss Le Neve on that ship. Or was it her shape, for I believe the captain said much the same of her as Sainte-Beuve said of George Sand, viz 'She had a great soul and a perfectly enormous bottom'? I always felt sorry for Crippen; he had tremendous courage and the day before his death wrote a very good letter to Miss Le N.

Did you know that when the search for him was on, and his picture was everywhere, some Etonians got hold of a photograph of Michael Bland[1] and sent it up to Scotland Yard? There was certainly a strong likeness.

You interest me about Birkett. The fashion is to say he is splendid. I heard him give a good literary lecture once, and he likes watching cricket, so he cannot be all bad. He is or was a much nicer man in court than that coarse and truculent Patrick Hastings was. I never met him, but once, as someone's guest sat near him at lunch at the Garrick. He was being very crusty about his food. I was lunching with old Pellatt[2], and on our way out he had a brief chat with Seymour Hicks, who said more really witty things in a shorter time than I have ever heard. Pellatt said he was always like that. If I lived in London that is the club I should like—and should probably be blackballed for it, as old Agate was. I think that was one of the few things that he felt permanently sore about. I can imagine that a 'queer' who had to pay away hundreds a year in blackmail would not be *persona grata* to a good many members.

I haven't seen what happened at your London Library meeting. Who *was it* who said to me recently that 'if anybody can defeat the Inland Revenue it will be R.H-D', but he was not optimistic. I am afraid they win much more often than not. Shall we ever see T.S.E. at the Lit. Soc. again? By an odd coincidence, it was only a week ago that my sister-in-law refused a plateful of raspberries and cream on the same grounds. But surely dental plates should be more pip-tight than that? I wear a plate, but gollop raspberries whenever opportunity offers. Mouth-roofs of course vary. A leading retired general near here cannot find a plate which does not cause him acute agony whenever inserted. He will have to get his gums like those of Caesar's soldiers, i.e. hard enough to bite anything after the teeth had worn away.

How long is your liquor-embargo to last? Old Heythorp in his prime wouldn't have stood it as long as you have. I wonder why you don't mind more.

Do you know anything about one Paul Johnson, deeply dyed in the *New Statesman* colours? In a recent article he had the impudence to

[1] Eton master.
[2] Headmaster of a prep-school.

reproach the Queen for attending a race-meeting while Parliament was discussing those Mau-Mau floggings. Can stupidity and malice combined do better than that? I see your supporter Angus Wilson says he is going to vote Labour because his family's Toryism infuriates him. It seems a poor reason. But almost every day something in the papers sends my temperature soaring. I wonder if there will be any papers soon. I doubt if Birkett or anybody else will do much. Why do I associate printers' holidays with a mysterious word viz 'wayzgoose'? I must look it up again, -nth time.

P.S. I have rheumatism in the left wrist and am shortly to have electric treatment from a man called Prodger—a name straight out of H.G. Wells or Dickens.

19 July 1959   *Bromsden Farm*

I can't resist sending you Adam's last letter (please return it). I particularly like 'the maddening crowd' and his modesty in explaining that the wicket was easier when he went in.[1] Now, on the strength of his performance, Adam is playing in the final of the House Cup, where Wykes's are again the opposition, and sound likely to win.

This weather suits me fine, except in London, where it is hellish. All this week-end I have been in the garden wearing bathing-pants and basking. Only nine turned up for the Lit. Soc. and we dined in the small room. Contrary to all tradition, Tommy insisted on my sitting on his right. Jonah has recently had pneumonia, but seems little the worse. We had *consommé en gelée*, cold duck with orange salad, fruit with ice-cream, and a cheese soufflé. I ordered a huge jug of iced barley-water for myself and got through pretty well, though I was delighted to go home at 9.30. I find prohibition no worry at home, but it seems to make me tire easily in company.

Your experience correcting papers on Shakespeare reminds me of the days when I stood at the back of the Old Vic stage, carrying a

[1] Coleridge's won the Junior Cricket cup by an innings and 92 runs. They scored 156 to their opponents' 38 and 26. Adam made 43 and took 7 wickets for 4 runs.

halberd and wishing all Shakespeare was as good as the best. For instance, the three casket scenes in *The Merchant of Venice* are almost intolerable to listen to, night after night. All I can say for Beatrice and Benedick is that when Gielgud and Diana Wynyard played the parts they seemed very witty, but at no other time. You're right about Seymour Hicks: he was always wildly funny, and in the Garrick took as much trouble with the dimmest young new member as with his own cronies. The Garrick is very hot against homosexuals (though one or two have slipped through): they say it isn't so much the chap himself as the sort of friends he's likely to bring to the club, and some knowledge of the Savile, where there is no bar, makes me think they're probably right.

The Annual General Meeting of the London Library passed off smoothly. T.S.E. presided with grace and grave charm. A tiresome old fellow called Waley-Cohen said he'd taken a book out of the Library which was full of anti-French propaganda, and would we please return it to its publisher. I told him we couldn't be responsible for the contents of all 750,000 books in the library, but that I would 'look into' the matter. Our rating appeal has now been put off till the autumn. We lodged it more than a year ago: the law's delays do not grow shorter.[1]

I haven't yet got to the execution of the King, but the pace is quickening, and I know the best is still to come.

You are right to associate wayzgoose with a printer's holiday, since that is exactly what it means. This year I hope it chokes them.

Apart from the resultant financial loss, and the certain prospect of a frightful scrum of books in the autumn, this period of stagnation suits me very well, since it is enabling me to tie up innumerable loose ends in Oscar before he goes to the printer. Last week I got *eight* new letters: none of surpassing interest but all worthy of inclusion. The total is now well over 900.

[1] In 1957 the London Library, which had for eighty years been immune (as a charity) from paying rates, was suddenly informed by the Inland Revenue that it would in future have to pay £5000 a year. An appeal to the Lands Tribunal was dismissed, and when in October 1959 the Court of Appeal upheld that decision, the Library already owed the Inland Revenue upwards of £20,000. Hence the immediate appeal for money which is mentioned later in these letters.

So sorry to hear of your rheumatism: Prodger sounds just the chap for it.

Tomorrow evening Ruth and I are being taken to Gielgud's Shakespeare recital. I'm pretty sure I shall enjoy it, since he does all the best bits, and his verse-speaking is always a joy.

I wouldn't at all mind seeing Olivier's *Coriolanus*; I've never seen the play acted; but the journey to Stratford and the need to book tickets months ahead rule it out. Olivier, to my mind, has no idea how to speak verse, and never will have, but he has other qualities, and I don't care what anyone does to *Coriolanus*.

Did I tell you that Comfort is going to France with her mother for a fortnight on August 11? Adam goes to stay with friends in Scotland on the same day, and we're hoping to nip back to Swaledale for ten days or a fortnight. It depends on the strike, the office, my partners' holidays etc. So far I haven't liked to raise the question, so soon after my long absence.

I can't pretend I'm mourning that foul-mouthed old horror Munnings:[1] his conversation in the Garrick was like a stopped-up-drain released, and I'm not at all interested in horses.

23 July 1959   *Grundisburgh*

I don't see how this is to help being a scrap, since mainly through the incompetence of the G.C.E. pundits at 'the older and more splendid university' I have been sorely pushed these last few days. And I was just hoping that the work this morning would go on wings, when I came upon thirty papers on *Eothen*[2] done by young women who knew the book by heart and rewrote most of it with astounding speed and disheartening illegibility. So I have again fallen behindhand, and to-morrow the worst paper of all comes in—nearly three hundred of them. This was the paper last year which produced *forty-eight* sides from John Betjeman's daughter, who was at that convent school at

[1] Sir Alfred Munnings (1878–1959), President of the Royal Academy from 1944. Painted mostly horses.

[2] *Eothen, or Traces of Travel brought home from the East* (1844) by A. W. Kinglake (1809–1891).

Wantage where apparently it is *de rigueur* to write about three–four words a line in enormous handwriting. It is almost impossible to mark with any confidence an answer that extends to eight pages; one has forgotten the beginning as one nears the end.

A near neighbour of ours who lost her husband very suddenly a month ago had her house burnt down on Tuesday—'Father-like He tends and spares us.' Nobody knows why, though wiseacres are pursing their lips and shaking their heads over a Russian maid, 'a chain-smoker of cigarettes' they say. The next house to this one has a thatched roof, and the owner of it and his wife are always in a dither about fire. I suppose you saw about the train which puffed fifteen miles to Felixstowe, followed by a fire engine. Pretty well every yard of the banks on the railway from here to London is black. And the heavens are as brass.

A lawyer friend of mine won't have it that they don't like Birkett, and wonders where your information comes from; he says if B. cannot patch up the strike, no one can. Is there a more up-to-date text in the Bible than 'Jeshurun waxed fat and kicked'?[1] The worker has plenty of money now, so goes on insolently demanding more—and good men like you and Christopher Hollis are heavily mulcted.

The Lit. Soc. dinner sounds very toothsome—but you don't say whether it was wild duck or the tame villatic fowl: I suspect the former as you mention orange salad. I don't like your still being on the waggon. All wrong. How long, O Lord, how long? The body 'that handful of supple earth and long white stones with sea-water running in its veins' may be a thing to marvel at, but it goes wrong too easily and too often. Prodger's ante-room is a 'sair sicht'. I am easily the most lissom mover.

Of course you are right. Shakespeare needs to be *acted*. Beatrice and Benedick I do remember liking years ago, at Birmingham if you please, where they don't act as well as D. Wynyard and J. Gielgud. D.W's sister was gym-mistress at the school where Diana and Rose went and got all D's old clothes. The real surname is Cox, which is harmless. In my youth there was a pin-up called Olive May; her surname was Meatyard. Names are fearfully important. Just imagine if *Paradise Lost* had been written by Hobsbawm.

[1] Deuteronomy, xxxii, 15.

I too shed no tears over Munnings. I met him here shortly after his famous Academy speech. He went on with it interminably, and (like his speech) without a happy turn of phrase, or scrap of wit anywhere. A tedious old man. Talking of the foul-mouthed, I have just read the life of Frank Harris.[1] Max B's cartoon of himself and F.H. at dinner is the best thing in the book. Have you read his autobiography? Unprocurable by the layman, but I always imagine publishers can get anything they want. Do the Yanks allow it? I see some old Judge in U.S.A. has just been very broadminded about *Lady Chatterley*, which, apart from what George Forsyte called 'the nubbly bits', seemed to me a tremendously dull book. But I have never been able to do with D.H.L. Bedside reading *pro tem* is D. Henley on that dreadful old virago Lady Carlisle.[2] All the worst Victorian *grandes dames* rolled into one, with an extra pinch of temper, snobbishness, and intolerance.

I was stung on the lip last week by a wasp in my port, lunching at the Cranworths'—ten minutes after old Lowther—Speaker's son—had been stung by a different one in *his* port. A completely unique incident. For the next twelve hours I resembled the late Ernest Bevin.

I do hope Prodger will cure your rheumatism. Seventy-six is no age these days, and I thank Heaven that you are otherwise flourishing. My old friend Arthur Ransome (whom I visited at his Putney home last week) has been bedridden for seven months with some kind of rheumatoid arthritis. He is seventy-five, and I begin to fear he will never walk again. So does he, and the other evening, when his wife was out of the room, he said in a woeful voice: 'I'd always hoped to end respectably.' His wife, a large and vigorous Russian woman of sixty-five, refuses to have any kind of 'help', and the task of nursing, cooking, cleaning, shopping etc is clearly wearing her out. It's all most distressing, but my visits seem to cheer them up and I am going again soon. The journey from Soho Square takes an hour each way, unless I

[1] By Vincent Brome (1959).
[2] *Rosalind Howard, Countess of Carlisle* [1845–1921] by Dorothy Henley (1958).

hire a car (which I did a fortnight ago, dreading the heat-wave rush-hour in the Underground). It took half an hour and cost 24/-.

My information about Birkett came from a Judge of the Appeal Court, but let it pass. Perhaps the old boy will settle the printing strike in the end. I fear the Lit. Soc. duck was tame—so sorry! Where does the 'handful of supple earth etc' come from?

I'm sure that long ago I told you of the collection of bad and funny book-titles made by me and William Plomer in the 1930s. I've just found a new one for the collection—a slim volume of Nineties verse called *Vox Otiosi* by David Plinlimmon. Can't you see it? And how well the title would suit a thousand other books!

Last Monday Ruth and I were taken to John Gielgud's Shakespeare recital, which proved to be an evening of rare pleasure. Wearing a dinner-jacket on an empty stage surrounded by red curtains, he recited and acted many of the loveliest speeches, interspersing them with Sonnets, and with extremely apt comments of his own on what was coming next. It was wonderful to hear a whole evening of S's supreme poetry, without any of the boredom and nonsense that so often intervene. He spoke all exquisitely, so that one heard and understood every syllable. I wish you could have heard it. Afterwards we supped with the great man at the Ivy. He was in excellent form and most amusing. When I commented on his admirable restraint in Romeo's balcony and death scenes, he said: 'You've no idea how much easier it is without a Juliet. When there's a beautiful girl above you on a balcony, or lying on a tomb with candles round her, naturally the audience look at her the whole time, and Romeo has to pull out all the stops to get any attention.'

My dictionary says that the origin of Wayzgoose is 'obscure', and it's not in Johnson. I'm sure that tiresome fellow Eric Partridge would have an opinion ready. But Ivor B. is your man.

Last week I also visited Donald Somervell in the Queen's Gate Clinic. He has had part of one kidney removed and is now undergoing four weeks of prostrating ray-treatment. It sounds terribly like cancer, but he was very cheerful, reading a life of Cardinal Manning by day and P.G. Wodehouse in the evening. I said I'd go again next week. Luckily he has a nice woman-friend to look after him.

So sorry about your lip, but if you *will* dine in noble houses these days, I suppose you must expect the port to be full of wasps. Believe it or not, I am *still* battling with Oscar, finding more and more that needs doing. You'll certainly waste some days when that comes along! I've no evening engagements next week, thank goodness. London buildings are not organised for heat-waves.

30 July 1959   *Grundisburgh*

You mustn't be compassionate about my paper-markings. No schoolmaster is so resentful of drudgery as other human beings. A lot of rot has been poured out. The pay isn't all that meagre, and the woman who said her husband had been sacked for making a mistake of half a mark in eight hundred papers was—in Swift's courteous phrase —saying the thing that was not. I have in fact had two grimmish days —fifty-seven scripts from Downside, where the young papists, knowing, like Father Brown, the paramount necessity for obedience, had learnt their five books practically by heart, as no doubt they had been ordered to, and wrote volumes of decidedly stodgy but undeniably accurate and comprehensive information. I felt definitely grateful to the occasional one who wrote a few pages of scanty drivel—and of course to the one who wrote lyrically of Keats's unsurpassable adjectives, e.g. '*bearded* bubbles winking at the brim'. What I, as an examiner, call a really good school is e.g. Clayesmore, where their answers are like the prayers of those who mourned Sir John Moore—'few and short'.

Prodger's efforts are so far as unavailing as the tears and sighs of the ungodly, filled with guilty fears, who behold His wrath prevailing —an awfully silly line surely? If God is omnipotent he could have easily made them less ungodly, and if omniscient why that outburst of angry rage? Really Hymns A. and M. *are*! But Prodger is quietly confident; he has the air of a sworn tormentor of old who knew that if his thumb-screw didn't make much impression his rack certainly would. My doctor hinted the other day that at seventy-six one must not expect aches and pains to vanish as they used to, and that I am very lucky, especially as internally my heart is like a rainbow shell that paddles in a halcyon sea.[1] When are you going to be let off the waggon? That is a much more serious affair. And it looks as if after Bank Holiday your nose will once more be to the grindstone; no doubt Wayzgoose will prevail over the week-end. I am glad, by the way, it *was* a tame duck—much more toothsome eating than wild, though I believe one mustn't say so. I don't know where the 'handful of supple earth' comes from. I happened on it as *quoted* by Rider Haggard. It is less contemptuous than Webster's 'a box of worm-seede at best'.[2]

That Gielgud evening sounds fine. This morning I hear from Routh who too was there, and echoes your praises of it with a few grace-notes of his own thrown in. He says that he *and* his two neighbours (hard-faced city men, he says) were *all* in tears at the *Lear* passage. I like to remember that old Johnson, when editing Shakespeare, refused to read *Lear* again, as he simply couldn't face it (or 'up to it,' as *all* G.C.E. candidates say, as well as 'meet up with' etc. What the *hell* are their English teachers doing?). Routh also says that he came away convinced of the *extraordinary* beauty of *All's Well*. So I am again wrong. Minorities usually are ('About things on which the public thinks long it commonly attains to think right'. Dr J. may be taken to apply to Shakespeare). That is an interesting remark of Gielgud's about *Romeo and Juliet* and manifestly true. I suppose he has thought out everything he does. Do they all? I remember Agate recording how he complimented Benson[3] on some inflection or gesture, and B. candidly said he had merely done what he did without thinking. But no doubt lots of the big things in words or action are instinctive. What news of D. Somervell—though they do take a kidney out for other reasons. But those who know always pull a long face if they hear of deep-ray treatment. I do hope he will be all right. Prodger, if you please, had half his lung removed last winter; that *was* cancer, and he is quite sure it came from smoking cigarettes. But he is *very* cheerful—and optimistic.

Nice little silly joke—Parson to choirboy mentioned ethics. Boy looked blank. 'Don't you know anything about ethics?' Boy: 'No, Sir; I live in Thuthex'. Sorry!

[1] Christina Rossetti, 'A Birthday'.

[2] *The Duchess of Malfi*, act iv, scene 2.

[3] F.R. Benson (1858–1939), Shakespearean actor. Knighted 1916 on the stage of Drury Lane theatre.

It is Bank Holiday morning, eleven o'clock and all's well. Yesterday I spent entirely in the sunny garden, occasionally nipping indoors to provide Oscar with another or a better footnote. Ever since I got the top copy of the typescript ready for the printer, more and more things have turned up demanding additions and alterations. Also I am finding, just as I did with *Hugh Walpole*, that the books one read at the beginning of a five-year job yield a lot more if re-read at the end. One doesn't completely know what one's looking for until the work's in final shape. How bored you must be with all these minutiae of editorship—and how little the results will be noticed by most of the book's readers! Though, in fact, good editing, like good printing, should be so suited to its subject as to be taken for granted.

Several of our main printers are on holiday (wayzgoose to you) till today week, and we shan't get much out of them till the end of August. Ruth and I are hoping to nip up to Kisdon on the 12th or 13th for the best part of a fortnight: exact details next week. My American friend Leon Edel, the Henry James expert, arrived with his wife last week. They are spending a month in England, based on Ruth's house in Hampstead.

I can't follow Routh's remark about *All's Well*, since it didn't figure in Gielgud's programme. Someone has blundered. J.G. has certainly thought out and perfected every syllable and gesture: did you read that interesting interview with him in Friday's *Times*?

I spoke to Donald Somervell again on the telephone. He sounded much better, and is now spending most of the time in a friend's house in St John's Wood, returning to the nursing home only for his daily ray-treatment. Sparrow has offered him some comfortable rooms in All Souls, and he may go there to recuperate.

Last week in London was mercifully quiet, with the evenings dedicated to Oscar. I can quite see how such a task could become an obsession without end. I am *still* deep in *The French Revolution*: the King has just been executed, and I ought to finish on Kisdon, where I have another (pocket) edition. Otherwise my reading is all for Oscar. Tomorrow I must trek out to Putney again to sup with the Ransomes, and on Wednesday I am giving dinner at the Garrick to my bibliographical advisory board, i.e. John Carter, John Hayward and Tim Munby, the Librarian of King's.

The crossword in this week's *Listener* is a teaser, combining ordinary clues, mathematics (which Adam solved in a twinkling) and much information about Norse mythology. What a lot of time you save by not doing them!

6 August 1959   *Grundisburgh*

Mea culpa. I slipped the pen. Not *All's Well* but *Much Ado* was what Routh delighted in at the Gielgud recitation. (Another gaffe! I wrote *As You Like It*!) I had been looking over scores of *As You Like It* scripts; my brain is in a Shakespearean fog. And *en passant* how infinitely I prefer Rosalind to Beatrice—or in fact any other Shakespearean lady. Beatrice no doubt would have been fun to sit next to at dinner, but every day, no thank you. Cleopatra for half the twenty-four hours. Do you remember the lady in the Bülow memoirs who might have married Isvolsky the Russian foreign secretary; after he had reached that eminence, she said, regarding what she had missed: '*Je le regrette tous les jours; je m'en félicite toutes les nuits.*' It is *ad rem* to mention that Isvolsky resembled one of the plainer species of toad (*bufo disgustans*). I read that excellent thing of Gielgud's in *The Times* with great interest. Technique in almost every art and craft always enthrals me. I remember a picture-restorer at Hagley once showing us how he knew a most convincing old picture-frame to be a fake. All forgotten now of course, except that the little worm-holes were so situated that a worm who goes into secret places behind and under the moulding couldn't have made these holes which were all so to say frontal—and were made with tiny shot from an air-pistol. Also wood a hundred and fifty years old brown with age will not—as this did—show white if you take a sliver off the surface with a pen-knife.

How could I possibly be bored with your struggles with Oscar? Surely that must be a best-seller? I shall be taking *E. Marsh* to Cambridge to read in the intervals of deciding whether Pincus and Squance ought to pass and Bytheway and Mange ought to fail. These are actual recent names. One could easily play Cardus's game with them, one eleven, i.e. Beauties—Sunlight, Nice, Bravery, Lettice, Brilliant, Allbless, Mellody, Friendship, Bee, Flowerdew, Divine, v. Beasts—Puddepha, Quass, Jellinek, Sogno, Gutch, Twohig, Bew, Beeny, Beeby, Bobby, and Bones. Tosh and Toh umpires, Mutton and Mimpriss scorers, groundsmen Gasper and Gorbally. Unbelievable but true. The oddest, perhaps of all is apparently quite common in Burmah: it is simply 'Ng'. I should be flummoxed by that at Absence.[1]

I say, how good Ivor is in the new *D.N.B.* on old Agate. I read it in the smallest room in the house this morning—decided in fact that the *D.N.B.* is the perfect lavatory literature. Why does the man Crossman express satisfaction at the gentle debunking, as he calls it, of Henson? Even he and other Wykehamist prigs never wrote a more meaningless sentence. The notice doesn't debunk at all, and why should anyone want H. debunked? He was an excellent bishop, and wrote very much finer English than Crossman ever did or will. How I do hate judgments and prejudices of this kind. And in both *New Statesman* and *Spectator* (a deplorable paper now) the reviews and comments are becoming increasingly cryptic. Are they *all* undergraduates, resolutely showing off? How can Peter F. be happy in that *galère?*

The waggon till September at least? *Very* serious. Did you only just avoid cirrhosis of the liver? You refuse to take it very seriously, but I believe you had a jolly grave illness. Must have been.

Prodger says my wrist is better, and is unmoved by my asking 'Then why does it ache just as much as ever?' His answer is perilously akin to that ancient humbug: 'That shows it is getting better,' but not quite. He is a good man.

The cornfields here look superb, every haulm standing beautifully at attention, so different from last year when every field was as tousled as a third-former's head.

Love to Ruth. I rather think I didn't send it last week, so this is a double lot. So look out, my man.

---

[1] Eton name for roll-call.

Thunder is rolling round, rain is falling. By the mercy of providence this didn't happen yesterday, when four of us set off at 8.15 a.m. and drove sixty-seven miles to Aldwick, near Bognor, where some old friends have a house on the sea. The sun shone uninterruptedly, and it was so hot that I bathed *four* times. The tide was conveniently high, we took an excellent picnic lunch with us, and the roads (whatever the papers may say) were no worse than any other summer Saturday. Altogether the outing was a thundering success, enjoyed by all. We got back at 8 p.m. Tomorrow morning Duff leaves for Greece, Comfort and Adam go their separate ways on Tuesday, and Ruth and I plan to drive to Kisdon either on Wednesday or (more probably) Thursday. Anyhow write there this week. I can scarcely believe we'll be there so soon. I'm sending this to Cambridge to make sure of its reaching you.

There does not seem to me much chance of Oscar's hitting the best-seller list. It's going to be an enormous book costing several guineas. I hope for extensive reviews, and perhaps translations into foreign languages, but I can't see the common man (whoever he is) rushing out to buy it. Never mind, no doubt pure scholarship is its own reward. I'm still deep in last-minute addenda and corrigenda, but I can see they won't be finished by Wednesday, and the two large cartons of typescript will make their third journey to Kisdon Lodge. I love your lists of candidates' names—clearly much more interesting than the stuff they write. I don't promise to read *How Green* until Oscar has passed out of my control, but we'll see. The *Spectator* has indeed reached rock-bottom, and Fleming has retired to the decent obscurity of an occasional contributor. He drives to Argyllshire tomorrow, ready for the first *battue* on the Twelfth. Once a year they shoot over Kisdon, but most of the grouse are well away from us and we're not bothered.

I had an agreeable dinner last week with my bibliographical friends, but a large jug of the nicest and coldest barley-water doesn't take the place of a glass of wine, and I found myself getting tired and bored before ten. I also journeyed once again to Putney and supped by Arthur Ransome's sickbed. Tomorrow Ruth and I are going to the new Noel Coward play, which I feel may be more amusing than the critics admit: you shall hear.

In bed recently I have re-read *Malice Aforethought* by Francis Iles: it is nearly thirty years old, but I enjoyed it again. Did you ever read it? Otherwise it has been Oscar, Oscar all the way. If this book is nothing else, it will be a mine of information, a sort of *Who's Who* of the Eighties and Nineties in certain circles, social, literary, dramatic etc. I think in your copy I'll have to put an asterisk against the names of all homosexuals in the index (which itself will be hellish long and ever so informative).

(Duff has just rung up to say he's run out of petrol a mile away, and Bridget has driven off with the mowing-machine petrol to his rescue.)

How well do you remember the Marconi scandal? One of my authors is writing a book about it, and I find it most interesting. I was only five when it happened, so missed it as news and have never seen it exhaustively dealt with as history. Rufus Isaacs was, I should say, a pretty slippery customer.

University Arms Hotel
Cambridge

13 August 1959

This really must be a scanty contribution to a correspondence which in quantity, quality and regularity has already reached majestic proportions—because I arrived late last night and your letter which awaited me cannot be dealt with properly till—I suspect—after the post has gone this evening. We shall see.

Cambridge is quite horrible—costive with humanity or at least as Serjeant Buzfuz put it 'beings erect upon two legs and bearing the outward semblance of men and not of monsters'[1] (and the women are worse—damp, bulbous, coffee-coloured). The hotel is grossly over-heated 'because the Americans like it so'. We have just ended the first day's work, in the usual state of complete inability to see *how* we can possibly finish in a week. Did you know that practically all the schools in England begin with B. or C. or W.—and all of them send in several thousand candidates. And of course it becomes clearer every

---

[1] *Pickwick Papers*, chapter xxxiv.

year that *examination* on set English books is absurd, meaningless, and demoralising to all concerned—the cheque that comes at the end is the only sound and sensible thing about it.

I have brought a Trollope to read in the intervals, viz *Can You Forgive Her?* What fantastic titles he did light on. But *how* good they are—*real* people and you really want to know what is going to happen to them. *Miles* better than AUSTEN (Hush!)

Did you see my letter in Saturday's *Daily Telegraph*? Very odd. Everyone I ask says they read the *D.T.* Not one saw the letter. It was merely a little tale about an old Lord Chief Justice which hit a certain nail on the head. Perhaps nobody ever reads the correspondence column. It is usually full of rubbish.

Malice Aforethought I remember thinking awfully good, but I never can remember who F. Iles really is. I like your plan about 'my' Oscar (bless you) with the starred homos: it will look like Baedeker.

In re Marconi, look up the poem by Kipling beginning 'Well done Gehazi', addressed to Rufus Isaacs. It was a sorry show, full of stout lying.

16 *August 1959* *Kisdon Lodge*

Our dear farmer is not at the moment milking up here, so we no longer have our milk and post brought up for us, but yesterday we went down to shop at Hawes, and there was your letter waiting at Keld post office—which is also the local Youth Hostel, kept by an admirable Yorkshireman and his wife. He comes from Keighley, but despises his fellow West Riding men as busybodies and much prefers the people here. He is great friends with our farmer, who lives next door to him.

You seem a little harassed in your letter, and I only hope that strong doses of Trollope taken at bedtime will preserve your health and sanity. T's titles are excellent, but so were others of the time. I particularly like *What will he Do with it?* and *Red as a Rose is She*. To my mind these are almost as good as *Have With You to Saffron Walden*,[1] surely the best ever.

[1] By Bulwer Lytton; Rhoda Broughton; Thomas Nashe.

Alas, I never see the *Daily Telegraph* unless it is sent in mistake for *The Times*. Have you a copy of your letter? I would return it faithfully.

You seem to have been much less surprised at the B.B.C. Advisory Council[1] than I was. Anyhow I shall look forward to discussing greyhound racing with the Bishop of Manchester, and the steel industry with Gubby Allen—and you shall hear all about it.

I think it was Maurice Baring (but you will correct me) who said he had decided that the *Iliad* and the *Odyssey* weren't written by Homer, but by another man of the same name. The saying, *pari passu*, goes for Francis Iles, whose real name is A.B. Cox.

Today has been pure joy: brilliant sunshine and a deep blue sky with the whitest cotton-wool clouds flying over the mountains. We had breakfast, lunch and tea outside and didn't speak to anyone else all day. I think I told you that when we first came here we discovered, deep under the turf which came right up to the cottage door, a fine set of huge flagstones forming a little terrace in front, and on either side a path to coalshed and E.C. Well, today we found a lot more, buried even deeper, which complete and enlarge the path to the coalshed. We had tremendous fun digging them out in the sunshine, and I can see that the rearrangement and levelling of them will take us ages. If we have another hot day we plan to drive about sixty miles to a place called Saltburn-by-the-Sea, which we once briefly visited and liked enormously. It is a small, entirely Victorian seaside place, designed for the toiling millions of Stockton and Middlesbrough. It is south of Redcar and north of Whitby. It has sands and a little pier, and there is a thin black line of coal-dust at the edge of the water. The drive to it is all countrified.

Having been up here only six weeks ago, we dropped back quicker than ever into the delicious rhythm of the place, and our only complaint is that the hours fly past too quickly. Oscar still claims every possible moment, and even as I write this Ruth is looking through our vast typescript for this and that. Finding one letter or reference may take hours. Outside in the sun today I read all through the 600-page bibliography of O's writings, and found a mass of tiny things I had missed earlier. Clearly one could go on like this for ever, but I *must*

[1] Of which I had just been made a temporary member.

reach some sort of conclusion by the end of this month, or the publishing business will wither.

At night I am *still* Carlyle-ing, and have now passed Charlotte Corday. Ruth is reading Henry James by day and a detective story in the evenings. We had sausages, fried potatoes and beans for lunch, followed by apple pie and stewed blackberries. An occasional grouse, hare or curlew passes by: there is a water shortage in all the Dale villages, but our spring trickles on, and all the fields are incredibly *green*. The brown tops of the fells are now purple with heather. All the hill-farmers are so used to taking three months to get their hay in, because the weather is never right, that this year, when every field was harvested by mid-July, they don't know what to do with themselves in August: a few days' beating for the local shoots perhaps.

Did I tell you that Ruth's son is going to be married to a charming American girl in October? Anyhow the young couple are coming up here next week-end to spend a day with us. We are meeting them at Richmond (thirty miles) and have got them rooms at an inn about halfway from there. Although it's an intolerable nuisance having *anyone* here, they're both delightful, and their arrival will give us an opportunity to clean and tidy everything, so as to show off the cottage at its best. We pray for a fine clear day like to-day—when one could see into Westmorland, and almost watch Roger making impish comments at his desk—but I expect they'll get a drizzling day with no visibility.

Alas, there seem to be no sales while we're here. Since the local paper didn't appear for seven weeks, I daresay many sales were postponed and will now take place just too late for us.

Ruth says she much enjoys the affectionate messages you send her —and would send a lot back if only the censor would pass them.

21 August 1959   *Grundisburgh*

It hasn't happened often before, but I am afraid this letter won't arrive till Monday. Your letter was not coughed up by the hotel until Wednesday evening, and we had a great rush all that day and Thursday, which left us all rather limp. You never can tell in this awarding;

if you run up against a mad examiner you may spend three hours on work which should take one. On Wednesday a man (ex-don) turned up who quite often gave eight to an answer that was worth sixteen. He evidently was marking fifteen–sixteen-year-olds on a Tripos standard. Curses both loud *and* deep accompanied the re-readership of his scripts. But all is over now and we are home again—Pamela from Holland which she much enjoyed. The Lawrences were in their caravan and she nearby in a sort of Dutch council-house—far cleaner than an English ditto would be, though quite primitive. Another thing which struck her was the enormous amount the Dutch eat; her landlady was convinced that P. must surely starve to death after seeing what an infinitesimal portion she ate of the six thick slices of bread, the two eggs, ham, cheese (!) etc which they put on the breakfast-table.

Your address. Do you suppose that though away from home I have not got it in my pocket? And now in fact it is pretty secure in my head, though that may become a blank at any moment. *Can You Forgive Her?* just lasted out the bed-time reading night and morning. A rum lot the Vavasors—and that old stick Planty Pal; and one could make a lot of adverse comments, but how *readable* it all is. How little many people have read, whose job one would have thought needed a good deal more—e.g. an English Lit. examiner of fifty or so, who was reading *Howards End*, 'the first one of Forster's I have ever read'. He teaches Eng. Lit. too, at some not wholly dim school. That would not happen in Germany surely? And my colleagues, who know all about John Osborne, Lawrence etc., had never even heard of Father Damien and the Stevenson letter. And one of them foams at the mouth at the memory of having once been asked to read Carlyle's *Life of John Sterling*—on the odd grounds that he hates Carlyle's 'Teutonism', of which there is no more in *J.S.* than there is any of Kipling's jingoism in *The Jungle Books*. Fancy any Eng. Lit. teacher not knowing Carlyle's description of Coleridge at Highgate!

Do you include in your good titles *Is He Popenjoy?*[1] which I can't quite swallow, though I seem to remember it as excellent reading. I remember little nowadays of anything recently read.

[1] By Anthony Trollope.

I was stupidly thinking 'Well done, Gehazi' was the first line of the poem. No, here it is in R.K.'s collected poems simply called 'Gehazi' (1915). It is pretty blistering, but I suppose Rufus Isaacs blandly ignored it. Has A.B. Cox ever written under his own name, or any other but *Malice Aforethought* under F. Iles? It was very good. Don't I remember a masterly first sentence, something like: 'It was during the Vicarage Garden party that X decided to murder his wife'? Tell me, by the way, about Simenon. They all say he is so good, but I must have struck some of his offday stories, e.g. *Maigret in Montmartre* which I read on yesterday's journey. It seemed to me well enough, but not more, and Maigret himself showed no particular genius. What would you recommend of Simenon's?

I met Bob Boothby at Cambridge and liked him; he was excellent company and very friendly. What good stories they tell of old Beecham the conductor. I like his 'What an artist!' when a donkey brought into some opera rehearsal brayed, followed by 'And what a critic!' when it copiously evacuated on the stage. No doubt you knew it.

I once went to Saltburn, though I cannot remember when or why. I don't recollect the coaldust at the water's edge. In your letter you make it sound like an additional attraction. I like to hear that Ruth keeps two books going at once, because I always do (I *have* had three). Tell me of any really good recent Penguins. Otherwise I shall really have to re-read in bed W.W. Jacobs, *Earlham* and *The Irish R.M.*—not that there are not worse fates than that (my Cambridge colleagues, by the way, think nothing of the last, but I suspect they haven't read it—in the Quiller-Couch sense of 'reading').

My letter in the *D.T.* I merely, via an old hero, hit a full pitch to leg. Some ass had suggested that the Tories after nine years are tired and 'voters should give the others a run'. I recalled the old Lord Chief Justice who, his friends hinted, should retire, one reason being that he often went to sleep on the Bench. He grunted and then asked who would succeed him. When they said 'X', he snorted and said: 'Well, let me tell you, I do much less harm asleep that X would do awake.'

Love to Ruth. Good news about her son. One knows such sad tales of a mother finding her son's choice of a wife wholly wrong.

You were quite right, and your excellent letter reached me only this morning. In fact this suited well, since our week-end was much occupied with the visit of Ruth's son and his intended. On Saturday (the last day of a week of superb sunshine) we drove to meet them at Richmond (which is *not* thirty miles away, as I told you last week, but only twenty-three), picnicked with them on the moors and brought them back here. Yesterday they came back for lunch, after which we drove them back to Richmond. By then the weather had broken, and the mountain-tops (including ours) were blanketed in damp clouds. Today a gale is raging, and by ill luck this is the evening on which we arranged to climb down the hill and sup with our benevolent farmer and his family. So I may not be able to post this till tomorrow.

As usual, we have decided to steal an extra day here, and will now drive south on Thursday. The next day (Friday) is my fifty-second birthday, and Ruth is planning a little dinner-party in her Hampstead house, at which Comfort (who returns from France that day) will be present. On Saturday morning C. and I will go down to Bromsden, where I shall hope to find your letter waiting.

Gradually, in the evenings and at odd moments, we are filling up the lacunae in the Oscar notes, and I am re-writing the worst of them. Ruth is now reading the whole damned thing through, with the notes, to make sure they are in the right places etc.

A.B. Cox has, so far as I know, never published anything under his own name, but many years ago he wrote a number of quite good detective stories as Anthony Berkeley (which I suppose are his Christian names). As Francis Iles he published one other suspense-story, called *Before the Fact*. I haven't set eyes on a copy for ages, but remember thinking it good, if a trifle inferior to *Malice A*. Simenon is excellent at his best, but he has written so much that, although I've read most of them, I can't now remember which is which. You may well have struck an inferior one. I should try some more—perhaps non-Maigret ones, for M. is, as you say, not wildly exciting. Simenon's greatest gift is that of conjuring up the feel and atmosphere of French seaports and small towns in the minimum of words and almost without adjectives. Maupassant had this gift, but S. is even more successful at it. My favourite Beecham story is of the instrumentalist who played a wrong note at rehearsal. Beecham tapped for silence and then asked: 'What's your name?' 'Ball, Sir Thomas', said the culprit. 'H'm,' said Beecham, 'singular!' Cardus, a great friend and admirer of B's, has a fund of good stories about him. And now I see he has married another young girl—well, well!

(Now I must change and descend the mountain. More anon.)

10.45 p.m. We have just staggered up the hill, blown out by endless home-made cakes etc. Luckily we borrowed a powerful flashlight from our hosts, for the night is pitch-black, with a gale blowing.

Last Monday we duly drove to Saltburn (sixty-two miles, all country) and spent a happy day on the beach. I bathed three times, R. once. The rest of the week we simply basked outside the cottage, all meals alfresco, and we are both sunburnt as though by Riviera sun. At long last I have finished *The French Revolution*, and I somehow doubt whether, for all its splendid flashes, I shall ever read it again. When I get home I shall start on *Past and Present*: searching for Oscar's quotations is certainly enlarging my scope, and I don't need much excuse to launch out into well-worn but by-me-neglected paths.

I imagine you are likely to be invaded by grandchildren for the next few weeks, and can see you sheltering from them in your summer-house. Alas, we haven't taken any more snapshots for your delectation: hot sunshine begets a delicious lethargy in which reading *The Times* is a hard day's work—even yesterday's *Times*. And often we don't breakfast till 10. Lingering over breakfast is the office-worker's first step to liberation. Do you remember Birrell's remark: 'Chippendale, the cabinet-maker, is more potent than Garrick, the actor. The vivacity of the latter no longer charms (save in Boswell); the chairs of the former still render rest impossible in a hundred homes.' I copy it out irrelevantly because I have just come across it quoted by Oscar and enjoyed it. Now it is time to light our candles and go up to bed. The wind is raging outside: otherwise there is no sound save the quiet tick of the grandfather clock. This is the place for us.

Ruth insists on sending her love.

Good! The old rhythm is re-established—systole and diastole don't they call it? I don't know exactly what they/it mean(s), and strongly sympathise with the embryo science-student who wrote that in all human affairs could be observed a regular movement of sisterly and disasterly. How G.K.C. would have loved that and brilliantly demonstrated the profound truth of the remark—just as he did of the apparently faulty definition that an optimist was a man who looked after one's eyes and the pessimist one's feet.

I am in the summer-house—after a month during which it was far too hot. And of course this would be the day on which Pamela is turning me out of it and entertaining; and all the afternoon and evening the garden will be full of shapeless old women, led by a vivacious nonagenarian named Mrs Shadrach Gray. She used to darn my socks and when I questioned her charge of one penny per sock as being absurdly small, she replied firmly that it was what she charged in 1897 and why should she change?

Odd about your gale. Suffolk has known nothing but sunshine and calm for weeks, and my frame of mind approaches that of Keats's bees[1] —and *my* cells have been pretty clammy of late. At anything over 78° I am like the psalmist, poured out like water. Marking papers has really been as good an occupation as anything more active. I have not quite finished yet—nothing from British Guiana having turned up, and I await without enthusiasm about 180 lucubrations on *Great Expectations*. And I want to hear no more about Joe Gargery or Magwitch as long as I live.

That is most interesting about A.B. Cox, because I always read any Anthony Berkeley I could get hold of. I wonder why he is so anonymous? And weren't you impressed by my remembering the first sentence of *M.A.*? I haven't seen it for twenty-five years. I had it, but some brute of a boy pinched it. I will try some more Simenon but you don't raise my hopes very high. Maigret is an impostor. Lestrade and

[1] In his 'Ode to Autumn'.

even Athelney Jones[1] would have thought nothing of his work in the Montmartre book. His atmosphere I agree is good. Thank you for the Beecham quip—very typical. Send me any more you come across. None so far reported is below first-class, unlike many in the Eddie Marsh book in which I am at the moment submerged. Not at all bored, though it really is too long, and the beer at times is very small. I find myself beginning to like E.M. You knew him no doubt—and will be able to tell me why he was always spoken of with more or less genial mockery. Was it the combination of eyeglass and voice and eyebrows or what? He had a far better head and heart than most of those who sneered at him.

Of course you won't read *The French Revolution* again—but you will sometimes dip into it in search of some half-remembered gem of phraseology or characterisation. What a vivid power the 'thrawn old peasant' had. Do you know his life? I never read the immense one (Wilson), but once knew Froude pretty well. The best short one I know is Garnett's—not in the English Men of Letters. You will like the past part of *Past and Present* and put Abbot Samson among your heroes. I never much took to Jane C. (nor did Browning!) and find her famous letters over-praised. Recently I was pleased to be told (by whom?) that she traded on her repute as a raconteur and could be very long-winded and boring. Wasn't that Geraldine Jewsbury association all rather dubious?

Talking of length, the Ipswich library, pursuing its policy of acquiring the most expensive and least readable literature, has just got three obese volumes of Theodore Dreiser's letters. I browsed on them for half-an-hour yesterday with very little pleasure or profit. A dullish dog surely? He wrote in 1941 that he would prefer to see the Germans established in England rather than the continuance in power of aristo-cratic fox-hunters. In brief he was pontificating without sense or point. Some friend at his English publishers protested and D. replied, addressing him more than once as 'darling', sticking to his views but hoping for no loss of friendship. I was pleased to see no further letter from or to this good man.

[1] 'When Gregson, or Lestrade, or Athelney Jones are out of their depths—which, by the way, is their normal state—the matter is laid before me,' said Sherlock Holmes (*The Sign of Four*, chapter one).

The garden swarms with offspring and I contemplate them as Macbeth did the descendants of Banquo, though considerably less horrified.[1] Pamela of course is in her element, ceaselessly busy, and obviously enjoying every moment.

P.S. Millions of good wishes for your birthday. Let me tell you fifty-two is just about the prime of life in many more ways than not. Of course if you still want to high-jump or waltz all night it isn't, but for calm enjoyment of the passing show, for freedom of taste, and indifference to fashion, it is the right age.

Love to Ruth. I have carried myself several inches taller since she 'insisted' on sending her love!

30 August 1959   *Bromsden Farm*

Your letter was faithfully awaiting me yesterday, on top of a fort-night's worth of bills, newspapers and circulars. Systole and diastole were repeatedly used by Carlyle to describe the action of the guillotine, so I suppose it will do to describe the ebb and flow of our correspondence—ah well, the tide's out here, as the talkative lady in *Juno and the Paycock* declared, holding out her empty glass.

Leaving Kisdon was agony, as ever. Our last day was gloriously hot and sunny, as was the day of departure. We locked the door of the cottage (after stopping the grandfather clock) at 10.30, ate our lunch and tea by the wayside, took it fairly easy, and reached Soho Square at 9.30 p.m. Friday was a mass of visitors, correspondence and other nonsense. Ruth's birthday dinner in Hampstead had to be postponed till 10 p.m., when Comfort belatedly arrived from France. The noise of London once again seemed intolerable, its air foetid, after the silent freshness of Kisdon, and next June seems a very long way off. I was indeed impressed by your memory of *Malice Aforethought's* opening, and would have been even more so if you had got it right! The immortal sentence runs: 'It was not until several weeks after he had decided to murder his wife that Dr Bickleigh took any active steps in the matter.'

[1] 'What, will the line stretch out to the crack of doom?' (*Macbeth*, act iv, scene 1).

I can't at the moment remember any more Beecham quips, but I recall Cardus describing how B. once rang him up from Leeds (or somewhere even more distant) and discoursed for half an hour, apropos of nothing, on English music from Purcell to Delius. Knowing B's dislike of Elgar, Cardus at last interjected 'What about Elgar?' To which Beecham: 'What about him? Is he ill?'

Your reaction to the Eddie Marsh book was exactly mine, but I read it on Kisdon in paradise, where critical judgment is blunted by joy. I knew Eddie for many years, and it was impossible not to laugh at his squeaky voice, extraordinary gestures and general twitter.

I began *Past and Present* last night in bed, but sleep overcame me after two chapters. I've got the huge Wilson biography, but it's in fact a gigantic source-book rather than a biography. Froude is excellent, though now factually suspect in places. I'm sure Mrs Carlyle must have been hell, but the old boy can't have been too easy to live with. Have you ever visited their house in Chelsea? It's a museum containing all their furniture and many relics—austere, uncomfortable and very interesting. The nicest great-man's-house I've seen was Napoleon's Malmaison, where the library is a gem.

Theodore Dreiser's books are enough to stop me in my tracks, never mind his letters—that slovenly turgid style describing endless business deals, with a seduction every hundred pages as light relief. If he's the great American novelist, give me the Marx Brothers every time.

I loved your description of my age as the prime of life, and only wish I had more time for 'the calm enjoyment of the passing show.' Next week is already hideous with engagements, and I can see the doors of the prison house inexorably closing. Chaos still follows the printing strike, and we shall have to put off ten books to 1960. In a way this is a good thing, since it will obscure what would otherwise have been the hiatus caused by my three-months absence and the non-acceptance of any books (if you see what I mean) during that time. I usually publish just under fifty books a year—almost one a week, so we would normally be twelve short for next year. I'm not sure whether *The Lion* has gone to you yet: if not it shall go next week, when fresh supplies are promised.

300

Peter looked in this afternoon. While he was shooting in Scotland he was attacked by pleurisy, refused to pay any attention, went on shooting, and seems none the worse. He is an extraordinary chap.

At the birthday dinner on Friday I had my first glass of wine since April, didn't enjoy it much and felt no better for it, so I think I shall continue my teetotalism a little longer.

The garden here is unusually ablaze with flowers, particularly zinnias, which love the sun. Most of the grass is parched, and Comfort is having great trouble in transplanting seedling wallflowers. To-morrow Ruth and I are going to *The Aspern Papers*, on which I will report next week.

I had a feeble hope that membership of that ridiculous B.B.C. com-mittee would include a new radio set, but it seems they only run to free copies of the *Listener* and *Radio Times*. I can't wait for the first meeting.

2 September 1959   *Grundisburgh*

Well!! I could have almost *sworn* in a law-court that at least there was something about a garden-party in the first sentence of *Malice Aforethought*. And I have no copy, and it is out of print. Why isn't it in the Penguins? There are very many worse. I grant you it is not *very* impressive to remember a thing wrong. The number of things I am certain about diminishes rapidly; the day no doubt approaches when I shall have forgotten who played for England at Edgbaston in 1902— the side that Plum thinks the strongest that ever did. And we lost the rubber!

I have finished *Eddie Marsh*, and it is my considered opinion (as the specialist said in the advertisements of Lamplough's Pyretic Saline) that it would be hard to mention half-a-dozen people who did more good (using the word in Aristotle's sense, viz from a good motive, in a good way, and with good results) in a lifetime than he did. Your word 'twitter' holds the reason of his absurdity. About many (most?) of his written judgments there is no twitter at all. The way he stuck to his opinions, generally *very* sound ones, is admirable. As to voice, it is odd to remember that Bismarck, of all people, had a thin falsettoish voice.

It should have been that of Stentor, or at least Frank Harris. There is not much sign of Winston or Somerset Maugham laughing at E.M.

Yes, poor old Carlyle, as his mother said, was 'gey ill to deal wi' ', which Froude, in his loose way, often writes as 'to *live* with', which is very different. I have twice been over the Carlyle House, as well as the one at Ecclefechan (*not* Craigenputtock!), as you say an ugly uncomfortable house, with its absurd sound-proof room on the top floor, which was a complete failure, as anyone could have told him it would be if the ceiling wasn't doubled like the walls. They didn't know much about dyspepsia then (do they now?) but surely some doctor ought to have stopped him having what he calls an 'innocent spoonful of porridge' just before going to bed. Did you ever hear of a stranger 'nightcap'?

I am trying to set a paper on *Julius Caesar* in which no question is repeated that was set in any of the *four* papers in the last five or six years. And it is really not possible, as whoever thinks there are more than sixteen questions that can be asked on the play is like the cricket enthusiast who claimed that Trumper had seven different ways of dealing with a yorker. I think I shall try a quotation from old Agate, viz that Brutus is 'a magnanimous ass,' but it won't pass the revisers —I tried it on before. J.A.'s calling Richard II 'a muff' was objected to on the grounds that many candidates would not know what a muff was. It is true that the number of candidates who don't understand plain English steadily increases. 'Reading' was once set as one of the essay subjects, and produced several answers all about biscuits.

Sorry about your getting only the *Listener* and *Radio Times* for your good counsel on the B.B.C. committee. The former is as often as not unreadable. *Punch* is completely so. I understand hardly a thing in it. Does anybody read it? And who is the new editor of the *T.L.S.*? Pryce-Jones passed out of it very quietly.

Apart from professional football, is there anything more boring than everything about an election except the actual results? Roger's fatuous [Liberal] party is going to dish a good many Tory marginal M.P.s. I wish I had the smallest belief in democracy in action as opposed to in theory, in which of course we all believe. Old Inge in his *Evening Standard* articles had a nice right and left, one from Creighton: 'Socialism won't work till all men are perfect, and then it won't be needed', and 'A Labor program is one which leaves out "u" and "me"'. We live in the constituency of Eye, and our member is much the stupidest man in the country. Who is your member? I should be quite prepared to hear that you don't know, holding with the Doctor the sound if rather cacophonous view: 'How small, of all that human hearts endure, That part which laws or kings can cause or cure'.[1]

There *is* a garden party at the beginning of *Malice Aforethought*, so you weren't so far wrong. The trouble about Eddie Marsh was that, despite all the goodness you so rightly praise, he seemed (and in many ways *was*) exceedingly *silly*. For instance, his handling of Mrs Brooke (impossible old bitch though she was) was maladroit in the extreme. H.G. Wells and Arnold Bennett both had squeaky voices, but they weren't silly: perhaps impotence has its own brand of silliness.

The unreadable *Punch* has asked me to be drawn for 'a posy of publishers' which they are planning. I have graciously consented, so look out! The new *T.L.S.* editor is a charming chap called Arthur Crook, who has long been doing all the work there.

I propose to take as little notice as possible of the General Election. Henley is a safe Conservative seat, and the sitting member, John Hay, has some minor ministerial job. They say he's pretty good, but how do I know?

Last Tuesday my old father (age 81) drove to the Grand Hotel, Eastbourne, for a fortnight's holiday. He was accompanied by a twenty-four-year-old waitress called Iris, posing as his niece. Until recently he took such about with him for dalliance, but now it's simply, I fancy, for companionship, though how a cultivated man can long endure the conversation of an illiterate Cockney girl is rather baffling. Anyhow, the very first night the old boy fell over in the bathroom and (it appears) pulled a muscle, or something of the sort. He spent the next three days in bed in the hotel, and on Friday I heard that he was being moved to a nursing home. Iris then left for home, and as my sister is

---

[1] Dr Johnson, 'Lines added to Goldsmith's *Traveller*'.

away in Scotland I thought I ought to visit the old fellow. So yesterday morning I left here at 9.15 in our old Morris station-waggon and drove the hundred miles to Eastbourne. The roads were crammed with sea-going traffic, and the journey took me three and a half hours. Several times I thought I must be behind a funeral, and eventually I found I was! It was a glorious day, and the countryside (all crops harvested) looked benignly autumnal—plenty of mellow fruitfulness, and thank God no mists. I hit the sea-front at 12.45, immediately plunged into the sea (which I always adore), and then sat on the beach for a couple of hours, eating the excellent lunch Comfort had given me and reading a book about Oscar—very enjoyable. Then I visited my father. The nursing home is a Catholic one, run by Irish nuns, and since he is a violent Agnostic I was amused to find him surrounded by holy pictures and statues of the Virgin. I took him some flowers and books, and was reassured by his comparative comfort and the bottles of whisky with which he had come armed. I stayed an hour with him, ate an excellent tea, and drove home. There was so much less traffic that the return journey took three quarters of an hour less than the outward one, and I was home by seven, slightly tired but ever so virtuous. All of which puts me further back in my manuscript-reading etc.

Last Monday Ruth and I took our American friends to *The Aspern Papers*, which is first-rate—continuously dramatic and perfectly acted. I know you never go to the theatre, but I know you'd like this if you could hear it. On Tuesday I trekked out to Putney, and was delighted to find old Ransome much improved. He was able to get out of bed and totter with two sticks into the dining-room. His wife is thinking of taking him to Brighton for a change: he has been in bed since Christmas, and I was beginning to fear he would never rise again.

One day I lunched at the Ritz Grill, one with some rich City merchant-bankers, one with the wife of a millionaire—all for business reasons—so you can see that I am rapidly being dragged back into the whirlpool. London is full of visiting Americans and Canadians, who take up a lot of time, and I can't tell you how I long for the peace of Swaledale and my one perfect companion.

Donald Somervell is out of the nursing home, but he doesn't sound at all well. I'm going to see him tomorrow.

Oscar *still* hasn't gone to the printer, but it's no good trying to be a perfectionist if one hasn't got the time.

9 September 1959   *Grundisburgh*

Well anyway there *was* a garden-party. But I am still slightly put about at having misquoted so badly, rather (to compare small things with great) like the great scholar Ingram Bywater when someone reading a commentator's note came across the Latin word *'sicilicus'* I.B. lugged down a dictionary (I quote R.W. Chapman) and read out *'sicilicus*: It means the forty-eighth part of an *as*, and, by metonymy, a comma'. Then replacing the book, and turning to his audience, in accents of unfeigned dismay—'I didn't *know* that!' But the memory in old age! I remember the shock when C.M. Wells a few years ago recalled how Percy Lubbock and Alec Cadogan sat next to each other in Sixth Form. But Alas! A.C. came to Benson's a half or two before P.L. left. And C.M.W. had the Cambridge trait (defect?) of never making a statement unless he was sure of its truth.

Talking of misquotations, I hope you saw that my admirable nephew[1] after visiting Stevenson's grave in Samoa offered £50 to have the misquote 'home from *the* sea' put right on his headstone? I call that a good gesture, but I have no doubt that one of the sillier socialists, like that ass among the apostles, will grumble that it wasn't put into the poor-box.

E. Marsh. Yes, I see. That silliness. I suppose Winston and Maugham were cute enough to see through it. He certainly sounded rather silly when I met him at Roger's. But he was very old then, and spent most of the evening to, from, and in the water-closet, his bladder having clearly thrown up the sponge, literally and metaphorically. I wonder if Mrs Brooke was manageable at all. Perhaps we enter there that dim cave of physiological spleen, breezily referred to by a medical friend of mine who stated that—as he put it—'*all* women instinctively dislike a eunuch'. Do you know anything of this? Surely it must have been the theme of many manuscripts offered to you.

[1] Charles John Lyttelton, tenth Viscount Cobham (1909–1977), Captain of Worcestershire cricket side 1936–1939, Governor-General of New Zealand 1957–1962.

I am interested to hear what you say about the modern treatment of jaundice. New since my day (nine years ago). I don't expect it has reached Suffolk yet. My own doctor is a charming man, but knows very little. I hope you will be back in the convivial world at the October Lit. Soc.

How good you are about visiting invalids! Tell me about D. Somervell. He is a bright spot at the Lit. Soc. And your bankers and millionaires. Are these last ever happy? A few days ago the *Daily Telegraph* had a picture of the richest man in the world—capital £700m. A face with *no* expression except gloom, worry, and dyspepsia. Bankrupts *per contra* invariably look plump, hilarious, and obviously without a care in the world. It is a solemn thought that on Wednesday you are about two million pounds richer than you were on the previous Wednesday. Isn't Nuffield about the only *actively* benevolent millionaire we know of? What a reflection on those Mellons etc. Perhaps, like Bernard Shaw they are all convinced in their old age that they are ruined.

13 September 1959   *Bromsden Farm*

Thank goodness *The Lion* has reached you at last: I only hope it doesn't disappoint you. Adlai Stevenson should be on its heels, 'but with unhurrying chase and unperturbed pace'—forgive me; I have just agreed to open the Francis Thompson centenary exhibition at Preston on October 29, and am brushing up my memory of that remarkable poem,[1] parts of which (as much as you would let me) I once recited to you so as to escape Early School. Luckily I still think *very* highly of F.T., so should be able to fill thirty unforgiving minutes of jaw about him.

I missed the news of your nephew's splendidly quixotic offer about the misprint on Stevenson's tomb, but what a fine gesture!

You simply mustn't start worrying about the General Election, which, except for casting my vote before swine, I propose to ignore. Did you see the (I think Giles) cartoon of the man, promised daily election talks, junking off his television set to the rag-and-bone man?

[1] 'The Hound of Heaven'.

The possibility of switching the machine off is seldom mentioned, but then I've never had a set and am ignorant of its seductive power. As for Mrs Brooke, Eddie, and the proposition that all women instinctively dislike a eunuch, alas, I lack experience to answer you, but it seems quite likely.

If you haven't read *The Aspern Papers*, you must do so at once: it's one of H.J.'s best. None of his own plays had any success at all—and rightly, for they were no good. His stories are packed with drama (now being exploited by others), but he lacked the one essential dramatist's gift—an instinctive sense of exactly what will *go* in the theatre.

I visited Donald Somervell again last week—in a friend's house in a noisy part of St John's Wood, miles beyond Lord's. He was up and dressed, and we sat out on a flower-filled balcony, but he looked terribly thin and pale, and his whole state sadly reminded me of another friend who died of much the same thing (a growth on the bladder) some months after undergoing the agonising deep-ray treatment which Donald has just endured. However, I pray the cases may be quite different, and he was cheerful enough, though when I left, his lady protector said he hadn't laughed like that for weeks. I shall try and go again.

I've no idea whether bankers and millionaires are ever happy, but my luncheon hostess told me that Mr Clore takes as much trouble about buying a picture for £20,000 (£4. 10. 0 to you or me) as in acquiring a business for several millions. Sounds kinda dreary to me. But the Mellons have given away countless millions in the U.S.A. The National Gallery itself, in Washington, was financed by them.

I'm ashamed to tell you that Oscar *still* hasn't gone to the printer: more and more letters and facts keep cropping up, and it seems silly to run up unnecessary bills for proof-corrections if I can do them now. And I have very little time. The other day Shane Leslie told me that one of Oscar's boys was caricatured in Michael Arlen's *The Green Hat*, so I re-read it (the first time since it appeared when I was at Eton) and was astonished to find how readable and interesting it was. The plot is ridiculous and much of the dialogue fantastic, but the book has a definite quality beyond the curiosity of a period piece. I remember in 1930 asking Somerset Maugham what he thought of Arlen's books, and he said 'The first thing to remember is that he's an Armenian, an Oriental'. I now see that he was right: this book is like something by the author of *The Arabian Nights* set down in London and Paris of the 1920s. I hesitate to suggest your reading, or re-reading, the book, and simply report its unexpected effect on me. Into what unexpected places do the rigours of research carry one! (Incidentally Shane Leslie was right, and I got the reference for my note.) At the same time I'm plodding through *Past and Present*, and so far plodding is the *mot juste*, but I suspect there is better to come. I've got more than a dozen books out of the London Library, all containing Oscar references which I haven't yet had time to consider. The job, I fear, is endless.

Here the garden is Sahara-dry and even the sun-loving zinnias hang their heads till the reviving hose is brought their way. Adam shoots the squirrels as they come for the walnuts, which aren't any good anyhow. All our apples are dropping off, but I revel in the sunshine and dread the end of summer-time. Peter can't wait for October and the pheasant's death-knell. They are taking up most of Soho Square with a pneumatic drill.

16 September 1959   *Grundisburgh*

I had forgotten that your Early School exemption choice was the Hound. A very good one too. And you have never forgotten it—which of course was my *raison d'être*. Luckily the authorities never found out, or I should have been scuppered. They would have asked for a ruling, and of course the whole arrangement was *ultra vires*. I never did any action of the entire rightness of which I am more certain. I should like to hear your jaw. Will it be taken down? If so—!

I shall tell my nephew of your reaction, which will please him immensely. It certainly ought to be widely known that one Governor-General has a right sense of values.

How right you are about the election. I wish I could be as philosophical, but I am like Ovid, '*Video meliora proboque, Deteriora sequor*'[1] (he was writing of morals!). There was a very good article by Hollis in the *Spectator* in which he pointed out that the scurrilities used to be

[1] I see and approve better things, but follow worse (*Metamorphoses*, vii, 20).

308

confined to *hoi polloi*, while the leaders of the parties thundered high-mindedly in the upper air, but TV etc has changed all that; leaders have to talk to the Eatanswill voters in the voters' own language. *Hinc illae lacrimae*. It is an odd thought that Mr Gladstone could and did address a working-class audience for one and a quarter hours in the open air on the subject of the disestablishment of the Irish Church —and held their attention. Can the present bigwigs do that? No. They carry no ice, as Jimmy Thomas said to Eddie Marsh, who corroborated it by adding 'and cut no guns'.

I note what you say of *The Aspern Papers*. I suppose if poor old H.J. had collaborated with Pinero or Sardou his plays might have run. I doubt if I ever read the book. What a persistent posthumous success the old boy is having.

I withdraw *in toto* my smear about the Mellons. I had no idea old Andrew had been such a patron of the arts. Must have confused him with someone else.

You will not, I hope, omit to drink to the immortal memory on Friday. Half the papers seem to think the Doctor was born on the 13th. Why? Have we monkeyed with the calendar since his day? And has the dinner taken place, with old Powell as cheer-leader? We ought to get some American fan to endow the club handsomely, so that it could really provide a good dinner in the famous room, and not among the spittoons and cigarette-ends of the Cheshire Cheese. But such nice things don't happen.

20 September 1959   *Bromsden Farm*

I sincerely hope that my Francis Thompson 'jaw' will not be taken down—even for your edification. In about three weeks' time I shall bitterly regret having accepted their invitation, and thank goodness I had the wit the other day to decline to address two hundred French schoolmasters in London, welcoming them to London in an *hour's* talk! The French Embassy offered to pay my 'usual fee', but a joke's a joke.

I'm all for harnessing the sea, but I should hate its salt to be removed, since it must be that very salt I so much enjoy in sea-bathing.

I care little for swimming in rivers, and abominate swimming-baths. Give me 'the unplumb'd, *salt*, estranging sea.'[1]

If I had any money I should take every possible step to make sure the Government didn't get it at my death. A close friend of Comfort's married (as his second wife) a charming old boy who was old enough to be her father. He was clearly wealthy and they lived in style, but she never liked to ask him about money. When he died (in his eighties) he left £400,000, of which the Government took £300,000. She was wild with rage and couldn't understand why he hadn't given their two children large presents. Nor can I.

Adam went back to Eton on Wednesday, and yesterday I drove over to take the three things he had forgotten—his portable wireless, his *braces* and the funds (some £3 in a small tobacco tin) of the Eton College Chess Club, of which he is (however unsuitably) treasurer.

Last week I again journeyed to Putney to sup with the Ransomes, but he is so much better that they are going to his sister's in the country for a change, so I shan't have to visit them for a few weeks.

I had a note from Donald S. to say he has gone to his brother's in Kent, so my visiting list is mercifully reduced. My old father is back in London, so I suppose I shall have to look in on him one day.

Peter is flying north tonight for three more days of grouse-shooting. Shooting is like a religion to him—something solemn and ritual, which can scarcely be joked about. When I occasionally suggest that it's a very expensive form of self-indulgence he is pained and shocked. Are all shooting-fans like that? I see no reason why people shouldn't do it (or hunting) if they like, but I can't quite swallow all their stuff about its being good for the birds and foxes. Or are you so ancestrally deep in the *mystique* that you think me iconoclastic?

23 September 1959   *Grundisburgh*

I spent a long evening after finishing my last G.C.E. paper (the author of which had the impressive name of Amelia Macdoom) reading *The Lion* from beginning to end, and relishing it vastly. I suppose the reviewers are right in saying the mystical and the factual are inade-

[1] Matthew Arnold, 'To Marguerite, continued'.

quately blended, but I got several good thrills out of it. The first encounter with King left me literally breathless. The author conveys —as Blake did in 'The Tiger'—the deadly terror roused when his eyes changed 'from soft gold to a glacial yellow,' and makes the dealings of the girl with King entirely convincing. I was sorry when he had to die.

You will be amused to hear that my nephew's gesture apropos of Stevenson's tombstone *did* produce a letter of protest in a New Zealand paper on the grounds that there were many causes worthier of £50, and the inscription as it stood did adequate justice to its subject. Charles hasn't stopped foaming at the mouth since he saw the letter. I have replied by pointing out that, though not at first sight strongly resembling Mary Magdalene, he is being misjudged exactly in the same way as she was over that spikenard. I remember a young Socialist years ago condemning Shakespeare as valueless because 'he wrote nothing about the class-war'. But is it only senile pessimism on my part which sees the defence of worth-while values becoming a tougher job every year?

To-morrow we go to listen to our sitting Tory. I didn't want to, but Pamela insists. I think she sees me being tarred and feathered by the local diehards if I don't go. I hope he will be heckled.

I giggle over what Adam left behind—as cheering evidence that boys don't alter. Braces and the Chess Club money are supremely right. Was it in your day that the Hon. Sec. of the Shakespeare Society took the minute-book with him to Cambridge, and Luxmoore had eventually to get the Cambridge police to extract it from him?

I didn't know Peter was a gun-fanatic. I never was, but there were a good many in Worcestershire in the early 1900's. A man who shot accidentally a young pheasant in September was not actually cut by the county but apt to be vaguely referred to as 'poor Tom', the underlying inference being that he couldn't be 'all there'. There is a very good scene in a book of R.H. Benson's, *The Conventionalists*, describing the awful solemnity with which the 'veterans of the smoking-room' discuss the 'problem of the second barrel'. The host presides, with great tact and geniality while chiefly engaged in 'smoking a cigar as well as it could be smoked'. R.H.B. could do such episodes superbly, but I expect he was before your day. Like hunting-men and foxes, shooters, without actually averring that the pheasant enjoys being shot at, are quite sure that the bird if offered the choice of living to be shot or not living at all, would vote for the former. Ask Peter.

At the library yesterday I picked up a book called something like *The Craft of Letters*, a symposium in which John Lehmann put the *Life of Hugh Walpole* at the top of modern biographies, so there!

I must stop. My doctor this morning thought to reassure me about the itch with the information that 'the skin is one and indivisible', which I thought was only said of God and peace. But at least it seems to mean that there is every hope that my ailment is *not* leprosy. I am rather like C.M. Wells (now 88) who was always convinced that every ache spelt cancer or paralysis, and every sneeze pneumonia.

27 September 1959   *Bromsden Farm*

Once again the hot sunshine kept me out in the garden all day, and I am behindhand with everything, so you won't get much of a letter, I fear. I have just finished reading Gissing's surviving letters to H.G. Wells. I suppose I shall publish them, but truly they're very dull— which I fear is the epithet that fits all Gissing's work. Have you read any of his novels?

No reviews of Jonah yet: it's just as well he doesn't get back from Italy till the end of next week. Did I tell you that he's now trying his hand at short stories? He simply can't stop writing, has exhausted his memories, knows that no-one will publish his books on religion, is tired of verse, and so falls back on fiction. What will it be like?

So glad you enjoyed *The Lion*: didn't you think the opening very good: all the animals in the morning?

I can see you're going to be much more involved in the Election than I am. I love the way you say 'sitting Tory', as though he were something protected by decent feeling, like a sitting pheasant. I fancy I have inadvertently disfranchised myself by failing to apply in time for a postal vote, but Henley's Tory is safely sitting and won't miss my X.

The Craft of Letters was *edited* by John Lehmann, but the gratifying remarks in it about my book were by J.I.M. Stewart, a Christ Church don who writes excellent detective stories as Michael Innes.

Let me tell you of my latest piece of Oscar-hunting. In 1929 an incredibly addle-witted society woman called Mrs Claude Beddington published a rubbishy book of memoirs, full of wind, famous names and split infinitives. In the middle of it she irrelevantly printed four excellent letters from Oscar to someone called 'Harry', written in 1885. Seeing Mrs C.B.'s name in the telephone book, I wrote to her (she must be very old) asking if she had the original letters, and whether she could now tell me who Harry was. No answer, so I rang up. She proved to be a vitriolic old tartar: 'I certainly shan't tell you who he was, no matter how often you ask me!' She then wrote me an abusive letter, accusing me of 'stirring up muck' to make money, which seemed a little hard since after all she printed these letters first. Nettled by the old bitch, I determined to find out Harry's name without her. The only clues in the letters were that he had been a Bluecoat Boy and was up at Cambridge in November 1885. I wrote to a dear old man at Christ's Hospital (retired beak, now in charge of the library, met through Edmund Blunden) asking if he could give me a list of Old Blues who were at Cambridge in November '85, and had Harry or Henry as Christian name. Back in a quaking hand came the answer: 'There was only one—H.C. Marillier (1865–1951)'. This was a great stroke of luck, and a glance at *Who Was Who* showed that he was clearly my man. But I still wanted the originals, so while I was busy Ruth went down to Somerset House and looked at his will. He left everything to his second wife, and the will was witnessed by 'Ernest H. Pooley, Barrister'. This rang a bell, and sure enough I found in *Who's Who* that Sir Ernest Pooley married in 1953 the widow of H.C. Marillier!

All this happened last week, and on Friday I wrote to Lady Pooley, asking whether she had the original letters, and if there were more (Mrs Beddington in our telephone duel told me that 'Harry' had a suit-case full!). I can't wait to get her answer. Meanwhile Mrs Beddington, softened by the reasonable answer I sent her, shows signs of weakening, but I'd love to be able to tell her that I not only know who Harry was, but have got the originals. See what a lot of time I enjoyably waste!

Mrs Beddington seemed to think that to have received a letter from Oscar would brand anyone as a pervert down the ages. I told her

I had letters to 250 men and women, including Browning, Gladstone, Matthew Arnold, Irving, Ellen Terry, Whistler, Bernard Shaw, Ruskin etc etc, and she really couldn't think them *all* queer. Harry, she told me, was '200% normal' (sounds terrifyingly unbalanced, doesn't it?) and twice married. 'Why do you worry then?' said I.

Goodnight, dear George, another exciting instalment next week.

1 October 1959   *Grundisburgh*

The majestic splendours of September's passing equalled or even surpassed its incomparable prime. Lord's at 4.30 yesterday afternoon was not a cricket-ground of this world, though the committee-room was earthly enough. Poor old Plum really does 'mop and mow' now. Does the passage of time really insist on a jaw that wags and wags, and that eyelids shall be rimmed with geranium-red? I am not sure they were not more sensible in medieval times when the holy maul was kept behind the church-door with which to brain the senile when they were beyond a joke. *Pro tem.* and judging by what daughters and friends say, I *am* a joke, so nothing need be done for a year or two.

Gissing I read quite a lot of fifty years ago. Dreary stuff I seem to remember, except—*what* was that book called he wrote when at last he wasn't starving? I then thought it rather beautiful, but haven't seen it for years.[1] The late Headmaster of Wolverhampton, one Warren Derry, an amiable and definitely intelligent man, has nearly finished a life of Dr Parr.[2] He thought of approaching the O.U.P. but is rather off it. I told him I would tell you about it. Not that I held out any hopes, but said, which is true, that it sounded a book which would interest you. He told me some very good things about the old pedant. But I expect you have your own plans and are up to the neck for years.

Your Oscar episode is absorbingly interesting—a rare piece of comedy ending with your discovery of Harry's identity, Lady Pooley and the weakening of Mrs Beddington. Mind you tell me all the rest

[1] Probably *By the Ionian Sea* (1901).

[2] The Rev. Samuel Parr (1747–1825), schoolmaster at Harrow, where he taught Sheridan, and other schools. Voluminous writer, in Latin and English, on politics and religion.

as it happens. After all some day these letters of yours to me will be a largely complete autobiography. Very few such have any stories so good. And there are plenty of others.

I remember Roger being as indignant as he can be (which is nothing much!) at old Queen Mary and George VI objecting to his mentioning that Q. Victoria's dress on a certain occasion was too low. ('Why lug this in?' H.M. pencilled in the margin.) It had already appeared un-objected-to in print: Greville, I guess.

I came back from Cambridge yesterday where I was for one night at a hotel in a garden bordering the river. There was a largish bade-lynge of ducks which one guest out of every three fed with bread. The ducks were clearly socialist ducks. Whenever one got a larger bit than the rest a dozen at once pursued her and tried to bag it. The possessor eluded them and won but only by dint of bolting the morsel, so in the end it did no good to anyone. I enjoyed the air of meek triumph which it assumed the moment after victory. You could *hear* it saying 'Sucks to you' (there is a pun somewhere here).

I am always amused at your reception of any name I suggest for the Lit. Soc. (not I grant you with any great conviction or partisan urging): so far they are either homos, or drunkards, or bores, or aesthetically (to eye or ear etc) repulsive, or all of these at once. Do you think my Extra Studies had somehow a homosexual influence? So many of my audience have gone that way. But it is of course well on the way, judging by our novelists, to becoming a *virtue*. Our philosophers appear to be agreed that there are no absolutes in morals, so the vice of one century may be the virtue of another.

Harry Altham, the new M.C.C. president, told me to-day that he has copied out and given to at least six people, old Jonah's poem on Eton in *A La Carte* and they are all thrilled by it. And no one has ever heard of it! Did not his publishers do pretty poorly about the book? As you know, it is of first-rate quality and the reviews said so when it came out. I feel dubious about his stories somehow, but who can tell? I wrote and told him how much I liked his book, but he won't have got it yet.

There was an excellent dinner-party here last night, and I particu-larly enjoyed a good crack with Joan Astley who is splendid company. I told her I was writing to you and she enjoined me to send you abundant good wishes. There was also a charming American lady, Mrs du Boulay, whom you may know—merely for the reason that there seem to be jolly few people you don't know.

How you will mock me when you hear that on leaving Cambridge temporarily bookless I spent half a crown on the Penguin *Lucky Jim* to see if on a second reading it was—as I thought—the earnest record of trivial people doing and saying trivial things, with no particular wit or felicity of style in the writing. And it is in its thirtieth edition—has a page of ecstatic press-statements about its brilliance. It might be the book the world is waiting for.

4 October 1959   *Bromsden Farm*

Do by all means suggest to Warren Derry that he should send me his life of Dr Parr, if possible without raising his hopes. Sparrow is a great expert on Parr, and if necessary I might get his advice. Although I am persistently overwhelmed by books and manuscripts, I never in fact have *enough*, and each time one of my half-yearly lists appears I wonder how on earth the next one is to be composed.

On Tuesday I got a charming answer from Lady Pooley (*çi-devant* Mrs Marillier) saying she had *no* O.W. letters and remembered her late husband (Harry) saying he had never had them back from Mrs Beddington! Accordingly I wrote to Mrs B, saying I now knew who Harry was, and that his widow believed Mrs B still had the letters, and wouldn't she have another look for them. No answer from her yet. Another good O.W. letter (to W.L. Courtney) turned up last week from a friend in America.

Did you see that the leading article in the current *Spectator* recommends its readers to vote Liberal, or failing that Labour? Surely there will be a flood of abuse and resignations from the far-flung rectories? I have already cast my True Blue vote by post, since I shall be in London on Polling Day. The *Daily Telegraph* is giving its usual all-night party in half the Savoy, with unlimited food, drink, dancing, and dreary results flashed onto a huge screen. I have been to two of them and shall avoid this one. My daughter Bridget, who is dying to go, is planning to get herself in on my invitation card.

And as for your endemic masochism—deliberately re-reading *Lucky Jim*—well! I look back in pity.

Summer-time, winter-time, it makes no difference to the delicious mid-day heat, and today I picked *sixty lbs* of quinces from our one tiny tree.

Last night Duff arrived back bronzed and cheerful after six weeks in Greece. He had driven a thousand miles in three days, but seemed none the worse. On Friday he returns to Oxford for his last year, and on Saturday plays for Fred's Old Boys against the Field. Adam says that none of the doors in the new house shut, and there is no hot water in the showers. He is now *Secretary* of the Chess Club, so some other boy's parents will have to stump up when the £3 in the tobacco-tin disappears.

Last week Ruth and I were taken to Graham Greene's play *The Complaisant Lover*, which we both enjoyed. Ralph Richardson gives an excellent performance in it.

When we meet on the 13th (Tommy, alas, can't come to the dinner) I shall have come almost straight from a committee-meeting of the London Library, at which a tricky question has to be answered. The Trustees of Carlyle's House in Chelsea (Harold Nicolson is one) have asked the Library to lend them for an indefinite period Carlyle's sofa and armchair, which for many years have stood in an obscure corner of the Library, unlabelled; indeed I doubt if half-a-dozen members even know they're there. Committee-members leave their hats and coats on them: that's all. My strong feeling is that they should go to Cheyne Row, where they will be seen and known (perhaps even admired) for what they are. Clearly H.N. will back me up, but the Librarian tells me there will be opposition. No doubt the impish Fulford will have a Liberal word to say. You shall hear all about it.

Next Saturday is the wedding, and Ruth is overwhelmed with preparations. It's at a village called Stoke-by-Nayland, beyond Colchester, and the expedition will take all day. Comfort is coming too, and my sister.

The electric drilling in Soho Square is jolly nearly insupportable: it has already been in progress for a month, curse them.

I copied out an incredible paragraph from the egregious Mrs Beddington's memoirs, but stupidly left it in London, so you'll have to wait a week for its doubtful pleasure.[1]

Peter's agent here—a nice active man of thirty-five—was stricken last Saturday with violent polio, and has been in an iron lung for a week, almost beyond hope. Now the fact that he has survived so long apparently brings a little hope. He has a wife and three small children. Adam and Bridget have been inoculated, but Duff never had his second jab, which I'm now ordering him to arrange immediately. I suppose one day they'll find a cure.

7 October 1959   *Grundisburgh*

How infallibly tiresome human beings can be—especially those who regard themselves as high-minded. Your wretched Mrs Beddington of course should let you have all the O.W. letters she has apparently pinched. But she won't, having (as one reads between the lines) the wrongheaded obstinacy of such folk, half fool and half knave. Perhaps Lady Pooley could use legal pressure to get the letters? It is an engrossing story.

I *greatly* enjoyed Jonah's book, and wrote to tell him so; he has a delightful style—light and firm. But won't the chorus of indolent reviewers talk about waste-paper baskets, scraping the barrel, etc? So easy, now that the 'belles lettres' essay or causerie is out of fashion. Birkenhead, though, was quite pleasant in the *Sunday Times*. But he is an O.E. Kingsley Amis is not, and *Lucky Jim* is very unlike Jonah's work. I like your Maxian expression 'endemic masochism,' and plead guilty, secure in the comfortable knowledge that if and when your letters are published, practically nobody will know the meaning of either word. But I didn't spend much time over the vapid complications of what it is putting it too high to call the love-affairs of some of

---

[1] 'Mrs Cornwallis-West's daughter, Shelagh, had married Lady Grosvenor's son, the present Duke of Westminster, and George Wyndham's brother, Guy, was the husband of Mrs Cornwallis-West's sister, Minnie; thus Mrs Cornwallis-West was the mother-in-law of Lady Grosvenor's son as well as the sister-in-law of Lady Grosvenor's husband.'

(Mrs Claude Beddington, *All That I have Met*, 1929, p. 171.)

the most insignificant and boring people that ever breathed. The grim truth is, however, that I am no nearer than before to solving the mystery of its immense success. But, as Birrell said, one needn't worry if modern stuff doesn't appeal, as there is always Boswell to read thoroughly. Do you know at all what happened at the Johnson Club meeting, at which grave matters were to be discussed? The club cannot go on as at present.

Of course that sofa and chair should be in Cheyne Row,[1] and why should anyone object? But of course they will. I hand you this from Bishop Creighton, which you may be able to use. 'After we have let the ape and tiger die in dealing with ourselves, there remains the donkey, a more intractable and enduring animal.' You could also say that a fellow-founder of the London Library with Carlyle has a grandson (G.W.L.) who is sure his grandfather would have approved of the transfer. How did the two things ever get to the Library? Are there relics of all the founders?

Stoke-by-Nayland is not at all far from here. I wish Ruth could look in here. She would refresh us far more than a week's rain for which we pant, but no doubt she has not a moment. Oh yes and of course you too; I hadn't realised you would be there. Stupid!

I think I grow steadily stupider. Last week I attended a committee-meeting of the Governing Bodies Association, and was bewildered by the ease and confidence with which portentous knights like Sir Griffith Williams and Sir William Cleary threaded their way among the intricacies of the English educational system. They really do know the difference between a direct-grant and a grant-aided school which to the normal man is as much a mystery as the difference between a Republican and a Democrat in the U.S.A. However *Who's Who* reveals that they have been in or about the Board of Education most of their lives, where I suppose such knowledge is essential. I now understand the slightly frosty look on the jowly visage of Sir Griffith when I said a certain action of the minister's apropos of Woodbridge School was 'bogus'. It is not impossible that he formulated it. My suspicion that I had put my foot in it was aroused by the impish grin on the Archbishop's face. I like his boyishness, though many no doubt would say archbishops should not be boyish. But it is an effective and lubricatory

---

[1] They now are.

element of his admirable chairmanship. He would be a better companion on a desert island than Sir Griffith.

Last night I began *Dr Zhivago*, but rather doubt if I shall persevere. I am *not* good at the Russians—'fluid puddings' as Henry James called their great novels. I don't understand *why* they say and do the things they do. I expect you took it in your stride and put it at the top of twentieth-century fiction. The plain truth is that I am too old, too dull-witted, too inattentive, too out of date. None the less I am coming to the Lit. Soc. on Tuesday. And I am writing to Warren Derry—when I can find his address.

11 October 1959   *Bromsden Farm*

Only a half-length letter to-day, alas, but I shall see you on Tuesday, and just now things are crowding in on me. All yesterday was taken up by the wedding of Ruth's son: all went well, and the bridegroom's mother looked exquisitely beautiful. It's too bad that we couldn't take advantage of our comparative nearness to you, but it wasn't possible.

At 10.30 tomorrow the Court of Appeal will begin its hearing of the London Library's rating-appeal, and I must be there to listen. After keeping us waiting fifteen months for a date, they finally gave us four days' warning. T.S.E. was (still is) on his way to America, but I managed to telephone to him in his cabin before the *Queen Mary* sailed, and he angelically said I could put his name to any letter I thought suitable for *The Times*. If we lose our appeal, it seems sensible to try and float our public appeal for money on the wave of sympathy which we shall surely receive, so there probably won't be time to send a draft letter to the U.S.A. for T.S.E.'s approval. This afternoon Simon Nowell-Smith and I roughed out a rather pedestrian first draft. They expect the hearing to end on Tuesday, and the London Library committee meeting is fixed for 2.45 that day. So I look like having a busy couple of days.

No answer from Mrs Beddington: I fear she has finally gone to ground. On Thursday evening I sat alone in the flat, unwillingly hypnotised by the election-results, which were mostly 'No Change' and pretty dull. I went to bed only when Gaitskell 'conceded' the election. So your gloomy forebodings were happily unjustified. Jonah came to see me and proudly showed me your letter, which was the first thing that greeted him on his return home from Italy and gave him untold pleasure. The Johnson Club meeting isn't till October 27, so those weighty issues remain undecided. I don't think I could use Bishop Creighton's excellent phrase at the London Library meeting without some member of the committee taking it personally. Did you hear of the parson who began his sermon: 'As God said—and rightly —...' It grows on one.

I have never attempted *Dr Zhivago*, and doubt whether I ever shall —so there!

All football was stopped at Eton last week, as each game on rock-hard ground produced a crop of broken bones.

15 October 1959   *Grundisburgh*

A *very* good evening again. And how well and svelte (*le mot juste!*) you were looking and how lovely was Ruth. We had good talk at our end. The wicked knight[1] was in excellent form (I am *not* referring to Tim!) and I am certain enjoyed himself. Jonah kept him well in play, but four or five joined in. Afterwards I had a talk with John Sparrow about Dr Parr and his prospective author, whom he knows quite well and approves of. And yesterday I wrote to Derry and encouraged him to get into touch with you—at the same time making it clear that he mustn't take your flawless affability and courtesy and interest as any sign that your professional judgment was bamboozleable (a *good* word. M. Banck was before your day at Eton who told his division, 'I stand no boozlebam from little English boys', with the result of course that he had to stand it—and much else—for the next eleven years.) Then Ivor, Jonah, Sparrow, and I sat until after 10.30, when all you sissies were tucking yourselves up. No, I exempt *you*, who never face less than two men's work every morning. An interesting point was that during the entire evening not *one* word was said about the election, though many topics were tossed about. Flash Harry bet Peter Fleming

[1] Sir Malcolm Sargent.

half a crown that the word 'spikenard' does not come in the New Testament Mary Magdalene episode. Surely F.H. will lose. As the 'little judge' said in the Bardell case[1]: 'How could I have got it on my notes?' i.e. why do we know the word at all if it is in no gospel? He seems to know the Bible as well as he knows Beethoven—but he *didn't* know the saddest and shortest biography ever written, which is in it. I think I have told it to you. The late Lord Jowitt was delighted with it.

What does 'Judgment Reserved' mean? I hope that the holy three are putting their heads together to defeat the letter of the law—but I don't suppose I am more optimistic than you are. The law is so often a ass (only seven people in England ever quote Mr Bumble correctly —and I am one of them!).

The next case of any real interest may well be 'Lyttelton v. X.Y.Z.', to wit my solicitors, who have for a year and a half had £4500 of mine, from the redemption of some gilt-edged stock, and forgot either to ask my trustees about re-investing, or even putting it on deposit. Really men of law and business are more inept, careless, doodle-witted, opinionated and mendacious than parsons, schoolmasters and publishers!

18 October 1959 *Bromsden Farm*

Having had a delightful hour of you beforehand I can resign myself to the fact that it is so often the *other* end of the dinner-table that you are keeping a-roar. You were in splendid form on Tuesday, and clearly enjoying yourself, to my great delight. While you were hobnobbing with Sparrow and Co I had withdrawn to an upper chamber with the amenable Roger, and between us we re-wrote (for the fifth time) the draft letter to *The Times* about the London Library. 'Judgment Reserved' means that we shan't know the verdict for about a fortnight— which gives me time to send the draft letter to T.S.E. for a sixth revision by the master hand. I have asked Masefield to back up our letter with another on the following day, when the time comes. Roger

[1] In which Mr Pickwick's landlady Mrs Bardell successfully sued him for breach of promise. The little judge was Mr Justice Stareleigh (see *Pickwick Papers*, chapter xxxiii).

came to the Court of Appeal for the tail-end of the hearing on Wednesday morning. I hear rumours, through our solicitor, that our admirable Counsel, Geoffrey Lawrence, may charge nothing at all for this whole appeal! His normal fee would be about £700, so his waiving it would be a tremendously generous gesture: surely the least we could do would be to make him an honorary Life Member of the Library.[1]

On Wednesday the Court of Criminal Appeal was hearing the Podola case in the next court.[2] The wretched man himself wasn't there (for which Ruth was rather thankful), but we pushed our way through a phalanx of coal-black law-students and others to have a look at the court—and very impressive it was, with five judges in wigs and scarlet gowns ranged in line with the Lord Chief Justice in the middle. The Attorney General (that ass Manningham-Buller) was reading a mass of argument about 'true amnesia', but the scene was none the less dramatic. (A B.B.C. announcer has just said 'controversy—God help him!)

I fancy Flash Harry will lose his half-crown over spikenard, which, according to Cruden, occurs in two of the Gospels. I wouldn't have expected P.F. to know any more of the Bible than F.H. Please tell me (you never have) the saddest and shortest biography.

For goodness' sake take some firm steps to recover your £4500 before your solicitors abscond. The first solicitors I ever had to deal with bore the splendidly Dickensian name of Smith, Rundell, Dodds and Bockett. Don't you love the way it begins quietly with the simple Smith (clearly an alias) and works its way gradually into top gear with the improbable Bockett? J.M. Keynes said he considered solicitors as a class to be ignorant, stupid and ineffectual—and who are we to dispute the great man's word?

Peter looked in to-day. His agent is still (after three weeks) desperately ill with polio, and has to be artificially fed since he can't swallow. There's no knowing when or if he'll be able to work again, which is a great nuisance for Peter.

[1] We gratefully did.
[2] Guenther Fritz Podola, a German–Canadian, had murdered a police sergeant while on the run from a blackmail charge. He pleaded hysterical amnesia, but was convicted. His appeal was dismissed and he was executed on 5 November.

Fred's old boys were beaten 3–2 by the Field, and Duff scored the 2. He is now in digs at Oxford and planning to work for his Schools next June. He took a lot of excellent colour-photographs in Greece and is hoping to lecture with them at prep-schools for a fiver a time, as he successfully did after his Russian trip. We are encouraging him to apply for a Commonwealth Fellowship, which would mean a year at an American university.

Adam reports shamefacedly that the school were beaten at chess by Mill Hill!

I am now two-thirds of the way through *Past and Present*: some of it is pretty dull, but as always with T.C. there are memorable moments when the grumbling thunder gives place to a flash of lightning, and Abbot Samson is a nice new friend. I'm also much enjoying George Painter's new life of Proust, which is full of wit and scholarship. Ronald Knox and Queen Mary await my attention.

Did I tell you that last week I heard of twenty-five new Oscar letters in Texas?! Photostats are on their way, and expectation is high. It begins to look as though I shall print the best part of a thousand letters—but when? you ask, and my answer is an apologetic and explanatory mumble.

Sparrow told me at dinner that G.M. Young is now in an old men's home at Goring-on-Thames, quite gaga and not properly recognising Sparrow when he goes there: very sad, but it's a great relief not to have him at All Souls, as one can imagine.

Didn't you think Jonah looked very pale and old the other evening? I fear that pneumonia in the summer aged him a little. He is rather upset because Harold Nicolson hasn't reviewed his new book in the *Sunday Times* (nor has anyone else), and I try to comfort him.

On Friday I was drawn (or caricatured) for *Punch*: I'll let you know when the result is going to appear, but I daresay you see that dismal hebdomadal regularly. Last week I won a dictionary from the *Spectator* for solving their crossword—or rather Ruth did, for I always send in solutions in her name, so that she'll have the fun of getting the prize if there is one.

Have I missed Diana's baby in *The Times*, or hasn't it appeared yet? How many grandchildren will that make?

Goodnight, beloved patriarch. I must do some work.

324

As if whenever I glanced down *your* end of the table I didn't see one vast chuckle, every face a-wreath with smiles! Our roars were mainly the work of Jonah and Flash Harry, who was in fine salacious fettle. Yes, I did enjoy every moment, but then I always do. It is a warming thought to reflect what an amount of great and continuing happiness *you* have poured into my senescent years—letters, Lit. Soc., books, *Ruth*—isn't that a pretty good cornucopia? This very morning two lovely fat books, obviously bursting with good qualities. No return that I can make for these rich benevolences looks anything—*is* anything—but derisory in comparison. As Pamela said at breakfast, the luck of finding such generosity in the book-world just when reading is one's chief pleasure is simply fantastic.

I *do* hope you will defeat those brigands. I keep an eye wide open for your letter. A slightly less momentous one from me is in to-day's *Times*, which I expect you missed; it is shamefacedly tucked away on page 3. It will be interesting to see if anyone answers. It may light such a candle, Master Ridley, among all the more purpled and dew-lapped members of the M.C.C. Do you think that *all* the famous sayings, last words etc were invented? I have written to Plum Warner that my nephew said he was told by Rhodes that Trumper never said 'For God's sake Wilfred, give me a moment's peace' in the 1903 Test Match at Sydney, when V.T. made 185 and Rhodes bowled all afternoon on the plumbest of wickets; and I urged Plum to let us know the truth, which he must know.

Later. A postcard from Plum, mainly illegible, and the only decipherable thing is that *none* of any of the sayings attributed to cricketers is true. We must fall back on old Agate's view that there are two truths to everything—factual and artistic, the first being what *did* happen and the second what *ought* to have happened, or alternatively what Achilles actually did, and what Homer recorded his doing. Agate's great example of this theory was Cardus's superb description of Tom Richardson at Old Trafford in 1896—T.R. standing dazed, like some great animal, by the failure of his heroic effort—the factual truth being that when the winning hit was made he was legging it to the pavilion and had downed his quart before anyone else had got there.

Geoffrey Lawrence sounds a good man. Why are barristers usually spirited and interesting chaps and solicitors exactly the opposite? I don't think mine will abscond—yet, anyway. My brother is hot on their trail. The head of the firm is straight out of Dickens or Wells. He bites his thumb, not as a sign of contempt but to give him an air of deep thought; he makes notes about what one is saying on his blotting-paper, and once, I know, there was certainly no lead in his pencil (may I remind you of the Staffordshire squire who begat an heir when over seventy and mocked at the disappointed heir-apparent for 'thinking I had no lead in my pencil'. Hush!).

I like the names of your first solicitors. All in jail now I suppose? They are almost in the class of Quirk, Gammon, and Snap in Warren's *Ten Thousand a Year*. My father had an old friend whose name had the reverse trend—a majestic start—and a weak finish. Ferdinando Dudley Lee Smith. But Keynes was right. Solicitors are always getting wrong exactly what we pay them—rather heavily—*not* to get wrong, e.g. wills. My uncle Bob was a solicitor—and far the stupidest of all the eight brothers. He did all the family business and cost them thousands through his blundering. Still, I recollect with gratitude an item on the bill he sent my cousin: 'To conversation on telephone about Captain X's pension, and agreeing that it would be a small one: £1. 6. 8.' I class that with Pamela's bill from a vet 'to attendance on cat 1/6; to removal of cat 1/-; to burial of cat 1/6 = £0. 4. 0.' Which brings me to Jehoiachin. Look up *II Chronicles* xxxvi, 9, because if I merely quote you won't believe me.[1] You will be interested; so will Ruth (and I suspect, that like me, it will move her just a *little* way in the direction of tears!). What *could* the poor imp have done? I suppose he catapulted the postman's dog or something of the sort. It must be admitted that the same king in the *Book of Kings* is given *eighteen* years, but no one has thought of correcting *Chronicles*, and there it remains. I imagine the

---

[1] 'Jehoiachin was eight years old when he began to reign, and he reigned three months and ten days in Jerusalem: and he did that which was evil in the sight of the Lord.'

poor lamb was knocked on the head after a reign of three months and ten days—just about a Michaelmas half.

Jonah writes cheerfully, but says he is being kept indoors for breathlessness, which doesn't sound too good. He *did* look rather battered on Tuesday, but was in good form and stayed late.

I hope the dictionary Ruth won was the thirteen-volume Oxford. But probably you have that. I could never run to it.

Yes, Diana's second son turned up *on* the day (characteristic!) and all goes well. And Rose reports No 5 should appear in April (our nineteenth. At the moment it is nine boys, nine girls, and *all* sound in wind, limb, *and* mind. There is no 'poor Dorothy' thank God).

Yes, of course a lot of *Past and Present* is entirely out of date now. But as you say, through all the dead grey lava the old volcano sometimes erupts finely. Abbot Samson is alive all right, also Willelmus Sacrista and his potations. Little things stick in my memory, Richard's 'tornado' oaths and a tiny snapshot of John 'in cramoisie velvet', was it? And you know there are some jolly good things in his fierce *Latter-Day Pamphlets*. *All* the abuses of government, Parliament etc which he savages are still alive. Read—it won't take you two minutes—the Pig Philosophy in the article 'Jesuitism' and say if you can that we have outgrown all that. And on lots of other pages he might be talking of the late d-d General Election!

I have just been reading about Courvoisier[1] and Wallace in the book of Mrs Yseult Bridges, who fancies her detections.[2] I suppose there cannot be much doubt that Wallace did kill his wife, but the Appeal Court were surely right. The evidence just fell short in point after point—but only just. Wallace's face gives *me* the shudders. Surely those eyes are not those of a sane man. I am sorry for Adam's sake that W. was a very keen chess-player. No Mill Hill champion would have beaten him! Mrs B hints that his murdering Mrs W. may have been

---

[1] François Benjamin Courvoisier, a Belgian valet, murdered his employer Lord William Russell in May 1840 and was publicly hanged outside Newgate prison on 6 July. Thackeray was taken to the execution and was so distressed by it that he wrote a strong anti-death-penalty article 'On Going to see a Man Hanged', which was published in *Fraser's Magazine*.

[2] *Two Studies in Crime* (1959).

in his eyes like a chess-problem, i.e. to block all police-moves as Alekhine foresaw and frustrated all moves his opponent might make. Will that wash?[1]

A splendid four-pager, with a two-page rider this week. I can't conceal from you the fact that Jonah's book isn't selling anything like as well as its predecessor, though I try to blur the facts to Jonah himself by vaguely encouraging noises. Still, he has had a pretty good run with his reminiscences, and I never expected great sales for this volume.

No news yet of the Court of Appeal's decision—and, more tiresome, no answer from T.S.E. in America. I have a nasty feeling that the whole thing will break between 2.30 on Wednesday (when I attend my first B.B.C. General Advisory Council Meeting) and 2.30 on Thursday, when I address the burghers of Preston on Francis Thompson. A busy week seems likely.

I think all the bright law-students must go to the Bar, leaving their duller brethren to be solicitors. I imagine that few barristers would get very far without some of those qualities which solicitors so signally lack.

Jehoiachin's story is certainly pitiful: I will give Ruth the reference tomorrow. No, I haven't got the big Oxford Dictionary, but the firm gave one to Arthur Ransome in reward for much help, and he has left it to me in his will, he says. I hope that many years will pass before I get it, since I am A.R.'s literary executor designate, and I don't want any more work just now.

So glad Diana's baby arrived safely: what a brood you have engendered!

---

[1] In 1931 William Herbert Wallace, a Liverpool insurance agent, was convicted of battering his wife to death, but the evidence was purely circumstantial, and the Court of Criminal Appeal quashed the verdict on the ground that it could not be supported, having regard to the evidence. Wallace died two years later, a broken man.

I obediently read and enjoyed 'Pig Philosophy', and am still wading through *Past and Present*.

Yesterday we drove to the Cotswolds to lunch with Comfort's stepmother, and afterwards I spent a delightful hour with Katie Lewis. She is 81, daughter of the first Sir George Lewis, the solicitor, and the only person I know who actually knew Oscar. True, she was only a child, but her memory is excellent, and since she seems to have known everybody since, she is splendid company. Just now she is mourning old Berenson, to whom she was devoted. Her parents were close friends of the Burne-Joneses, and her house is full of his pictures, as well as others, including a fine Rossetti drawing of Mrs William Morris. I wished I could have stayed longer. On the way we stopped for half-an-hour in Oxford and I snapped up a few secondhand books at Blackwell's. In term-time now it's almost impossible to park a car anywhere in the centre of the city: I suppose Cambridge is almost as bad. Nor will any number of ring-roads help to solve this problem. But driving in this country simply isn't fun any more: the wide deserted roads of France are another matter.

I'm just finishing the manuscript of a book I shall certainly publish. It's the first volume of the autobiography of John Morris, who recently retired from being Head of the Third Programme. It's an unusual book and he an unusual man. A contemplative recluse-type, he spent most of his life as an officer in the Indian Army (Gurkhas) and was on the first Everest expedition (1922). He is—or was—homosexual, and he treats this subject explicitly, with quiet dignity and good sense. I think it will interest you. It's called *Hired to Kill*—from Swift: 'A *Soldier* is a *Yahoo* hired to kill in cold Blood as many of his own species, who have never offended him, as he possibly can'.

But you know that already. If only all manuscripts were as acceptable! I rather look forward to the train-journeys to and from Preston, as undisturbed times for reading, though on the way up I shall doubtless be desperately preparing my speech. Why on earth did I ever agree to go? Ruth says I'm congenitally unable to say NO, but I *am* getting better at telling swift lies to telephoning hostesses, and long only to be left alone.

The Duff Cooper Prize for this year is looming up, and goodness knows who we can get to give it away. So far we've had Winston, the

Queen Mum and Princess Margaret: where do we go from there? Perhaps Diana will have an idea. Her second grandchild is expected daily—in Beirut, where the expectant father is recovering from amoebic dysentery. Now I must finish John Morris.

29 October 1959   *Grundisburgh*

I think you are right about solicitors and barristers. My uncle Bob would have been a hopeless barrister. It is true he was a hopeless solicitor too, but his firm didn't go bankrupt and he remained in it. He would have been disbarred in no time. He had in his prime a certain flair for words (e.g. Cobden's match[1]) and he loved rolling over his tongue words like 'reversionary legatee' though the family suspected he didn't know what either of them meant.

We go in a fortnight or so to *Trial by Jury* and *Pinafore*. I am President of the local G. and S. Society and have just written 250 words to be printed in the programme. *T. by J.* I haven't seen for over fifty years and remember thinking not very good. I am surprised too to find that *Pinafore* had a longer run first go than any of them (700 nights. *Mikado* came next with 672, but easily beat *P.* in all the revivals). What a tedious man Gilbert must have been—always in a huff about something, and brandishing his solicitor in every other letter.

What a pity the horse-whip is out of fashion. Did you ever know it used? I did—on an (eventually) eminent civil servant who jilted an old-fashioned and hot-tempered man's sister. I still meet him at Lord's sometimes. He is riddled with arthritis and couldn't horse-whip a mouse now.

You must have had a good spell with Sir George Lewis's daughter who 'saw Shelley plain', so to speak. Wasn't O.W. great fun with children, or did I imagine that? My hat, there will be good reading in your book when it comes. *Will* it come? Remember, as warning, the Balzac story in which an artist spent so long perfecting his picture that it ended as an almost complete blur, save for one tiny foot of breath-

[1] His stirring account of the University Match of 1870, published in the Badminton Library volume *Cricket* (1888), edited by A. G. Steel and the Hon. R. H. Lyttelton.

taking loveliness.[1] But surely it *must* be a best-seller on both sides of the Atlantic: or have tastes been finally corrupted by *Lucky Jim* and *Rooms at the Top*?

Have you ever picked up a real bargain at Blackwell's or Foyle's? John Bailey haunted the Charing Cross Road for years, but had no luck, till one day in Paris he picked up a book of poems with on the fly-leaf 'William Wordsworth from his friend Robert Southey'. I don't know what happened to it.

John Morris is new to me, but *Hired to Kill* sounds good. Did you ever read Taine on Swift with his 'terrible wan eyes'? Taine is very vivid—superb on the Elizabethans, but completely mystified by the English admiration of Dr Johnson. He would be. The leading miller of Ipswich recently announced in the Club that 'Dr Johnson was a bore —not that I ever read Boswell of course'. Yes the horse-whip ought certainly to be revived.

All Saints Day 1959   *Bromsden Farm*

Jonah looked in on Friday, less pale and gaunt than he was at the Lit. Soc., but still very breathless and able to mount the stairs only one at a time with a rest between (it's a mercy he wasn't bound for the flat!). His doctors tell him that his heart and lungs are fine, and perhaps some form of anaemia is his trouble. Meanwhile he is hard at work writing short stories: what will they be like? He is being most good-natured and philosophical about the moderate sales of his last book.

Each time you mention Gilbert & Sullivan I confess that I have never witnessed any one of their works, but clearly you think I exaggerate. How can I convince you? Wagner, yes, but my parents cared nothing for G. and S., and no close friend or chance circumstance has since lit up my ignorance. I've read most of the *libretti* and heard all the music, but an opera in a theatre—no. Clearly I should repair this omission, grit my teeth, and go to the whole lot, one after the other,

[1] In Balzac's *Chef-d'Oeuvre Inconnu* there is no loveliness left. '*Je ne vois là [dit Poussin] que des couleurs confusément amassées et contenues par une multitude de lignes bizarres qui forment une muraille de peinture.*'

next time they're in London, but shall I? Perhaps *Patience*, with its Oscarian allusions, would set me rolling down the slippery slope?

I'd adore to see your arthritic old friend trying to horsewhip a mouse, after limbering up by breaking a few butterflies on the wheel.

Oscar was indeed excellent with children, but then he was excellent with everyone, and all fell beneath his spell—even as I have fallen, sixty years after his death. Yes, the book will definitely appear, though I still can't say exactly when.

My best bargain at Foyle's was a copy of Edward FitzGerald's (anonymous) *Readings in Crabbe*, inscribed by him to a friend. I got it for sixpence. In the old days on the Farringdon Road barrows (which nowadays I have no time to visit) I was always finding for sixpence or a shilling books worth several pounds, and I can still remember the first edition (four vols, one shilling each) of *Middlemarch*, which I had to leave because I could carry no more. Next day, not unnaturally, they had gone.

I have accepted *Hired to Kill* and am now preparing the manuscript for the printer—a wearisome task.

My first meeting of the General Advisory Council of the BBC was rather amusing. Imagine a huge Council Chamber, arranged like this:

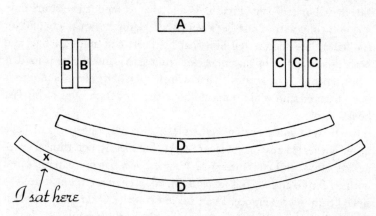

A. housed the Chairman (Norman Fisher—very good), Sir A. fforde (Chairman of Governing Body) and Sir I. Jacob (retiring Director General)

B. Governors

C. Massed BBC executives.

D. The Council.

332

I sat with two other 'new boys', Andrew Devonshire and Margaret Lane (Lady Huntingdon). A lot of questions (some interesting) were asked and more or less answered. The people who spoke most were Lord Strang (ex F.O. and very twitchy), a retired Governor of Nigeria called Sir James Mackintosh, Sir Hugh Linstead M.P., George Woodcock (of the T.U.C.), that horrible Patrick Gordon-Walker, the Bishop of Manchester, a chap called Hoare (something to do with the Cinema), Prof Mansergh (on Commonwealth relations) and, I'm delighted to say, Mr Gentle, head of the Greyhound Racing Association. When I crept away after two hours it was still going strong. Thelma Cazalet was the only Governor I knew. Gubby Allen is no longer on the Council.

On Wednesday, armed with sandwiches and coffee provided by Ruth, I travelled to Preston: the train was exactly an hour late. I stayed at the Victoria & Station Hotel (which must clearly take second place to the Hotel of the Immaculate Conception & the Post Office at Lourdes) and next day was lunched heavily by the (female) mayor and a mass of aldermen. Afterwards I spoke for half an hour in the Public Library to an audience of two hundred or so. Since my talk was almost purely literary, and most of them were utterly illiterate, little pleasure was enjoyed, except by the Library staff, who had arranged the Francis Thompson manuscripts and books most intelligently. (F.T. was born in Preston in 1859.) Sadly clutching a ham roll and a bar of chocolate I travelled back to London in a state of exhaustion.

5 November 1959   Grundisburgh

I can tell from my own feelings pretty well how angry you must be feeling about this Philistine triumph as the nice contemptuous little leader in *The Times* puts it. Shall you appeal to the House of Lords, or are they bound to say the same? How damnable it all is. English civilisation *deserves* to go down the drain. I hope Hodson[1] in his summing-up showed both sympathy and shame.

Jonah's health doesn't sound very good to me, who preserve the old belief that oarsmen's hearts are apt to go pop. I wonder how anaemia can cause breathlessness. What odd remote causes they

[1] Charles Hodson (b. 1895), then a Lord Justice of Appeal.

discover nowadays. I have occasional itching on elbow and ear. It is being put right by my wearing elastic stockings, believe it or not. I feel dubious about dear Jonah's short stories. So do you!

Odd your never seeing a Gilbert and S. play. Too late now, I suspect. Gilbert's prose is dreadful, and Sullivan's tunes are widely held to be 'twee'. They asked me to write 250 sparkling words on G. and S. for the *Pinafore* and *Trial by Jury* performances next week. I sent them (and thought they were rather good!) and have had neither acknowledgment, nor thanks. These are the times that try men's souls! Are you as aware as I am of the very strong movement in favour of *not* answering letters, *not* acknowledging, *not* thanking? It grows apace (I am reminded of a candidate who in a recent G.C.E. exam wrote in a *Richard II* paper that 'Bolingbroke was fond of trying not to annoy people'. (N.B. If you do go to a G. and S. play choose *Patience*, *Iolanthe*, or *Mikado*.)

Your B.B.C. General Advisory Council sounds from its personnel 'fine confused feeding'. No doubt whatever sensible and civilised measures you advocate will be turned down. Your vignette of Lord Stamp ('ex F.O. and very twitchy') brings him out very clearly—like Carlyle's Secretary the long-suffering Foxton, described by his master as 'very talky, scratch o'plastery, but good, compared with nothing'.

I see by the way that the rating of Lord's is probably going the same way as the London Library's. The M.C.C. want it to be £3500, the rating brigand £9000 odd, fortified no doubt by someone's suggestion (roughly) that a single-wicket match between Marilyn Monroe and Diana Dors would fill the stands. How I do hate all jacks-in-office—as you must have hated the Preston audience. But that in its turn may be senile pessimism. Books do seem to be increasingly read; they cannot all be drivel. A fan of Ian Fleming's said I *must* read his last one, and I did, but—! I.F.'s recipe is cards, wines and dishes (as costly as possible), torture, a seasoning of breasts and thighs, and a series of ludicrous strokes of luck and escapes by that very unattractive Bond from impasses in which his chief, who may have eyes of chilled steel and jaw of ditto, but certainly has a brain of cotton-wool, is always landing him. Can one really shoot a man in the back while playing baccarat in a crowded casino, without anyone hearing or suspecting till the murderer has vanished? What does P.F. think of I.F.'s books?

Last month my pre-Lit. Soc. letter missed you, so this time I plan to post on Sunday. To-day the country seems to have been swathed in fog, except just here, where we had bright hot sunshine all day. At noon I sat outside reading, with no summer-house to protect me. Adam is home for Long Leave: we are mercifully absolved from St Andrew's Day this year, since Adam is largely in charge of a 'Conversazione' which is being laid on in the Science Schools, and is unwilling to be disturbed. One of the highlights, I gather, is to be a working still, supplied by Guinness, with stout for the assistants. Adam seems quite happy in the new house, but says that the boys definitely don't get enough to eat.

The final scene in the Court of Appeal was on the drab side: since one can appeal only on points of law, the verdict is purely legal, without occasion for sympathy or shame. Although our two main (and vital) points were disallowed, so that a further appeal to the House of Lords is pointless, two minor points were given in our favour, and may well be a great help to other bodies in similar plight. (1) They ruled that the word 'annual' in the phrase 'annual voluntary contributions' could refer to the recipient, so that legacies can be included, provided one can show a settled pattern of such receipts. (2) They agreed that to a library a gift of books is just as much a 'contribution' as a gift of money. These are two basic changes in the law, for which others may bless us.

After the verdict I asked an usher if there was a room in which I could have a brief consultation with the Librarian, our solicitor, etc. He said 'You can go in here', and ushered us into THE LORD CHIEF JUSTICE OF ENGLAND'S COURT (as was proclaimed by the entrance). In these impressive surroundings we licked our wounds and decided to put in motion the appeal for money. We received just over £1000 in the first twenty-four hours after the letter in *The Times*, which seems quite hopeful. This included another £400 from Donald Somervell, bless him (he has had to have a second operation and is now in a Canterbury hospital). Masefield's letter I kept up my sleeve, so as to get it printed on the following day. I hope that the leading article on the book-page of next Thursday's *Times* will be devoted to the Library, and the *Guardian* rang me up yesterday about a piece they are preparing. I'm sure the great thing is to get as much publicity as we can as quickly as possible. I am having two thousand offprints of our *Times* letter, to use as ammunition. All this takes up a lot of time and energy.

In the middle of it I dashed to Broadcasting House and recorded three minutes' worth of drivel about Jonathan Cape's eightieth birthday. This you can hear tomorrow week (Sunday 15th) in a programme called The World of Books, though it will, as they say, bore the pants off you.

My writing is getting illegible—it wasn't Lord Stamp but Lord STRANG who twitched at that meeting.

I'm sure I warned you that Ian Fleming's last book was pretty poor: Peter is the soul of fraternal loyalty in these matters.

Yesterday morning I discovered, after months of patient tracking, that a Pall Mall bookseller has got nine excellent Wilde letters (which, ironically enough, I sold in Hugh Walpole's library at Christie's in 1945. Then they fetched £50, and now the bookseller wants £1000 for them). I went along to see him and he let me read the letters: at least two of them are first-rate, and somehow I *must* get them for my book (the bookseller would rather sell them as 'unpublished' and so is unwilling to let me copy them). I have already written to an American millionaire (who bought some other letters so that I could see them) and am hoping I can find a purchaser somewhere. How this book does grow! I'm still waiting for the final two batches of photostats from California.

Last week I was also much plagued by visiting American professors —three of them in one day left me breathless and exhausted. All nice and learned chaps, you know, but better taken in small doses.

Ruth won another crossword prize of 15/- last week, and since she and I have now received prizes from four papers lately, I've started sending in solutions with my sister's name and address.

I am told that *Queen Mary* and *Lolita* (blest pair of sirens) are carrying all before them in the bookshops, and we petty men must walk under their huge sales and peep about to find ourselves dishonourable graves. (Adam has just returned proudly bearing a partridge, after a day's shooting with friends.)

The Duff Cooper Memorial Prize is looming up again, and I am endeavouring, by very remote control, to snaffle Princess Alexandra as presenter.

N.B.   PROBATE, DIVORCE AND ADMIRALTY DIVISION
CHINESE MARRIAGE DECLARED VALID
WOU V. WOU (WOU OTHERWISE COLLINGWOOD INTERVENING)
WOU (OTHERWISE COLLINGWOOD) V. WOU

12 November 1959   *As from Grundisburgh*

Again an excellent evening—though less good as lacking the hour beforehand. The old acid drop[1] was in pretty good fettle on the whole, though he wasn't going to admit approval of much. He said, *inter alia*, that I was very deaf (untrue), that the Lit. Soc. now mainly consisted, as far as he could see, of novelists whom nobody read (untrue), that, yes, Donald Somervell was a nice enough chap—but he saved his face by adding 'he was a very bad Attorney General' (probably untrue, and I thought of the equally sour Housman, when told that X said he was the best Latinist in Europe: 'That is not true, and if it were, X would not know it'). The flavour of Tommy's conversation on the other side had the additional freshness of contrast—a nutty claret after quinine. And what a nice fellow Alan Moorehead is. I like to meet a chap who really does take the fall in the hippopotamus population to heart.

Roger bustled off earlyish, having promised to see home Harold Nicolson whom he described as 'very tottery'. Do you agree? Jonah was momentarily deprived of breath on rising from the table, Bob Brand had special dishes all through the meal, and as I told you, Sir C. would describe me as deaf as a haddock.

What a foul city you live in! To breathe this afternoon is to inhale vaporised pennies—old ones. Everyone was delayed in getting to the Abbey School G.B. meeting and I had to take the chair. Like all school G.B. meetings the main topic was finance, but one item of the agenda was the rather incongruous one, for what sum should we sell the

[1] Cuthbert Headlam.

337

stuffed head of a bison which we mysteriously acquired with a recently bought house? I did what I could to keep them dallying with this, and just when short-term mortgages were looming, thank God the Chairman arrived and the bison was indefinitely consigned to limbo.

I am intrigued by Adam's temporary entry into the world of stout. Bid him remember that it is a *food*, and a barrel in his room will at least keep starvation at bay. Why should Fred's cook produce less food in the new house than she did in the old? School diet is a constant headache, though there is, I gather, a less unanimous conspiracy by all boys to say the food is 'muck' than there used to be. At a girls' school I know, the general cry always has been that the girls are not given enough to eat. But in the same breath the complainers admit that their daughters are radiant with health and energy and happiness. So what ought we to do? A century hence perhaps the faculty will be saying that eggs and bacon are the main cause of cancer, consumption, rheumatism and corns. But I hope they will last my time. Do I know your *bêtes noires*? I think I should. Mine are parsnips, artichokes, Brussels sprouts, ginger, boiled mutton, macaroni, sago, skate, pike, and whale—not only because Dr Summerskill recommended it, though that could surely be held ample reason.

I am in the middle of the Druon book[1] and after a slow start, enjoying it. But do they really copulate as much as that in France—or die so frequently? And I wanted to ask you about *Lolita*. Need I read it? *Dr Zhivago* smothered me before half-way. And tell me all about Middleton Murry, whom no doubt you knew. Dislike of D.H. Lawrence makes me incline to like M.M. but I suppose he *was* a rum cuss. Not, surely, a very bad critic of Shakespeare, Keats and Co., at his best? But 'everything by starts and nothing long.'[2]

I turn steadily into Mr Pooter. Yesterday evening I bent to light a spill and a shout of ribald laughter announced that the seat of my trousers had a rent in it, one of those silent unannounced rents that come to thirty-year-old trouser-seats just before they give up the ghost. Has it ever happened to you? I inherit it. My mother used to send my father's oldest clothes to jumble bazaars in Worcestershire. My father used to visit the sale and buy them all back. Charles Fisher

---

[1] *The Curtain Falls* by Maurice Druon.
[2] Dryden, *Absalom and Achitophel*.

(killed at Jutland) and a friend found a jacket of my cousin Ted Talbot's at the tailor's, sent for cleaning. They got hold of a handful of buttons, two small bits of old cloth, and some shreds and patches, borrowed the tailor's note-paper and sent the stuff up to Ted T. saying 'Dear Sir, We regret to inform you that after cleaning the enclosed articles are all that remains of your jacket'. A good joke I think. Please agree.

Surely *some* very rich man will buy really worthwhile immortality by establishing the London Library. An American?? It *cannot* be allowed to fade away or even alter. Your (and T.S.E.'s) letter was a very good one. So was Masefield's.

Shall you tell anywhere the whole story of the Wilde letters? It is enthralling. What a fantastic number he must have written.

I shall not read about dear Queen Mary, who (oddly?) does not interest me, any more than her second-rate son (eldest) did. She and the bearded saint, as Roger called him, must have been very indifferent parents. But much may be forgiven him for (a) when asked what film he would like to see when convalescing, answering 'Anything except that damned Mouse' and (b) when the footman, bringing in the early morning royal tea, tripped and fell with his load and heard from the pillow 'That's right; break up the whole bloody palace'. The old autocratic touch.

14 *November 1959*   *Bromsden Farm*

I've decided that I prefer writing on Saturday when I can: there's less pressure of time, and I can still nourish the comforting illusion that all my publishing work can be done on Sunday. This week I also have to draft a 'press release' about the new Phoenix Trust[1], of which (unless my draft is unprintable) you should read something in the papers during the next fortnight. And I must compose a speech for Jonathan Cape's eightieth birthday dinner on Monday. I inadvertently misled you about that broadcast, which was in fact this afternoon, but you didn't miss much, and I am still recoiling from the horror of hearing in cold blood what my daughter assures me is my

[1] For the origins and objects of this Trust, see volume three of these letters.

339

own voice—ugh! My *coup* of the week was to persuade Winston (through his wife) to write to *The Times* about the London Library. I expect you saw his letter this morning. I only hope it brings in a few more cheques: so far we've had upwards of £3500, and there's a long way to go. Alan Pryce-Jones wrote an article for *The Times's* Thursday book-page (where he operates as George Cloyne—what a name to choose!), but the editor said the Library had been given enough space —two brief letters and a tiny leader! So now I'm trying to get the article on to the back page of the *Lit. Supp.* I very much missed our monthly crack in Soho Square, but thank goodness I caught you in time to prevent your standing impotently on the rainswept pavement with the handle of your favourite bell adrift in your hand.

It's really high time Cuthbert was mercifully put away: he's a misery to himself and a ghastly nuisance to everyone else. When he left he was still complaining that 'the whole atmosphere of the club has changed' (if he hates it, why not resign?), and when he claimed to have lost his hat and coat (with the strong implication that they had been deliberately stolen) I slipped quietly out into the night. Roger was charming at dinner, and so was Andrew Devonshire. Before dinner Cuthbert asked Brand: 'What claim has the Duke of Devonshire to belong to the *Literary* Society?' To which Brand mildly replied: 'About as much as I have', which temporarily shut the old curmudgeon up. I thought Jonah looked very ill, but he rang up next day to explain that he was perfectly well except for his breathlessness, but breath seems to me rather an important thing.

You're clearly much fussier about your food than I am. I positively like all your *bêtes noires*, except pike and whale, which I've never consciously eaten and certainly don't yearn for. I think the only things I positively dislike are brains, tripe, black pudding, trotters, hearts and a few other varieties of so-called edible offal. I always avoid fish with lots of little bones, and remember with sympathy the entry in an old book of etiquette about eating game, which began: 'Tantalising though these small birds may be . . .'

I read the Druon trilogy twice—once in French and once to correct the translator's worst howlers—and I still think it jolly good. What about that blind old man following the staghunt on his relief map— and his later marriage to his old mistress?

I'm sure you *will* read *Lolita*, but you will be bored and disgusted, so now you know!

Middleton Murry I only *just* knew, when Cape was his publisher and I was there. As a man he was a weak and pathetic mess, but as a *literary* critic he was often very good—on Keats, Shakespeare and Swift, for instance.

Too bad about your Pooterish trousers, and I loved the story of the joke played on T. Talbot. Some of my clothes are certainly old enough to split, but none have yet.

The only joke I've so far collected for my speech is this:

PATIENT: 'I can't think what's the matter with me these days, Doctor. I can't remember a thing.'

DOCTOR: 'Dear, dear, when did this start?'

PATIENT: 'When did *what* start?'

I expect you heard it at your prep-school, but it'll have to do for Monday, *faute de mieux*. I'm also told that the latest popular game in America is called Incest—all the family can join in! As they say these days, how funny can you get?

My bird-table is back in action, and the nuthatches seem ravenous. Also I surprised a green woodpecker in the garden today. When, as I hope, you pay us your Christmas visit, you will find the library transmogrified by the introduction of new curtains and chair-covers—its first ever, since the old ones were bought for our London house well over twenty years ago, and were hanging in strips like old flags in military chapels.

The penultimate batch of Oscar photostats arrived from America last week, and Ruth and I are busily grappling with them. The book is getting bigger and richer steadily. What shall I do without it? The answer is the thousand and one other things I ought to be doing now.

18 November 1959   *Grundisburgh*

Yes, Sir Cuthbert in the matter of geniality, tolerance, broadmindedness, and even ordinary understanding, is *not* improving—at least judging by what he says. But I suppose the fact that he does come shows that he hates and despises us less than he pretends.

I don't think *The Times* has really done you very well about the London Library. A tiny leader, and surely it was lumpish to put Winston's letter in small print. You will get the money surely. Let some U.S.A. tycoon immortalise himself. Why not that ridiculous Getty whose capital I read is 700 million? I suppose he has twenty cars and a thousand shirts.

I enjoyed my London spell, but found it rather tiring. Highgate village *is* a long way off, and a journey underground with perhaps two changes (and what a lot of walking one can do underground!) then a mile in a bus, and ending with a 440 yards walk aren't all that fun. I had a pleasant dinner at Gerald Kelly's one night—he knows almost as many people as you do. For one evening, at any rate, he is good company. I sat next to a nice Russian lady, wife to a genial American whose friends range between Stalin and my Humphrey. He said Stalin's Russian was abominable—worse than the worst Cockney.

I love your story of the man who lost his memory—and laughed out loud when alone, which is the ultimate test of funniness (P.G. Wodehouse passes it repeatedly). And the new American parlour game went down well at lunch in the Ipswich club yesterday.

Pamela returns tomorrow from staying with Roger and wife. My youngest daughter has arrived safely from Malaya and is with a sister at Eton. Her three children demanded to be taken back to Malaya, on the intelligible grounds that England in mid-November was the foulest thing they had struck. To explain to them that to have no snakes, scorpions, tarantulas, sleepy sickness or Malayans constitutes a definite 'bull' point has so far had no success. Of course it would be about eight degrees colder every day than a normal November. I am writing at 3.50 and it is almost pitch-dark. And the shortest day is over a month away. Bah!

Next day. P. has returned from Barbon. She reports that Roger also thought that of course Winston's letter should have been in big print —and the first letter too in the chief column. Will, won't, the Government do something about these exorbitant rates? I see Dr Barnardo's homes are being squeezed now. Damn all jacks-in-office. Also backbenchers who worry mainly about flogging and TV. The coming years are going to be a great test of Macmillan, who must wage ceaseless war against his own Philistines in Parliament and Press. What *would* old Carlyle have said about the squalor and selfishness and stupidity of 1959, seeing how fiercely he attacked those of a hundred years ago? I have been re-reading in Froude's *Life* at meals and found any number of good things. What he called 'men's cussed ways of going on' really did make him miserable—helped no doubt by dyspepsia, but quite obviously genuine. But, as he more than once said, he wasn't always being murdered when he cried out. And after all he did live eighty-five years, before he began 'twinkling away' after longing for his *Dimittis* ever since Jane died. Ruskin's summing-up always strikes me as good. 'What can you say of Thomas Carlyle but that he was born in the clouds and struck by lightning?' Like Johnson it must have been fun to listen to his talk, provided that you carefully refrained from crossing swords.

22 *November 1959*   *Bromsden Farm*

Once again I have been forced by circumstances to retreat to Sunday writing. On Monday I duly delivered my speech after Jonathan Cape's eightieth birthday dinner: there were no others, so I can safely say mine was the speech of the evening. Anyhow it seemed to please the old buzzard and his assembled friends, and thank God it's over. On Tuesday I heard that Hugh Walpole's sister Dorothy had died suddenly of a heart attack in Edinburgh, where at the age of seventy-two she was still practising as a doctor. I am one of her executors, so on Thursday afternoon I travelled north (comfortably reading in a first-class Pullman) and stayed the night with my co-executor, a nice intelligent fortyish Edinburgh lawyer (W.S.). Dorothy, bless her, left me £1000, which will safely cover the rest of Adam's Eton bills, and so relieve me of a perpetual headache. I don't think I've ever bothered you with my financial worries, but in fact I haven't (never have had) a penny of capital, and since my income is only just enough for our modest expenses, all school-fees have always had to be conjured out of the air. Somehow we have struggled on from half to half (once it was almost Long Leave before I got the money) and a week ago the total

343

in my reserve (school-fees) account was £125—not enough for the next Eton bill, and I have also to find £200+ a year for Duff. So you can imagine what a blessing this legacy is. Also, when Robin, the surviving brother, dies, all Hugh's copyrights and royalties (if there still are any) are to belong to me. Robin is sixty-seven and so simple as to be scarcely capable of looking after himself. He has lived with Dorothy for the past ten years and she looked after him. Now I fear my co-executor will have to bear the brunt. Dorothy was deeply religious (their father, you remember, was Bishop of Edinburgh) and on Friday I attended *three* services (all in the rain)—one at the little church she went to, one at the crematorium, and one at the burial of the ashes in a charming country churchyard at Dalmahoy, where the parents are buried. A delightful old Scotch canon conducted all three, reading and speaking beautifully, and the Bishop of Edinburgh gave a goodish address at the first one. He ended with this prayer, which I had never heard before:

Go forth upon thy journey from this world, O Christian soul,
In the name of God the Father Almighty who created thee,
In the name of Jesus Christ who suffered for thee,
In the name of the Holy Ghost who strengtheneth thee,
In communion with the blessed Saints, and aided by Angels and
 Archangels and all the armies of the heavenly host.
May thy portion this day be in peace, and thy dwelling the
 heavenly Jerusalem.

Very beautiful, don't you think? I later copied it from the Scottish Prayer Book, where it appears under 'The Visitation of the Sick', though the Canon told me it is seldom so used, since its recitation doesn't exactly encourage the sick person.

After spending the rest of the day with Robin, and trying to explain everything to him, I caught the 10.50 p.m. train, on which I had booked a sleeper, and got to London fairly exhausted yesterday morning—and so down here, where I have slept a good deal.

The London Library has now received close on £5000, and there seems a good chance of Christie's holding a special sale on the Library's behalf. T.S.E. gets back next week.

I lived at Highgate for some years, but wouldn't do so again. Either right *in* London (over the shop in Soho Square) or right in the country, I should say, unless one has cars and chauffeurs.

The final batch of Oscar letters arrived from America last week, but when shall I find time to assimilate them? Tomorrow Ruth and I go to *Rosmersholm*, on which I will report.

Did you see the one-shot serialisation of my Dickens book in to-day's *Sunday Times*? They paid £500 for it (£450 to the author, £50 to R.H-D. Ltd) and I hope the publicity will sell out the first edition. Your copy shall go to you tomorrow. It comes out next Friday.

Last week we won another dictionary and a 15/- book-token with my crossword solutions. There's nothing like wasting one's time in a profitable way. I've almost finished *Past and Present*, and am inclined, after what you say, to go on to Froude next. Although G.M.Y. had become a nuisance (not to me)

> Men are we, and must grieve when even the shade
> Of that which once was great is passed away.[1]

I am trying to persuade Sparrow to edit a short memorial volume of his letters etc.

It 'ails from the prime foundation', as Housman put it about some much lesser wrong, that you should ever be harassed about money. I positively ache with sympathy, because I know how much it would depress me and get between me and anything I was doing—and you never show any signs of it. So I rejoice heartily over the Walpole £1000, and wish it was ten times the size. Don't go and plonk a single penny of it on the London Library. That just cries out for a millionaire with quite ordinary good sense and feeling to put it out of reach of all harm with a scratch of his pen. Odd to me that one hasn't already done so. There must be good Carlyleans in the States in spite of his derisive summing-up of their civil war as a smoky chimney which had caught

[1] Wordsworth, 'On the Extinction of the Venetian Republic'.

fire. I cannot believe you wouldn't enjoy Froude's *Life*, though I cannot remember meeting anyone who finds such rich enjoyment in it as I always have. They just never mention it. There is of course too much groaning and grousing, which is not easy to skip, though desirable, because brilliant flashes may lighten the darkness at any moment, and no one could relish them more than you will. You keep on coming across things like the juryman who stuck out against the other eleven, his head 'all cheeks, jaw, and no brow, of shape somewhat like a great ball of putty dropped from a height'; on Margaret Fuller, 'a strange lilting, lean old maid, not nearly such a bore as I expected.' There is any amount of his grisly laughter. Meanwhile I note that the sympathy and conviction that the London Library must be saved is unanimous and growing. The law is much less rigid than it used to be about wills, and clearly should be about rates levied on institutions like the L.L. and Dr Barnardo's homes.

I was sorry to see G.M. Young's death, though I didn't know him except through those *first-rate* little books that were about the first of your fairy-gifts to me. A big batch of extracts from his observations on men and things found their way into my commonplace book and from that to my Governor-General nephew in N.Z. who uses them in his speeches (which recently were called in a N.Z. paper the best ever made by a N.Z. Governor-General!). I can well believe it, as they (G.M.Y.) are never commonplace or platitudinous, and platitude is the occupational disease of G.-G.'s.

I *say*, Rupert, *The Curtain Falls*!! I finished it nicely balanced between fascination and horror. *Superb* descriptions, but what frightful people, and the author's disgust and pleasure in depicting the loathsomeness of the human body, male and female, especially of the old, and his almost gloating over their dreadful deaths is positively Swiftian. Was the degradation of inter-war France really as bad as that? And do tell me what did/do the French think about the book? It surely is an appalling picture, no other word for it. I literally could not put it down. The reviews I have seen don't seem to realise the size and strength of Druon, do they?

Very busy today. New car arrived, and Pamela was shown the ropes. She will have to get used, by trial and error, to the brake and the accelerator having changed places, which no doubt is as it should be, but error might be costly. Then P. had to cook lunch for our Bishop against time. At 1.20 no Bishop. I rang him up, and in words stifled by compunction and the bread and cheese of his own lunch he explained that his secretary for the first time in donkey's years had made a muddle. Extending forgiveness to a Bishop is a luxurious experience. Have you ever had it? And on the top of it I ate his lordship's lunch, so all ended on a happy note.

I have been reading in bed Evelyn Waugh's life of R.A. Knox with ambiguous feelings—as one has, or I do, in reading about Newman. Does God want all that endless heart-searching about Him and how to worship Him? I am a thousand miles away from understanding what those profound minds are at in their ceaseless meditations on such matters.

There is a lovely blunder in the index. Was Bishop G.A. Selwyn laughed into oblivion before your Eton day? He used to be rammed down our throats by visiting preachers as the perfect model all Etonians should copy? I fancy R.A.K. and Co. may have laughed him out of court, and the Headmaster would warn preachers not to mention him. Well, he is mentioned in the pages dealing with R.A.K.'s schooldays. The index has 'G.A. Selwyn (eighteenth-century wit)'. They mixed him up with the other George Augustus who was sacked from Oxford for blasphemy, and spent his time attending executions, visiting morgues and being mildly (and generally indecently) witty. How R.A.K. himself would have enjoyed this supremely rich gaffe!

28 November 1959   Bromsden Farm

An American visitor this week produced the ultimate Yellow Press headline: it runs: TEEN-AGE DOG-LOVING DOCTOR-PRIEST IN SEX-CHANGE MERCY-DASH TO PALACE.

A complicated story, you may think, but no more involved, I assure you, than my life has been since I last wrote to you. Monday was all right—a normally busy day, ending with an enjoyable evening watching Peggy Ashcroft's lovely acting in *Rosmersholm*—and on Tuesday the trouble began. We were slowly preparing the press-release of the Phoenix Trust to be put out early in December, when

347

the *Evening Standard* (goodness knows how) got the whole story. I refused to tell them anything, but on Wednesday they printed two long and accurate paragraphs about the scheme, and immediately the other papers were round me like a swarm of hornets. To avoid antagonising them all I was forced to rush out an official statement in a couple of hours. Almost all the other Trustees were unobtainable, so I had to get the statement into final form, duplicated, and sent round by hand with covering letters to seven newspapers and press agencies. I daresay you saw it in Thursday's *Times*. That afternoon, while I was being interviewed by a young lady from the *Sunday Times*, the secretary of the Pilgrim Trust (Lord Kilmaine) rang up in a towering rage to say I had no business to say the Phoenix Trust had been 'founded and endowed' by the 'Pilgrim', since all they had done was to lend their name, give us £500 and nominate a Trustee. He calmed down a little when I pointed out that the offending words were the ones from his own Charter which he had read out to me as the Pilgrim T's authority for helping us, but I had to agree to send out a correction, again by hand, to the same seven places. Next morning (Friday) appeared that savagely malicious leader pouring scorn and ridicule on the new Trust. It seems, don't you agree?, an extraordinary thing for *The Times* so to attack a philanthropic scheme directly it's announced, and I can only imagine that the article was inspired, if not written, by some tight-fisted and self-important person (probably a publisher) who fears his pocket may be endangered. I felt the article must be answered, and I drafted a letter, which I hope they will print on Monday. A.P. Herbert was most helpful with telephonic advice. Meanwhile I had to stay up last night to appear (or rather be audible) for eight minutes on the Home Service, talking about the Phoenix Trust. I don't suppose you heard it. Pretty dull, I fear: I only hope comprehensible. The worst thing about such jobs is the time they take: for those eight minutes I was in Broadcasting House for just on two and a half hours! This morning I had to find someone to type my *Times* letter, take it myself in a taxi to Printing House Square and dash to Paddington. You can imagine how much literary or publishing work I have done this week. Though by using *three* secretaries I managed to keep almost abreast of my correspondence. And in the middle of everything I got a cable to say that the wealthy Bollingen Foundation of New York has agreed to finance a multi-volume complete edition of Coleridge's works, for which I've been scheming for several years.

Ruth has been a tower of strength and devotion all the time, bless her.

T.S.E. is back in England and we are to meet to discuss the L.L., on whose behalf I am laying traps for tycoons.

The Duchess of Kent has agreed to present the Duff Cooper Prize on December 17.

So glad you couldn't put down *The Curtain Falls*: the French loved it, and the first volume was awarded the Prix Goncourt.

Just now I took down Cobbett's *English Grammar* for fun: I have the second edition (1824), in which are bound advertisements of all Cobbett's books, obviously written by him. Of the *E.G.* he writes: 'This work has been published to the amount of *fifty-five thousand copies*, without ever having been mentioned by the old shuffling bribed sots, called Reviewers.' That's the stuff! I must read him again. Take care of yourself in London, and don't go near Regent Street after dark. Forgive this hurried letter: I simply *must* read some manuscripts.

St Andrew's Day 1959   *67 Chelsea Square*

But they tell me you *are* coming on Thursday, and if that is so I will spare you a letter. I like to see you in large print and the chief place in to-day's *Times*—where Winston's letter about the London Library should have been. There is no whirlpool of which you are not the centre.

I shall be coming to the Lit. Soc., but I will *not* sit next to the old death'sheadlam twice running. How nice it will be to see you on Thursday.

5 December 1959   *Bromsden Farm*

Paris was worth a Mass, said Henry of Navarre, and surely two postcards are worth a half-length letter. It was angelic of you to bring

349

back my umbrella, and I'm only sorry that I missed you. I remember Hugh Walpole saying of Clemence Dane: 'If that woman leaves her umbrella in my flat *once more* I shall murder her'. So I mustn't do it again. I thoroughly enjoyed my evening, and rejoiced to see you and Pamela looking so well, not to mention the radiantly lovely Diana.

Comfort suggests your coming to lunch on the Sunday, 27 December. Let me know on Tuesday if it suits. It might be as well if you telephoned to Soho Square on Tuesday morning to make sure that Ruth will be there at 6 to let you in if I am kept at my meeting. She has every intention of being, but I don't want to chase you across London as I did last month. I shall think of you on Monday night, beaming benevolent and Chips-like at Old Boys whose names you can't quite remember—or are there none such?

The Phoenix Trust is attacked again this morning, by a disgruntled and professionally agin-the-Government author. I hope someone will answer, and so keep the controversy alive. R.A. Butler was very sympathetic to the London Library when I saw him last week at lunch at the Birkenheads'. We discussed the Dilke case, and when he admitted that Joe Chamberlain probably did nothing to prevent D's disgrace and disappearance, I said: 'It's a dirty game, politics'. 'Yes', he answered simply; 'You see, it's for power.' He struck me as immensely self-satisfied, but fundamentally right-minded. His new wife is most charming and easy to talk to.

Adam, though nothing like as good at games as Duff, seems to have the valuable gift of being on the winning side: after his winning captaincy in the Junior Soccer League and Junior Cricket, he has now been in the side which last week won the Second Fives cup for Fred's. Adam says the cup is hideous, but honour is satisfied. Duff returns from Oxford tomorrow, so there is much cooking to be done. I have brought down a great chunk of Oscar, having decided that he must be despatched to the printer before Christmas, finished or unfinished.

Diana Cooper looked in on Friday: she is spending the week-end at Petworth, where the P.M. is shooting. Diana is determined to make him take action about the London Library.

350

Tuesday was even better than usual—beginning with the lovely vision of Ruth at the foot of the stairs and ending, if you please, with a long and good crack with Roger, Ivor B., and Jonah till 11.30, all three in excellent form. Earlier in the evening your ears should have tingled, for your heroic work for the London Library is seeping into the consciousness of men, as of course it should and must. And as your reward you had old Cuthbert to yourself with no relief from his other side! I hope those who say they are coming and then don't have to pay up? It is bad clubmanship. We shall have none of poor old Jonah till the summer, as he tells me he has been ordered abroad for his chest—Portugal I think—for the next four months. What will Cuthbert say about that? I suppose the leeches know what they are doing.

On Friday I take the chair at a village brains-trust. The first question sent in is 'Would you in the next world prefer to be a dog, a cat, or a budgerigar?' I suppose you know the right curtailed pronunciation of budgerigar on the Cholmondeley = Chumley principle? Three guesses.

Love to R. Would she or you object if I said she was a darling? *Yes.* So I won't (but she is all the same).

Cuthbert was much less disagreeable on Tuesday, but he's not exactly a life-enhancer. Gerry Wellington wrote and apologised for not turning up, and Jo Grimond telephoned during the dinner, but Harold N. simply failed to turn up. It's Cyprus that is to harbour Jonah—perhaps they'll elect him President!

Next morning Ruth said: 'There's only one word for George—lovable.' I could think of a few others, but I let it pass.

The best news is (1) Adam has won the Chess Cup—not only the biggest in the school, but apparently bringing with it a fiver in cash! (2) I think I have succeeded in wheedling £1000 for the London Library out of the B.B.C.! But mum is very much the word until the news is official. Privately they asked whether we would mind publicity about the gift. I said on the contrary: it might stimulate other donors. That would bring the total to £6500. Meanwhile the Christie's sale goes forward, and Henry Moore has promised to give a small bronze, which should bring in a few hundred pounds. Soon I must tackle goodness knows how many other possible benefactors. It's a job to know what to do first.

In an attempt to polish off Oscar I brought down an almost unliftable suitcase containing two complete copies of the manuscript, with many attendant books and papers. I've worked on it almost all day, but there's still a helluva lot left to do.

Have you read the Dickens book yet? On Wednesday one of the author's main pieces of evidence was blown sky-high by a Cambridge don, and I had to spend most of that day sorting things out. You'll probably see a couple of letters in tomorrow's *Sunday Times*. Undeterred, the Critics are going to discuss the book *next* Sunday on the radio.

On Wednesday evening I took the Librarian of the London Library to dine in the House of Commons with Leslie Hale, the Labour M.P. who is going to organise a deputation of the thirty-six M.P.s who are members of the Library. He's a vigorous, frank and engaging fellow— a country solicitor from Leicestershire, who has the reputation of speaking faster than any other M.P. In fact they say he can make a speech in the middle of Mr Paget's speech (he's the slowest of all). Unfortunately our host had ordered a mass of wine (sherry, white, red), and it was all opened and decanted, so I simply had to ignore my teetotalism and drink it. A nasty headache all next day seems to prove that I should still keep off it.

After dinner it transpired that the Librarian had never been in the House before, so I asked Hale to give us two tickets for the Strangers' Gallery, where we spent a very dull hour listening to Mr Maudling fluently spouting about Unemployment to a largely empty chamber. Fancy spending one's working life there—ugh!

I was most touched by Roger's kind words at the London Library. Most of the committee are like lumps of driftwood, moving sluggishly with the current, so R's intervention was as unexpected as it was encouraging, bless him.

Duff has got another story (a short amusing one) in the Christmas number of *Argosy*. He has developed a painful boil on his leg and has spent today in bed, very sorry for himself. I think they'll all three be here at Christmas: let me know if the Sunday's okay.

Diana Cooper has sent me most of her third volume—in the roughest form—and I shall have to spend some of the Christmas holiday trying to get it into preliminary shape. Her servant-problems at Chantilly would make a book of their own: she's had dozens of every age, sex and colour—Chinks, Philipinos, West Indians, French, Italian, English. A pair of refugee Poles, who arrived penniless on a tandem bicycle, left two years later with a three-ton lorry full of loot. They went back to Poland, but didn't like it, and came back the other day. Diana said they could inhabit the lodge as soon as the sacked French gardener left. He now refuses to budge, and the Poles are squatting querulously on the top floor of the house. Meanwhile the Algerian cook, who was sacked last week for striking Diana's French maid ('*il m'a giflé!*'), was murdered next day by another Algerian. Never a dull moment! Next week Diana is coming over for the presentation of the Duff Cooper Prize, which this year is being given by the Duchess of Kent to Paddy Leigh Fermor for his book *Mani*, a large tome about southern Greece. Ruth and I have had to arrange everything and send out all the invitations. Diana's list was written in pencil, all names spelt wrong and no addresses.

She tells me that last week-end at Petworth she gave the P.M. a memorandum about the London Library (I'd love to have seen it) and he seemed most sympathetic and interested—as I'm sure he is. One can't have too many irons in this particular fire.

All the same, I wish I was with Ruth in Kisdon Lodge, reading another chapter of *How Green* by the open range! June seems a long way away.

> It is not many miles to Mantua?
> No further than the end of this mad world.

I bet you don't know where that comes from!

353

This weak utterance comes to you so to speak *de profundis*. Not that I have been seized with 'intestine stone or ulcer, colic pangs' or any species of 'wide-wasting pestilence,' but simply because I have to deal with a large batch of scripts by a monstrous regiment of young women. The questions are on 'Narrative Poems of To-day' and to every question the young women write, in that horrid looping, swooping hand so many of them affect, voluminously, never quite on or off the point, enthusiastically, insipidly. The after-effects are what you get from immersion in a very large bath, quite full of luke-warm water, and I recall Arnold Bennett's recipe for the right treatment of Mrs Humphry Ward's heroines, i.e. that they should be gathered in a besieged city about to fall, all armed with revolvers to protect them from the cruel and licentious soldiery, that the city falls, the soldiers burst in—and all the revolvers turn out to be unloaded.

I see the M.C.C. has followed the L.L. down the rates-drain—and I doubt if M.C.C. has an R.H-D to salvage them. *The Times* strikes the right note of angry contempt for the framers of this degraded law.

Please congratulate Adam from me on his Chess Cup. Yes I remember it—far the largest. But there was no cash with it in my day. Not that I ever won it. I was in the final, *aetat* eleven, at my prep-school, lost, and burst into tears. How often one is *very* unhappy at the age of ten. And on the whole what hateful places prep-schools, anyhow, were, especially if situated, as mine was, among the brickfields near Uxbridge.

Your Oscar saga is really enthralling. You could make a grand production by simply telling your experiences while compiling it, incidentally pillorying that morose and curmudgeonly old b-tch you told me about. It must surely be a best-seller.

I am sorry about your still being on the waggon. Your jaundice was aeons ago. Are you sure it wasn't D.T. or cirrhosis of the liver? Doctors can be very tactful. And there goes old Winston, positively pickled in alcohol, and never having an ache or pain. All men are *not* equal.

The servant problem really is—! Yesterday we lunched with the Bishop. He opened the door, carved and handed round everything and whisked the joint out to, I think, the gardener. Diana Cooper's experiences are thrilling. We haven't yet got to cooks killing each other.

Your Mantua quotation beats me. Whence is it? I forget more and more, quicker and quicker.

19 December 1959   *Bromsden Farm*

This brief note is not to be answered till *after* your visit here—and in the meantime a Christmas truce or moratorium will prevail. I have been working all day at Oscar (on Monday he goes to the printer) and am so sleepy and cloth-headed that I think I'd better go to bed and write more in the morning. I'm reading *Coningsby* in bed and so far enjoying it greatly.

Sunday morning—rain, gale and all.

I wanted to write a brief footnote about *Coningsby*, and the simplest way seemed to be to read the book—footnote-hunting is now my only excuse for reading anything decent. When I was at Eton we were given *Sybil* for a holiday-task, and I was surprised at how much I liked it. So far I have read only the Eton section of *C*, and will report further next week.

Adam got another Distinction in Trials (his fifth), but missed the Trials Prize by nineteen marks, his conqueror being a lad named Motley, whom he beat in the final of the Chess Cup.

The best news is that the B.B.C.'s cheque for £1000 reached the London Library last week, with a very nice letter from Sir Ian Jacob. This I hope to use as a lever to prise open the coffers of ITV. Also, to my great surprise, the *New Statesman* responded to my appeal with a cheque for £250! The Library has now received £7000 in all, and I am pressing on. The Phoenix Trust will just have to wait. Like the man pursued by the Hound of Heaven, I feel 'trellised with intertwining charities'.

The presentation of the Duff Cooper Prize went off well. Evelyn Waugh (who has promised a manuscript for the Christie sale) is now very fat, glassy-eyed, and carries an ear-trumpet! I told him it suited him and he should never be without it.

I saw S.C. Roberts for a moment at the Jepsons', benign and charming as ever. Those two lines about Mantua were written by Maurice Baring, and you're supposed to think they come from *Romeo and Juliet* —which indeed they might.

I still haven't got a single Christmas present, so my next few days will be busy. I shall think of you in the midst of your progeny, taking credit for all the individual presents that Pamela has so cleverly bought. Have a nice time, and turn up here some time before one on Sunday. I think the whole family will be here to greet you.

Now I must tidy up Oscar for his journey.

New Year's Eve 1959   *Cambridge*

H.K. Marsden motored me here on Monday—the dullest drive in England variegated by H.K.M.'s jumpy nerves. Once he braked so suddenly that the car behind gave his a kick in the pants; he didn't even get out to look, but sourly assumed it was the bumper.

I dined with old Gow who was in fair form considering he was the next morning to have a wisdom tooth out, which the leech said the X-ray *might* show to be 'impacted', i.e. grown into all the surrounding bones and only separable with a hatchet under chloroform in a nursing home. In old days I suppose one just mildly died of phossy jaw (spelling?).

Last night we went to a film—*Great Expectations*. Excellent. All the setting and scenery etc were masterly. Mrs Gargery was made too savage. She didn't merely give Pip a cut or two with 'Tickler' but *thrashed* him, thereby making one despise Joe, who stood by doing nothing. Joe irritates me in fact in both book and film.

I suggest *Sybil* is really a much better book than *Coningsby*, but it is decades since I read either.

A don here told us—not knowing I knew you—that 'Hart-Davis was doing wonders about raising money for the London Library.' I didn't contradict him!

Yesterday I was given a lovely Penguin, *Yet More Comic and Curious Verse*. An excellent volume—full of things I had never seen or heard of, though of course you have. You won't mind being reminded of the couplet:

> God in his wisdom made the fly,
> And then forgot to tell us why.

We are off to another film this evening, I don't know what, but they swear it isn't rubbish. I'll believe it when I see it. Last night I was smoking one of Alexander's cigars, and the slightly bibulous attendant exclaimed 'Lummy, here come the millionaires'. Just the effect we were aiming at!

INDEX

Abel, Bobby, 106
Agar, Herbert, 83
Agate, James, 59, 84, 143, 194, 216, 231, 232, 272, 276, 284, 287, 302, 325
Agnew, Geoffrey, 161, 163
Ainsworth, Harrison, 146
Akenside, Mark, 207
Alanbrooke, Lord, 36
Albemarle, Lady, 70
Aldington, Richard, 78
Alexandra, Princess, 337
Alice in Wonderland, 219
Alington, C. A., 52, 73, 212, 214
Alington, Hester, 39, 40, 43, 44, 52, 63, 87, 101
Alington, Lavinia, 52
Allcock, 106
Allen, G. O. (Gubby), 179, 291, 333
Altham, H. S., 247, 252, 265, 315
Altrincham, Lord, 39
Amis, Kingsley, 21, 31, 123, 194, 264, 318
Amory, Thomas, 259
Amsler, Dr, 12, 211
Annan, Noel, 188, 190, 217, 220
Anselm, Archbishop, 36
Aprahamian, Felix, 231
Argyll, Duke of, 13, 15
Aristophanes, 59
Aristotle, 301
Arlen, Michael, 307-8
Arlott, John, 231
Arnold, Dr, 69, 120, 242
Arnold, Matthew, 76, 96, 98, 100, 102, 130, 310, 314
As You Like It, 275, 286
Ascham, Roger, 107
Ashcroft, Peggy, 76, 147, 347
Aspern Papers, The, 301, 304, 307, 309
Asquith, Raymond, 77
Astley, Joan and Philip, 161, 179, 315
Astor, Gavin, 141
At the Drop of a Hat, 1, 10

Attlee, Clement, 16, 182
Aurora Leigh, 130, 131, 133
Austen, Jane, 132, 136, 157, 162, 204, 290
Austen-Leigh, R. A., 122
Aylmer, Felix, 213

Bacon, Sir Francis, 272
Bagehot, Walter, 220
Bailey, F. M., 213
Bailey, John, 68, 331
Balcarres, Lord, 16
Baldwin, Oliver, 115, 116
Baldwin, Stanley, 16
Balfour, A. J., 16, 77
Ballantrae, *see* Fergusson
Balzac, 330-1
Banck, M., 321
Baring, Maurice, 291
Barrie, J. M., 115
Barth, Karl, 172
Bartok, Bela, 156
Bates, H. E., 97, 159
Bayley, John, 21, 39, 256
Beaton, Cecil, 54
Beauclerk, Topham, 8
Beaverbrook, Lord, 139, 143, 162
Beddington, Mrs Claude, 313-4, 316, 317-8, 320
Beecham, Sir Thomas, 120, 294, 296, 298, 300
Beerbohm, Elisabeth, 67, 80, 134, 183, 188, 209
Beerbohm, Max, 16, 29, 58, 119, 134, 136, 138, 141, 149, 153, 155, 172, 174, 183, 209, 213, 281, 318
Beethoven, 9, 77, 269, 322
Behan, Brendan, 174
Belloc, H., 87, 92, 93, 94, 269
Benaud, Richie, 186
Bennett, Arnold, 28, 131, 185, 303, 354
Benson, A. C., 110, 120, 135, 136, 220, 224, 228-9, 241, 273, 305

Benson, E. F., 5, 241
Benson, F. R., 284
Benson, R. H., 241, 311
Bentley, E. C., 159
Berenson, Bernard, 329
Berkeley, Anthony, see Iles
Bernard, see Fergusson
Besant, Annie, 198
Betjeman, Candida, 105, 108, 115, 279
Betjeman, John, 16, 105, 108, 163, 175, 176, 199
Bevin, Ernest, 281
Birdwood, General, 207
Birkenhead, Lord, 16, 318, 350
Birkett, Lord Justice, 77, 274, 276, 277, 280, 282
Birley, Robert, 43, 234, 235
Birrell, Augustine, 42, 296, 319
Bismarck, Count, 76, 123, 301
Black Beauty, 1
Bland, Michael, 276
Bliss, Arthur, 231
Blunden, Edmund, 43, 97, 111, 112, 114, 140, 141, 144, 147, 152, 187, 249, 313
Blunt, Wilfrid, 12, 62, 241
Bodkin, Sir Archibald, 8
Bogan, Louise, 69
Bonham-Carter, Lady Violet, 174, 231, 233
Bonnor, George, 25
Boothby, Bob, 57, 61, 104, 177, 294
Boswell, James, 177, 241, 244, 296, 319, 331
Bourchier, Arthur, 193
Bourne, R. M. A. (Bobby), 14, 47-8, 53, 59
Bourne, Rose, 177, 280
Bracken, Brendan, 113, 114, 115, 133
Bradley, A. C., 143, 145, 193
Bradman, D. G., 141
Brahms, Johannes, 222
Brain, Sir Russell, 8, 9, 38
Braley, E. F., 21
Brand, Lord, 67, 337, 340
Brewster, H. B., 240
Brewster, Julia, 241
Bridges, Lord, 217, 220
Bridges, Yseult, 327
Briggs, J., 186
Bright, John, 196
Briginshaw, 268, 271, 272
Brinton, H., 28, 119, 153

Britten, Benjamin, 166
Brooke, Mrs, 303, 305, 307
Brooke, Rupert, 263
Broughton, Rhoda, 290
Brown, "Estimate", 214
Brown, Ivor, 47, 51, 53, 58, 65, 83, 146, 185, 219, 221, 231, 236, 237, 243, 249, 252, 256, 258, 282, 287, 321, 351
Brown, T. E., 78
Browne and Kennedy, 58
Browne, Patrick, 93, 104
Browning, Oscar, 219-20
Browning, Robert, 24, 66, 84, 98, 167, 232, 298, 314
Brunner, Sir Felix and Lady, 271
Bryant, Arthur, 41, 44, 54, 83
Burke and Hare, 58
Butler, R. A., 179, 201, 350
Butler, Dr Samuel, 22
Butterwick, J. C., 29, 261
Byron, Lord, 78, 169, 170
Bywater, Ingram, 305

Caccia, David, 267
Caccia, Harold, 16, 267
Cadogan, Alec, 59, 114, 161, 163, 305
Cadogan, Lady Theodosia, 161
Calder-Marshall, Arthur, 108, 186
Caldwell, Erskine, 123, 126
Cameron, Ian, 44
Cape, Jonathan, 204, 258, 336, 339, 341, 343
Cardus, Neville, 77, 79, 179, 227, 228, 230, 236, 286, 296, 300, 325
Carey, Clive, 47
Carlisle, Rosalind, Lady, 193, 281
Carlyle, Jane, 238, 298, 300, 343
Carlyle, Thomas, 27, 29, 39, 40, 44, 45, 46, 48, 51, 58, 101, 119, 142, 154, 181, 190, 196, 226, 228, 232, 238, 260, 292, 293, 299, 300, 302, 317, 319, 324, 334, 343
Carner, Mosco, 231
Carroll, Lewis, 25
Carter, John, 203, 204, 253, 254, 255, 286
Casanova, 169
Cassandra, 88, 105
Castle, Barbara, 158
Castle Dangerous, 194, 195
Cattley, T. F., 108, 109-10
Cavaliero, Roderigo, 113
Cazalet, Thelma, 333

Cecil, Lord David, 21, 28, 66, 135
Chamberlain, Joseph, 167, 350
Chamberlain, Neville, 150, 229
Chamson, André, 37
Chapman, Hester, 10, 37
Chapman, R. W., 39, 207, 305
Charles I, King, 192
Charles II, King, 199
Charteris, Lady, 176
Charteris, Martin, 79, 176
Chaucer, 41, 118, 238, 245
Cherry-Garrard, A., 246
Chesterton, G. K., 73, 167, 194, 221, 297
Chiang Kai Shek, 139, 143
Chippendale, Thomas, 296
Christie, Agatha, 44, 244
Christie, John, 52, 223
Church, Richard, 37
Churchill, E. L. (Jelly), 153, 168, 235
Churchill, Lord Randolph, 143
Churchill, Winston, 9, 16, 23, 25, 57,
  63, 77, 139, 171, 204, 228, 229, 236,
  263, 302, 305, 329, 340, 342, 349, 354
Chute, J. C., 208, 239
Cicero, 204, 205, 207
Cinquevalli, 264
Cleary, Sir William, 319
Clore, Charles, 307
Clough, A. H., 7
Cobbett, William, 349
Cobham, Viscount (Charles), 16, 246,
  305, 306, 311, 346
Coburn, Kathleen, 67
Cohen, Harriet, 113
Coleridge, F. J. R. (Fred), 26, 27, 45,
  57, 80, 164, 189, 190, 195, 197, 251,
  271, 317, 338, 350
Coleridge, S. T., 32, 214, 293, 349
Collins, Churton, 248
Colman, Mrs Geoffrey, 76
Colquhoun, A., 182
Colvin, Sidney, 155, 158
Coningsby, 355-6
Connolly, Cyril, 74
Conrad, Joseph, 21, 270
Cooke, Alistair, 20, 67, 71, 76, 78, 254
Cooper, Diana, 2, 10, 14, 16, 19-20,
  27, 30, 32, 34, 38, 54, 60, 64, 73, 75,
  83, 100, 134, 138, 150, 170, 173, 176,
  188, 195, 235, 237, 239, 251, 253,
  330, 350, 353, 355
Cooper, Duff, 10, 78, 81, 92, 93, 168,
  175, 176, 238, 239, 249, 256, 268

Cooper, Lettice, 33, 158
Courtney, W. L., 316
Courvoisier, F. B., 327
Cousins, Frank, 272
Coward, Noel, 289
Cowdrey, Colin, 186, 265
Cox, A. B., see Iles
Cox, Mary Stewart, 55
Cozzens, J. G., 172, 174, 175
Crabbe, George, 232
Cranworth, Lord, 264, 281
Crawford, Mrs, 167
Cream, Neill, 8
Creighton, Bishop, 302, 319, 321
Cricket Country, 249
Crippen, H. H., 275
Crook, Arthur, 303
Crossman, R. H. S., 260, 262, 287
Cubitt, Sonia (née Keppel), 128
Curtain Falls, The, 338, 340, 346, 349
Curzon, Lord, 5, 21, 162
Cuthbert, see Headlam

Damien, Father, 200, 293
Dane, Clemence, 350
Dante, 64
Darwin, Bernard, 24, 216, 233
Darwin, Charles, 154, 155
Davson (Glyn), Anthony, 169, 171
Day, Mr Justice, 232
Day-Lewis, C., 197
De Beer, Esmond, 214
De Haviland, R. S., 154
De la Mare, Walter, 8, 10
Denman, Mr Justice, 126
Dent, Alan, 210
Derry, Warren, 314, 316, 320, 321
Devlin, Christopher, 112
Devonshire, Dowager Duchess of, 161
Devonshire, Duke of, 333, 340
Dexter, E. R., 179, 184
Dickens, Charles, 62, 103, 160, 192,
  213, 216, 217, 226, 277, 289, 322,
  326, 345, 352
Dickson, Lovat, 62
Dilke, Sir Charles, 154, 163, 167, 168,
  183, 350
Disraeli, 74
Dobrée, Bonamy, 239
Doctor Zhivago, 320, 321, 338
Donne, John, 269
Doughty, C. M., 167

Douglas, Lord Alfred, 64, 82, 84, 90, 149, 161
Doyle, Conan, 8
Dracula, 261, 263
Dreiser, Theodore, 174, 298, 300
Driberg, Tom, 174
Drinkwater, Daisy and John, 113
Druon, Maurice, 145, 338, 340, 346, 349
Dryden, John, 338
Du Boulay, Mrs, 65, 316
Dulles, John Foster, 139, 171, 249, 250
Durnford, Walter, 122
Dykes, J. B., 123
Dynasts, The, 114, 116, 119

Earlham (by Percy Lubbock), 119, 294
Echo de Paris, 204, 207, 209
Edel, Leon, 34, 35, 37, 41, 45, 47, 51, 55, 285
Eden, Anthony, 16
Edward VII, King, 129-9
Eisenhower, President, 57, 163
Elephant Bill, 109
Elgar, Edward, 122
Eliot, George, 42, 232
Eliot, T. S., 3, 5, 8, 37, 59-60, 93, 95, 104, 134, 140, 142, 145, 147, 159, 171, 183, 274, 276, 278, 320, 328, 339, 344, 349
Elliott, Claude, 115
Ellis, Havelock, 108, 109, 110, 111-2, 113, 156, 186, 189-90, 191, 194
Elton, Lord, 42
Emerson, R. W., 19, 22-3, 24-5, 58
Emma, 132, 133, 135
Eothen, 279
Epstein, Jacob, 140, 159, 170
Eton Poetry Book, An, 212, 214
Eugénie, Empress, 226
Evershed, Lord, 88
Evy, *see* Jones

Faber, Geoffrey, 14, 15
Faerie Queen, The, 15, 40
Fagg, A., 248
Falstaff, 189
Farouk, King, 165
Farrer, Sir Leslie, 103
Feinburgh, Wilfred, 210, 212
Fergusson, Bernard, 5, 38, 51, 53, 88, 161, 219, 240
Fforde, Sir A., 331

Fisher, Archbishop, 36, 66, 182, 210, 211, 215, 349
Fisher, Charles, 101, 115, 338
Fisher, James, 67, 70, 71
Fisher, Margery, 67, 70
Fisher, Norman, 70, 332
FitzGerald, Edward, 9, 167, 206, 232, 264, 332
Flash Harry, *see* Sargent
Flecker, J. S., 9
Fleming, Ian, 46-7, 49, 159, 334, 336
Fleming, Mrs Ian, 174
Fleming, Peter, 5, 17, 24, 39, 72, 74, 76, 91, 106, 108, 110, 141, 149, 163, 169, 170, 185, 188, 191, 205, 211, 213, 227, 235, 236, 246, 254, 266, 268, 271, 272, 287, 288, 301, 310, 311, 312, 318, 321, 323, 334, 336
Flint, Bet, 7
Fonteyn, Margot, 54
Ford, Edward, 165
Forster, E. M., 109, 159, 217, 220, 223, 293
Forster, John, 62
Forsyte Saga, The, 22, 88, 97, 105, 122
France, Anatole, 66
Fred, *see* Coleridge
French Revolution, The, 227, 228, 230, 232, 267, 274, 278, 285, 296, 298
Freyberg, General, 208
Froude, J. A., 298, 300, 302, 343, 345, 346
Fry, C. B., 141, 142, 186, 224, 243
Fry, Roger, 66
Fuchs, Sir Vivian, 137, 138
Fulford, Roger, 5, 6, 25, 40, 51, 80, 133, 139, 141, 162, 199, 219, 244, 245, 292, 302, 305, 315, 317, 322, 337, 339, 340, 342, 351, 352
Fuller, Margaret, 346

Gaitskell, Hugh, 321
Galsworthy, John, 105, 114, 224
Gandhi, 9
Garnett, David, 52
Garnett, Edward, 205
Garnett, Richard, 298
Garrick, David, 144, 296
Garten, Dr, 209
Gatty, Hester, 144
Gentle, Mr, 333
George II, King, 25
George III, King, 256

George V, King, 154, 257
George VI, King, 315
George, Daniel, 97, 100
Georgian Afternoon, 4, 13, 22
Getty, Paul, 342
Gibbon, Edward, 80, 82, 84, 95-6, 97, 139, 141, 218, 268
Gielgud, John, 191, 193, 278, 279, 280, 282, 284, 285, 286
Gilbert & Sullivan, 152, 154, 156-7, 330, 331, 334
Gilbert, W. S., 8, 12
Giles, Frank and Kitty, 17
Gissing, George, 312, 314
Gladstone, W. E., 42, 65, 114, 139, 143, 204, 229, 309, 314
Glasgow, Earl, 161-2
Glass, Douglas, 34
Glenconner, Lady, 174
Godden, Rumer, 104, 106, 109, 111, 112, 123
Goering, 15, 58
Goethe, 132
Golding, Louis, 113, 115
Goldsmith, Oliver, 24, 161
Gollancz, Ruth and Victor, 162
Gordian, Emperor, 218, 221, 223, 268
Gordon-Walker, Patrick, 333
Gore, Bishop, 43, 237
Gosse, Edmund, 141
Gow, A. S. F., 206, 219, 236, 240, 257, 260, 261, 262, 264
Gower, John, 247
Grace, E. M., 268
Grace, W. G., 141, 144, 223, 253, 268
Graham, Harry, 10
Grahame, Kenneth, 211, 216, 233
Gransden, K. E., 145
Grant, Douglas, 112
Graves, C. L., 257
Graves, Robert, 177-8, 180
Gray, Mrs Shadrach, 297
Gray, Thomas, 207
Great Expectations, 297, 356
Green Hat, The, 307-8
Green, Peter, 213, 233
Greene, Graham, 24, 148, 317
Greville, Charles, 315
Grillparzer, Frans, 40
Grimond, Jo, 162, 351
Gromyko, 161
Grover, Tony, 192, 195, 210
Guedalla, Philip, 128

Gunther, John, 250

Hagen, Walter, 223
Haggard, Rider, 284
Hakluyt, Richard, 138, 141
Haldane, J. B. S., 74
Hale, Leslie, 352
Hale, Lionel, 33, 83
Haley, Sir William, 209
Hambleden, Patricia, 166
Hamilton, Hamish, 6, 169
Handel, G. F., 56, 57, 58
Hansall, Henry, 150, 154
Harcourt, Sir William, 237
Hard Times, 190, 191
Hardy, Thomas, 56, 111, 112, 114, 232
Harland, Henry, 155
Harris, Frank, 64, 149, 151, 281, 302
Harrison, Rex, 230
Hart-Davis, Adam, *passim*
Hart-Davis, Bridget, 20, 22, 54, 64, 80, 90, 96, 99, 102, 159, 169, 176, 245, 289, 316, 318
Hart-Davis, Comfort, *passim*
Hart-Davis, Duff, *passim*
Hart-Davis, Richard, 13, 60, 169, 222, 226, 254, 303, 304, 310
Hartley, L. P., 33
Hastings, Patrick, 276
Hawes, Stephen, 229
Hay, John, 303
Hayward, John, 214, 217, 234, 286
Hazlitt, William, 259
Headlam, Cuthbert, 51, 53, 65, 66-7, 163, 165, 243, 253, 337, 340, 341, 351
Headlam, G. W. (Tuppy), 128, 132, 153, 207, 233, 239, 244, 247
Headlam, Walter, 220
Heber, Bishop, 203
Helbert, 196, 198
Hemingway, Ernest, 151
Henley, Dorothy, 281
Henry VI, King, 256
Henson, Bishop Hensley, 17-8, 19, 21, 22, 25, 287
Herbert, A. P., 61, 91, 113, 163, 177, 179, 191, 213, 348
Herbert, George, 138
Herodotus, 227
Heroes and Hero-Worship, 226
Herrick, Robert, 138, 204, 205, 207
Hesketh, Phoebe, 218, 221
Hetty Wesley, 267, 269

Heygate, A. C. G., 11
Heygate, John, 11, 13
Heygate, Liza, 6, 10
Heygate, Mrs, 11, 12
Heywood, Thomas, 138
Hicks, Seymour, 276, 278
Hilbery, Mr Justice, 164
Hill, Clem, 68
Hill, M. D. (Piggy), 11-2, 14, 73, 76
Hill, Maurice, 217
Hill, Ted, 268
Himmler, 58
Hinton, James, 190
Hirst, George, 142
Hitler, 15, 150, 185, 256
Hobbs, J. B., 141
Hodson, Charles, 333
Hofmann, Heinrich, 255
Hogben, Lancelot, 52
Holland, H. Scott, 43
Holland, Vyvyan, 231
Hollis, Christopher, 35, 38, 207, 269, 280
Holmes, Mr Justice, 157, 239
Holmes, Sherlock, 8, 81, 82, 109, 298
Home, Lord and Lady, 161
Homer, 169, 238, 291, 325
Hood, Alexander, 128, 131, 149, 179
Hood, Diana, 36, 58, 127, 128, 129,
    131, 133, 135, 149, 179, 185, 247,
    280, 324, 327, 328, 350
Hopkins, G. M., 112
Horace, 128
Horder, Lord, 202
Hordern, Michael, 190, 195
Hotson, Leslie, 217
House, Humphry, 112
House, Madeline, 188, 217
Housman, A. E., 44, 69, 94, 105, 132,
    173, 203, 204, 206, 207, 236, 237,
    239, 253, 255, 257, 264, 268, 337, 345
Housman, Laurence, 198, 206-7, 255,
    257
How Green was my Valley, 35, 38, 39, 40,
    82, 86, 89, 121, 124, 255, 256, 258,
    260, 265, 288, 353
Howard, Michael, 160
Hugh-Smith, John, 133, 135-6
Hunt, Leigh, 259
Hurst, George, 9
Hutton, Sir Leonard, 186, 189
Huxley, Aldous, 74, 237

Ibsen, 156

Iles, Francis, 289, 290, 291, 294, 295,
    297, 299
Inge, Dean, 302
Irish R. M., 200, 239, 294
Irving, Henry, 143, 144, 195
Irving, Laurence, 16, 271
Isaacs, Rufus, 289, 290
Isvolsky, 286

Jackson, Henry, 206
Jackson, R. L. (Joe), 76, 78
Jacob, Gordon, 9
Jacob, Sir Ian, 331
Jacobs, W. W., 124, 126, 128, 130, 131,
    133, 136, 294
Jaffé, Michael, 217, 220
James, Henry, 12, 27, 28, 30, 31, 34,
    35, 39, 47, 50-1, 52, 53-4, 55-6, 119,
    155, 156, 158, 172, 218, 237, 241,
    261, 263, 292, 307, 320
Jonson, Ben, 250
Jowett, Benjamin, 14, 15
Jowitt, Lord, 322
Julius Caesar, 74, 302
Juno and the Paycock, 299

Kean, Edmund, 145
Keats, John, 283, 297, 338, 341
Kelly, Gerald, 342
Kemsley, Lord, 34, 38
Kenealy, Dr, 8
Kent, Marina Duchess of, 349, 353
Kessel, Joseph, 188
Ketton-Cremer, Wyndham, 205, 207,
    209, 213, 214
Keynes, Geoffrey, 147, 216-7
Keynes, J. M., 217, 219, 323, 326
Keynes, Margaret, 216
Kilmaine, Lord, 83, 348
King, Bishop, 43
King, Cecil, 241
Kingsmill, Hugh, 56, 110
Kipling, Rudyard, 21, 48, 59, 163, 223,
    255, 290, 293, 294
Knox, E. V., 16
Knox, R. A., 324, 347
Kortright, C. J., 25
Kruscheff, 58

Lady Chatterley's Lover, 281
Lamb, Charles, 148, 157
Lancaster, Karen and Osbert, 96
Landon, Perceval, 261

Landor, W. S., 269
Lane, Allen, 83
Lane, Margaret, 333
Lang, Andrew, 237
Lang, Bishop, 43
Langland, William, 238
Lapsley, Gaillard, 215
Lascelles, Sir Alan (Tommy), 6, 10, 17, 18, 33, 41, 54, 58, 83, 109, 163, 183, 185, 191, 194, 199, 221, 243, 245, 277, 317, 337
Lascelles, Joan, 10
Laski, Harold, 16, 47
Latter-Day Pamphlets, 327
Laud, Archbishop, 182, 211
Laver, James and Veronica, 113, 163
Lavinia (*née* Lascelles), 10
Lawrence, Aubrey, 182
Lawrence, D. H., 95, 120, 281, 293
Lawrence, Geoffrey, 90, 93, 108, 116, 323, 326
Lawrence, Helena and Peter, 182, 293
Lawrence, T. E., 78
Leadbeater, Bishop, 196, 198, 203
Leavis, F. R., 24, 56, 98, 123, 158, 203, 219, 239, 264
Lecky, W. E. H., 73
Lehmann, Beatrix, 191
Lehmann, John, 166, 312
Lehmann, Rosamond, 37, 64, 76, 83
Leigh Fermor, Paddy, 353
Leishman, J. B., 2
Le Neve, Ethel, 275
Lenin, 9
Leslie, Shane, 307, 308
Lever, Charles, 76
Lewes, G. H., 32
Lewis, Sir George, 155, 329, 330
Lewis, Katie, 155, 329, 330
Lincoln, Abraham, 199, 203-4, 205
Lindwall, Ray, 189
Linklater, Eric, 46, 49, 74, 80, 83, 96, 150, 185, 210, 254
Linklater, Magnus, 74, 80, 96, 159
Linklater, Marjorie, 74, 80, 254
Linstead, Sir Hugh, 333
Lion, The, 300, 306, 310, 312
Llewellyn, Richard, 35
Lloyd George, D., 201
Lloyd, Selwyn, 249
Lockhart, R. Bruce, 67, 68, 79, 171, 243
Lockwood, W. H., 106, 142
Lolita, 177, 179, 191, 336, 338, 341

London Library, The, *passim*
Longfellow, H. W., 57, 58
Longman, George, 15
Longman, Robert, 15
Lovell of Queen's, 219
Lubbock, Percy, 28, 30, 32, 47, 56, 70, 72, 92, 93, 98, 132, 224, 241, 255, 260-1, 263, 305
Lubbock, S. G., 14
Lucas, E. V., 264
Lucas, F. L., 28, 30, 31
Lucky Jim, 316, 317, 318, 331
Lusty, Bob, 83
Lutyens, Mary, 147, 191, 197, 198, 203
Luxmoore, H. E., 62, 223, 311
Lydgate, John, 238, 242
Lyttelton, Alfred, 48
Lyttelton, Anthony, 222
Lyttelton, Edward, 85, 240
Lyttelton, first Lord, 207
Lyttelton, Humphrey, 36, 55, 57, 133, 154, 156, 177, 184, 227, 229, 342
Lyttelton, Oliver, 57, 222, 268
Lyttelton, Pamela, *passim*
Lyttelton, R. H. (Bob), 326, 330
Lyttelton, Spencer, 5
Lyttelton, Thomas, 154
Lytton, Bulwyer, 290

MacArthur, General, 57
Macaulay, Lord, 15, 55, 74, 98, 116, 146, 234
Macaulay, Rose, 162
Macbeth, 181, 187, 190, 193, 194, 299
Macdoom, Amelia, 310
Mackintosh, Sir James, 333
Macleod, K. G., 243
Macmillan, Harold, 16, 105, 109, 111, 141, 176, 183, 224, 342, 350, 353
Macnaghten, Hugh, 293
Madan, Geoffrey, 202, 211, 213, 215, 228
Madariaga, Salvador de, 143, 145
Maitland, Thomas, 205
Malice Aforethought, 289, 290, 294, 295, 297, 299, 301, 303
Malory, Thomas, 242
Mannheim, Mrs, 65
Manning, Cardinal, 282
Manningham-Buller, R. E., 323
Mansergh, Prof., 333
Marford, Charlie, 201
Margaret, Princess, 175, 176, 330

Marillier, H. C. (Harry), 313, 314
Marsden, H. K., 153, 356
Marsh, Eddie, 255, 258, 260, 263, 269, 271, 273, 286, 298, 300, 301, 302, 303, 305, 307, 309
Martyn, Edward, 155
Marvell, Andrew, 192
Mary, *see* Cox
Mary, Queen, 315, 324, 336, 339
Masefield, John, 180, 193, 195, 272, 335, 339
Mason, Kenneth, 92
Maudling, Reginald, 352
Maugham, W. S., 42, 53, 159, 168, 170-1, 228, 239, 245, 302, 305
Maurice, F. D., 41
Maxton, James, 260
May, Olive, 280
May, Peter, 186, 265
Mellon family, 306, 307, 309
Menuhin, Yehudi, 76
Meredith, George, 10, 12, 35, 44, 45, 48, 59, 85, 119
Merrick, Leonard, 215, 217
Middlemarch, 32, 40, 42, 86, 89
Midsummer Night's Dream, A, 189
Miller, Keith, 189
Milton, Ernest, 144
Milton, John, 59, 74, 177
Misleading Cases, 191, 194, 195
Moiseiwitsch, Benno, 231
Mold, A., 186
Molotov, 161
Moltke, Count von, 164
Montague, C. E., 193, 237
Montague, Elizabeth, 174
Montgomery, Lord, 235
Moore, George, 3, 42, 48, 85, 149, 155, 169
Moore, Henry, 352
Moore, Sir John, 283
Moorehead, Alan, 10, 337
Moorehead, Lucy, 96
More, Thomas, 111
Morgan, Charles, 17, 18, 19, 21, 23, 25, 37, 62, 63, 64, 103, 107, 130, 136
Morgan, Hilda, 18, 19, 130
Morris, John, 329, 330, 331
Morris, William, 167
Mortimer, Raymond, 191, 268
Muggeridge, Malcolm, 110, 224
Muir, Percy, 103
Mulholland, Mrs, 10

Muller, Max, 74, 78
Munby, A. N. L. (Tim), 286
Munnings, Alfred, 279, 281
Murdoch, Iris, 39, 256
Murray, Dr John, 115
Murray, John G. (Jock), 39
Murry, J. Middleton, 59, 228, 239, 338, 341

Napoleon, 69, 94, 300
Nashe, Thomas, 290
Nasser, 58, 89, 100
Newcastle, Duke of, 25
Newman, Ernest, 231
Nicholson, Edie, 140
Nicholson, William, 50, 141
Nicolson, Harold, 4, 20-1, 58-9, 103, 114, 133, 162-3, 249, 317, 324, 337, 351
Nightingale, Florence, 98
Nisard, J. M. N. D., 40
Norah (Fahie), 173
Nowell-Smith, Simon and Marion, 37, 320
Nuffield, Lord, 306
Nugent, Tim, 51, 72, 185, 246

Occleve, Thomas, 247
Olivier, Laurence, 279
O'Neill, Eugene, 184
Orwell, George, 59, 74, 239
Osborne, John, 12, 194, 264, 293
Overbury, Sir Thomas, 271
Ovid, 308

Paget, Bishop, 43
Paget, R., 352
Painter, George, 324
Palmer, William, 8
Pardon, Sydney, 189
Parks, J., 248
Parr, Dr Samuel, 314, 316, 321
Partridge, Eric, 282
Past and Present, 296, 298, 300, 308, 324, 327, 329, 345
Pater, Walter, 261, 263
Pattison, Mark, 75
Pavia, Leo, 206
Pavy, Salathiel, 250
Pearson, Hesketh, 8
Pellatt, Tom, 276
Pepys, Samuel, 8, 244
Peter, *see* Fleming

Petrarch, 98
Pfeiffer, Karl G., 245
Philimore, Lord, 160–1
Phoenix Trust, The, 113, 339, 347, 348, 350, 355
Pinero, A. W., 309
Pitoeff, Madame, 145
Pitter, Ruth, 67, 70
Plinlimmon, David, 282
Pliny, 227
Plomer, William, 33, 35, 62, 64, 66, 129, 131, 166, 282
Plum, see Warner
Podola, G. F., 323
Pooley, Sir Ernest, 313
Pooley, Lady, 313, 314, 316, 318
Pooter, Mr., 185, 338, 341
Pope, Alexander, 185, 218, 244
Porson, Richard, 4, 238
Posh, 232
Potter, Stephen, 40, 41, 49–50, 80, 83, 103, 198, 231
Pound, Ezra, 3, 95
Powell, Anthony, 31, 33, 34, 65, 113
Powell, Dilys, 145
Powell, L. F., 38, 214, 309
Priestley, J. B. and Jacquetta, 141, 145
Prodger, Dr., 277, 279, 280, 281, 283, 284, 287
Proust, Marcel, 324
Pryce-Jones, Alan, 5, 18, 20, 31, 75, 113, 253, 302, 340

Queen Mother, The, 330
Quickswood, Lord, 197
Quiller-Couch, A., 294

Rabelais, 246
Raleigh, Professor Sir Walter, 47, 172
Ramadhin, S., 189
Ramsay, A. B., 18, 244
Ranjitsinhji, Prince, 141, 142, 186, 247–8
Ransome, Arthur, 11, 116, 159, 184, 235, 254, 281, 285, 288, 304, 310, 328
Ratchford, Fannie, 37
Ravensdale, Lady, 162
Raverat, Gwen, 216
Rawlins, F. H., 236
Ray, Gordon, 56, 64
Raymond, John, 31
Redgauntlet, 190, 191, 194, 195, 200, 203, 205, 210, 221, 223

Reeves, Miss, 159
Regler, Gustav, 208, 212
Renan, Ernest, 33
Rhodes, Wilfred, 15, 325
Rhondda, Lady, 26, 103
Richardson, Ralph, 317
Richardson, Tom, 106, 142, 223, 325–6
Ridley, Cecilia, 203
Ridley, Ursula, 13, 203
Roberts, Denys Kilham, 83
Roberts, S. C., 35, 38, 172, 183, 188, 207, 209, 214, 236, 356
Robertson, Field-Marshal, 28
Robespierre, 32
Robins, Elizabeth, 155–6
Roger, see Fulford
Rose, see Bourne
Ross, Martin, 50, 136
Rossetti, Christina, 284
Rossetti, D. G., 329
Rothenstein, Will, 117
Rothermere, Lord, 241
Routh, C. R. N. (Dick), 136, 137, 138, 204, 272, 284, 285, 286
Ruskin, John, 25, 42, 48, 124, 127, 131, 314, 343
Russell, Bertrand, 14
Russell, Conrad, 239
Russell, Leonard, 145
Ruth, see Simon
Ryan, A. P., 109
Rylands, George (Dadie), 37, 217, 220

Sackville-West, Vita, 162–3
Sadleir, Michael, 249
Sagan, Françoise, 37
Sainte-Beuve, 275
Saintsbury, George, 40–1, 43, 44
Sancroft, Archbishop, 36
Sand, George, 275
Sanders, C. R., 68, 69
Sardou, Victorien, 309
Sargent, Malcolm, 3, 5, 6, 8, 17, 219, 231, 321, 322, 323, 325
Sartor Resartus, 27, 29, 30, 32, 39, 101
Sassoon, George, 144
Sassoon, Siegfried, 140–1, 142, 144, 145, 147
Savant, A., 69
Say, J. B., 228
Sayers, Dorothy, 242
Schreiner, Olive, 190
Schreyvogel, Joseph, 40, 44

Schubert, 187
Scott, Sir Walter, 76, 242
Searle, Ronald, 213
Secker, Martin, 46
Sedgwick, Adam, 211
Selwyn, Bishop G. A., 347
Shakespeare, 7, 89, 132, 136, 172, 174, 239, 240, 272, 277, 282, 284, 338, 341
Shaw, Bernard, 25, 73, 78, 114, 156, 306, 314
Shawe-Taylor, Desmond, 231
Shearman, Mr Justice, 94
Sheen, Gillian, 252
Shelley, 14, 110, 128
Sheppard, D., 179
Sheridan, Clare, 9
Simenon, Georges, 53, 54, 56, 294, 295, 297
Simon, Oliver, 117, 118
Simon, Ruth, 95 et passim
Simon, Timothy, 292, 294, 295, 320
Sitwell family, 180
Sitwell, Edith, 23, 25, 98
Sitwell, Osbert, 203, 254
Slater, E. V. (Sam), 239
Sligger, see Urquhart
Smith, J. G., 8
Smith, James, 33, 65, 66, 103
Smithers, Peter, 173
Smyth, Ethel, 210, 226, 240, 241, 242, 245
Snow, C. P., 159
Socrates, 98
Somervell, Donald, 5, 17, 33, 80, 82, 90, 96, 97, 160, 166, 282, 284, 285, 304, 306, 307, 310, 335, 337
Somerville, E. Œ., 49, 50, 76, 128, 136, 200, 239
Southey, Robert, 238, 331
Sparrow, John, 73, 75, 77, 170, 171, 213, 230, 234, 285, 321, 322, 324, 345
Spencer, Herbert, 69, 71-2
Spender, Stephen, 37
Spring, Howard, 247, 249
St Joan, 145, 146
St John, Christopher, 226
Stalin, 342
Stanley, Molly, 186
Stephen, Leslie, 42, 260
Stephenson, Sir Guy, 8
Stevenson, Adlai, 306
Stevenson, R. L., 47, 101, 155, 157, 158-9, 200, 215, 293, 305, 306, 311

Stewart, J. I. M., 312
Storey, Graham, 217
Storrs, Ronald, 55, 57, 58
Strachey, Lytton, 68-9, 141, 143, 146, 164, 242
Strang, Lord, 333, 336
Streicher, Julius, 110
Strong, L. A. G., 33, 119, 122
Strong, Tommy, 43
Suicide among Cricketers, 106
Sullivan, Arthur, 123
Summerskill, Edith, 158, 338
Surrey, Earl of, 138, 238
Sutherland, Prof., 188
Swetman R., 179
Swift, Jonathan, 283, 331, 341, 346
Swinburne, A. C., 44, 65-6
Swinnerton, Frank, 47, 53, 159, 247, 250
Sybil, 355, 356
Synge, J. M., 63, 256

Taine, Hippolyte, 331
Talbot, Bishop, 43
Talbot, Ted, 339, 341
Talleyrand, 256, 258, 268
Taste of Honey, A, 210, 212
Taylor, A. J. P., 235
Temple, Archbishop, 36, 73, 115, 219
Tennyson, Lord, 9, 42, 68, 84, 102, 139, 167, 181, 237, 274
Terry, Ellen, 193, 195, 314
Thackeray, W. M., 56, 60, 62, 64, 192, 223, 233
Thesiger, Tony and Virginia, 10
Thomas, Edward, 207
Thomas, Gwyn, 33
Thomas, Jimmy, 309
Thompson, Edith, 94
Thompson, Francis, 306, 309, 328, 331
Thompson, W. H., 206
Thorndike, Sybil, 145, 146
Thornycroft, Hamo, 141, 142
Tim, see Nugent
Time and Tide, 24, 25, 26, 30, 47, 103
To be Young, 191, 194, 196, 198
Tolstoy, Leo, 132, 167, 173, 174
Tommy, see Lascelles
Toynbee, Arnold, 44
Traherne, Thomas, 18
Trevelyan, G. M., 115
Trevor-Roper, Hugh, 235
Trollope, Anthony, 28, 244, 290, 293

Trott, Albert, 106
Trueman, Fred, 179
Truman, Harry, 57, 58
Trumper, Victor, 15, 68, 141, 144, 302, 325
Tuppy, *see* Headlam
Tynan, Ken, 71, 146

Udall, Nicholas, 135
Ulysses, 78
Uncle Silas, 261, 263, 265
Upjohn, Mr Justice, 10
Urquhart, F. F. (Sligger), 196, 198, 200

Van Oss, Oliver, 62
Vansittart, Lord, 88, 91
Vaughan, E. L. (Toddy), 11
Vaughan, Henry, 182, 183
Vaughan, Mrs, 49
Vaughan Williams, R., 156
Veale, Douglas, 257
Verney, John, 17, 19, 21, 24, 39
Verrall, A. W., 95
Victoria, Queen, 315
Virgil, 238
Visiak, E. H., 2

Wagg, Alfred, 222, 224
Wagner, Richard, 331
Walkley, A. B., 153, 155
Wallace, W. H., 327-8
Walpole, Dorothy, 343, 344
Walpole, Horace, 25, 207
Walpole, Hugh, 32, 42, 53, 55-6, 61, 104, 107, 111, 118, 204, 249, 285, 312, 336, 343, 344, 350
Walpole, Robin, 344
Walter, Bruno, 231
Ward, Mrs Humphry, 69, 354
Warner, P. F. (Plum), 25, 221, 223, 224, 225, 226, 301, 314, 325
Warre-Cornish, F., 135
Warre-Cornish, Mrs, 94
Wass, Tom, 106
Watts-Dunton, T., 65-6
Waugh, Evelyn, 251, 258, 347, 355-6
Wavell, A. P., 170
Webb, Beatrice, 32, 45, 158
Webster, John, 284
Wedgwood, Veronica, 103, 205, 207
Weidenfeld, George, 177
Welldon, Dean, 18, 228

Wellington, first Duke of, 77
Wellington, seventh Duke of, 351
Wells, C. M., 18, 25, 34, 44, 106, 167-8, 223, 224, 226, 228, 230, 305, 312
Wells, H. G., 8, 27, 28, 30, 31, 32, 35, 42, 47, 169, 192, 200, 220, 277, 303, 312, 326
West, Anthony, 42, 43
West, Rebecca, 28, 52, 73, 143
Westminster, Loelia Duchess of, 16
Wheeler-Bennett, J. W., 148, 149, 154, 185
Whistler, J. McN., 314
White, Joseph Blanco, 214-5
Whitney, John Hay, 37, 176
Whitworth, Rex, 114
Whymper, Edward, 81
Wickham, A. K., 14
Wieler, Brigadier L. F. E., 145
Wigwam, Dr Virgil, 32
Wilberforce, Octavia, 156
Wilde, Oscar, *passim*
Wilkes, John, 169
Wilkinson, Ellen, 260
Willey, Basil, 214
Williams, Griffith, 319, 320
Williams, Harold, 40
Williams, Mrs, 7
Williams, Sir William, 83
Wills, Mr Justice, 95
Wilson, Angus, 271, 273, 277
Wilson, Colin, 27, 172
Wilson, David, 298, 300
Wilson, J. Dover, 143, 145
Wingate, Orde, 240
Wise, T. J., 37
Wodehouse, P. G., 52, 136, 197, 282
Wolfenden, Sir John, 201
Wollheim, Richard, 217, 220
Wood, Henry, 3
Wood, Rev. J. G., 227
Woodcock, A., 224
Woodcock, George, 333
Woodcock, John, 231
Woodruff, Douglas, 23
Woolf, Virginia, 32, 105, 212, 215, 240, 241
Wordsworth, William, 8, 21, 35, 53, 124, 331, 345
Wright, Aldis, 206
Wrong Box, The, 215
Wyatt, Woodrow, 174
Wyndham, George, 232

Wyndham-Goldie, Grace, 145
Wynyard, Diana, 278, 280

Yeats, W. B., 59, 71, 101, 115, 160, 209, 269

Young, G. M., 44, 141, 220, 228, 230, 233, 234, 236, 324, 345, 346
Young, R. A., 239
Younghusband, Colonel, 213